In the eyes of modern man, Egypt remains predominately a strange world where pharaons and gods, sometimes monstruous, sometimes charming, are found in the act of accomplishing strange rites, in the centre of hieroglyphic inscriptions charged with mysterious significance. This scene from the temple of Kom Ombo in Upper Egypt is characteristic in this respect.

But this bas-relief also illustrates other more positive aspects of Egypt. It shows in its manner a civilisation which, through all changes, was able to conserve and develop traditions which come from the beginning of history (it should be mentioned that the present scene dates from the beginning of the Christian era). Il also reveals men who attempted to construct a coherent explanation of the world and to record it by means of art and architecture to the best of their abilities. It was finally made known through a highly subtle and logical instrument of thought and communication : hieroglyphic writing.

Egypt

GUIDE-POCHE UNIVERS

Egypt

408 pages
16 coloured photographs - 8 coloured maps
92 figures - 135 maps and plans

LEHNERT & LANDROCK

ART PUBLISHERS

K. LAMBELET, Succ.

CAIRO

1981

This guide was prepared by the Editing Service of Editions Marcus. Paris.

The collaborators in the original edition were : Hans Strelocke, author ; Franz Huber, Gert Oberländer and Arnulf Milch, maps and plans ; Vera Solymosi-Thurzo, illustrator.

Alain-Pierre Zivie prepared the French Edition and provided photographic illustrations.

Barbara Adams and Angela P. Thomas prepared the English translation, adaptation and revision.

Robert Segond checked the revision of the maps and plans.

Guy Montagnana made up the pages and designed the cover.

The Delegation of the Tourist Office of the Arab Republic of Egypt in England provided valuable information and documentation.

The details in this guide reflect the latest information obtained by our collaborators and are given **without guarantee.**

EXPLANATION OF SYMBOLS

⌂	De-Luxe Hotel	⌂	Youth Hostel
⌂	First Class Hotel	🚂	Railway
⌂	Second Class Hotel	🚌	Cars and Buses
⌂	Tourist Class Hotel	⛴	Sea or River Connections
ⓣ	Tourist Office	✈	Air Connections

The numbers or letters in bracket after the place names or sights correspond to those on the different plans. The distances in kilometres (and miles) which may follow the name of a place start from the commencement of each excursion.

Contents

The Libyan Desert Oases

Plans, Maps, and Coloured Photographs

Practical Information

Tourist Information by Region

Information on the Transport, Hotels, Restaurants, Amuse-
ments, Museums, etc., of the Towns mentioned in the Principal
Itineraries :

Detailed Index

Introduction

Egypt is the most ancient tourist country in the world. Among the first travellers who visited the pyramids, the temples and the other marvels of the Nile valley, can be counted such men as Herodotus, Strabo, and the Emperor Hadrian. These and others enthused over the monuments and a civilisation which, even in their epoch, was already very old. The rediscovery of Egypt is meanwhile relatively recent ; it was revitalised by Bonaparte, who, in 1798, before the Battle of the Pyramids, used this now celebrated phrase in the address to his soldiers : « Soldiers ! In the height of the pyramids you are gazing on 40 centuries ! ». Since then the flood of educated visitors, but also tourists, has never stopped. The number of those who remain impressed by the astonishing sight of the masses of stones raised in the honour of the gods, kings and the dead has never ceased to increase.

The country where one of the most ancient and greatest human civilisations formerly developed is today a gigantic open-air museum. It possesses a very rich heritage of ancient relics, the equal of which can scarcely be found elsewhere. To be a success, a journey along the banks of the Nile should be thoroughly prepared. The more knowledge that the visitor has of the life of the ancient Egyptians, their art and their civilisation, the more the experience of the visit will make a deep impression. This guide will therefore be doubly useful to the tourist ; it will serve as a serious preparation for the visit and at the same time be a faithful companion in the country itself, a daily record of the unforgettable splendours.

At the begining an introductory chapter on « the Land and the People » will be found. Then a résumé of the history of the Nile valley from prehistory to the present day, giving the rudiments necessary for understanding the country's evolution through time and for placing the antiquities visited in their historical context. To begin with, in the chapter « Art and Civilisation », is a presentation of the history of Egyptian art. In order to familiarise the layman with the essential notions which will permit him to understand the art and civilisation of the pharaonic era, the guide gives a alphabetic lexicon of the principal terms used in these subjects, also an account of the religion and the funerary cult of ancient Egypt. A chapter is devoted to Islam, the religion of the majority of the present Egyptians.

After the information for preparing the visit comes the guide proper with descriptions of the sites and itineraries. The last part is devoted to general or particular practical information on each town which will facilitate the organisation of the journey. Finally, a detailed index permits better use of the book.

The Land and the People

Egypt is properly thought of as part of the Sahara, because more than 95 % of its surface consists of stone, sand and desert. However, in the middle of this expanse, the Nile flows in a south-north direction. Also, as far as the flood extends, the Nile valley gives the impression of a perfectly coherent oasis landscape. There one of the most ancient and greatest civilisations of mankind could develop, the imposing remains of which still give rise to admiration. Civilisations may be superimposed, but Egypt survived however through the millenia as that which was, according to the still famous phrase of the Greek historian, Herodotus, a gift of the Nile.

The Nile is the vital artery of the country because it is its water alone which confers a proverbial fertility to the relatively narrow band which is the Nile oasis. The rest of Egypt is situated in the arid zone which extends from the Atlantic to the interior of Asia. Only slight effects of Mediterranean climate touch the northern edge of the country, in the Nile Delta. This brings with it some rainfall : 7 in. a year at Alexandria, 1 in at Cairo and only ¾ in. at Asyût in Upper Egypt, which corresponds to about 30 days of annual rainfall at Alexandria, 6 at Cairo and, at the most, 1 at Asyût. Whereas the rainfall becomes rare towards the south, the temperature rises : the annual mean rises to 19 °C in the Delta littoral, to 21 °C at Cairo and about 30 °C at Asyût. However, when the hot wind, the *Khamsîn* blows from the desert, especially in the spring, temperatures of more than 45 °C are not unusual.

Position and Extent

Egypt (Arabic *Masr)* is situated in the north-east angle of the African continent, but it also encroaches on Asia in the Sinai peninsula. It reaches the Mediterranean in the north ; at the north-east the Sinai peninsula is joined to Palestine (the largest part of which today forms the State of Israel) and is bordered by the Red Sea. The southern frontier with the Sudan is essentially a straight line which follows latitude 22° degrees north. The western frontier reaches across the Libyan desert, with the exception of a relatively restricted area between the Siwa oasis and the Mediterranean ; the border between Egypt and its neighbour Libya is this time a straight line situated on longitude 25° degrees west. The country has an area of 1,002,000 Km², (465,000 sq. mi.) it is slightly bigger than France, Belgium, Netherlands, West Germany, Austria, Switzerland and Liechtenstein put together. The greatest distance from north to south is 1,025 km (637 mi.) and from east to west 1,240 km (770 mi.).

Geology

The heart of Egypt, the narrow Nile valley, is closed at the east by the *Arabic Desert Plateau* and at the west by the often restricted and precipitous *Libyan Desert*. Facing the deep fracture of the Red Sea, which descends to about 2,190 m (7,185 ft.), are mountain chains, the height of which may reach 2,000 m (6,562 ft.), consisting of granite, schist, diorite and gneiss on the summits. In this region, between the rift valley of the Red Sea and the Nile valley, the pharaohs mined towards the centre for volcanic porphyry and on the edges for limestone and marl, necessary stones for architecture and sculpture. On the other side, the western Libyan desert is formed of a limestone plateau (which turns grey towards the south) about 300 m (984 ft.) high, which, much further towards the west, is covered with dunes of light sand, sometimes as high as 60 m (197 ft.) resting in western and southern beds. Between the virtually sterile deserts the sediments from the annual flooding of the Nile have been deposited on the original sand and gravel, in the course of geological periods, as a silt of alkaline and fertile clay. The layers have accumulated today to a height of often more than 10 m (33 ft.) and they have formed a fertile soil which shaped Egyptian civilisation. Towards Cairo they were formed of compact conglomerates of sand, gravels and plant remains, also of nummulitic limestone dated to the Eocene ; this was the material used for the facing blocks of the Great Pyramid, for statuary and by stone workers. Down stream from Cairo, the Nile is subdivided and forms the *Delta*, a vast area of 22,000 km² (8,500 sq. mi.) consisting of fertile soil.

With its 6,671 km, (4,145 mi.) the Nile (Arabic : *Bahr el Nil*) is the longest river in the world. The largest quantity of water comes into it from the *White Nile*, the source of which is situated in the Victoria and Albert Lakes, 621 m (2,037 ft) above sea level. In the east Sudanese plain it receives the marshy tributaries of the *Gazelle* and the *Giraffe*, also the *Sobat*. Then it flows along a sinuous course through Upper Sudan. At Khartum it is joined by the *Blue Nile* coming from the high plateau of Abyssinia, which gets its name from the particles of dark coloured soil which are carried with it. At last comes the addition of the rapid flow of the *Atbara*, the last Nile tributary. Then, the river crosses the desert plateau and after having conquered the last rapids of the *cataracts*, it comes to the level of Aswan (slightly above the Tropic of Cancer) into a valley the width of which varies between 1 km (0.60 mi.) (at Aswan) and about 25 km (15 mi.) (at Cairo) and which forms, up to the mouth of the Delta at the Mediterranean, the most populated and fertile part of Egypt. Further south the Nile now flows into the gigantic, artificial lake created by the new Aswan Dam. Lake Nasser is already immense extending 100 km (60 mi.) south of the Sudanese frontier at Wadi Halfa. Finally, in the Delta, the Nile divides and forms the Rosetta and Damietta branches (without counting the other secondary channels) united by numberless canals.

The area covered by the river reaches a total of 2,803,000 km² (108,000 sq. mi.) Navigation commences at Lake Albert. It is often impeded, along the upper course, by barriers of water plants, *Sudd* and it is interrupted in the Sudan by the granite cataracts.

It has been millenia since man profited by making use of the natural rhythm of the high and low waters of the. Nile. They lived by the power conferred by its fertility and gave it divine characteristics. The ancient Egyptians called the Nile god (or rather the Nile flood) *Hapy* and because of its proved fecundity they represented him with female breasts and a generous abdomen.

In summer, during the rainy season, in the tropical region of Africa, an enormous quantity of water falls in the great lakes on the high plateau of Abyssinia, which (augmented by water from the melting snows) then flows towards the Nile which begins to rise. Its flood, the flood of the Nile, reaches Aswan with fairly good regularity between the 15th and 18th June and Cairo after another 6 to 12 days (according to the height of the water). At that time the river has risen some 7m (23 ft.) at Aswan and about 5 m (16 ft.) at Cairo, which is approximately twenty times the water of its normal flow. At the beginning the colour of the water is greenish because of the numerous particles of algae in suspension, then, at the time of the highest water it has a brownish-red tint which comes from the silt washed from the high plateau of Abyssinia.

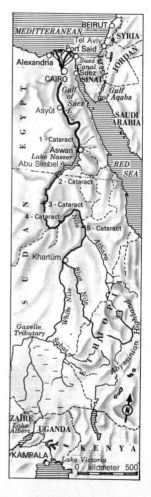

During Antiquity this Nile flood was measured in cubits in the *nilometers*. the normal level of the water in the Graeco-Roman period was 16 cubits. According to meticulous calculations, the sediments may be estimated at about 3.6 tons per cubic metre (35.32 cu. ft.) of the fluvial bed which forms a layer which raises the Nile valley and its basin about 10 cm (4 in.) every century between Aswan and Cairo, being a layer of sediments of 52 million tons per annum. As well as the mass of water which only waters the banks which are in direct contact with it, large quantities of supplementary water filter into the soil (up to 12 cubic kilometers per annum) and augment the water table; as a consequence numerous deep wells are excavated on the borders of the desert and in the oases.

The Nile flood was always the most important time of the year for the Egyptians and above all for agriculture and it was designated as the beginning of the year: inundation, winter, summer. With the fall of water at the end of September the peasant sowed in the still wet soil and after four difficult months he was able to work and harvest his fields; a little quicker on the border of the desert, longer near the river. Then, between March and June, the earth lay fallow and dead and waited for the new inundation.

That the highest level possible should always be reached (without however being excessive and destructive) was always the prayer of the Egyptians for whom it determined the « fat » or « lean » years. But this state of affairs has ceased and the rising now stops south of Aswan because, in the 19th and 20th centuries, reservoirs and containing barrages were constructed in order to stop dependance on the height of the flood by the use of continual *irrigation* (the barrages and dam of *Aswan, Esna, Nag Hammâdi, Asyût* and *Qalyûb*). The modern high dam of *Sadd el-Ali* (new Aswan dam) as well as being used in other spheres and techniques, will also serve to complete this plan with more certain irrigation.

Flora and Fauna

The present day exploitation of vegetation is amazing. Gardens or the cultivation of flowers and plants are not encountered, the *fellah* has little use for them. Forests and grassland are completely absent. Only the groves of palm trees form well circumscribed groups; and then it will be date palms which are predominant. The best quality grow in the oases far from the sea and around Aswan, because there the Saharian continent climate with its slight humidity favours a proper maturity of the plant. The harvest takes place from August to October. The Nilotic acacia grows mostly next to the banks, next to eucalyptus, sycamore, tamarisk, mulberry, mimosa, poinsetta *(flamboyants rouges)* and carob. Every type of fruit comes to maturity with suitable height and quality because of good irrigation of the gardens and plantations.

The cultivation of foodstuff and cereals is most important, oils, green vegetables and spices, such as aniseed, fennel, pepper and cumin. Around *Nag Hammadi* and *Kom 'Ombo* there are extensive plantations of sugar cane ; in the hot and humid Delta, fields of cotton.

In general the widespread idea that the country is rich in wild life is not quite correct. There are no more crocodiles living free. Hippopotami, lions, ostriches and giraffes went more than a millenium ago to the African interior. Wild animals only live now in the desert regions. The numerous types of lizard, desert jerboa and chameleon are harmless. Poisonous snakes and scorpions should be guarded against. You should avoid copses and piles of stones and not slide your hand under flat stones or in cracks in walls. Wear closed shoes in hot sand because vipers like to hide themselves there. There are roebuck in Sinai.

Vultures and kites hover over the populated zones, even above Cairo.

On the water course, in the migration period, the birds which come down from Europe mingle with the water birds of Egypt. The white heron is almost a domestic animal for the peasant, which rids his animals of vermin. Domestic animals comprise cattle, sheep and nanny goats ; the *gamus* (water buffalo), camel and donkey serve as beasts of burden or draught beside the small, swift and patient Arab horse. Pigs and dogs are despised ; the cat, on the contrary, is, as in ancient Egypt, the beloved fireside companion (less in the country). Breeding is rare. The maintenance of useful animals, apart from those mentioned above, is restricted to the breeding of pigeons, chickens, ducks and geese which, in large groups, confer a picturesque animation on the Egyptian villages.

Climate

Apart from the Mediterranean climatic zone which affects a part of the Delta and the north coast, a subtropical desert climate reigns over the rest of Egypt with a blue sky and a hot and dry atmosphere during the day followed by a night chill. Cairo (over which the sky is very often overcast as in other large cities) has only six days of rain a year ; in Upper Egypt it rarely rains ; in Alexandria and the Delta there are abundant winter rains. Between March and May, the *Khamsîn* (Khamsîn = 50) can blow over the land. It is a burning wind which comes from the south, similar to the sirocco of North Africa ; it makes

one feel tired and lazy or, on the contrary, rather nervous. The *Sobaa* is an even more violent wind the effects of which can be worse. It carries masses of sand which obscure the sky to the point of removing visibility, so that the train and air timetables cannot be followed (airports may have to be closed). When you are caught in the Sobaa you have to protect your eyes (and your camera equipment), look for a safe shelter and wait for the end of the tempest.

The following table gives the average minimum and maximum temperatures for each month of the year for the most important places.

Minimum temperatures in degres Celsius (° C)

	J	F	M	A	M	J	J	A	S	O	N	D
Mersa Matruh	8,3	8,4	9,9	12,2	15,0	18,5	20,6	21,2	20,0	17,4	13,8	10,2
Alexandria	9,3	9,7	11,2	13,5	16,7	20,2	22,7	22,9	21,3	17,8	14,8	11,2
Port Said	11,3	12,1	13,5	16,1	19,6	22,4	24,1	24,9	23,9	21,8	18,4	13,7
Ismailia	8,0	9,0	10,5	14,0	17,0	20,0	22,0	22,0	20,0	17,0	13,5	9,0
Cairo	8,6	9,3	11,3	13,9	17,4	19,9	21,5	21,6	19,9	17,8	13,9	10,4
Minya	3,9	5,4	7,8	11,7	16,7	18,8	20,2	20,5	18,6	15,9	11,5	7,0
Luxor	5,4	6,8	10,7	15,6	20,7	22,5	23,7	23,5	21,5	17,7	12,3	7,9
Siwa	4,1	5,5	8,2	12,2	16,6	19,4	20,7	20,6	18,3	14,8	10,2	5,8
Dakhla	4,6	6,1	9,7	14,4	19,6	22,4	23,0	22,9	20,7	17,4	12,0	6,7
Hurghada	9,7	10,1	12,4	15,9	20,8	23,5	24,8	25,0	23,2	20,0	15,6	11,4

Maximum temperatures in degrees Celsius (° C)

	J	F	M	A	M	J	J	A	S	O	N	D
Mersa Matruh	17,9	18,8	20,0	21,9	25,3	27,4	28,8	29,6	28,5	27,0	23,6	19,5
Alexandria	18,3	19,2	21,0	23,6	26,5	28,2	29,6	30,4	29,4	27,7	29,4	20,4
Port Said	18,0	18,7	20,2	22,6	25,8	28,5	30,4	30,9	29,2	27,4	24,0	19,9
Ismailia	19,5	20,5	24,0	29,0	33,0	35,0	36,5	36,0	24,0	31,0	26,0	21,0
Cairo	19,1	20,7	23,7	28,2	32,4	34,5	35,4	34,8	32,3	29,8	21,1	20,7
Minya	20,6	22,5	25,4	30,2	35,4	36,3	37,0	36,6	33,4	31,2	26,6	21,7
Luxor	22,9	25,5	29,0	34,8	39,4	40,7	40,8	41,0	38,9	35,1	28,9	25,0
Siwa	19,7	21,7	25,1	29,8	34,2	37,3	37,9	37,8	35,1	31,8	26,4	21,2
Dakhla	21,5	23,9	27,9	33,0	37,4	38,8	39,0	38,9	36,1	33,0	28,0	23,0
Hurghada	20,4	20,8	22,8	25,8	29,4	31,2	32,5	32,9	30,4	28,2	25,3	21,7

Agriculture

Agriculture is still, as in the distant past, the principal part of the Egyptian economy and it gives up to 62 % of the population their means of subsistance. Although the modern state is seeking to improve the quality of the soil with scientific methods in order to increase the quantity and the quality of agricultural production, it will be a long time, however, before all the population benefits from the results.

The Egyptian peasant (Arabic : *fellah*) still works, in effect, essentially like his predecessors of 4,000 years ago, above all in the case of tools : two cattle pull his wooden plough, the clods are broken up with a simple metal harrow and the earth is only lightly turned over by the slightly penetrating wooden plough. Nevertheless, the fertile and well-watered soil gives two harvests each year ; then the fellah really works with the universal Egyptian tool, the short handled hoe. In summer rice, cotton, sorghum (a type of millet) ; in autumn in the Delta maize ; in winter wheat, barley, clover, onions and beans, without counting the numerous types of vegetables destined to satisfy local needs. As a general rule, the corn is still cut with a sickle, or grubbed up, then thrashed with a sledge pulled by animals or with a spiked harrow before being winnowed in the air so that the wind separates the chaff and grain. The grain silos are made of clay, as they were in archaic times and as they can still be seen in the tomb scenes of the early dynasties.

As well as the cultivation of plants necessary for subsistance and internal consumption, there is always a large area given over to industrial cultivation, which brings money into the country, of which cotton must be ranked first. In spite of the reinforcement of its cultivation by other very important products, the cultivation of cotton constitutes the most important part of the agricultural activity of the country. Cotton is the chief export, Egypt's principal source of foreign currency (85 % of the total export.) It is estimated that about 50 % of the world's production of cotton, of « Karnak-fibre » type comes from Egypt, about 50,000 tons produced from 80,000 km² (30,000 sq. mi.) fields.

Apart from cotton, Egypt exports rice, dried and fresh onions, sugar, sesame, lemons, dates and grapes. Sugar cane, introduced into Egypt by the Arabs in the year 700, is cultivated particularly in the south of the country ; the harvest is about 500,000 tons per annum.

Egyptian livestock is of little importance. The water buffalo *(gamus)*, cattle and goats are considered as beasts of burden or simply utilitarian animals, and reach a total of 6 million. The donkey is chiefly the economic and patient animal which carries men and burdens, although the dromedary carries the heavier loads. No « impure » pigs are found (except in some farms kept by Christians), but there are many dogs, cats and above all poultry and pigeons. The latter provide a first class fertiliser for the vegetable patch, although in the poorly wooded areas, cattle and goat manure is used as fuel. Throughout the country pigeon-houses which overlap the houses can be seen, the construction of which varies according to the region. Besides this the walls of dried mud and the organic dust which is found in the ruins of ancient sites, are ransacked for *sebakh,* a fertile manure rich in ammonia, soda ans saltpetre, which horrifies archaeologists because of the damage done to ancient sites.

Irrigation

The ancient system of irrigation, known since the predynastic period, is simple and full of good sense and it is still used today. The banks of the Nile are reinforced and the area which extends behind the river is divided into *hods* which are flat basins separated from each other by banks of earth about 30 cm (1 ft.) high, and with areas which vary, according to the owner, from 400 to 17,000 hectares (988 to 42,000 acres). These are joined together by canals between them, the first of which, « the upper canal » is found up-stream. When the river has risen, the Nile water pours into the canals in the basins, waters them according to a fixed distribution and stays there about 40 days while the banks are opened by hand and with hoes. This is obviously a method which is only possible to apply when the ground is level.

But, for watering the fields some distance from the river, situated higher than the Nile, sometimes 300 or 400 m away, (330 - 430 yd.) appropriate systems were invented in early times to draw and raise up the water. Drawing up water by means of a leather bucket, *nattaleh* is the most primitive method. It is laborious and its effect is feeble. By employing this method a maximum of 2,500 m² (3,000 sq. yd.) can be watered each day.

The *tunbûr*, also known under the name « Archimedean screw », is a hollow cylinder made of wood or metal, with a spiral arrangement inside (similar to a never-ending screw), which, when it is inclined to about 30°, can raise up water to about ¾ m (2 ½ ft.). The output is a maximum of 6,000 m² (7,176 sq. yd.) of earth watered a day.

The *sâqiya*, a type of wheel machine, has been known since the Ptolemaic period. It has a harnessed team (cattle, camels) which turns a horizontal « gear » 9 m (10 yd.) in diameter, which itself turns a vertical wheel which draws up the water by means of clay vases fixed to it. At each turn the vases fill up with water from the lower level and, when they have gone back to the highest point, empty it into the canal system. The output with a machine a little less than 3 m (10 ft.) high is approximately 2,000 m² (2,400 sq. yd.) each day.

The *tâbût* is a light wheel of wood or metal that, like the *tanbûr* raises the water with a circular compartment fitted in the interior. It is employed particularly with regular levels of water, in Middle Egypt and the Delta. Output with a rise of 1.5 m (5 ft.) : about one hectare (2,500 acres) a day.

The *shâduf* is an apparatus for lifting water made of a long balance with a bucket or pocket at one end which brings up the water and, at the other end, a block of clay or stone which serves as a counterweight. With several *shâdufs* arranged one above the other water can be raised to 4 m (13 ft.). The work, carried out by one or two men working at the same rhythm, is very tiring. Output : about 4,000 m² (4,800 sq. yd.) per day.

Water wheels *(noria)*, are worked by the force of the current, and for this reason they can only be used in the Fayûm where a current exists caused by a level different to the valley. Animated mechanically *(kabba)* they nevertheless make it possible to bring up water very quickly. Where it is possible they are still used today.

The modern rotary pumps are the most apt for getting the best possible results. But as they are too expensive for the fellah, they are only used periodically with public money, serving most of all to irrigate the cane sugar plantations which need an enormous amount of water. At the time of inundation the sluice gates of the Aswan Dam stay open ; in November, when the waters go down again, they are reclosed for the time necessary to replenish the reserve lake. Then it is allowed to rest so that there will be water against the drought until the arrival of the new inundation. With this system and with the masses of water imprisoned by the *Sadd el-Ali* it will be possible to water progressively all the land which will extend the cultivation to 80,000 km² (30,000 sq. mi.) and permanent irrigation to 800,000 hectares (2,000,000 acres).

Industry

The young Egyptian industry depends on the price of raw materials and the supply of energy necessary for their transformation. In the case of electricity, an appreciable result is expected from the full functioning of the turbines of the High Dam (10 million kilowatts per annum).

The textile industry is of prime importance, concentrated in Lower Egypt (Kafr el Dauwar, Mehalla, Alexandria) and Cairo. Production concentrates on cotton thread and textiles with a cotton base, which attains a total of 100,000 tons. On the other hand, light Egyptian tobacco is made into cigarettes. Helwan produces cement and several refineries treat sugar. The setting up of a really heavy industry was started by the steel works erected by the G.F.R.

and with Soviet co-operation. The steel works now work fully and produce crude steel ; they are supported by the works at Aswan which use on the spot minerals extracted in the region. These works function with current produced by the turbines of Sadd el-Ali.

Coal mines were detected and put into operation in Sinai. It is also possible to drill for petroleum there and also on the border of the Red Sea. The importance of the growing cinema industry, which is concentrated at Giza, should not be neglected ; it is becoming known as the Hollywood of the Arab world. The films which are produced there (about 200 per annum) hold the principal place in the cinemas of the Arabic speaking world.

Communications

The communication routes naturally have Cairo at the centre. Alexandria is the turning place of maritime traffic. Nearly 10,000 km (6,200 mi.) of surfaced roads, 15,000 km (9,300 mi.) of unsurfaced roads and tracks run everywhere in the country ; in the Delta region the network is very dense, while the connections are looser on the north-south route and with the oases.

The road system is used by commercial and private vehicles and supplied with a network of petrol stations and garages.

The railways go from Cairo to nearly all the important places in the country and connect to the neighbouring countries : by the coast to Libya, by the Suez canal to Haifa (closed since 1948) and south, partly by boat, to the Sudan.

The new international airport of Cairo at Heliopolis is used by more than twenty-five airlines. It is the base of the national airline company « Egyptair » (Arabic : *Masr el-Tayaran*) which has numerous connections with Europe. This airline also has internal flights to Aswan, Luxor, Abu Simbel and other places outside the valley.

Population
and Social Structure

The present population of Egypt is more than 37 million which is a density of more than 1,000 inhabitants per square kilometre (0.3861 sq. mile). But, if only the Delta and the Nile valley are counted, where habitation is concentrated, Egypt is without doubt one of the most densely populated countries in the world. The number of inhabitants has increased by practically tenfold in one hundred and fifty years, whereas the habitable surface has barely doubled. The gain in agricultural land anticipated with the construction of the Sadd el-Ali could only momentarily cope with requirements because of the population explosion.

The State has instituted an agricultural reform which limits the ownership of land to 80 hectares (197.68 acres) and which fixes the minimum land required to support a fellahin family to 2.5 hectares (6.177 acres). Up to now this has hardly reduced the gap which separated rich from poor. The Egyptian fellah still belongs to the least favoured class of humanity. Little has changed since the pharaonic period.

The fellah is probably an authentic enough descendant of the inhabitants of ancient Egypt, the number of which must have reached more than eight million at certain periods. The fellahîn have kept until now certain ancient customs to which they sometimes give a new meaning. They live in their own setting and lead a tranquil and laborious life with frugality and resignation, the roots of which go back thousands of years. Their clothing is picturesque consisting of a cotton gallâbîya which resembles a type of long shirt, a short

pair of trousers in the same material underneath, possibly a wool overcoat on the top, a turban or small coloured hat on the head (if anything), possibly sandals on the feet and a solid stick in the hand. The fellahîn, who constitute at least 70 % of the population, have thus been able to retain more or less the same existence through the different civilisations which have succeeded through time.

Besides the peasants, there are another half a million workers. These are most often men who were originally peasants who have left the overpopulated countryside to work in the towns. The inhabitants of the cities are therefore, for the most part, of the same origin as the fellahîn and the descendents of different conquerers who passed through Egypt must also be distributed in the towns and the countryside. Lastly, the Bedouins are on the way to becoming sedentary, becoming peasants as well as workers.

The social status of women is adapting itself to modern life. According to Islamic tradition women lived isolated in the bosoms of their families, but now they participate more and more in social and professional life, and tend to have more responsibility. As a general rule, Egyptians practise monogamy and the already very low percentage of polygamy (mostly in the countryside) is diminishing. The pre-eminent role of the mother in the family is also tending to decrease. The veil is no longer worn, but the countrywomen still sometimes have a tendency to hide their faces in front of strangers. The established feminist movement allows equal career opportunities, at least in principle. In the legal system, equal rights are not yet totally and definitively acquired. As regards marriage, it is still quite usual, in the country-side, for girls to be married by their parents at 16, hardly knowing their husbands. Female excision is still a custom among the peasants.

Whith more than 4 million people, the Christian Copts form an important minority, some of them taking administrative and political responsibilities. They have an important cultural tradition, the history of which is displayed in the Coptic Museum, which the visitor should not fail to see. However, the majority of them are poor city-dwellers and peasants. They live in large numbers in the older parts of Cairo, near Fustât, also in Alexandria, and in Middle and Upper Egypt, where they sometimes form the majority, especially in the towns of Minya, Asyût, Abu Qurqas, Sohag, Girga and Luxor.

Apart from the Copts, the existence of a minority of about 100,000 other Christians should be mentioned, they belong, for the most part, to different Oriental churches, orthodox or attached to Rome. Lastly, *Jews,* who at all times formed an important minority in Egypt, have, for the most part, left the country and their community is on the way to extinction.

The nomadic *Bedouins* who live in the deserts on the Red Sea, in the oases and in Sinai are being encouraged more and more by the State to settle ; sometimes they become workers. There are no more than about 50,000 who move from pasture to pasture with their herds or who practise camel breeding. Although they are all Muslims, the Bedouins are aware that they are very different to the settled fellahîn.

Nubians are certainly the least favoured ethnic group in Egypt. Practising Islam also, they have an origin, a language and customs entirely different to the other Egyptians. Now, because of the drowning of their land by the waters of the two Aswan barrages, they have been forced to leave and move to totally strange environments where they have to begin a new existence (see Kom Ombo, p. 301). Lacking resources, the men have for some time been obliged to go to work in the large towns where they are servants or porters, in spite of the fact that their families often stay in the southern villages.

The Language

In ancient Egypt they spoke *Egyptian* which belonged to the Hamitic-Semitic language group. Although this language has become fairly well known since the work of Champollion (see p. 90), there is only some idea of its pronunciation because the vowels were not transcribed in the writing. With the introduction of Christianity, the last stage of Egyptian writing was *Coptic*. Its usage was lost bit by bit as Arabic took over and it has not been spoken since the thirteenth century, but it has remained the liturgical language of the Coptic church.

In modern Egypt an Arabic dialect, which is one of the branches of the Semitic group of languages, is spoken. But in administration, inscriptions, literature, large newspapers and on radio, they use a more or less literary Arabic which is the language of the Koran and which is understood in principle in all the Arab countries. The pronunciation of Egyptian dialect may vary according to the region. The common language is rich in words of Coptic, Turkish or even European origin (culinary vocabulary for example).

In the principal tourist places and in the large towns visitors can always find people who speak English or French (particulary in business) and sometimes Italian or Greek.

Arabic Alphabet

The Arabic alphabet consists of 28 consonants (of which three may also serve to lengthen the vowels) which may take four different forms according to their position in the words. Vowels are not transcribed, except in the Koran and in some other cases where they are indicated by the use of small signs put above or below the consonants. Arabic is read and written from right to left.

Pronunciation of Egyptian

Naturally only an approximation of Arabic pronunciation can be transliterated into the Latin alphabet. Arabic includes a series of vocal sounds which are unknown in Indo-European languages and, for this reason, they can only be transliterated in a very imprecise manner. In this handbook we have transliterated the Arabic sounds with English sounds which most clearly correspond and in the simplest possible way. However, for certain place and personal names, as well as certain names peculiar to Arabic, we have used the English transliterations most frequently used on plans and maps, or those which have passed into common usage. In this way, the transliteration of Arabic words is always a sort of compromise which aims for practical use, rather than authenticity.

The following list gives some practical examples of the pronunciation of special or difficult sounds :

sh as in English (*shop*)
g generally pronounced hard (*good*) but often soft in Upper Egypt as in other Arab countries.
gh a guttural resembling the French rolled *r*.
kh like *ch* in the Scottish word *loch*, or the German *ch*.
dh like *th* in the.
th like *th* in thing.
û as *oo* in *fool*
î as *ee* in *been*
u as in *full*
q a very guttural *k*.
â as in *father*
ei as *a* in *lane* (*sheikh* is pronounced *shake*)

The Arabic ain is a harsh and peculiar guttural sound sometimes transliterated as *a*.

The Arabic definite article is *el* (sometimes pronounced *al*) for all genders and numbers. It is used in the names of places and before a large number of the consonants the *l* is

Name	Equivalent	Independent	Final	Medial	Initial
Alif	', a	ا	ل	ا	ا
Bā'	b	ب	ـب	ـبـ	بـ
Tā'	t	ت	ـت	ـتـ	تـ
Tha'	th	ث	ـث	ـثـ	ثـ
Jim	j	ج	ـج	ـجـ	جـ
Hā'	h	ح	ـح	ـحـ	حـ
Kha'	kh	خ	ـخ	ـخـ	خـ
Dāl	d	د	ـد	ـد	د
Dhāl	dh	ذ	ـذ	ـذ	ذ
Rā'	r	ر	ـر	ـر	ر
Zāy	z	ز	ـز	ـز	ز
Sin	s	س	ـس	ـسـ	سـ
Shin	sh	ش	ـش	ـشـ	شـ
Sād	s	ص	ـص	ـصـ	صـ
Dād	d	ض	ـض	ـضـ	ضـ
Tā'	t	ط	ـط	ـطـ	ط
Zā'	z	ظ	ـظ	ـظـ	ظ
'Ayn	'	ع	ـع	ـعـ	عـ
Ghayn	gh	غ	ـغ	ـغـ	غـ
Fā'	f	ف	ـف	ـفـ	فـ
Qāf	q	ق	ـق	ـقـ	قـ
Kāf	k	ك	ـك	ـكـ	كـ
Lām	l	ل	ـل	ـلـ	لـ
Mim	m	م	ـم	ـمـ	مـ
Nūn	n	ن	ـن	ـنـ	نـ
Hā'	h	ه	ـة ـه	ـهـ	هـ
Wāw	w	و	و	و	و
Yā'	y	ي	ـي	ـيـ	يـ

· = 0	● = 5	١· = 10
١ = 1	٦ = 6	١١ = 11
٢ = 2	٧ = 7	١٢ = 12
٣ = 3	٨ = 8	٢· = 20
٤ = 4	٩ = 9	٣· = 30

assimilated (for example el-Qasr is pronounced eq-Qasr).

In contrast to the letters, Arabic numbers (which are the remote ancestors of our Arabic numerals) are read and written from left to right. Some knowledge of the numbers would make the visit easier.

Government and Administration

Since the first of September, 1971, Egypt has had the official name *Arabic Republic of Egypt* (before then it was known as the *United Arab Republic*). From that time it has been part of an association with Libya and Syria under the name *Union of Arab Republics*.

The head of the Arabic Republic of Egypt is the President of the Republic who is also the commander-in-chief of the armed forces and leader of the National Defence Council. He determines State policy and appoints and revokes the Prime Minister and the members of the Cabinet.

The legislative body is the National Assembly. On its motion, the people elect the President with a mandate of six years. The deputies of each of the 175 districts of the country form the 250 members of the National Assembly for five years. Half of them must be peasants and workers. The *Arab Socialist Union* is the only political party.

Egypt is subdivided into 25 administrative regions. Five of them are the towns of Cairo, Alexandria, Port Said, Ismailia and Suez. The Delta consists of eight provinces (Tahrir, Beheira, Qalyûbiya, Sharqîya, Damietta (Dumyât), Kafr esh-Sheikh, Garbieh, Dakhalîa), the same as Upper Egypt (Aswan, Qena, Sohâg, Asyût, Minya, Fayûm, Beni Suef and

Gîza). The four frontier districts (Southern Desert, Eastern Desert, Red Sea and Sinai) depend directly on the Ministry of the Interior, whereas the towns and provinces have restricted autonomy.

Broadcasting, Television and the Press

The State Broadcasting organisation plays an important part because it is the central organisation of telephone, telegraph, broadcasting and television. The information service approved by the government as « the Arab voice » is not only broadcast to the Arab world, but is transmitted in 19 different languages to large parts of Asia and Africa.

Since 1960 all the Egyptian newspapers have been nationalised. Among the principal newspapers are : « El-Ahram » (« The Pyramids »), « El-Akhbar » (« The News »), « El-Mesa » (« The Evening ») and « El-Gumhuriya » (« The Republic »). There is also a daily newspaper in English, The Egyptian Gazette and two in French, Le Progrès Egyptien and Le Journal d'Egypte where English or French tourists can find extracts of the Arab press translated into their languages and certain useful local information. All the newspapers come out in Cairo.

Education

Since 1933, children between 7 and 12 have received, in principle, a general elementary education. Since 1950 school has been free. The « elementary school » is followed by « preparatory school » of 3 years, to which the « high school » or « vocational school » is connected. After three more years, the holder of a school leaving certificate may study in one of the five Universities : in Cairo at Gîza, Ain-Shams or the American University ; at Alexandria ; at Minya or at Asyût. One of the oldest universities in the world, the Koranic University of El-Azhar in Cairo holds a special position ; it has long played an important role in the Islamic world and it has also become a general university where virtually all the modern disciplines are taught.

Food and Drink

Egyptian cooking

Egyptian cooking is Oriental-Arabic, with Turkish, Greek and Italian influences. The food is fatty and strongly spiced or conversely very sweet. Mutton and veal, as well as poultry, form the basis of many dishes. Meat is grilled or roasted. It is accompanied by a salad dressed with oil, tomatoes and onions. The following list gives some of the special Egyptian dishes in alphabetic order.

Ataiyef : dough filled with walnuts or almonds, fried and dunked in syrup.

Baklawa : heavy and fatty puff pastry, stuffed like *Ataiyef,* baked and covered with syrup.

Bamiyah : a type of vegetable, shaped like a cone-shaped shell, baked in a tomato sauce *(dimma).*

Cossa : courgettes stuffed with chopped mutton.

Dolma : vine-leaves stuffed with meat hash.

Ful-medammes : boiled beans, served hot with oil and lemon.

Kebab : pieces of grilled lamb or mutton, served on parsley.

Kalauwi : grilled offal on parsley.

Kufta : balls of minced meat often accompanying kebab.

Konafa : sweet vermicelli-shaped dough with syrup, almonds and walnuts, fried in oil or butter.

Mahallbiya : a type of rice pudding with dried fruit and attar of roses.

Taameyya : patties made with ground bean dough.

Tehina : sesame seed paste flavoured with lemon.

Here are some Arabic words which may help you when you order your meals :

fetoor : breakfast
gadda : lunch
asha : dinner
Shurba : soup
bade masluk : boiled egg
samaka : fish
lakhma : meat
rosto : roast
farkha : chicken
khodar : vegetables
patates : potatoes
ruzz : rice
salata : salad
pandurah : tomatoes
basal : onions
set : oil
zibda : butter
khall : vinegar
felfel : pepper
sukkar : sugar
gibna : cheese
fakha : fruit
toffah : apple
mishmish : apricot
fraulah : strawberry
kommetra : pear
tien : fig
krees : cherry
mango : mango
battikha : water melon
kawun : cantaloupe melon
bortukaan : orange
khakh : peach
barkuh : plum
khainab : grapes
yûssef effendi : tangerine

DRINKS

Coffee and above all tea are the national beverages. Coffee *(kahwa)* is prepared like Turkish coffee ; it is drunk *sokkar ziâda* (sweet), *masbuth* (medium) or *saâda* (without sugar). Tea is always fairly strong and may be flavoured with mint.

Egyptian beer is very popular (trademark *Stella*). It can be accompanied with a glass of date brandy. The wine, which comes from Lake Mayût is quite good. The best is *Gianaklis*

and the better vintages are *Pharaons, Omar Khayyam* (red) *Rubis d'Egypte,* (rosé) and *Cru des Ptolémées* (white).

Fruit juices, served well-chilled, are refreshing. Mango juice is particularly worth trying as well as lemon or lime juice. It is possible to stop often at the numerous bars where fruit juices are prepared (costing only a few piastres). In the streets you sometimes come across sellers of water or *ere-souz*, a type of liquorice juice which is the favourite drink of the country.

History

The story of Egypt covers about 5,000 years of human history. Up to the thirteenth century B.C. this history is simply that of the Nile valley, but after that, it also becomes the history of Egypt's changing relations with the important powers of the Mediterranean and the Oriental empires up to the Persians, Greeks and Romans who came after the Pharaonic empire. After them, Egyptian history becomes partially integrated with the history of the Islamic world and most recently has been one of the trouble spots of the modern world.

Ancient Egypt

The Egyptian priest Manetho (305-285 B.C.) wrote a history of his people in Greek and, for this purpose, arbitrarily divided the succession of sovereigns known to him into 31 dynasties ; a division which is preserved for convenience by modern historians. Manetho's chronology for the Old Kingdom and Middle Kingdom is, in almost every case, too high. The modern chronology for these periods is founded on comparable and established dates from finds and the study of correspondence, treaties and documents which have been found in Egypt itself and the neighbouring Mediterranean and Asiatic countries.

With the restriction that these dates give for the Old and Middle Kingdoms, which means they may have to be closed up eventually, the his-

torical summary given in this guide corresponds to the present state of Egyptological knowledge. Each of the following section gives, at the beginning, the dates for the period, then the principal historical events, the religious trends, a list of the notable monuments and finds of the period considered and, finally, a king list.

RECENT PREHISTORY
(from circa 5000 B.C.)

Nomadic hunters, the carriers of the Neolithic culture, settled in the Nile valley. In their religious representations, the Nile flood and the fertility rites which were associated with it (offering a young girl to the river god) played a great part. They also developed a belief in an after-life and in gods with definite personalities. The first calendar was created. Finds : Settlements and cemeteries of the cultures of Badari and Naqada.

ARCHAIC OR EARLY DYNASTIC PERIOD
(3000-2780 B.C.)

Ist and IInd Dynasties.
The upper Egyptian king known to history as Menes, who can perhaps be identified as the historical pharaoh Narmer, united Upper and Lower Egypt ; Memphis became the capital. The increased use of copper dates to this period. Hieroglyphs, a combination of pictographic and

phonetic signs appeared and their use developed. Religion : The sky god was Horus and his incarnation was the king. Finds : Annals on tablets, stelae, seals, slate palettes, red and buff pottery, stone vases.

> *King List*
> Menes or Narmer, Aha, Djer Uadji, Udimu,...Semerkhet, Hotepsekhemwy..., Khasekhemwy (the list is still not well established and is only partially cited here).

OLD KINGDOM
(2780-2270 B.C.)

IIIrd Dynasty (2780-2723 B.C.). The king reigned autocratically over a country divided from the beginning into provinces or nomes. Administration was well organised. Religion : Sophisticated theological systems were established at Heliopolis and Memphis. Monuments : The Step Pyramid of Djoser at Saqqara, built by Imhotep, is the most ancient stone building in Egypt ; funerary reliefs, statues of Djoser, wood panels of Hesy-re.

> *King List*
> Djoser (Zoser) or Neterkhet, Sekhemkhet, Khaba, Huni.

IVth Dynasty (2723-2563 B.C.) Prosperity reigned over the land, arts and crafts flourished. Straight lines, plain surfaces and massive supports were used in architecture. The stone cutters and engravers worked limestone and granite. Religion : The Memphite •doctrine predominated. Solar barques were constructed for the dead king's journey in the after-life. Monuments : The Bent pyramid and Sneferu's pyramid at Dahshûr, pyramids and funerary temples of Cheops, Chephren, and Mycerinus at Gîza, Great Sphinx at Gîza, necropolises and mastabas, Abu Roash pyramid, statues and stelae.

> *King List*
> Sneferu, Cheops (Khufu), Redjedef, Chephren (Khafre), Mycerinus (Menkaure), Shepseskaf.

Stela of the Serpent King from Abydos (Ist Dynasty).

Vth Dynasty (2563-2423 B.C.). The influence and the power of priests and officials increased. The *Pyramid*

Texts appeared in the reign of the last king of the dynasty, covering the walls of royal tombs to ensure the survival of those within. Religion :

The king was officially called the « Son of Re » (= the sun). The cult of the god Re became the state religion. The belief in survival in the after-life deepened ; funerary ritual became fixed. Monuments : Solar temples at Abu Gurob, pyramid of Unas at Saqqara (with texts), mastabas of Ptah-hotep and Ti at Saqqara, limestone reliefs, wooden or stone statues (for instance the *Sheikh el-Beled* or « village mayor » in the Cairo Museum).

> *King List*
> Userkaf, Sahure, Neferirkare Kakai, Shepseskare, Neferefre, Nyuserre, Menkauhor, Djedkare Isesi, Unas.

VIth Dynasty (2423-2263 B.C.). The power of local princes increased ; royal power diminished ; the establishment of a type of feudal system. Organized expeditions to the land of Punt (on the horn of eastern Africa) to bring back incense and other products. Voyages to Africa : a pygmy was brought back to delight Pharaoh. Religion : The elaboration of moral maxims which appear in the « Instructions », a didactic genre of literature. Monuments : Pyramids and mastabas at Saqqara, Dahshûr and Maidum. Mastabas and rock-cut tombs in Middle and Upper Egypt.

> *King List*
> Teti, Userkare, Pepi I, Merenre I, Pepi II, Nitocris.

FIRST INTERMEDIATE PERIOD
(2263-2040 b.c.)

VIIth and VIIIth Memphite Dynasties, more or less fictitious.

IXth and Xth Dynasties at Heracleopolis. The period seems to have been full of social unrest, violence and civil war ; less in the north and in Memphis. Infiltration of Asiatics in the north. The princes of the nomes took more and more power. The literature is full of pessimism and scepticism. Religion : The importance of Osiris, the god of the dead, with whom, not only the king, but each mortal could claim assimilation, increased. Finds : Models illustrating daily life, groups of wooden soldiers.

> *King List*
> Most of the kings remain unknown. Three kings with the name of Kheti and one with the name of Merikare.

MIDDLE KINGDOM
(2133-1785 B.C.)

Toilet Scene on a Princess's Sarcophagus. Dyn. XI.

XIth Dynasty (2133-1991 B.C.). The Theban princes took the country's difficult situation in hand. Finally, Mentuhotep II reunified Upper and Lower Egypt. The royal residence was transferred to Thebes. In statuary and relief the ancient style enjoyed a veritable renaissance. Religion : This is the period to which the very long *Coffin Texts* are dated. Monuments : Tombs of Mentuhotep III and IV, Deir el-Bahri tombs, ship models.

> *King List*
> Several kings had the name Inyotef or Mentuhotep

XIIth Dynasty (1991-1785 B.C.). The residence was established once again in the north, near the mouth of the Fayûm. The Middle Kingdom reached the zenith of its power with conquests of Palestine and Nubia (down to the second cataract). Religion : Amun became the principal god and his name entered into the composition of royal names (Ammenemes means : « Amun is at the front »). They also began to tolerate foreign deities. Ammenemes I wrote a more or less pessimistic instruction (in fact apocryphal) for his son Sesostris. Monuments : Lisht pyramids ; Heliopolis obelisk, Dahshûr pyramid, Beni Hasan paintings, Aswan tombs, Hawara « Labyrinth », Tanis sphinx.

> *King List*
> Ammenemes I (Amenemhat), Sesostris I (Senusret), Ammenemes II, Sesostris II, Sesostris III, Ammenemes III, Ammenemes IV, Sobekneferu.

SECOND INTERMEDIATE PERIOD
(1785-1575 B.C.).

XIIIth and XIVth Dynasties (1785-1680 B.C.). Multiple causes and complexities led to the decline of the country ; the period is incompletely known.

> *King List*
> More than thirty kings many of whom were named Sobkhotep, Ammenemes, Sesostris etc.

XVth, XVIth and XVIIth Dynasties. (1680-1575 B.C.). The Hyksos, who came from Asia, infiltrated into Egypt and made themselves masters of a large part of the land. During their domination, the horse, the chariot and new military techniques were introduced into Egypt.

The XVIIth dynasty of Theban princes was partially contemporary with the XVth and XVIth dynasties which were purely Hyksos. Religion : Importance of the god Seth in the north, assimilated to Baal. Monuments : Very few have survived of this troubled time ; statues.

> *King List*
> The Hyksos kings were often named Apophis, the Theban kings Inyotef, Seqenenre or Kamose.

NEW KINGDOM
(1575-1085 B.C.)

XVIIIth Dynasty (1575-1308 B.C.). The Theban prince Amosis crushed and drove off the Hyksos and reunified the country. With Tuthmosis III, Egypt became a great international power. The territory extended up to the fourth cataract and into a large part of Syria-Palestine. A fever of construction took over the country ; numerous works of art were produced of an excellent style. In the time of the « heretic » king Akhenaten « Amarna » art prevailed, intimate and full of life. Religion : Amun became god of the empire ; the temple of Karnak was continually enlarged. Existence of a rich funerary literature (Guides for the afterlife). Akhenaten introduced a type of monotheism ; the cult of the Aten, the solar disk, and made his capital at Amarna. After his death the ancient religion was restored. Monuments : Temples of Karnak, Deir el-Bahri, Luxor (partly ancient), colossi of Memnon, tombs in the Valley of the Kings, finds from Amarna.

King List
Amosis, Amenophis I, Tuthmosis I, Tuthmosis II, Hatshepsut (Queen), Tuthmosis III, Amenophis II, Tuthmosis IV, Amenophis III, Amenophis IV(= Akhenaten), Smenkhkare, Tutankhamun, Ay, Horemheb.

XIXth Dynasty (1308-1186 B.C.) A new dynasty which sprang from generals of the Delta. The kings who followed installed the royal residence in this more strategic region. There were numerous military campaigns, above all that of Ramesses II against the Hittites. Period of power and great buildings. Religion : The theology of Amun continued to develop (with beautiful hymns to the god). The Hebrews left Egypt about this time (Exodus). The foreign cults continued to develop (Baal,Astarte). Monuments : Temples in Nubia (Abu

Simbel), Karnak, Luxor, Abydos, royal and private tombs in Thebes, funerary temples.

King List
Ramesses I, Sethos I (Seti), Ramesses II, Merneptah, Sethos II, Amenmesses, Siptah, Tewosret (Queen).

XXth Dynasty (1186-1085 B.C.). The « Sea Peoples » and the Libyans who tried to invade Egypt were repulsed ; a long period of peace followed. With the increase in the power of the priests, the empire collapsed. The State within a State which was the priesthood of Amun predominated and the last Ramesside kings stood aside faced with the rise of the priest-kings. Monuments : Buildings at Karnak, Medinet Habu temple, royal and private tombs at Thebes.

King List
Sethnakht, Ramesses III, Ramesses IV to Ramesses XI

THIRD INTERMEDIATE PERIOD (1085-664 B.C.)

XXIst Dynasty (1085-945 B.C.). In Upper Egypt power was held by the High priest of Amun in spite of the fact that kings reigned simultaneously in the Delta. Monuments : Tombs and treasures of Tanis

King List
Smendes, Herihor, Psusennes I, Pinudjem, Amenemope, Siamun, Psusennes II

XXIInd Dynasty (945-730 B.C.) Kings of Libyan origin, the Bubastides, replaced the Tanite kings. Jerusalem was attacked by Sheshonq I (the Shishak of the Bible) and the temple of Solomon was pillaged. Religion : Importance of local divinities. Monuments : Buildings at Thebes and Tanis, royal tombs.

King List
Sheshonq I, Osorkon I, Takelothis I, Osorkon II, Sheshonq II, Takelothis II, Sheshonq III, Pami, Sheshonq IV

XXIIIrd Dynasty (817-730 B.C.). This dynasty was contemporary with the preceding dynasty. The Nubian kings pillaged Upper Egypt and continued their advance up to Memphis. Bronze-working techniques became more perfected.

King List
Petubastis and several kings named Osorkon and Takelothis.

XXIVth Dynasty (730-715 B.C.). The Saite kings held the north of Egypt and tried to oppose the aims of the « Ethiopian » kings (=Sudanese), but finally they were defeated by them. The two kings of this dynasty later passed into legend and literature.

King List
Tefnakhte and Bocchoris

XXVth Dynasty (750-656 B.C.). The Ethiopian king Piankhi had already conquered Egypt in 730, but incompletely. His successors completed his work. They also struggled against the growing strength of the Assyrians who in their turn finally took possession of Egypt. The Sudanese kings retained Egyptian civilization and their reigns correspond to a revival, chiefly in Upper Egypt. The ancient strength of the god Amun was restored at Karnak and his « divine adoratrices » played a great part. Monuments : Great buildings throughout the land, chiefly at Thebes.

King List
Piankhi, Shabaka, Shebitku, Taharqa, Tanutamun.

LATE PERIOD
(663-332 B.C.)

XXVIth Dynasty or Saite Period (663-525 B.C.). The prince of Sais, Psammetichus, expelled the Assyrians who themselves had vanquished the « Ethiopians ». The royal residence was at Sais in the Delta. The dynasty favoured the arts and every type of production and gave rise to a veritable national renaissance. The arts attained a certain perfection, particularly sculpture, which was given an incomparable realism. Under Necho, a canal was cut between the Nile and the Red Sea. The Greeks began to settle in Egypt as merchants (at Naucratis) or as mercenaries in the royal army. Monuments : Numerous tombs at Thebes or at Saqqara, buildings throughout the country.

> **King List**
> Psammetichus I, Necho, Psammetichus II, Apries, Amasis, Psammetichus III

Statue of Nespekeshuti (XXVIth Dynasty)

XXVIIth Dynasty (525-404 B.C.). The Persian Empire dominated the Orient and attacked Egypt which Cambyses conquered and put under the control of a *satrap*. The Greek traveller Herodotus visited the country.

In spite of the foreign occupation, which was not supported by the Egyptians, architecture, sculpture and literature flourished. Monument : The Temple of Hibis in the Khârga oasis.

> **King List**
> Cambyses, Darius I, Xerxes, Artaxerxes I, Darius II

XXVIIIth and XXIXth Dynasties (404-378 B.C.). After numerous local revolts in the Delta which were severely repressed, the Egyptians succeeded in defeating the Persians under the leadership of Amyrtaeus who is the only king of the XXVIIIth Dynasty. Other men, who came from the town of Mendes, finally took power and formed the XXIXth dynasty. Egypt attracted more and more Greeks who played an important role in the country. Monuments : Numerous traces of architectural activity throughout the country.

> **King List**
> Amyrtaeus, Nepherites I, Psammetichus, Nepherites II

XXXth Dynasty (378-341 B.C.). A new dynasty, originating from the town of Sebennytus, took the throne. Egypt knew its last brilliant period under indigenous rule ; the kings manœuvred between the powers of the period and maintained the appearance of Egypt's grandeur. They fortified and reconstructed the towns and their temples. A building fever took possession of the land. The arts were favoured.

> **King List**
> Nectanebo I, Teos, Nectanebo II

Second Persian Domination or XXXIst Dynasty (341-332 B.C.). The Persian kings finally re-took possession of Egypt. Their domination was brief and very badly supported. Alexander the Great was favourably received.

> *King List*
> Artaxerxes III, Ochus, Arses, Darius III Codoman

GREEK OR PTOLEMAIC PERIOD

(332-30 B.C.). Alexander the Great made himself known as a pharaoh by the oracle of Amun at Siwa. He founded Alexandria, the success of which was rapid. At his death, his generals disputed his empire and Egypt fell to Ptolemy, son of Lagus, a Macedonian, the successors of whom were the Ptolemies or Lagides. For three centuries Egypt was the centre of Hellenistic culture because of the considerable role played by Alexandria, where a cosmopolitan Greek-speaking population cultivated the arts and sciences. At the same time the Egyptian population followed its habitual life, but between the two cultures, indigenous and Greek, were reciprocal influences. The Ptolemies exploited the land for their profit, but pleased the Egyptians with an intelligent religious policy (numerous constructions of temples). Finally, the numerous dynastic disputes and the rise of Rome caused the end of Greek domination. Monuments : Temples of Edfu, Philae, buildings at Saqqara and Alexandria. Demotic and Greek manuscripts, etc.

> *King List*
> Alexander the Great, Ptolemy I to Ptolemy IX with queens called Berenice and Cleopatra.

ROMAN PERIOD

(30 B.C.-395 A.D.).

The last Greek queen, Cleopatra VII became a temptress to stop the Romans. She succeeded in this way with Julius Caesar and Mark Anthony, but the future Emperor Octavius Augustus won the naval battle of Actium in 30 B.C. and the queen committed suicide. Egypt became a province of Imperial Rome and subject to the vicissitudes of the Roman empire with its moments of glory and its difficulties. Trouble broke out regularly in the country. The emperors however wisely favoured the Egyptian religion and continued to construct large temples. The influence of the language and the spirit of the Greeks continued to spread, whereas Egyptian influences reached Rome (cult of Isis). Very soon Christianity penetrated Egypt and reached Alexandria. It was persecuted in the beginning, then popularised by Constantine and above all by Theodosius who, in 392, ordered the closure of all the pagan temples in Egypt. Christianity was expressed in the Greek or Egyptian language (this was written in the Greek alphabet and became Coptic). Monuments : Temples of Dendera, Philae, Kalabsha, Kom Ombo, buildings at Alexandria.

> *Emperor List*
> From Augustus, all the emperors who reigned in Rome up to the death of Theodosius.

BYZANTINE PERIOD

(395-641 A.D.)

On the death of Theodosius, the Roman empire was divided into a western and an eastern empire. Egypt was part of the Greek-speaking eastern empire. Christianity was the official religion. On the fall of Rome, the eastern empire, the capital of which was Byzantium, was called the « Byzantine Empire ». Christianity was firmly established in Egypt and the last bastions of paganism became more and more reduced. Numerous religious disputes which led to doctrinal schisms originated in Egypt ; it took a long time for them to come to an end (Council of Chalcedon in 451). The numerous political vicissitudes weakened Egypt and she retired within herself. Extreme religious currents developed (monks and anchorites became more and more numerous and it was Egypt which gave rise to the first uniform monastic life). A fairly rich Coptic literature developed, mostly consisting of translations of the sacred texts and the lives of saints and martyrs. Monuments : monasteries on the Red Sea, in the Wadi Natrun and a few in Egypt. Coptic churches in Old Cairo.

> Emperor List
> All the Byzantine emperors from Arcadius to Heraclius I

Arabic Egypt

From the Umaiyads to the Mamelukes

641. The Byzantines resisted the Arab troops led on behalf of the Caliph by Amr Ibn el-As who finally conquered the whole of Egypt. He founded Fustât which now corresponds to Old Cairo. The country became Islamic fairly rapidly.

658-750. Dynasty of the Umaiyads of Damascus, the most ancient Islamic dynasty. A governor, usually a prince, governed Egypt. Marwân II, the last Umaiyad was assassinated in Egypt.

750-868. Dynasty of the Abbasids of Iraq. Mamûm, son of Hârûn er-Rashid, quelled the resistance of the Copts and Bedouins. Then the power of the Caliphs declined and Egypt was independent for a short time.

868-905. Dynasty of the Tulunids. The sultan, Tûlûn, a Turk who was governor under the Abbasids, conquered Syria and Mesopotamia.

905-969. Dynasty of the Ikhshidids, also founded by a governor of Turkish origin, Ikhshid. His descendants were ruled by an Abyssinian eunuch, Kâfûr, who took power and seized Syria and Palestine. Under the weak Ahmad, the Fatimids arrived in the land.

969-1171. Dynasty of the Fatimids of Maghreb. Gohar founded Cairo. Under El-Muizz and El-Aziz there was a certain prosperity and brilliance. The strength of the Fatimids then decreased with a brief respite under El-Gamali. Amalrich I, king of Jerusalem, entered the Delta and sacked Fustât.

1171-1250. Dynasty of the Aiyubids. The Kurd Saladin (Salâh el Dîn), founder of the dynasty, built the Cairo citadel. He conquered Syria and recaptured Jerusalem from the Christians. After his death, during the rule of El-Kâmil, the Christians were victorious at Damietta. Saint Louis (Louis IX of France) recaptured Damietta in 1249, but on the way to Cairo, he was captured by Tûrânshâh and taken prisoner. When the sultan Tûrânshâh was assassinated, the leader of the bodyguards, Ed-Durr, took the throne.

1250-1382. Dynasty of the Bahrite Mamelukes. The ancient body-guards and slaves (of northern origin bought in the slave markets of the Near East) took power. Of the twenty-five sultans of this period, only five reigned for more than ten years, the others were assassinated before that time.

1382-1517. Dynasty of the Circassian Mamelukes. The royal crusade to Jerusalem was suppressed. Beibar made Mecca dependant on the sultan of Egypt. El-Ashraf Khalil completed the victories over the last Christian princes in the Holy Land. Plague epidemics raged in Egypt. In this period the Christians had to wear dark blue costumes, black turbans and a wooden cross weighing five pounds around their necks, while the Jews had to wear yellow costumes, black turbans and a heavy black ball hung from their necks. The Mameluke sultans repulsed the Turks and the Portuguese. The last sultan, Tumân Bey, was executed when the Turks entered Cairo.

1517-1798. Domination of the Turks. The Sultan Selim I conquered Egypt which became a province of the Ottoman empire. An economic and cultural decline made itself felt throughout the land. The *pashas* (who represented the Turkish sultan) exploited the fellahîn and the authority of the Turks diminished while that of the Beys of the twenty-four provinces became more and more influencial. Soon the bodyguards, the Mamelukes, took power once again, but they remained officially loyal to the sultan of Constantinople.

REFORM AND REVOLUTION

1798-1799. In order to block England from the maritime route to the Indies. the French government charged Napoleon Bonaparte to lead an expedition to Egypt, which fitted in with the ambitions of the young general. He defeated the Mamelukes at the Battle of the Pyramids and conquered Egypt entirely in a very short time. After the English victory gained at Abuqîr by Admiral Nelson, the French had to capitulate and leave Egypt. The French intellectuals who accompanied Bonaparte's army indirectly founded Egyptology and emphasised the birth of modern Egypt by their studies.

1805-1952. Domination of Muhammed Ali. The Albanian Muhammed Ali fought against the French, was promoted to general, and then, in 1805, pasha and governor of Egypt for the Turks. In 1807 he forced the English to leave Egypt. During a banquet given in the citadel of Cairo, he murdered 480 important Mamelukes. Muhammed now had a free hand to move along the path of reform. He took the Sudan and made war in Syria, Arabia and Greece. He reformed the army and agriculture by constructing the retaining barrages and also improved the irrigation of the Delta. Having surrounded himself with European counsellors, even though they were working in his interests, Muhammed Ali appeared as the founder of modern Egypt.

1848-1879. Ibrahim Abbas I, Said and Ismail, the successors of Muhammad Ali, detached themselves progressively from Turkey which was weak. Ismail took the title of Khedive (viceroy). Under his reign, in 1869, after ten years work directed by the French engineer Ferdinand de Lesseps, the Suez canal was opened and inaugurated on the 18th November, 1869 in the presence of the Empress Eugenie.

1879-1892. The khedive Taufiq (Tewfiq). Profiting from a nationalist revolution (Arabi Pasha) the British installed themselves in Egypt in 1882. In 1883 the rebellion of the *Mahdi* broke out in the Sudan which resulted in the death of general Gordon when he tried to retain the Sudan in Egypt.

1892-1914. Khedive Abbas II Hilmy. General Kitchener defeated the army of the Mahdi in 1898. An important part was played by Lord Cromer. The first Nile dam was constructed. Prosperity spread through the land.

1914-1917. The Turks became allies of Germany, the British proclaimed martial law in Egypt and nominated Husein Kamil as sultan. The Sudan was annexed.

1917-1922. Reign of the sultan Ahmed Fuad.

1922. The British recognised the independence of Egypt which became a sovereign State, the sultan assumed the kingship as Fuad I. In spite of this nominal independence, the British High Commission continued to play an important part. The British held the Suez canal, occupied the Sudan and were responsible for the country's defence. Independence movements gained strength.

1937. Faruk I mounted the throne. His authority began to be disputed, particularly by the army. Egypt became more and more modernised. A cosmopolitan society took the economic fate of the country into its hands. Difficult relations between the national *Wafd* movement and Nahas Pasha.

1940-1942. The German troops commanded by Rommel advanced towards Egypt. The allied troops under Montgomery blocked their advance at El-Alamein.

1946. Faced with the nationalist movement, the British evacuated their troops from Egypt, but continued to occupy the Suez canal.

1948. Egypt took part in the Arab war against the new State of Israel.

1952. The « free officers » and general Nagib overthrew king Faruk who was banished from the country after his abdication. Agricultural reform was instituted according to a quinquennial plan.

1953. The monarchy was abolished. The Republic of Egypt was proclaimed on the 18th June.

1954. Internal political pressure caused the fall of Nagib. Colonel Gamal Abd el-Nasser took power. British troops began to leave the Canal zone.

1956. The Sudan became independent. Nasser became President. The last British troops left the country. In order to construct the new Aswan Dam Nasser nationalized the Suez Canal Company. After a long delay, airborne French and British troops were parachuted into the Canal towns. For her part, Israel was in open conflict with Egypt. Under Russian-American pressure the UNO ordered the evacuation of the three armies and put an end to the conflict.

1958. Egypt and Syria were unified under the name « United Arab Republic » (U.A.R.) of which Egypt formed the « South province ». The USSR aided the construction of the new dam.

1960-1961. Work began on the Aswan Dam *(Sadd el-Ali)* with important Russian aid. The value was enhanced by the development of Tahrir province in the western desert. Nasser practised state socialism by nationalising and sequestering foreign property and important concerns. Egypt became the leader of the third world. In 1961 Syria left the UAR.

1964. A phase in the construction of the new dam was completed.

1967. Tension arose in the Gulf of Aqaba (Sharm el-Sheikh) and in the Gaza strip (withdrawal of UNO troops) which provoked the escalation of a new conflict with Israel on the 5th June (Six Days war). The Israelis occupied the Gaza strip and the Sinai peninsula, to the Suez Canal.

1970. Death of Nasser. The new President was Anwar el-Sadat.

1971. Sadat inaugurated the new Aswan Dam.

1972. Egypt and Libya drew closer. In 1973 the UAR became the ARE (Arab Republic of Egypt) which with Libya and Syria form the « Union of Arab Republics ».

1973. The out-break of the fourth Israeli-Arab war in October (Yom Kippur). Egypt bridged the Canal with boats and took back part of the east bank, even though the Israelis established a bridgehead on the west bank. Under pressure from the great powers, the UNO arranged the cease-fire again.

1974. An agreement between the two armies resulted in the Israeli withdrawal to a line 20 km (12.4 miles) from the bank of the Canal (Dr Henry Kissinger's mission). Egypt undertook to put the canal zone in order.

1975. On the 5th June, Anwar el-Sadat re-opened the Canal, cleared and demined with, among others, help from the British Navy. In the summer a new agreement was sought between Egypt and Israel. The negotiations took place with American help and proved to be difficult, but succeeded in August.

1977. Président Sadat travelled to Jerusalem to re-open peace negotiations with Israel.

1979. Following further American participation a peace treaty between Egypt and Israel was signed in Washington in March.

1980. Political and cultural associations with Israel were extended ; embassies were established in both countries and discussions on the implementation of the peace treaty were continued.

Art and Civilisation

Historical Survey of Egyptian Art

PREHISTORIC PERIOD
(c. 5,000 - 3,000 B.C.)

During the Palaeolithic period before 5,000 B.C., although different climatic conditions existed in North Africa, the vast deserts along the length of the Nile Valley had already been formed and were much as they are today. From the Red Sea across to Libya flint tools and *rock carvings* of armed men, animals and hunting scenes have been found on the rock ledges. In the hunting scenes, the figures are elongated to express movement, but are smaller and closer together in domestic scenes. From the latter it is clear that cattle, goats and pigs were domesticated. The dead were buried in cemeteries. In the archaeological survey of Nubia before the rising of the great lake behind the new dam, some of these Predynastic cemeteries were excavated. The painted decorations on the characteristic red pottery found there depicted men and animals. During the Prehistoric period, which lasted throughout the fifth and fourth millenia, rock carvings were executed in the Libyan desert, in the Nile Valley and in the Wadi Hammamat. The composition of the scenes in the rock carvings is already very characteristic of that in later Egyptian art. One can recognise the elegant profile drawings of human beings as purely Egyptian.

During the Predynastic period in the fourth millenium the Badarian, Amratian and Gerzean (Naqada I and II) cultures developed, in which there was a progressive improvement in technical ability due to the introduction of metal-working. As changes in climate resulted in more and more of North Africa becoming desert, the Nile Valley became a desirable place for permanent settlement and civilisation began to develop there. The famous slate cosmetic palettes of Nekhen (Hierakonpolis), an early settlement and the first capital of Upper Egypt, belong to the transition between the Predynastic and Archaic periods.

ARCHAIC OR THINITE PERIOD
(3,000 - 2780 B.C.)

The natural barriers of the Mediterranean Sea and the deserts enclosed the Valley of the Nile and its people. This isolation created a kind of austerity in the thoughts of the Egyptians. They soon began to worship numerous gods under the guidance of powerful priests and began to believe in a life after death.

They called their tombs « Houses of Eternity » and furnished them with food and drink and all the necessary equipment for an after-life, which was envisaged as similar to life on earth. Art was essentially for the decoration of tomb and temple. For nearly three thousand years the forms of this art were perpetuated without any great basic changes. Such changes as did occur were slight for art continued to serve the same purpose, the needs of divine and funerary cults. Art was always very closely associated with religion.

A Crocodile on a Dish (Naqada I)

It is significant that it is the stone structures, which were primarily religious buildings, which have survived, whereas in general the mudbrick domestic and secular buildings have not.

Architecture, craftsmanship and painting were all aspects of this religious art. The prehistoric grave was replaced by a tomb which had a mound over it and this in turn developed into a tomb with a larger superstructure - the *mastaba* (see p. 63). The mastaba tomb had an underground burial chamber and rooms above in the superstructure to store the funerary equipment and offerings. The room containing the offerings communicated by a slit in the wall with another room, the *serdab*. This contained a cult statue of the deceased who thus had access to his offerings.

OLD KINGDOM
(2780 - 2270 B.C.)

The *pyramid,* in origin a stepped mastaba or one mastaba on top of another, began to develop towards its final form in the Old Kingdom. It formed part, and one part only, although the most important, of the royal funerary complex. It was the massive superstructure whose function was to cover and protect the royal burial chamber and its sarcophagus. The first pyramid and also the first building entirely in stone was the *Step Pyramid* at Saqqara (see p. 169). The pyramid of *Sekhemkhet* (p. 172) and the *Maidum* pyramid (p. 182) and finally the three pyramids at Giza (p. 134) represent the stages in the development and evolution of the pyramid which followed. The fully developed type of pyramid contained the burial chamber at the centre, corridors, wells and chambers and usually the entrance was situated in the north face. In the complex associated with the pyramid were various cult buildings. The Valley Temple on the water's edge was linked by a long causeway to the Mortuary Temple situated alongside the pyramid. Also in the complex were subsidiary pyramids and solar boats (on the techniques of their construction, see p. 136). These huge complexes demonstrate how completely the Egyptians had mastered the art of monumental building in stone. The result is imposing in its austere simplicity and at the same time reveals the absolute power of the king.

All the mortuary temples are similar in size and in the simplicity of their architectural form. The outlines are straight and sharp. The foundations are of granite, often highly polished. Heavy blocks used as architraves lie on the square, monolithic columns, against which statues are placed. These statues are usually monumental in character and sculptured in granite or diorite. Sometimes they vary in size and are carved in softer materials such as alabaster or wood.

King Chephren with the God, Horus.

Some statues were made in precious metals. However, very few of these have survived as they would be melted down by the tomb robbers. The relief work of the Old Kingdom takes the form of raised reliefs in the early part of the period and of sunk relief from the Fourth Dynasty onwards. These reliefs were carved mainly on exterior walls, where the scenes were enlivened by the heightening effects of light and shade. Their prime purpose was not envisaged as decorative, but rather as a means of perpetuating through magic the religious rites and ceremonial.

Painting constitutes one of the most important elements of Egyptian art. Nearly all the statues were painted

and sometimes they had inlaid eyes made from semi-precious stones or glass. Walls were covered with a layer of plaster and then painted with colours derived from minerals and vegetable matter. Walls of mastaba tombs were either painted in this way or else carved with reliefs and then painted. The statues of Rahotep and Nofret in the Cairo Museum are typical examples of the sculpture of this period. The mastabas of Ti and of Ptah-hotep contain reliefs which are characteristic of the high standard of work which was produced.

MIDDLE KINGDOM
(2133 - 1785 B.C.)

Whereas in Lower Egypt, the mastaba and the pyramid were the predominant architectural forms, in Upper Egypt at the end of the Old Kingdom a new type of tomb began to appear - the *rock-cut tomb*. This was a tomb cut out in the cliffs, which followed a similar plan to the mastaba in having an antechamber, a chamber with a false door, a serdab and a burial chamber. The serdab in the rock-cut tomb was an open room with a niche for the statue. Good examples of such tombs are those which were built for the provincial nomarchs or governors at Beni Hasan and Aswan (see p. 276 and p. 249). An expressive simplicity is evident both in the funerary architecture and in the decoration of the tombs. The sculpture is delicate and fine. It tends to be a realistic portrait of the living person, the owner of the tomb who has been brought back to life by the ceremony of the « Opening of the Mouth » (see p. 80). The reliefs and paintings have various types of scenes which as a whole form a panorama of Egyptian life and thought. There are scenes evoking the occupations and activities of earthly life, scenes of religious and funerary rituals, the judgement of the dead and the entry into the life-after-death.

In these rock-cut tombs, in the later royal and private tombs of the New Kingdom and on the walls of the temples, the evolution of the *art of Egyptian portraiture* can be seen. The figures are not in any way stiff, functional or monotonous, although they are drawn according to certain conventions and a fairly precise canon of proportion. They have life and warmth and as animated portraits ensure immortality for the person concerned by *symbolic magic*.

Our view of perspective involves a distortion of reality in the sense that the forms which are reproduced are not quite those of the object we actually see. The Egyptians, in common with other ancient cultures and with young children, drew without perspective. Human beings, for example, are represented in profile but with the eye shown as if from the front. The upper part of the body is turned so that both shoulders are shown, the trunk and upper legs are in three-quarters profile and the lower legs are seen in full profile.

The idea was to show a true and totally complete picture of the object. This applies to sculpture, painting and design. Differences in the size of objects indicated their relative importance. Thus the King is always larger than other men and the nobleman is larger than his servants and so on.

Near the tombs of the nobles at Thebes lies the temple of the Eleventh Dynasty King, *Mentuhotep* (see p. 227). The temple exhibits some features of Old Kingdom

architecture and has a rock-cut burial chamber, a series of terraces and a small pyramid. Another famous building of the Middle Kingdom is the so-called *Labyrinth* in the Fayûm (see p. 266), which was in fact the great mortuary temple belonging to the pyramid of Ammenemes III. These temples of Mentuhotep and Ammenemes are similar in that their sculpture harmonises with their pure and simple plans. Typical examples are the seated statue of Mentuhotep and the statues from Tanis. All these sculptures have a distinct facial expression, which is stiff and severe, yet at the same time full of compassionate humanity, which becomes more and more disillusioned. During the Hyksos period, Egyptian art remained on much the same level of achievement as previously, even though politically the Middle Kingdom had come to an inglorious end. It was the Hyksos who introduced the war chariot and harness into Egypt. These newcomers influenced the type of heroic and epic scenes which were to be popular in the New Kingdom.

NEW KINGDOM
(1575 - 1085 B.C.)

A masterpiece of early New Kingdom architecture was the *Temple of Hatshepsut* at Deir el-Bahri (see p. 223). The horizontal and vertical lines of this temple synthesize perfectly with its natural setting in front of a high vertical rock face. The decoration of the temple, its sculpture and its paintings show a high level of artistic achievement. Although it resembles in style and construction the Middle Kingdom temple at Deir el-Bahri, the Hatshepsut temple has certain unique features, characteristic of the New Kingdom. The queen also built a temple at *Buhen,* near to Wadi Halfa in the Sudan. This was a *peripteral temple,* which had a porticoed sanctuary, a style of temple construction which became popular all over Egypt.

Tuthmosis III erected a *Festival Hall* at the temple of Karnak (see p. 208) which was perpendicular to the main temple axis. This was an achievement which inaugurated a new form of construction in temples - an elevated central nave supported on either side by columns.

A rapid development in the types of temple columns is very noticeable. These were derived from plant forms, the shaft representing bundles of stems lashed together and surmounted by umbel or composite capitals. These columns can be associated with religious ideas governing the erection of temples. They were a reminder that the temple was a symbol of the primordial mound, from which the natural world had emerged with its luxuriant vegetation. The chambers, which succeeded each other, became smaller in size towards the sanctuary as did the doorways. All the architectural features of the temple emphasized the Egyptian theology concerning the cosmos and its creation.

The buildings of *Tell el-Amarna* (see. p. 281), the new capital of the « heretic pharaoh », Akhenaten, are faithful to the principles of New Kingdom architecture for palaces and temples. However, Akhenaten, with a view to rapid construction, built mainly in sun-dried mud-brick and consequently, there is little to see of his buildings at Amarna today. What is evident in the art of the Amarna period is the emphasis on naturalism and the joys of nature.

This is apparent in the numerous gardens in the city and its palaces, which had small ornamental lakes and pools and also in the pleasing and delicate colours used in painting and on faience tiles. Amarna art portrays a convincing realism, particularly in sculpture and relief work. It does not hesitate to show ugliness and deformities, nor to caricature in order to give a true and accurate picture of individuals. Amarna reliefs are filled with tall, almost emaciated figures with elongated skulls, long, graceful necks, large eyes and full, heavy lips.

In *funerary architecture* the final development of the rock-cut tomb exhibited a T-shaped plan in the case of private tombs, and a tortuous plan of various corridors and pillared chambers in royal tombs. The mortuary temple of the king was separated from his tomb, which was designed and equipped in secrecy in order to prevent it being robbed.

The New Kingdom was a period of ostentation for Egypt. She dominated much of the ancient world. Thebes and then the Ramesside Residences in the Delta became capitals of great importance. Tuthmosis III, Amenophis III, Ramesses II and Ramesses III, the most famous warrior-pharaohs, built monuments and particularly temples on a colossal scale throughout the land. They decorated the interior and exterior walls of these monuments with polychrome reliefs or paintings and erected colossal statues before the pylon gateways. Ramesses II in particular brought the colossal to the forefront of Egyptian art, making his monuments especially striking to the modern visitor who marvels at their immensity. Excavations at Egyptian sites have, however, produced many small and delicate objects of art made during the New Kingdom.

To the attentive observer a certain carelessness is apparent in the execution, however detailed, of colossal artistic forms. The ability to work such enormous masses is admirable, even though the result may be an empty grandiloquence. Increasing religious piety during the New Kingdom had an effect on artistic concepts and led to the production of idealized representations and to a distinct balance of design in architecture, reliefs and painting. The *Great Hypostyle Hall* at Karnak (see p. 205) and the pillared hall at Abu Simbel (see p. 312) are good examples of this. *Medinet Habu* (see p. 236), built by Ramesses III as a mortuary temple, palace and fortress, can be considered as the last great building symbolising the power and grandeur of the New Kingdom pharaohs.

As well as the monumental architecture and sculpture of this period, the reliefs and wall-paintings should also be appreciated by the visitor. Between the scenes in the Fifth Dynasty tomb of Ti and the sculptured registers on the walls of the Eighteenth, Nineteenth and Twentieth Dynasties' temples, lies a period of centuries. But all of these scenes are similar to each other in fundamental form and basic style. The visual field of the Egyptian artist was limited during the Old Kingdom to the Valley of the Nile. It was enlarged in the Temple of Hatshepsut to include Somaliland, « the Land of Punt », and to depict the botanical room of Tuthmosis III at Karnak (see p. 208) and extended to Syria and Palestine for the representation of conflicts abroad.

There are numerous scenes showing fights against the Hittites, the Bedouins, Syrians, Libyans and Nubians. Often shown in detail and on a larger scale than anything else is the thundering war chariot carrying the pharaoh. He is the principal warrior, always victorious, and the central figure in the tumult and confusion of the battle. The many facets of such scenes do not require from the visitor a particularly discerning eye for detail, but rather some time to allow him to appreciate the true general quality of these rich and often immense reliefs. The depiction of the war chariot in a warlike age was of such great importance that a whole canon of rules governing its representation was developed. The discerning eye can see that the chariot wheels become larger and larger and that the spokes of the wheels are

Statue of Tuthmosis III

so regularly and perfectly spaced that the vehicle almost seems to be moving. Perhaps one of the most valiant moments of this period of Egyptian history is depicted in the reliefs of the battle of Kadesh on the great pylon at *Luxor*. Here, the Egyptian and Hittite chariots meet in battle. (see p. 197). This battle of Ramesses II, which was so nearly a defeat and during which the life of the King himself was in danger, was the subject of reliefs on several of his monuments. It was also the theme of several literary works. In the imposing scenes of this battle, the horses and their movements are extremely natural and realistic.

EGYPTIAN ART AFTER THE NEW KINGDOM

After the New Kingdom, Egypt was only ruled intermittently by native kings. The other ruling dynasties were of foreign origin - Libyan, Ethiopian, Persian, the long Greek domination and then Roman rule. However, the artists continued to produce throughout most of this period works which preserved the character of ancient Egyptian art. The links with ancient tradition were strong and were not forgotten. But political problems and the increasing role played by foreign cultures in Egypt eventually began to have an effect on art forms. At first, new sources of artistic inspiration were lacking and there was also a political reaction, and these two factors resulted in the artists looking to the past for ideas. Ancient works, termed by them as archaic, were copied, sometimes badly and sometimes with true genius. When foreign influences began to be felt by the Egyptian artist, he attempted to integrate them into his own culture. Sometimes this proved successful, but

more often it resulted in degraded artistic forms. However, it must be remembered that this development took place over a period of more than a thousand years. Until the end of the Ptolemaic period, the Egyptians continued to produce wonderful works of art.

In architecture there was no such decadence. The buildings of the late periods were in every way similar to those which had preceded them. The architecture of the Graeco-Roman period and above all its temples reveal a mastery in execution which is worthy of the great periods of Ancient Egypt. The visitor can still see the immense and well-preserved remains of the temples of *Dendera, Esna, Edfu, Kom Ombo, Philae and Kalabsha*. The walls of these temples are covered with reliefs and inscriptions, even the most inaccessible corners are inscribed. It is this systematic and abundant decoration which most impresses every visitor to these temples.

The tombs of the Late Period are very reminiscent in plan and decoration to those of the Old Kingdom. The reliefs and paintings in the large Theban and Memphite tombs of this period have borrowed much in subject, style and type of inscriptions from the Old Kingdom mastabas. Good examples of this are the tombs of *Ibi* and *Mentuemhat*. Later still there are some tombs decorated in a Graeco-Egyptian composite style of funerary art. The most famous of these is the tomb of *Petosiris* at Tuna el-Gebel (see p. 280), in which certain scenes are done in the traditional Egyptian way while others are distinctly Hellenistic in style. But such tombs are exceptional. In general, until the Christian, period the tombs were built and decorated according to Egyptian traditions, although with the passage of time the style became more and more decadent.

As in all the preceding periods, the concept in sculpture remained poised between idealism and realism, but this basic conflict was often resolved in an original and very successful way. Whether they were working in stone or in bronze, the sculptors of the Late Period produced real masterpieces. For instance, there is the bronze statue of Queen Karomana in the Louvre and the realistic portraits of men like those of Mentuemhat in Cairo Museum. It can truthfully be said that during the last four native dynasties, works of sculpture were produced which rival those of the earlier periods.

From the first century B.C. there developed a minor art which was popular not only in Egypt but throughout the Mediterranean region and the Roman Empire. This was the production of amulets or statuettes of gods in faience or bronze. So many were produced in the workshops that they constitute a definite industrial enterprise. A particularly popular bronze statuette was Isis, suckling her son, Horus. It is not improbable that the theme of Isis and Horus, which inspired deep religious feeling, had the effect of preparing the ancient mind to accept the similar image of the Virgin Mary and the child, Jesus.

All of the achievements of Late Egyptian art did not prevent it from foundering when the civilisation and religion to which it was linked began to fade. Deprived of its living inspiration, Egyptian art inevitably declined. However, in some ways, it lived on in other forms for at least several centuries.

COPTIC ART

Coptic art may be linked on the one hand with the final phase of Pharaonic art as influenced by Graeco-Roman styles, and on the other hand with Islamic art. At first it was very influenced by native and Hellenistic styles and the themes were derived from pagan mythology. But from the fourth to fifth centuries A.D., Coptic art began to employ Christian motifs and quickly became the art of Christian Egypt. The word « Copt » came to denote an Egyptian Christian. Coptic art often used Egyptian themes in a Christian sense. Thus Isis and her son, Horus, are transformed into the Virgin and divine child, the victory of Horus over the evildoer, Seth, becomes St. George killing the dragon, Thoth is identified with St. Michael, the pharaonic sign for life, the ankh, is transformed into a cross, and the great hypostyle halls of ancient temples influence the architecture of the basilicas Good examples of such basilicas are those at *Hermopolis Magna* (see p. 279) and *Abu Mena* (see p. 194). Coptic colums are important architectural features of these edifices. The capitals which resemble those of the early Roman period are covered with ornamental carvings of friezes and interlaced plant forms. The best examples of these are found in the *churches of the monasteries* of the Wadi Natrun (see p. 272), those near to Sohag (p. 287), in those in the Red Sea area (p. 334) and that of St. Simeon at Aswan (p. 251). The predominant themes of the reliefs are Christian - the Virgin Mary entering Jerusalem and stories from the Old Testament. They often seem rather naive. The central figures are shown full-face, whereas those of less importance and animals are shown in profile.

The *funerary stelae* more than anything else show the influence of late pharaonic traditions in the choice of motifs and their treatment. The legend of Isis continues to be a popular subject. Also popular are depictions of cherubs, often holding a pigeon in one hand and a bunch of grapes in the other. Works in bronze, silver and gold attained a high level of artistic achievement. But above all it was the weaving of *textiles* which became a true art of the people. Designs of decorative, stylized figures, very abstract and shadowy in form, were woven in linen and wool. These textiles were used for the vestments of monks or as mummy wrappings. The Copts continued to practise mummification even though they did not adhere to pagan beliefs.

Ivory comb. 6th century A.D.

In the churches and monasteries the *objects carved in wood or ivory* attain the same high artistic and technical achievement reached in textile weaving. These wood and ivory pieces are normally carved with reli-

gious scenes or have inlays with biblical motifs. Today, the best pieces are in museum collections.

But it was perhaps in *painting* that Coptic art had its greatest flowering. Ornamental frescoes adorn walls in monasteries, churches, chapels, and also in the houses. The paintings are done with fresh, gay colours and are often surrounded with a decorative border. The frescoes in churches are normally found in the apse and the cupola and have significant religious themes. The most popular are depictions of *Christ,* Mary, the Apostles, the resurrection or friezes composed of episodes from the lives of the Saints. Characteristic and good examples of Coptic frescoes are to be found in the funerary chapels at El-Bagauat at the Kharga Oasis (see p. 352), in the monasteries of the Wadi Natrun, and in the church at Faras in Nubia.

Coptic *icons* should also be mentioned. These are always portraits of saints. In style, they exhibit some of the characteristics of Ancient Egyptian art, but resemble more closely Byzantine icons. The portraits are executed in tempera painting. The predominant colours used are brown, red and reddish tints and less frequently violet and green. The bordering is black.

The art of calligraphy was practised in the monasteries. The oldest Coptic manuscripts date from the third century A.D. at the time when Christianity was beginning to spread throughout Egypt. These manuscripts, unlike those from Ancient Egypt, express the vocalization of the words and therefore give some indication of the pronunciation of the Egyptian language. Their historical and religious interest is also of great importance. A great number of manuscripts written on all kinds of materials have survived. Many of them have beautiful illustrations which much later served as models for those in Western manuscripts and books.

THE ART OF ISLAM
AND OF MODERN EGYPT

The art of the Arabs exhibits some Persian and many Byzantine features. In Egypt this art also absorbed the previous native Egyptian traditions. In every place conquered by Islam there was a great development

Ibn Tulûn   Qalâûn   Sultân Hasan

Minarets of Cairo mosques

in art. In architecture the arch was a very popular feature. All types of arch were built. Roofs were often in

the form of cupolas or domes. Mosques were decorated with slender minarets. The façades of buildings were colourful and profusely decorated with *arabesques* or geometric and stylized plant designs, or with artistically executed Arabic inscriptions. The usual materials employed were limestone, stucco, gypsum, wood, mosaic, and glazed brick. Many ancient architectural elements like columns and granite sills were reused in these buildings.

Under the Umaiyads (658-750 A.D.) the first mosques were Christian churches adapted for their new role. The chancel was replaced, where this proved possible, with a richly decorated prayer recess, the *mirhab*, oriented towards Mecca. The most important part of the mosque was the courtyard, the *sahn*, which had a fountain or *hanafiya* in the centre. The courtyard was surrounded by covered colonnades called *liwans* near to which were one or more towers called *minarets*, from the top of which the people were called to prayer. This basic form is known as the « courtyard mosque ». The decoration on the stonework was of interlaced mythical animal and abstract designs. Ornamental Islamic art developed and blossomed from these designs, those on the glazed tiles, the *kufic* inscriptions, and the wooden carvings on the sides of the throne, the *minbar*. Designs which included the representation of living things and above all human beings disappeared as this was expressly forbidden by Islamic law.

The period of the *Abassids, Tulunids* and *Ikhshidids* (750-969 A.D.) saw the introduction of Persian, Sassanid and Turkish elements of style in architecture. The courtyard-mosque of Ibn Tûlûn in Cairo is a good example (see p. 114). Clay bricks were replaced by stone, pillars of masonry linked by arches tended to replace the monolithic columns previously popular. Sassanid decoration employed intertwining floral motifs which became prominent. Stucco and carved gypsum replaced stone reliefs. The Kufic inscriptions, hitherto rather plain, became more elegant and flowing in style. Designs on tiles equally became more flowing and lastly woollen carpets and silk fabrics were used as decorative features.

Under the *Fatimids* (969-1171 A.D.) Moorish and Umaiyad influences are predominant. The arches and the elegant double columns are characteristic of this period. Here appears for the first time the so-called *stalactite* decoration which can be seen in Cairo in the El-Azhar mosque (p. 147), the Hakim mosque (p. 116) and on the façade of the El-Aqmar mosque (p. 123). The walls of Cairo were erected in a Romano-Byzantine style as may be seen in the three gateways of Bab el-Futûh (p. 116), Bab el-Nasr (p. 117) and Bab Zuweila (p. 145), which still survive. In the Fatimid era carvings completely cover any wood which is visible. The chair and minbar in the mosque at the monastery of St. Catherine in Sinai are typical examples of this (p. 329). But the Fatimid era is most famous for its achievements in the minor arts. Cups, plates, and rock crystal or faience vases were decorated with reliefs, often of abstract, flowing linear designs and sometimes figurative designs. Bronze vases were similarly decorated. Faience tiles were made in special workshops. Definite Asiatic and even Chinese influences are apparent in the style of this work.

Under the *Aiyubids* (1171-1250 A.D.) and particularly in the reign of Saladin, the founder of the dynasty, Seljukid influences reached Egypt. Religious buildings in the Syrian style were erected, such as the mausoleum of Shafi with his domes. It was during this period that the *nashi* writing appeared for the first time and that the type of mosque with cloisters, the *khanqa*, was introduced. Mosaics in gold are relatively common, as were wells of a complex structure such as the spiralled well of Joseph in the Citadel of Cairo (see p. 113).

During the period of the *Mamelukes* (1250-1517 A.D.) Turkish influences dominate the style of architecture with elements of Fatimid, Moorish and also European influences. Madrasa-mosques made their appearance, as did monumental mausoleums. Great domes were built, supported from the corners of the walls by pendentives. The façades were heavily decorated and built with magnificent coloured stones. The gateways were deeply inset in the façades. The minaret towered over the whole structure. In form it had developed from being octagonal on top of a tetragon to being entirely circular. Regularly spaced balconies indicated the number of storeys. Mausoleums were constructed in the form of a high catafalque underneath large domes. A stela was inscribed with the dates of birth and death of the deceased and with some verses to Allah from the Koran.

All of the interior rooms, whatever their purpose, were sumptuously decorated. The essential elements of this decoration included gilded, ornamental work, mosaics, fanciful designs of leaves and scrolls, faience tiles and carved wooden domes of various sizes. In the minor arts the work became more and more elaborate. Glazed items, vases and chandeliers were finely and delicately fashioned. The colours red, green and blue were much used for embroidery in silk or wool on tapestries.

Under the rule of the *Ottoman Turks* (1517-1802 A.D.) the style of Turkish mosques with their domes and very fine minarets was copied in the building of Egyptian mosques. The minarets were now completely circular in form and at the top was a circular balcony. The private houses also imitated Turkish types and were furnished in the Turkish style. Good examples of these in Cairo are Beit el-Kreatlia (p. 115), Beit el-Sahabi (p. 146) and Beit el-Sihaimi (p. 123). Elaborately inlaid furniture was very popular.

From the reign of *Muhammed Ali* (1805-1849) a mixture of Turkish and European influences affected Egyptian architecture. The mosque of Muhammad Ali (p. 110), although rather indifferent work, would not be out of place in Istanbul. The palaces of Cairo and Alexandria are built in a partly classical and partly baroque style with some details which are distinctly Italianate. The whole effect is grandiose and pompous. At this period Egypt, although open to the artistic influences of contemporary cultures, did not assimilate them. This was a relatively static period in terms of art, although some interesting works were produced.

In the last fifty years modern urbanism has come to Egypt. Large building programmes and ambitious road-building schemes have changed the plan and appearance of the cities and large towns. More recently the road along the river in Cairo with its promenades and large hotels was constructed. This has its attractions. The *Cairo Tower*, built about fifteen years ago, is characteristic of contemporary Egyptian architecture. In style it imitates Western examples but also incorporates native

The Cairo Tower

Egyptian inspiration and motifs. The search for a native art style has led the Egyptians to look back to pharaonic art. But the copying of ancient themes and decorative styles has often resulted in the production of very bad imitations, from which modern Egyptian art has gained little of value. Like many other countries in the world, Egypt is searching for an original style in art, which will take into account contemporary trends and also incorporate the best of its ancient artistic traditions.

Egyptian Artistic and Cultural Terms

Amulet. Object of glazed faience, glass, stone, bronze or gold, which by its form, or material procured a man's health, luck and power and warded off perils and demons. Placed in the bandages of mummies, amulets served to ensure the dead man's existence in the after-life.

Ankh. The handled cross is also the hieroglyphic sign which designates 'life'. The divinities were often represented with the sign of life in their hands, and the sign was placed like an amulet in the tomb in order to ensure for its possessor an eternal life. The lustration water used in ritual could also be represented as a stream of *ankh* signs.

Annals *(Room of)*. Room constructed by Tuthmosis III at Karnak. The walls have a precise record of the campaigns of this king and the booty brought back from them.

Apostrophic. Character of a formula, rite or an object which was intended to protect and avert possible dangers ; from the Greek *apostrophe* « a turning away ».

Badari. A prehistoric chalcolithic necropolis in Upper Egypt, which gave its name to a culture at the beginning of the fourth millenium B.C. Finds : Ivory vases, toilet spoons, magic female nude figures with mutilated hands and feet, inhumations in circular graves decorated with bracelets and necklaces.

Beard. As a general rule, the ancient Egyptians did not have beards. They were reserved for gods, kings and great people. The gods wore plaited beards bent up at the end. Mummy sarcophagi were also decorated with divine beards in order to symbolize the transformation of the dead into gods. Royal beards, mostly artificial, were straight, but sometimes also bent at the end. Artificial beards were also worn for ritual purposes. Otherwise the fashion was to be clean shaven, so that the profession of barber had a certain prestige. They used a copper razor.

Beer. The national drink of ancient Egypt for the gods. kings. the living and the dead ; beer made from barley was put in the tombs, sometimes mixed with date juice to make it sweeter. It was strong and intoxicating like wine which was equally appreciated in Egypt.

Bubastides. The name given to the sovereigns of the XXIInd dynasty, of Libyan origin, because their residence was Bubastis in the Delta (see p. 316).

Building *(Style of)*. It is not possible to speak of a marked style in ancient Egyptian architecture, but simply the differences due to the use of various materials (wood, stone or brick). The style of every building depended at first on its ritual intention or purpose and new architectural ideas never led to an abrupt break with the past, not even the buildings in Akhenaten's new capital at Amarna. It is obvious, however, that each period had its preferences and that an experienced person can date a monument by its style.

Calendar. The Egyptians divided the hour into sixty equal minutes for the first time in the Late Period. Before that, from the earliest times, the day was divided into two parts of twelve hours each (twelve longer hours in the day and twelve shorter hours in

Ankh   Djed-Pillar   Flail   Falcon

the night, varied according to the season). A month consisted of thirty days and there were twelve months in the year, making 360 days. The months were put in three groups and formed the seasons : inundation, winter, summer. Five days were needed to complete the year, so they added five supplementary days at the end, called *intercalary* days. Although the year was regulated and devoid of disparities or readjustments in its subdivisions, the calendar gained six hours annually. Copernicus worked on a calendar derived from that of Egypt. This regular division of time is a useful aid to research on Egyptian chronology (see that heading).

Canopic. A jar, often made of alabaster (calcite), in which the mummified viscera of the dead were placed close to the mummy. The lids of canopic jars, usually four in number, represented the four sons of Horus (see p. 71).

Cartouche. An oval ring (derived from a circular original) in which the birth name (nomen) and the coronation name (prenomen) of the king were written. Its form resembles amulets in the form of knots and conveys pictorially « that which is encircled by the sun ». The decipherment of hieroglyphs made great strides because the names of kings were identifiable in their cartouches.

Chronology. The chronology of ancient Egyptian history is a very difficult matter because, in ancient Egypt, the years were not counted consecutively but each new reign was considered as a break and each time a new count was begun. (for example, the dates were noted as : the third year of Hatshepsut).

It is made even more difficult by the fact that the numerical order of kings with the same name was not given (I, II etc.) so they can only be distinguished by the name they were given at the time of their accession. The first chronological framework was made from the writings of Manetho (see p. 31), the Turin royal papyrus, the royal lists at *Abydos* and *Karnak* and the « Palermo stone ». In addition astronomy has made an even more precise chronology possible because during the Archaic period specific astronomical phenomena were observed and recorded. The beginning of the Egyptian year fell at the same time as the beginning of the Nile flood, so important for the country. This corresponds to the day when, a little before sunrise, the dog star Sirius (*Sothis*) was visible on the horizon. But the year was set back by six hours with the solar year, so that the calendar became out of step and it took 1460 years for the helical rising of Sirius to coincide again with the new year. It is known for certain that this phenomenon occurred in 139 A.D., so that before that date it is possible to calculate and precisely date the previous coincidences that the Egyptians dated in their own way. But we do not have similar documents for the very early periods and this is the reason why the Old Kingdom dates are still disputed. It is possible that these dating problems may be resolved from C14 when absolute dates can be obtained.

Circumcision. In ancient Egypt, boys were often circumcised at puberty. Several representations of this operation still exist. Certain temple reliefs (Medinet Habu) show the Egyptian soldiers with collections of uncircumcised phalli in their camps taken from the bodies of their enemies, but they respected the circumcised bodies. The practice of this operation was never systematic however, neither did it have explicit religious signification.

Coffins and Sarcophagi. The covering which was intended to protect the mummy of the dead could be very simple : matting, a box or pottery. But they preferred to use a specially constructed coffin, in cartonnage, wood or stone. Great people and rulers often rested inside several superimposed coffins with the exteriors decorated with reliefs and inlay (gold and semi-precious stones). Wooden anthropoid coffins with a mask of the dead appeared in the New Kingdom. Box-shaped coffins often had a painted door by which the dead person was supposed to leave and return, or even eyes which were supposed to permit him to look out.

Columns and Pillars. Egyptian columns were almost always mounted on circular bases of varying height which could be decorated with inscriptions and representations. Be-

cause the Egyptian column was very often intended to signify the growth of vegetation from the primordial swamp towards the sky, the shaft of the stone column was equivalent to the stem, or bundle of stems, and the stone capital to a flower. While in the Old Kingdom the columns were almost always monolithic (like pillars), in the later periods they tended to make them in sections and then assemble the drums. Five horizontal and circular bands were incised at the top of the shaft, surmounted by the capital which itself was capped by a rather flat abacus of smaller size. The different categories of columns and pillars :

The *Palmiform Column* slightly conical, smooth cylindrical shaft and above the horizontal bands is a capital in the form of a bundle of palm leaves which bend slightly outwards (for instance in the temple of Sahure at Abusir, dated to the Vth dynasty, see p. 166 or in the temple of Kom Ombo, see p. 301).

The *Lotus Column* with bud capital has a conical form ; the shaft is smooth or more often composed of a bundle of stems fastened together. Above the horizontal bands the capital takes the form of a stylised lotus bud with the petals usually closed (for example in the mastaba of Ptahshepses of the Vth dynasty at Abusir, see p. 166).

The *Papyrus Column* has a tapered base, then a conical shaft made up of a bundle of stems tied together. The section may be shown in several ways. Above the horizontal bands the capital has the form a stylised papyrus flower with closed petals (see for example the portico court at Luxor, p. 198).

From the New Kingdom, the shafts of these columns were left smooth in order to receive inscriptions and figures. The leaves may envelop the base of the shaft.

The papyrus column with an open or bell-shaped capital is more rare. A characteristic example is in the gigantic colonnade of the hypostyle hall at Karnak which separates two groups of papyrus columns with bud capitals.

Palm Column   Lotus Column   Papyrus Column   Composite Column

Tent-Pole Column   Hathor Column   Protodoric Column   Osiris Pillar

The *Composite Column* is the last result of an evolution which brought together external influences and a combination of different types of columns. Its capital may consist of up to 27 different combinations of plants (examples in the temple of Kom Ombo, see p. 301, and the court of the temple of Kalabsha, see p. 253).

The *Tent-Pole Column* was not inspired by a plant, but by the primitive pole used to support tents. It is straight, rarely circular, with a smooth circular shaft and a sharply protuding capital.

The *Hathor Column* has a slightly conical, circular shaft with the capital in the form of a *sistrum* head (in actual fact the whole column is a gigantic sistrum), which is the privileged instrument of the goddess Hathor. It has the head of the goddess (with the ears of a cow) crowned with a chapel on its four sides. There are examples at Deir el Bahri, see p. 223, Abu Simbel, see p. 313, and Dendera, see p. 294. The same motif can be found on pillars.

The *Protodoric Column,* which has its origin in the pillar, is in fact a column with compacted multiple sides. It was dressed smooth with eight of sixteen grooves, but was sometimes unfluted (good examples in the tombs of Beni Hasan, see p. 276).

The *Pillar* was used above all in the Old Kingdom as a four sided, robust and rectilinear support which supported the ceilings of funerary temples with their strong monolithic architraves, giving an austere impression (see the lower temple of the pyramid of Chephren, p. 140). The surfaces of pillars could be decorated with representations or inscriptions (for instance in the Osireion at Abydos, see p. 291). From the XIIth dynasty the use of *Osiris Pillars* spread ; these are pillars with a free side against which a standing statue of the king in the clothes and attitude of Osiris is erected ; the pillar and the statue stand on a base, but only the pillar supported the abacus. Originally cut from one block, this type of pillar was constructed later on from several pieces joined together (examples of Osiris pillars at the Ramesseum, see p. 231, at Medinet Habu, see p. 237, at Karnak, see p. 262, and at Abu Simbel, see p. 311).

Colours. For a long time, only the base colours were used, it was not until somewhat later that blended and intermediate colours were employed. The colours also had a symbolic signification : a blue tint was used for the flesh of Amun (god of the azure), green for Osiris in his aspect as a god of regenerated vegetation, black when Osiris was envisaged as god of the other world and dead (colour of mummies), yellow and red could signify immortality, but red could also designate that which was bad or negative in general (thus Seth could be depicted red as well as a dog or sometimes an ass). Red was also used by the scribes for rubrics and the Lower Egyptian crown was red (alongside the white crown of Upper Egypt), proving that symbolism escapes a very simple classification.

Creation. The basic idea in the Egyptian doctrines on the creation of the world is that of a primeval mound which emerged from the waters that covered it. All the necessary elements to create the world were there. Often a god appeared on the hill (out of a lotus for example) who unaided, created himself and then undertook the creation of the world.

At *Hermopolis Magna,* Atum appeared who then engendered *Shu* (air), *Tefnut* (moisture), then the earth god *Geb* and the sky goddess *Nut.* At *Memphis,* the god *Ptah* formed the earth alone using his knowledge and his word. Elsewhere, men were supposed to have sprung from the primeval god's tears and the gods from his saliva. According to another system, the god *Khnum* fashioned the gods, men and animals on his potters' wheel. All the systems of the creation of the world had in common a progressive character and some absence of a fixed hierachy in the creatures.

Crown. There were many types of crown which adorned the heads of kings and gods, and their number was increased by the combinations which could be made from them. The *Lower Egyptian Crown* is red like the umbels of the Delta papyrus (which was the heraldic plant of the north) ; it is a type of mortar with a high extension at the back, with a type of crook at its front. The Upper Egyptian Crown is white like a species of lily which grows in thickets in the south (which is the heraldic plant of this region of the country). It is high and rounded near the middle and it sometimes has an uraeus serpent at the front.

The two crowns united become the double crown or *Peschent* which is preminently the symbol of the Egyptian monarchy. Sometimes it has the two royal protectors at the front, the vulture and the uraeus. The basic forms are the same in other crowns, but they may be augmented with various elements : solar disk, single or double plumes, cow horns, double uraei etc. The head-dress of Amun is made of a mortar surmounted by two high plumes ; that of Osiris, a type of white crown decorated on each side with ostrich plumes. From the New Kingdom the king might also wear a crown which is often called the « war helmet » because it was often worn on campaigns.

Decans (*constellations of stars*). In the inscriptions of the pharaonic period, 36 decans were known in the appearance of the stars, each of which could be seen in the sky for a little more than ten days. They were believed to be protectors and during the night they were used to calculate time. These stars were painted on the ceilings of many tombs.

Diorite. This grey-green rock was a material which the pharaohs liked to use for statuary (Chepren's statue in the Cairo Museum). Diorite quarries have been found in the Arabic desert and in Sinai. Special expeditions were organized to extract the stone, for example to *Mons Claudianus* (see p. 339).

Red Crown of Lower Egypt | White Crown of Upper Egypt | Double Crown | Plumed Crown | Blue Crown

Djed (pillar). It was perhaps originally a stylised representation of a tree without branches or a sculptured post ; its significance as a hieroglyph is based on the root « to be stable », « stability ». The djed pillar could also take the form of a coloured amulet which conferred perpetual good health. In any case, it was an emblem intimately linked with the god Osiris, the incarnation of which he could sometimes be.

Electrum. A much used alloy made of a mixture of gold and silver. It was used, among other things, to cap the points (or pyramidions) of obelisks which made them reflect the sun and enabled them to be seen from afar.

Ennead. A group of nine divinities which all the theological systems sought to isolate, but which appear in the clearest form at Heliopolis : *Atum* engendered the couple *Shu* and *Tefnut,* they bore *Geb* and *Nut* whose children were the couples *Osiris-Isis* and *Seth-Nephthys.* These gods and goddesses constituted the « great ennead », but a « small ennead » also existed. The number nine was invested with a magic significance (it represented the square of three, this number was also very important, see p. 66). Besides the ennead, other types of groups could exist, such as the ogdoad. (p. 64).

Exodus. The departure of the *Israelites* from Egypt probably took place in the reign of Merneptah of the XIXth dynasty (about 1200 B.C.). The numerous details of the biblical narrative are made very probable by the Egyptian sources, but no direct references to this event, which was so full of consequence for the history of the region and so important in man's memory, have yet been found in the latter.

Falcon. This bird enjoyed a divine dignity in Egypt and represented the royal power ; its penetrating sight was considered a royal quality. Several gods were depicted with a falcon head in representations and it is only their particular attributes which characterize and distinguish them from the falcon-headed *Horus.* The role of this god was to protect the king and very early on, the royal titulary accorded a great importance to Horus.

Festival. The Egyptian year was marked by festivals ; the cycle commenced with the New Year festival, then it was followed by the lively rejoicing which marked the sowing and reaping, with moreover numerous festivals of the local or regional gods, the royal jubilees and the festivals of the dead. The most renowned festivals which took place were the *Festival of Opet at Thebes* and the *Festival of the Valley* in the eastern part of that town. Types of mystery plays also took place at Abydos, but little is known about their subjects. The celebrated festivals at Buto and Sais in the Delta, Hathor at Dendera and Horus at Edfu should also be mentioned. On these occasions the priests carried the sacred barques with the divine images on long and solemn processions which went from temple to temple across the roads, or the god could travel on the Nile by boat. From time to time, offerings were made, incense was burnt and libations were poured. The festivals could last for several set days.

Flail. The kings held the crook and the flail in their hands as a symbol of royal power during ceremonies ; this is attested in numerous reliefs and on statues. This flail had its origin in a whip, and consisted of a wooden handle from which three ribbons

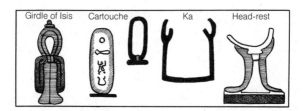

Girdle of Isis   Cartouche   Ka   Head-rest

hung down, made of more or less precious materials. Some flails, such as those of Tutankhamen, could be veritable goldsmith's works of art.

Girdle of Isis. Amulet in the form of the tied girdle of a robe. In the late period Isis was represented with a similar girdle on her breast. In fact the amulet recalls the shape of the handled cross ; its significance was a good luck charm in connection with stability ; this is the reason it is very often associated with the djed pillar.

Harem. In the houses of important people, but above all the royal palaces, one or more rooms were reserved for the wives or concubines. The women lived there in relative liberty. In the case of the king, a special administration was concerned with the harem where the « great king's wife », the queen, lived and reigned.

Head-rest. Head support, the upper part of which is semi-circular, forming a rest for the head during sleep. In museums there are often beautifully worked head-rests decorated with representations of protective divinities to guard the sleeper and to keep evil spirits away from him. Usually head-rests were made in wood, but the most beautiful are in stone (and particularly in alabaster (calcite).

Human Sacrifice. There was no human sacrifice in Egypt, although it is known that other ancient communities sometimes practised it. The well known scene of the king smiting his enemies before the gods was only a symbol of royal victories and had an apostrophic value.

Incense. The burning of incense was an important rite in the cult, like libation (see p. 63) ; it took place in front of the offerings and the divine statues. The numerous representations are alike : the kings holds the censer in his left hand and with his right hand puts a ball of incense in the flame. The censer is in the form of a bronze tube provided with an incense receptacle with one end in the form of a human hand and the other with the head of a falcon.

Ka. The lasting part of the individual, that which faithfully obtained the vital force for him, his favourite and his support, called the *ka*. There is no word in our language with which to translate this complex notion and it can only be imperfectly rendered with such terms as « double » or « vital force ». « To go to his ka » signifies « dead ». The ka must not be confused with the *ba*, another part of the individual which corresponds slightly to our « soul » and which is represented as a bird with a human head, fluttering between the tomb and the outside world.

Khepri. The scarab was the hieroglyphic sign used in the roots « to become » « come into existence ». In the Heliopolitan theology, this insect was assimilated with the god *Khepri*, the sun being reborn in the morning, often represented as a man with a scarab in place of the head.

Libation. As well as the burning of incense, water libations were often made at the beginning and throughout ceremonies. The king or priest poured the water from an ewer onto an offering table or into a vase placed on the ground.

Life (the gift of). In exchange for offerings and cult enacted in his honour, the divinity offered life to the king. This gesture, which was often represented, generally took the form of the god holding out an *ankh* sign to the king's nostril so that he could partake of the breath of life. The kings were generally described as : « given eternal life like Re ».

Mastaba. An Arabic word for « bench », *mastaba* came into use as the word to designate tombs in the shape of trapezoidal benches, dating to the earliest times. Mastabas were the private tombs of the Old Kingdom, a great number of which are found in necropolises, grouped around the royal tomb. The interior is composed of two parts : the rooms necessary to the funerary cult and the sarcophagus chamber. In the upper rooms (at ground level), the complexity of which varied according to the importance of the owner, were offering tables, cult statues and a statue of the *ka* in the *serdab* (see p. 68). All the walls were decorated with paintings and reliefs. After, the subterranean sarcophagus chamber was blocked up and the shaft was completely obstructed with stones.

From that time it became, in theory, inaccessible, The most interesting mastabas were found in the Saqqara necropolis (see p. 169 on.)

Monolith. Architectural element of great size made of a single block of stone, such as a pillar, architrave, obelisk or colossal statue.

Music. Ritual and banquets demanded music. This is the reason why many walls of temples and tombs represent musicians and their instruments. Among these instruments the following should be mentioned : *harp, lute, lyre, trumpet, flute,* a type of *oboe, drum* and *tambourine.* Metal rattles *(sistra),* jangling necklaces and other rattling instruments were also used more as a method of protection from evil spirits and a means to express joy than as musical instruments.

Naos and Naophoros. The first word may also be used to designate the temple sanctuary (the « holy of holies ») as well as the tabernacle of stone (or wood) in the form of a chapel, closed by a double door of wood, which served as the abode of the statue of the god. As regards *naophoros,* it is a statue representing a person kneeling or standing (generally a priest or an important person) holding a naos (tabernacle) and its divine image in front of him. Naophori were in vogue in the New Kingdom and especially in the Late Period.

Nefertiti. Representations of the wife of Akhenaten occur in statuary or on the walls of the tombs at Amarna. Among other portraits a particularly beautiful, unfinished, red quartzite head of the queen was excavated in 1914 (Cairo Museum). The polychrome limestone head is more well known, with its high mortar head-dress, which is in the Museum of Charlottenburg, in West Berlin. Its long neck is typical of the Amarna style, nevertheless without the exaggeration which sometimes occurred during this period. The right eye is inlayed with enamel, although the left is blank for an unknown reason. Both the Cairo head and the one in Berlin show a woman of superb beauty. She certainly merited her name, which means « the beautiful (one) is come », even although this name did not give an allusion to Nefertiti's own beauty.

Offering List. A hieroglyphic text which was inscribed on the walls of funerary chapels ; it was divided into numerous small regular rectangles in which the quantity and the quality of the different offerings necessary to the cult were indicated.

Offering Table. A stone tray of characteristic form and lay-out which was deposited in the funerary chapels or in the temples in order to receive the food offerings destined for the dead and the gods.

Ogdoad. Eight primeval divinities that were called the ogdoad, living in and personifying chaos before the creation of the world ; they were grouped in couples. Nun and Naunet ruled the primitive waters, Heh and Hehet infinite space, Kek and Keket darkness and finally Amun and Amunet invisibility. Hermopolis Magna was their cult centre, called « the town of Eight » in their honour. It was also said that they were interred under the mound of Djame at Medinet Habu. It was thought wrongly for a long time that Amun of Thebes was originally the Amun of the ogdoad.

Osiris Pillar. Architectural support with a square or rectangular section against which a figure of the god of the dead Osiris rests, standing, in the form of a mummy holding a sceptre and a flail (see p. 61) ; often the figure represents the king assimilated with Osiris.

Ostracon (plural : **Ostraca**). A Greek word which is used to describe flat and smooth fragments of limestone or potsherds, such as are found everywhere, on which it was possible to write when the use of expensive papyrus was to be avoided and which were thrown away after use. Ostraca could also be drafts which gave the correct basis for writing of literary texts (for example in the scribe's school), attempts at writing or drawing, accounts, plans of buildings and decoration, caricatures, etc. In west Thebes, and particularly at Deir el-Medina (see p. 232), thousands of ostraca were found dating to the New Kingdom which often contain invaluable information for historians.

Pectoral. Word originating from the Latin pectus « chest ». The pectoral was a piece of precious jewellery which was worn on the chest by kings and some important people. It is in the shape of a temple façade with its cornice at the throat and sometimes a winged disc and scarabs. Pectorals were made in expensive materials, gold and semi-precious stones, often with considerable skill. They were supposed to give magic protection to their owners. The pectorals of Tutankhamun are among the most sumptuous.

Persea. The god of the empire, Amun-Re, assisted by the god of writing, Thoth, wrote the name of the king on the fruits of this sacred tree to assure numerous jubilees for him and a long reign. This scene was often represented in temple reliefs, particularly in the Ramesside period. Amun is accompanied by other divinities and next to him the king kneels under the sacred tree.

Peseshkef. This instrument in the form of a fish tail with double cutting edge was used in the « opening of the mouth » ceremony. This magic ritual served to revive the body after mummification and the deceased's statue after the funeral ; it restored the senses and allowed nourishment to be taken (see p. 80).

Pomegranate. The pomegranate, *Punica granatum* was introduced into Egypt in the XVIIIth dynasty ; it came from Asia. Its fruit, the size of an apple, with its thick skin, numerous pips and sweet flesh, gave a juice which was used to make a highly appreciated drink which was even deposited in the tombs. The shape of the pomegranate inspired numerous artisans and goldsmiths.

Pylon. Monumental gates in the form of towers, similar to fortresses, which form the principal temple entrance. The two piers of the pylon have a pronounced trapezoidal form and a flat roof ; the walls are covered with reliefs and inscriptions. As a general rule, there are gigantic scenes showing the king smiting his enemies in front of the gods. There are deep grooves down the façades where the cedar poles stood (usually four) surmounted by flags. Inside the pylons there are often rooms and stairs.

Relief. A form of stonework in which the figures are raised up from the flat surface in which they are cut. The expression « figure in relief » clearly shows that it concerns in general the bas-reliefs which were often painted. But it may also be a question, in certain cases, of simple incised images in stone without any relief. The designer first sketched the contours of the figure in ink on the prepared surface, then the sculptor incised the image or made a bas-relief. In incised work the figures were sunk into the surface, in bas-relief the figures remained on the original level while the rest of the surface was cut away around them. A special form of relief which is only attested in Egyptian art is sunk relief ; the basic outline was first incised, then the figures were modelled within and the result was a relief sunk deeply into the wall. The decorators of Egyptian temples used sunk relief (or simple incision) for the external walls because the outlines are very clear in the deep shadows.

Rock Tomb. Tombs which are partially or totally cut in the rock face of a mountain. In the Middle Kingdom, this type of tomb was somewhat rare, being reserved for important people, consisting of a funerary chapel and a deeply excavated burial chamber. Pillars or columns cut out of the rock served as supports. In the New Kingdom, the tombs had a T-shaped plan. Private rock cut tombs are found throughout the country ; the best known are those of *Beni Hasan* (see p. 276), *West Thebes* (see p. 215) and *Aswan* (see p. 249) which are chiefly found on one bank of the Nile.

The royal rock-cut tombs of the New Kingdom are located in the « Valley of the Kings » at Thebes (see p. 215). Usually, these tombs consist of corridors and successive chambers with modifications in the general axis. The walls are decorated, as in private tombs, but above all with purely funerary themes (great funerary texts such as certain chapters of the « Book of the Dead »). In contrast to the ancient royal pyramids where the funerary temple and tomb itself were together, the funerary temples connected with these rock-cut tombs were far away and were built on the edge of the cultivation and without any architectural link with the tombs.

Sacred Lake. In direct relation with the myths of the function of the world and the theological systems and, at the same time, a symbol of the primeval waters, the sacred lake, inaccessible to common mortals, was a necessary construction for each temple ; it served as a place of purification for the priests and the scene for certain mysteries repeated at fixed times. The lake was most often rectangular (sometimes oval or crescent shaped) ; it was walled up along the edges and steps gave access to the water.

Serdab. Name given to a special chamber built in the tombs (above all in mastabas) to receive the *ka* statue of the deceased. It is possible to see this statue through a slot cut in the wall of the *serdab* which also permitted the *ka* to come out and partake of the food and drink left on the offering table.

Shabti. (ushabti, shawabti). An Egyptian term which, by a play on words, means « answerer ». They are small figurines in the form of mummies which were put in the tomb near the dead person so that, in the after-life, they could take his place in the agricultural work which awaited the blessed in paradise. They were often 365 in number, one for each day of the year, accompanied by 36 overseers.

Stone. In a country so rich in quarries, stone was used from the first dynasty for the construction of temples and tombs and manufacture of statues and obelisks. The hard rocks are *diorite* used for statues, *basalt* for temple pavements, pink or grey *granite* for obelisks, columns and architraves. The softer rocks are *breccia* (sedimentary with inclusions of older rocks and a tendency to break apart) used for sarcophagi and statues, *sandstone* for all architectural elements, very fine *quartzite* for statues, *limestone* for statues and architecture (casing of pyramids etc.), *alabaster (calcite)* for canopic vases, statues and minor objects, *porphyry* for statues and sarcophagi. The rocks were quarried with diorite pounders and wooden wedges which had been soaked so that they would swell, then they were worked with stone, copper or bronze tools and polished with sand.

Transparence. This term usually denotes the « permeability » of a wall or a sanctuary, the interior and exterior faces of which virtually correspond in the choice of decorative themes. Very often, the reliefs which ornament one wall face cannot be properly understood without reference to those which decorate the other face. The Egyptians were very fond of this type of connection.

Triad. The Egyptians gave the number three quite an important value (it was the plural number, two was known as a dual) and they had a tendency to associate it with their divinities grouped in three. So each town had a triad, generally composed of an important god or goddess (the « father » or the « mother »), his or her partner or « consort » and a « son » god. Among other examples, the following should be mentioned : the triad of Thebes (Amun, Mut, Khonsu) ; of Memphis (Ptah, Sekhmet, Nefertum) ; of Edfu (Horus, Hathor, Harsumtus) and finally the « divine family » : Osiris, Isis and Horus.

Udjat Eye. Much sought after and often used protective theme. It consists of the front view of a falcon's eye (the god Horus) with eyebrow and make-up lines underneath. The udjat eye was frequently used as an amulet made in many materials. This eye was connected with the complex myths concerning the eye of the sun. Its cosmic significance was such that it became the pre-eminent offering, the one the king offered to the gods to ensure that things went well.

Vizier. The highest official of the State, or the administrator of part of the country, something like a prime minister or a governor. Vizier is a word taken from oriental administration and conveniently used for ancient Egypt.

Wood. There was not very much wood in Egypt and it could not be used for some things because of its bad quality. They made coffins and statues from *sycamore* wood, everyday objects, ordinary furniture and boat equipment from *acacia* wood and woodwork from *palm* trunks. *Ebony* was imported from the southern Sudan and *cedar* from Lebanon. The latter, a heavy, hard and strong wood, was reserved for boat building, temple doors, great flag poles which decorated the pylons and the coffins of affluent people. Using only stone and bronze tools for woodworking, the Egyptian carpenters were able to achieve perfection in very difficult work and also execute inlay with other materials such as glass, stone and metal. Because of the perishable nature of the material, relatively few objects of wood are preserved.

Ancient Egyptian Religion

THE GODS

Amun was initially the local and relatively obscure god of Thebes. During the Middle Kingdom and particularly after the expulsion of the Hyksos by the Theban princes, he became a national god, the god of the Empire. With *Mut* and *Khonsu* he formed the Theban triad. He was the god of the wind and of the breath of life and therefore was recognised as being omnipresent. His increasing importance and that of his priesthood in State affairs lasted until the Amarna period, when Akhenaten introduced the cult of Aten. After the Amarna period the authority and influence of his priesthood was restored and became so great that the high priests eventually became kings (the « priest-kings »). With the Assyrian conquest and the destruction of his sanctuary (which nevertheless would know again its hours of glory) and above all with the decline of Thebes, the cult of Amun began to decline also and was replaced by those of other gods and particularly with that of *Osiris*.

Amun is represented in human form, and only rarely as ram-headed. He wears a high crown with two plumes and holds in his hand a *was* sceptre. This is a long wand, forked at the end and embellished at the top with a stylised animal's head (this is the sceptre of the gods, that carried by goddesses being a long stem of papyrus).

Anubis is the god of mummification, who stands at the side of Osiris, the god of the dead. As the protector of the tombs of the necropolis, he bears the epithets « Lord of the Necropolis », « He who is upon his mountain », « He of the embalming » and « He of the divine pavilion ». He was worshipped in nume-

Amun   Anubis   Apis

rous places, for example in the « Town of the Dog » (Cynopolis = Asyût) which was consecrated to him ; see also his chapel at Deir el-Bahri (p. 224).

He is habitually represented in human form with the head of a jackal or dog, or as a black jackal lying on a shrine. In tomb relief scenes he is often shown leaning over a mummy and restoring it to life.

Apis is a complex divinity who was increasingly popular in late times. He was particularly worshipped at Memphis, where he was recognised as a form of the god, Ptah, and later also as a form of Re. He is always depicted as a bull wearing a solar disk and uraeus on his head. A live bull, who was carefully chosen and then kept in an enclosure, was considered sacred and the incarnation of Apis. When he died he was buried with due ceremony in the Serapeum of Memphis at Saqqara. (See p. 173). There was also a famous Serapeum at Alexandria. In the

Late Period Apis became an extremely popular divinity both within Egypt and abroad.

Aten. A divinity of early origin symbolizing the physical disk of the sun, Aten was, however, an obscure god until the Eighteenth Dynasty. He began to play a more important role during the reign of Amenophis III. In the reign of the latter's son, Akhenaten, Aten assumed a considerable and in fact exclusive position. The King, motivated by sincere religious feelings and also by political sentiments, desired to raise the importance of the Aten above that of the cult of Amun and his all-powerful priesthood. He replaced Amun by Aten and the cult of the visible and concrete aspect of the sun's disk, in so doing establishing a type of monotheism in advance of its time. Akhenaten himself composed some beautiful hymns to his god, full of lyricism. He founded a new capital, called Akhetaten, « the horizon of Aten », at Tell el-Amarna. Here the

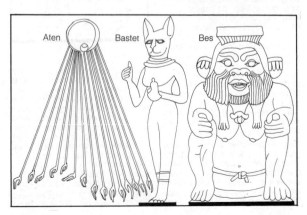

Aten   Bastet   Bes

temples were simply altars open to the sky. But the new cult only survived during the reign of « the heretic king » and for a few years after his death. Under Tutankhamun the cult of the god Amun was restored and all memories of the Amarna period were swept away.

Aten is always depicted in the form of a solar disk from which emanate rays terminating in human hands. As the deity was considered primarily as the source of all life, the hands often hold out the sign of life, the ankh, towards the nostrils of the king and queen, thus expressing in a relatively traditional way a characteristic idea of Egyptian religion.

Bastet. A cat goddess, who is the prototype of the peaceful and satisfied goddesses. In their more violent and earlier form such goddesses were depicted as lionesses. Bastet was closely associated with the town of Bubastis in the Delta, where joyful festivals were regularly held in her honour. She is nearly always shown as a woman with the head of a cat and wears one gold ear-ring. In her hands she holds a sistrum and a basket. Sometimes she is depicted as a seated cat, like the numerous and often very beautiful bronze cats which can be seen in many museums. In the Late Period Bastet was particularly worshipped in the form of sacred cats. When these died they were mummified and buried in special cemeteries. The goddess *Sekhmet* often symbolises the violent and unleashed aspect of Bastet.

Bes. A deformed and grotesque god, depicted with an obese body, short legs and an almost bestial face. Sometimes he is shown armed with a sword and a shield. His frightening and simultaneously comic appearance had the effect of dispelling evil

spirits which might be harmful to man under certain circumstances. In particular he was the protector of the marriage bed and of women in labour and was a powerful force against the dangers of venomous animal bites or crocodiles. To add to his peculiar appearance he is sometimes shown with his tongue hanging out.

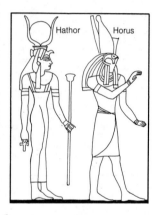

Hathor   Horus

Hathor. Goddess of life in its most exuberant and carnal form and thus the goddess of joy, love and dancing. During the course of time she was assimilated with numerous other goddesses and thus borrowed certain of her characteristics from them. According to the particular form she took or the place of worship concerned, she had numerous names or epithets : « Lady of the Turquoise » in Sinai, « Lady of the Necropolis » in her form as a funerary goddess, « The Luminous », « The Golden » etc. Her principal sanctuary in the Late Period was at Dendera (see p. 294). The Greeks identified her with Aphrodite.

Hathor is often represented as a cow, her sacred animal, or as a woman wearing a solar disk between the horns of a cow. A combined form of this is found on Hathor columns (see p. 59) where Hathor is shown with a female face but with cow's ears.

The Seven Hathors were the goddesses of destiny. They could predict the future and are often seen assisting at the birth of the divine child in the *mammisi* of the Graeco-Roman temples.

Horus. Originally he was the god of the sky and his eyes were the sun and the moon. However, from the First Dynasty he played the role of protector of the king and of the pharaonic monarchy in general. He could assume various aspects according to the different theologies in which he played a part. He is particularly well known as a participant in the Osirian legend. As the posthumous son of Osiris, murdered by Seth, Horus was reared by his mother Isis in the marshes of the Delta. When he became a man, he decided to avenge his father and contended with Seth to recover his rightful heritage, royalty over the earth. This myth explains why Horus came to be considered as the principal royal god, whom every pharaoh sought to imitate. Hence the importance of Horus or of the falcon Horus in the royal titulary and in royal names.

Horus could assume numerous forms depending on the places where he was worshipped or according to his different identities. At Heliopolis he was *Horakhty*, « Horus of

the Horizon », at Giza *Harmakhis*, « Horus in the Horizon », as the son of Isis he was called *Harpocrates*, as the protector of Osiris he was *Harendotes*. He is mainly depicted as a falcon-headed man, like several other Egyptian divinities. His main cult centre was at Edfu. His four sons played a special role as protectors of the canopic jars (see p. 56). They are usually represented as follows : Imsety, human-headed ; Duamutef, jackal-headed ; Hapy, baboon-headed ; and Qebhsenuef, falcon-headed.

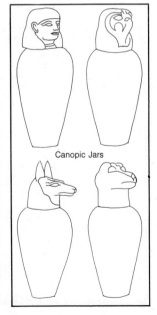

Canopic Jars

Imhotep was the vizier of the Third Dynasty King, Djoser, and was deified in the Late Period. His accomplishments were many. He had built the Step Pyramid at Saqqara (see p. 169) and thus had invented building in stone. He was a scholar, an author and a doctor. Therefore in late times he was considered as the protector of architects, scribes and doctors. The Greeks called him Imuthes and identified him with Asklepios. As a god, he was very popular, particularly at Saqqara, where his tomb was situated and where a sanctuary, the *Asklepeion,* was dedicated to him. He was even made a « son of Ptah ». He is usually shown in a serious pose as a seated scribe.

Isis was the sister and wife of Osiris, the mother of Horus and an important participant in the legend of Osiris. It was Isis who in the form of a bird helped to revitalise Osiris after his death. Originally she may have been a goddess associated with the divine or royal throne as her name is written with the hieroglyphic sign representing a seat. In the course of time her cult grew and developed greatly and in the early years of the Christian era she was worshipped throughout the Roman world. At *Philae* her cult persisted for several centuries after the advent and triumph of Christianity.

Isis is normally depicted as a woman with the hieroglyphic sign for a seat on her head and with a headdress similar to that of Hathor, or as a seated woman holding the child Horus on her lap.

Khnum. A creator god often represented as a potter fashioning men on his potter's wheel. At Elephantine he was associated with the goddesses *Satis* and *Anukis* and acted as protector of the sources of the Nile and of the cataract region. His other important cult centre was at *Esna*. His sacred animal was the ram and thus he is normally represented as a ram-headed man (criocephalus),

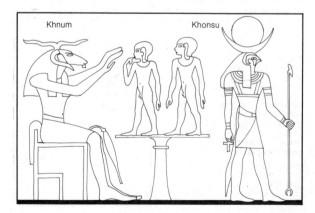

usually seated in front of his potter's wheel.

Khonsu, whose name means « he who crosses », was a moon god. His principal cult centre was at Thebes, where one of the Karnak temples was dedicated to him (see p. 210). He was a member of the Theban triad as the divine son of *Amun* and *Mut*. He could also assume an apostrophic role. He is shown in two main forms — as a young man with the sidelock of youth and like many other Egyptian gods as a falcon-headed man.

Maat. This goddess symbolised an important abstract idea to the Egyptians, one which is difficult to translate and explain in modern terms. Truth and justice perhaps summarise this idea fairly well, but it also referred to the notion of a correct order in the world. Basically Maat was the order which controlled the proper function of the creative world. Thus the pharaoh is often shown offering Maat to the gods, because Maat was the supreme offering. Similarly the vizier in his role as judge wore an image of this goddess on his breast. It was Maat who judged the merits of the deceased and determined whether he should enter into the after-life. She was the feather against which the heart of the deceased was weighed in the balance at the judgement of the dead. Maat was the daughter of Re, the legitimate offspring of the supreme god. She is depicted as a young and beautiful woman, either standing or seated, with a feather on her head, which is the hieroglyphic sign maat meaning true or just, and holds an ankh sigh in her hand.

Min was an ancient divinity who symbolized fruitfulness and fertility. He was also a local god in Upper Egypt who protected expeditions and thus was the god of the eastern desert and the Wadi Hammâmât. Coptos was his main cult centre and

Imhotep   Isis   Maat

great festivals were held there in his honour. The offering usually made to him was a variety of lettuce which increased his generative powers. He is depicted in a very characteristic way — he wears practically the same type of crown as Amun, who is often confused with him, but he is enveloped in a mummy cloth with one arm raised, sometimes holding a flail, and he is ithyphallic. His flesh is sometimes coloured black.

Montu. At one time the local god of Thebes and its principal divinity before he lost his pre-eminence to Amun, Montu nevertheless remained an important god in the Theban region. His cult was celebrated in several places, firstly at *Karnak* (North Karnak, p. 213) and also at three places nearby *Tôd, Medamud* and *Armant*. His essential character became more and more that of a warrior god and the king on his campaigns often invoked Montu's powers. At Armant the cult of his sa-

cred animal, the *Buchis* bull was very popular. Montu is generally represented as a falcon-headed god (hierocephalus) with two uraei, a solar disk and double plumes on his head.

Neith was an ancient goddess worshipped in the Delta, and more precisely in the town of Sais. It is possible that originally she was the protector-goddess of the Red Crown of Lower Egypt. With the passage of time her popularity grew. She became very important in the Late Period and particularly in the Twenty-sixth Dynasty, when the ruling family was Saite. She was associated with textile weaving and eventually with warfare and often carries some weapons. She is shown as a young woman wearing the Red Crown or a head-dress made up of the hieroglyphic sign used to write her name and sometimes holds a bow and two arrows.

Nephthys was a goddess associated in early times with the Heliopoli-

tan cycle and more generally with the myths relating to Osiris. She was in fact one of the four children of *Geb* and *Nut* and her husband was none other than her brother, *Seth*. *Anubis* was her son. She was a protector-goddess in the funerary rites. Because of her role in the resurrection of Osiris, she was closely associated with her sister, *Isis*, whom she greatly resembles, except that her head-dress is the hieroglyphic sign used to write her name.

Nut was a very ancient divinity who personified the sky and who was thought to give birth to the sun every morning. In the *Heliopolitan Ennead* she was the daughter of *Shu* and *Tefnut*, the wife of her brother, *Geb*, the earth, and the mother of *Osiris*, *Isis*, *Seth* and *Nephthys*.

As the sky-goddess she is usually depicted as a naked woman stretched out and leaning above the earth, which she touches with her feet and hands. The rest of her body

describes an arc over the earth. Her body is often decorated with stars and she is shown swallowing the sun at night and giving birth to it in the morning. The most complete scenes also include her husband, *Geb*, the earth, and the air-god, *Shu*, who comes between them and raises Nut with his arms. This symbolises the separation of the mythical union of the earth and the sky by the air. This particular scene often occurs in the royal tombs at Thebes. Nut also often appears on the exterior or interior scenes of coffins, as she held the promise of resurrection and was identified with the deceased being reborn as the sun was reborn every day.

Osiris was a very ancient Egyptian divinity connected with fertility and was probably originally from Lower Egypt. But he is known principally through the legend of which he is the central character and which was made famous by the Greek author,

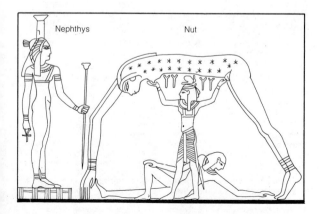

Plutarch. The role of Osiris in Egyptian religion often tends to conflict with the cults of Re and Amun. He was a god who attracted the worship of all men by touching upon the fear of death in each one of them. The death of Osiris, who was murdered by his brother, Seth, and his resurrection, which made him the god of the dead and the ruler of the after-life, were events with which the deceased sought to be identified. This identification with Osiris could only be claimed by the dead king in the Old Kingdom. But thereafter a democratization took place and eventually all the dead could claim the title « the Osiris... » which was equivalent to « the Late... »

The personality of the resurrected god, Osiris, was linked to his role as a god of fertility and agriculture. Occasionally Osiris-shaped beds were made of soil and seeds planted, which, when they germinated, symbolised his resurrection. Osiris was also connected with the rising of the Nile.

He was worshipped throughout Egypt, but had particular cult centres at *Busiris* in the Delta and at *Abydos* (see p. 288), where he was believed to have been buried. He is depicted as a mummiform figure with his face and hands coloured green or black. He wears an *atef* crown, which is the White Crown with two plumes, a false beard, and carries in his hands the insignia of royalty - the crook and the flail.

Ptah was a god particularly associated with the city of Memphis. Thus he was always connected with royalty as the god of the ancient capital of the country. But he had always been and remained a demiurge and craftsman, who according to the Memphite Theology had created the

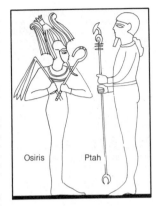

Osiris   Ptah

world. Thus he is recognised as the protector of artists and craftsmen and his high priest at Memphis bore the title of Chief of the Craftsmen. With *Sekhmet* and *Nefertum* he formed the Memphite triad. Ptah is generally depicted in human form wearing a long cloak which reveals only his hands holding insignia of office. He wears a false beard and has a tight close-fitting cap on his head.

Re. Initially Re was the sun itself and the god of the sun, as the Egyptians did not distinguish the one from the other very closely. But Re rapidly became a notable deity in the pantheon of Heliopolis, where he was more or less identified with the demiurge, *Atum*. The role of Re increased and developed to such an extent that all the gods could be and were assimilated to him, hence Amun-Re, Sobek-Re, etc. Osiris is also sometimes linked with him. Even Akhenaten borrowed several elements of the Heliopolitan theolo-

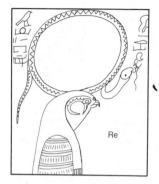

Re

gy for the personality of his solar disk, *Aten*. Re was profoundly associated with the king from earliest times. It was in the Fifth Dynasty that the title of « Son of Re » was first used by the king.

In tomb and temple reliefs Re is often shown either in human form with a solar disk head-dress or as a scarab beetle or as a man with the head of a beetle. He appears travelling in his barque in the company of other gods and crosses the sky by day and travels through the underworld of the dead by night. Re could assume several forms. In the morning he was *Khepri* and in the evening he could be *Atum*. One of the most popular representations of him shows him as a falcon-headed man wearing a solar disk on his head in his form as *Re-Horakhty*, « Horus of the Horizon ». Re was one of the four great gods of Egypt, the other three being Amun, Ptah and Osiris.

Sekhmet was a ferocious and violent lioness-goddess and the counterpart of the gentle cat-goddess, *Bastet*. She is also known as the wife of *Ptah* at Memphis. Her messengers

were fearful creatures who could inflict terrible scourges upon men, particularly diseases. There are beautiful black granite statues of Sekhmet at *Karnak* in the Temple of Mut (see p. 211). In the Temple of Ptah her cult statue still remains in situ (see p. 212).

Seth was originally the god who ruled over the land with Horus and whose particular domain was the mountain and desert regions. His character was violent and warlike and it was he who battled with the serpent, *Apophis*, the enemy of Re, on the solar barque. His violent and vicious nature soon characterized him as a negative god. This malevolent nature was emphasized by his role in the Osirian legend as the assassin of his brother, Osiris and as the seizer of his heritage, which Horus had to fight to regain. However, Seth's purely negative nature was not always predominant throughout Egypt. The Hyksos identified him with their principal divinity. He remained popular in the Eastern Delta region and the kings of the Nineteenth Dynasty who came from there worshipped him. The name Seti means « man of Seth ».

It was during the Late Period and in the Graeco-Roman Period that Seth came to personify all that was evil and was blamed for the invasions of foreigners like the Persians. The late temple reliefs often depict Horus contending with Seth, who is shown in the form of a hippopotamus or a pig. Seth is, however, more usually represented as a man with the head of a mythical animal. He was one of the great gods of Egypt who had fallen from grace and become a demon. Our Western conception of the Devil is partially derived from his character.

Thoth was the god of wisdom and of scribes and writing. As a moon god he was connected with the division of time into hours, days and months. He was also regarded as a god of justice and protector of laws. All of these aspects of his nature were complementary and often overlapped each other. Thoth was closely associated with Re, as the moon is with the sun, and was the heart and seat of all thoughts and therefore wisdom personified. He was the messenger of Re and this led the Greeks to identify him with their god, *Hermes*. He was known to them as *Hermes Trismegistos* or Hermes « thrice great », which was derived from one of the Egyptian epithets of Thoth.

Representations of Thoth closely associate him with his sacred animals, the ibis and the baboon. He is often depicted as an ibis-headed man holding a scribe's palette or in the act of writing. The many statuettes and amulets found of baboons and ibises attest to his popularity. He was patron of a profession, which was fundamental to the efficient administration of Egypt. Although worshipped throughout the land, Thoth had particularly important cult centres at *Hermopolis Magna* (see p. 279) and at *Bâh*, near to *Mendes* in the Delta.

Thoeris was a goddess particularly worshipped by women and above all by women in labour. She is often present in birth scenes. This protector-goddess with her relatively comic and friendly appearance is often depicted on reliefs in the *mammisi* of temples, where the divine royal birth is shown. Thoeris is represented as a female hippopotamus with swollen abdomen. She is always shown as a standing figure and leans on a magical knot.

Uraeus. This term could have been included in a lexicon relating to art and civilization as it is a religious symbol rather than an actual divinity.

Sekhmet   Seth   Thoth

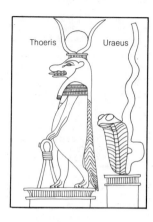

The uraeus could be the symbol of numerous divinities and should not be confused with certain serpent goddesses. It could personify the royal crown and was the symbol of its power and magic, hence its position on the royal brow. It was also considered as the eye of the sun and the force of its terrible heat. The uraeus also became a popular decorative theme particularly on friezes. It is easily recognised as it resembles a cobra with its neck puffed up and ready to strike.

BELIEF IN THE AFTER-LIFE AND THE FUNERARY CULT

« Death is today before me as the desire to return home, after long years passed in captivity », « The dwelling of those who are in the land of the west is deep and dark. There, there are no doors, no windows, no light to illuminate them, no wind to refresh their hearts. » These two very different phrases written by the Egyptians show that for men in the Nile valley, like those in every period, death was not a simple thing and it could fascinate or terrorize, according to the individual. But these sentiments were generally suppressed, particularly the latter, and the ancient Egyptians adopted a certain attitude in the face of death, which still always fascinates visitors to the country. The rites practised by the Egyptians are given below and the meaning which they may have accorded them, believing that death was not an end of pleasure and that it could be controlled if they took such care.

For the Egyptians, death was in principle only the stage which allowed entry across the threshold of death into another life, a type of sleep after which the soul, purified by judgement, regained the body and shared a normal life with it again, but this time in the empire of the dead, in amenty.

But to obtain this result, a certain number of precautions had to de taken even in life when the means were available. This involved above all the preparation and attribution of a certain area of ground which could constitute a funerary foundation. In the beginning, this was only possible for the king, the only true owner of the land, but rapidly it became possible for those close to him and that is why the pyramids were always surrounded by numerous mastabas for the ministers and courtiers. Therefore the royal palace with its organisation and etiquette was perpetuated in stone forever.

But at the end of the Old Kingdom, the royal power diminished and a middle class gradually rose who, after the period of scepticism which accompanied the social crisis of the

First Intermediate Period, preoccupied themselves with survival in the « west » and for that reason took great care during life. A site for the sepulchre was acquired and prepared, the construction of the tomb was quickly commenced, the decoration (reliefs, paintings, etc.) was started and continued for the necessary time and finally a contract was entered into between the owner of the tomb and the person (and his descendants) who was to occupy it after him. It is true that the mortuary duties fell theoretically on the eldest son of the departed (just as the king was in principle the only authentic priest in all the temples in the land), in general the services of a professional funerary priest were resorted to, the *servant of the ka*. He received a field from which he took products for the necessary offerings and his own subsistence.

This fact illustrates the economic importance and consequences of the Egyptian beliefs about death.

When death befell, the body was immediately carried to the « divine pavilion » where it was kept for 66 days (in the better cases) in order to be mummified (see p. 83), then it was returned to the family. Then the funeral ceremonies commenced, full of pomp according to the position of the deceased or very simple for the poor people (the majority) who very often did not receive a particular tomb.

The bodies of simple people were placed in mats. The dead were then piled in rock caves or sometimes in pits or in charnel-houses. These were the resting-places unless an individual belonged to the upper classes of society and enjoyed an Egyptian funeral.

In the latter case the women of the family and the mourners lamented ; they exposed and beat their breasts and threw ashes over their hair. Then the coffin was drawn up to the tomb on a sledge pulled by oxen and accompanied by the funeral procession. One woman was at the left of the coffin and another at the right, they played the roles of *Isis* and *Nephthys* mourning for *Osiris*.

Once in front of the tomb, the priests made purifications and recited prayers. Then the ceremony of « opening the mouth » followed, in fact a repetition of it, because the mouth of the deceased had already been « opened » previously at the time of mummification. The coffin and the statues of the dead were the object of the purifications, they were anointed and the mouth was restored to movement with special instruments such as the *peseshkef* (see p 65) and the adze. In this way the deceased was able to recover the use of his faculties : he could once again speak, eat and drink. Then the dead man's wife bade him farewell, kneeling and embracing the coffin which was then put in the burial chamber by the shaft. The entrance to the tomb was closed and sealed and the ceremony finished with a funerary banquet.

For his part, according to Egyptian beliefs, the dead man went to the other world for the judgment of the dead. A divine tribunal was held under the dais of the president *Osiris*, accompanied by *Isis* and *Nephthys* and assisted by 42 assessors, formidable genies of the after-life. *Anubis* led the deceased by the hand. His heart was placed on the pan of a balance to be weighed against the other pan which held a figurine representing the goddess of justice,

Maat, or an ostrich plume which served to write her name and to convey the conception which she personified. The ibis-headed god *Thoth* controlled the weighing with precision (the beam had to stay horizontal) and recorded the result on papyrus with his palette and his brush. At the same time the deceased recited his « negative confession ». He turned towards the 42 assessors and addressed each of

Funeral scene on papyrus. The wife of the deceased (above left) mourns while a funerary priest performs the ceremony of « opening the mouth » in front of the open tomb. The ka in the form of a human-headed bird descends a long shaft towards the sarcophagus chamber. It flys towards the mummy lying in his coffin (below right).

them with : « I did not (commit such and such a sin, according to the demon) ».

These magic invocations and formulas which he had to employ in the after-life in order to be able to repulse all the dangers which might be met with (demons, serpents, crocodiles, etc..) were put in writing in books or funerary rituals (above all the *Book of the Dead*), veritable handbooks of death. From the New Kingdom the funerary papyri accompanied the dead in the form of rolls covered with inscriptions, vignettes and large coloured drawings. They were generally put in the mummy bandages or placed next to them. These funerary texts are related to the *Pyramid Texts* of the Old Kingdom and the *Coffin Texts* of the Middle Kingdom, as well as being a link which connects them with much later and more numerous funerary books.

When the result of the weighing was unfavourable, the infernal and formidable animal with terrible fangs, *the Devourer*, sitting next to the balance, completely annihilated the deceased, whose second death was this time irredeemable, his body and his personality having been destroyed.

But if the result was favourable, then the deceased had the right to enter the after-life of the blessed. It was then permissible for the man who was triumphant in this way to enjoy, as in his first terrestrial life, the light, air, food, clothes, ornaments and furniture put in his tomb and he was able to continue to use them on condition that, on their side, the living continued to faithfully execute his funerary service. The Egyptian funerary cult was relatively formalised in spite of the fairly elevated

ideas on the judgement of the dead ; it demanded above all that the dead be permanently provided with all the necessary provisions. The destiny of the deceased depended on the living who would one day find themselves in the same situation.

The tomb paintings have scenes of situations drawn from the daily life of the deceased and enabled him to relive these earthly activities. They were intended to allow the dead to continue for ever his terrestrial life. His son, or the funerary priest, provided replacements and the permanent means of subsistence (offerings). Indirectly these cult ceremonies were a magical invocation which was supposed to transfer to the after-life the reality which was evoked by the representations in the tomb or the offerings which were placed there.

All the other offerings put in the tomb also served this plan ; the models which recalled the activities and gestures which were known to the deceased during his life with, in addition, the figures of servants who were supposed to assist him in the after-life. From the Middle Kingdom *shabtis* (or « answerers ») were placed in the tombs ; figurines of stone, faience or wood which were supposed to take the place of the dead in the after-life, when he was called to perform duties which even those in paradise did not escape. Very often, 365 shabtis were used, one for each day of the year.

Amulets of every type and scarabs were put in great numbers in the bandages of the mummy (and even in the body), the same ones that already played a great part in life on earth. The scarab was particularly appreciated because it was considered a solar symbol, it carried with it a promise of resurrection (like the sun which died each evening and was reborn each dawn) ; in addition it corresponds to the hieroglyph which signifies « become » « come into being », so that it confirmed this idea.

In the « beautiful west », the deceased lived happily ever after ; he could tow the solar barque as it travelled nocturnally through the underworld, or he could join the stars. His ka, the element of the personality which had accompanied him all his life since his birth and which was the incarnation of the life force, was able to blend with the statue which was its support and communicate with the exterior by the false door, the same at which the offerings of food were received, indispensable to continued existence. And, as the Egyptians were justly afraid of the indifference or forgetfulness of their descendants, they never hesitated to make « appeal to the living » by means of inscriptions destined for them ; they invited visitors to the necropolis to say the necessary prayers and symbolically furnish their offering tables, in return they promised thousands of blessings. Even the act of pronouncing the name of the dead or offering a libation in his favour was enough and greatly favoured the future life of those who consented to do it.

MUMMIFICATION

It is on the conception of survival in the after-life depicted above that the wish to conserve and protect the body from destruction is founded so that the soul and the ka might meet the body again and live with it. Great pains were taken to achieve this end and a long process was used to attain the desired result. It went so far

that there was no hesitation in « putting in order » with splints the limbs broken by the clumsiness of the embalmers or attempting to foresee the eventual misfortunes caused by tomb robbers.

The art of embalming was less part of medicine or craftwork than one of the series of ritual acts with religious and magic significance. Mummification performed in the best conditions (it should not be forgotten that even here the social strata gave rise to differences in procedure) lasted 70 days. The priests who may have worn a jackal mask to identify them with Anubis, their patron, took charge of the work and recited prayers and litanies at the same time ; they were assisted by the overseer of the house of embalming, often called the « tent of purification » or the « divine pavilion ». These special workshops were generally situated near the temples and above all near the necropolises.

The technique of embalming in its most accomplished form was long and at the same time fairly expensive. Also, this technique, which will be described in detail, was reserved for the first class of funeral, for pharaohs, important members of the royal household, ministers and very rich people. In all these cases the treatment to which the body was subjected was so sophisticated that it could last for thousands of years. The embalmers compared their first class results with the mummification of Osiris. They showed the customers models of wood painted and finished according to the chosen class with their details and prices.

In the beginning, mummification was reserved for kings and people of the royal blood. But soon it became popular with all the people and a

*The Body on the Embalming Bed (above). A Priest Wears the Mask of the God Anubis.
Below, Purification of the Body*

more and more complex and refined technique evolved. In the New Kingdom it attained its highest level of perfection and was surrounded with the greatest possible pomp. The example of Tutankhamun is revealing in this respect (even although the body of the king is one of the worst preserved because of the excess zeal of the embalmers) : numerous linen bandages were wound around the mummy which was then laid in three coffins encased in a stone sarcophagus itself enclosed by three concentric decorated wooden shrines.

It is known, because of the discovery of preserved viscera, that the mother of Cheops, the builder of the Great Pyramid, was mummified. Other excavations have produced evidence that mummification was practised before 3000 B.C. Even in the Christian epoch, the bodies of monks were summarily mummified. Because of their originally ritual practices the ancient Egyptian embalmers attained a relatively deep knowledge of anatomy and the siting of the organs in the body, which is revealed in the medical texts of the time. It is also possible that this science was relied on by Alexandrian medicine which made great progress in knowledge of the human body. In the Ptolemaic period, the art of the embalmer was linked with the teaching of practical medicine.

Numerous papyri are preserved ; Herodotus and the other classical authors described more or less in detail the embalming techniques. These sources, as well as the evidence from wall paintings, texts and detailed research enable the process of mummification to be reconstructed.

The embalmer began his work by emptying the skull of the deceased which presupposes a precise knowledge of its organisation. A hook was introduced through the nostrils which passed towards the base of the cranium and penetrated the brain which was then broken into pieces by the rotation and pulled from the skull through the nose. Very rarely the head was opened by a gash in the neck or even completely detached from the body. In the latter case, it had to be re-attached to it later by means of a piece of metal.

Now the lower part of the body had to be emptied through an opening made on the side. The men who practised this operation, following a precise ritual, were called *paraschists* in Greek and they belonged to a class of the population kept apart because of their activities which were simultaneously necessary and sacrilegious. It was in fact probably from their work and the fear of demons which might accompany them that they gained their bad reputation. They were avoided in the streets and they were always obliged to live separately in quarters reserved for funerary workers.

In contrast, the actual embalmers, compared to Anubis their divine patron, received more consideration and were grouped in the category of priests because of the pre-eminently religious character of their functions. With their bare hands they opened the abdomen and withdrew all the viscera, except the kidneys which were normally left behind the peritoneum and sometimes also the heart (which if removed could be replaced by a large magic « heart scarab » of stone). The heart and its reanimation evidently had a great importance and magic formulae were meant to help assure its preservation, one such is : « Isis speaks thus : your heart belongs to you ; it stays forever in its place ; it will never be stolen in the after-life ».

The viscera were then washed with palm wine and different spices and aromatics such as myrrh, then they were wrapped in long bandages and placed in special vases. These receptacles, known as *canopic jars* were meant to contain different organs (liver, lungs, etc.), and were held for this reason under the special guard of protective genies, the four sons of Horus, whose heads were represented on the lids of the jars. Very often the most luxurious of the canopic vases were in alabaster (calcite) and were carved with considerable skill (see p. 71).

Very rarely and mostly in the Late Period, the viscera were replaced in the body after being separately mummified. For the rest, there is every type of exception and mummies have been discovered which are « refilled » or only partially « emptied » without any trace of an incision to be seen. Even now, in fact, many details concerning embalming remain obscure.

After these operations, the next phase consisted of stuffing the chest and abdominal cavity with linen rags soaked in aromatics, resin and natron. The lateral incision was carefully reclosed with melted wax or resin and the nose, mouth and ears were sealed in the same way.

From then on the most important process of dessication could take place which really guaranteed the preservation of the body. This was not so much drying but the use of natron (of which Herodotus spoke) which removed water and oil from the body. This type of salt has been found in numerous vases, in the products of embalming and also in the mummy cloths and in the resin in which they were soaked.

Instead of a solution of salt which would have eaten into the skin and then have gradually destroyed it, dry natron was used and the body was placed in a large tank full of natron, constructed so that the head would emerge ; this has been gathered from the ritual texts.

Because of this dessication process, the skin shrank and the nails could separate from the fingers and toes. In order to prevent the loss of the nails the nail roots were sometimes pierced and held on with wire (sometimes gold). The kings often had their fingers and toes covered with individual caps of silver or gold.

After this operation the corpse left its natron bath and was washed with perfumed oils. The fingers and the hands were sometimes coloured red (possibly henna). All the body cavities which underwent muscular contraction because of the process were relaxed and padded with various pieces of linen or other materials so that the mummy would regain a « normal » appearance.

For the most important clients this process was performed by the best embalmers who answered directly to Anubis ; it took place on specially constructed tables several examples of which have been found. The mummified corpse lay on two wooden blocks so that the embalmer and later the bandager could work freely around it. A hole pierced in the middle of the table allowed the different products and body fluids to drain away.

Finally the mummies were wrapped in bandages made of linen cloth, which were often more than a hundred metres long. The fingers, hands and feet were bandaged separately, then the rest of the body and finally another exterior covering of larger, symmetrically arranged bandages was applied. All the bandages were soaked in products which gave the cloth a good appearance and a good smell to the body. (But the numerous oils and resins were, in the course of time, the cause of the brown or black tint of the mummies). Then on the outside (and sometimes in the bandages) the necessary amulets for the protection of the body were placed in predetermined places. Tradition governed this magic protection ; so that it was the *udjat* eye which corresponded to the ventral incision (because it signified integrity and the recovery of good health). All the usual forms were utilised. A pectoral might decorate the chest and a mortuary mask covered the face (the most famous is that of Tutankhamun).

Special formulae which accompanied the delicate rites of embalment were concluded : « You live again, you are henceforth endowed with eternal life, you are eternally young again ». « Your head is on your neck and Anubis has given new vigour to your body ». And Isis added : « I have removed your weakness from you ; you are standing again and you go everywhere as during your life ».

Very often the remains of bandages, the vases which had contained the oils and essences necessary for embalming and all the residues were gathered together and deposited in a corner of the funerary chamber. These remains have facilitated the research into mummification and on the ingredients employed in the process.

Writing and its Decipherment

The first tentative steps in the writing of words or thoughts is lost in the dim past. The figures and graffiti on the rock faces which are attempts at writing, however imperfect, date back to more than 5,000 B.C. But from the time of the unification of the land about 3,000 B.C. well defined Egyptian hieroglyphic writing existed. In the course of time it gave rise very quickly to other forms of writing, linear hieroglyphs and hieratic and, very much later, demotic.

HIEROGLYPHS

Contrary to the widely held opinion that hieroglyphic writing consists of a pictorial and inexact script, it should be stressed that on the contrary it is a truly phonetic script where the objects very often lose their concrete sense in order to convey simple sounds. In simplifying it can be said that each hieroglyph, except for a few exceptions, is a sound (but not necessarily a simple sound). But, from the historical point of view, it should be remarked that the evolution was from images which represented precise objects in the Egyptian environment which might simply keep their phonetic values, or undergo a progressive abstraction which made them ideograms.

As in all the Hamitic-Semitic languages, only the consonants were transcribed in Egyptian, without taking the vowels into consideration

(this is only possible in the languages where the word roots have an essential order). To eliminate possible doubts and ambiguities, one of the 150 interpretation signs *(deter-*

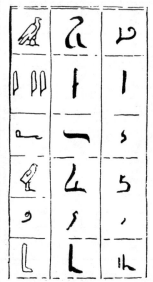

Left column : Hieroglyphs, Middle : Hieratic, Right : Demotic

Sign	Object represented	Phonetic value	Sign.	Object represented	Phonetic value
	vulture	Usually read as *a* In fact a glottal stop		wick of twisted flax	*h* emphatic
	flowering reed	*i* or *y* eg.in loyal		sieve	*ch* as in Scottish (*kh*) loch
	double flowering reed	*y*		animals belly with teats	*ch* as in German (ich)
	fore-arm	guttural sound usually read as *a*	or	bolt on folded cloth	*s*
	quail chick	*w*		pool	*sh*
	foot	*b*		hill-slope	*k* like *q* in queen
	stool	*p*		basket with handle	*k*
	horned viper	*f*		jar-stand	*g* hard
	owl	*m*		loaf	*t*
	water	*n*		tethering rope	*t* emphatic originally *tsh*
	mouth	*r*		hand	*d*
	reed shelter in fields	*h*		snake	*d* emphatic originally *dj*

Table showing the various phonetic signs used as an alphabet by the Egyptians.

minatives) was often put after the words, which, totally stripped of its phonetic value, was simply meant to convey precisely the meaning of the word. Therefore a man with his hands to his mouth or his front could determine the words meaning « eat », « drink », « think », etc. ; a man carrying a vase on his head (or a basket) indicates the idea of « carry ». Word signs, ideograms, determinatives and phonetic signs (one or several consonants) constituted this chiefly phonetic writing, which, in the course of time, was more and more refined with procedures such as phonetic complements for example. There is no separation between the words in the writing, or between the phrases. The direction of the writing can vary ; vertical (particularly in the early periods), right to left, but also from left to right (less often), and the purely decorative aspect which sometimes had priority over the others.

Hieroglyphs (in Egyptian « divine staves ») of the classic period comprised about 700 signs, certain of which were more common than others (the word signs and determinatives were not in principle limited). In the Ptolemaic and Roman period all the signs could have phonetic values and they were continually invented and modified, so that the signs employed became innumerable. The last hieroglyphic inscription dates to 394 A.D., it was inscribed on the Island of Philae during the reign of the emperor Theodosius.

The more or less sacred character attributed to writing and its decorative aspect was designed to cover, in the form of inscriptions or paintings, the walls of temples, pylons, coffins and tombs. The decorative aspect of the innumerable signs transcribed in

stone was reinforced by the play of light and shade which was different according to whether the inscriptions were in relief or simply incised.

HIERATIC AND DEMOTIC WRITING

The transition of actual hieroglyphs, which tended to be used exclusively for texts inscribed in stone, to the cursive form of hieratic, clearly appeared in the more linear cursive texts on tablets of wood, coffins and certain papyri. Written with brushes or reeds, later they sometimes became more light and elegant, and for this reason are called « cursive hieroglyphs ».

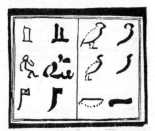

The hieratic script arose from a simplification of hieroglyphs

Hieratic was already formed and fixed in the Old Kingdom but its formal evolution was as great as that of hieroglyphs in the course of time. It is a writing which does not differ in its form or system from hieroglyphic writing. The appearance of this writing was profoundly modified because of the very graphic style which permitted the omission of certain elements of the original signs, so that very often the hieratic sign bears little resemblance to the original hieroglyph. The difference can be compared to the distance which separates the modern printed word and individual handwriting, with the difference that hieratic was simplified once and for all and that the different hands could not endlessly modify it.

Hieratic was used chiefly on papyrus and less often on wood or stone. It was used for religious texts as well as for profane or everyday writing (e.g. accounts). It was in use up to the Late Period and also up to the introduction of demotic, at least for religious rituals.

Demotic, the last form of ancient Egyptian writing, properly described as a new shortened writing, was even more sophisticated with the regrouping of signs. It is difficult writing in which the connections with hieroglyphs appear distant. It came into use about the VIII-VIIth century B.C. and the last attestation dates to the Vth century A.D.

COPTIC WRITING

As the Egyptians gradually became converted to Christianity, they abandoned the difficult traditional writing and created a new form (after several more ancient attempts), which was simply Greek writing to which seven ancient demotic signs were added. *Coptic* is in fact a fairly successful attempt to write the Egyptian language in the Greek alphabet. The first appearance of ancient Coptic was in the third century A.D., but there were already preliminary stages in the preceding centuries. It was Christianity which developed its use because the ancient writing was no longer really mastered and because the new religion

was conveyed largely in the Greek language. That was the reason for the use of seven demotic signs which served to denote Egyptian sounds unknown in Greek. Coptic also had a merit in that it more or less gives us the pronunciation of Late Egyptian (and its dialects) because this time the vowels are noted.

Coptic writing stayed in use in the country for as long as the Egyptian language (or Coptic) but rapidly declined after the Arab conquest, the conversion to Islam and the growing use of Arabic. Egyptian was spoken in the Coptic villages until the XVIIth century however and, at the present, Coptic language and writing is still used in the Christian liturgy of Egypt.

THE DECIPHERMENT OF ANCIENT EGYPTIAN WRITING

The key to Egyptian writing, chiefly hieroglyphs, was lost fairly soon after the country became Christian. There were numerous essays which tried to decipher them, but all were based on a vain symbolic interpretation. The Jesuit *Athanasius Kircher*, in the XVIIth century, had the fortune to understand the deep link between ancient Egyptian and Coptic (perfectly understood during his time), but did not make any more progress in the actual decipherment. With Bonaparte's expedition and specifically the discovery, by officer Bouchard in 1799, of a stela near Rosetta which became famous, the topic of hieroglyphs was current among the educated Europeans (among other workers was the English physician Thomas Young). But it was the Frenchman Jean-François Champollion who, because of precocious genius, detailed preparation and impeccable method, became the author, in 1822, of the great discovery of the reading and understanding of ancient Egyptian.

The Rosetta stone is inscribed with a decree of Ptolemy V in hieroglyphs, Greek and Demotic. This bilingual inscription was of great use to

The Rosetta Stone

Champollion who also used, among others, the copies of Ptolemaic inscriptions from Philae. His work was based on the royal names, enclosed in cartouches, which enabled him to read the simple signs. An immense work followed, and ten years after wards, Champollion finished the first Egyptian grammar, the publication of which was posthumous because he died young in 1832. The Egyptologists of the following generations have developed this immense work.

PAPYRUS

Papyrus used to grow in Egypt, particularly in the Delta and in the marshy regions ; it was prolific and of excellent quality. The stem with triangular section could reach up to six metres (19 feet) and was capped by an umbel. In stylised form, it was the sceptre of goddesses ; it served as the model for several types of stone columns which supported the roofs of temples and tombs ; on the other hand the papyrus forests were highly valued as hunting areas and finally its multiple practical uses were not ignored (construction of boats, ropes, mats, baskets and sandals, the extraction of juice). But the foremost use of papyrus was to furnish an excellent paper for writing. The Greeks called it *papyros* (from which *paper* comes) without doubt a slight modification of its Egyptian name which seems to have been *papuro* « royal », explained by the fact that the manufacture of papyrus was a royal monopoly in Egypt.

The papyrus stem was cut in sections up to 50 cm (20 in.), then it was separated into layers which were beaten with a hammer to flatten them, the layers were put side by side in two criss-crossed rows and wetted before being beaten again which stuck them together ; the leaves were then joined to others to form a roll. An average roll of papyrus comprised twenty leaves. The largest roll known is 40 metres long (131 ft). Both sides were often written on (the recto corresponds to the horizontal fibres and forms the interior of the roll). The Greeks and then the Romans learnt about papyrus in Egypt and used it a little, but it never took over from parchment (skins were more common than the exotic plant) and was supplanted by it at the end of the IInd century A.D. in Egypt itself.

The Religion of Modern Egyptians : Islam

In 640 A.D. the brilliant Arab general, 'Amr ibn el-'As, mounted his first expedition to Egypt. A member of the young Muslim community which was set on the conquest of the world, he shared its dynamism and enthusiasm. In 642 A.D., Alexandria, the great Christian cultural centre of Egypt, fell into his hands. Its fall made Egypt an Arab and Muslim country. A new capital was founded at Fustât, one of the quarters of old Cairo. The new faith, Islam, was implanted so firmly that today 90 % of the Egyptian population still adheres to it.

Islam is an Arabic word which signifies « submission, giving oneself totally to God », and is in itself a way of life.

Born in Arabia, in the Hejaz, during the 7th century A.D., Islam is a religion based primarily upon a sacred book, the Koran, which is a collection of divine revelations communicated to the prophet Mohammed, who was charged with their transmission to the whole world.

Mohammed was born in about 570 A.D. in the commercial milieu of Mecca, a rich city which lived off the traffic of caravans transporting precious merchandise, coming from India, via the Indian Ocean, to the West. It was also an important stop on the incense route and possessed a temple, in the shape of a cube, called the Ka'aba (cube), to which pagan Arabs went on pilgrimage. Made an orphan at an early age, Mohammed was brought up by his grandfather and then his uncle, and participated in this commercial life accompanying several caravans, until the day that he married Khadija, a rich widow for whom he was working. It was at this time that he received his first revelation. According to his own account, he heard a voice saying to him : « Recite », « What shall I recite ? », he replied troubled. After he had been tormented to exhaustion, the voice replied : « Recite ; in the name of your Lord who has created you ». And he recited. He pronounced the first phrase of what was to become the Koran. Later the voice said to him : « Preach, you are the Messenger of God ». Extremely distressed, doubting his mission, he returned home and confided in his wife, who comforted him and became the first to believe in him. More revelations followed and Mohammed preached. Several of his neighbours and his friends were converted. They formed the nucleus of the Muslim community whose members recognised in Mohammed the Prophet and Messenger of God. In this pagan milieu of Mecca, Mohammed preached of one God, Creator of the world and mankind, of a universal brotherhood and the equality of all men. This was a revolutionary prediction which rapidly aroused the hostility of his fellow citizens. Before long it was necessary for him to leave for a nearby city, Yathrib, which then took the name of Medina (from the word el-medina : the city of the Prophet). This became the first year of the Muslim era called « of the Hejira », the word *hejira* meaning emigration.

In Medina, where the inhabitants acclaimed him joyously, Mohammed became uncontested leader and progressively succeeded in extending his domination over a large part of Arabia. He defined the main tenets of the new religion which were to appear in the Medina Suras (the Suras are the chapters of the Koran) which reflect the work of a religious and social legislator. He formulated equally a constitution for the « umma » (community), defining the laws and obligations for each of the groups of which it was comprised : Muhajirun (the emigrants from Mecca), Ansar (the auxilliaries, inhabitants of Medina) and the people of the Book (Jews and Christians). He assured equally the material well-being of his people by organising raids against the enemy caravans from Mecca and continued the conquest by directing several campaigns against Syria. But the aim of the Prophet was to reconquer Mecca in order to make it his religious centre by associating his cult with the Ka'aba, which he wanted to return to honour, because of its connection with Abraham. An Islamic tradition mentions that the black stone, venerated by the Muslims, had been built into the wall of the Ka'aba by Abraham himself. After many battles and underhand dealings, Mohammed took possession of Mecca and made se-

veral pilgrimages to it. It was after his return from one of these pilgrimages that he died at Medina and where he was buried in 632 A.D.

Mohammed left Islam strongly established in the Hejaz and in less than a hundred years the new doctrine reached, in the east, the boundaries of China and the Indus, and in the west, the shores of the Atlantic. This swift progression of the Arab armies can be explained by the decadent state of the regions dominated by the two great empires of the time : the Byzantine and the Sassanid.

Islamic doctrine has its source in the Koran, which is presented as a divinely revealed code, closely inter-relating religious and Sociopolitical life. This code expresses itself in a religious law called *Shari'a* which applies to all of the community of believers. This is defined as a unique bond of faith in one God and in the mission of the Prophet. This double profession of faith is called *Shahada*. The formula itself is destined to be constantly made manifest and is repeated many times in all of the circumstances of the life of the Believers. The Muslim dogma has not received an official formulation, other than the *Shahada,* but the Muslim theologians have endeavoured to assemble the varied elements and to express them in theological treaties. The principal dogmas consist of the belief in divine unity, in the creation of the world by this one God, in the belief in angels and the prophets of whom Mohammed is the last and the culmination, in the final judgement when all men will appear before God, equipped with a book which will list all of their good and evil actions, and in the retribution : paradise for the good and the inferno for the wicked.

The legislation of Islam is based initially upon the Koran, but is completed and clarified by the *hadith,* which are the collections of the sayings of the Prophet, transmitted by his companions. These *hadith* have given birth to the oral traditions which exist essentially to verify the lists of transmitters in order to assure the truth of the latter. Once passing through the screen of criticism, these traditions were gathered together in a corpus which served as the basis for Islamic jurisprudence. This is expressed by four principal schools :

— *The Hanafite School :* founded in Mesopotamia (Iraq) in 767 A.D., predominant in Turkey
— *The Malikite School :* founded by the Imam Malik in 795 A.D., which is prevalent in Northern Africa, Western Africa and in Upper Egypt
— *The Shafi'ite School :* founded in Egypt by the Imam Shafi'i in 820 A.D., which is encountered in Lower Egypt, Syria and Southern Arabia.
— *The Hanbalite School :* founded by Ibn Hanbal in 855 A.D. which marks a reaction towards stricter traditionalism, and is the rite of Arabia.

These four judicial schools concern all the Sunnite faction of Islam, that is to say the orthodox majority. On the border of this orthodoxy Shi'ism is encountered which dominated Egypt for many centuries under the Fatimid dynasty (909-1171 A.D.). The Shi'ites claim a direct descent from the Prophet, through his son-in-law Ali (who was also his full cousin). They deem that they have been set aside unjustly by the Cali-

phate. which represented at the same time both political and spiritual power ; the Caliph was the leader of the community. The differences which exist between the Sunnites and the Shi'ites are more political than doctrinal.

THE OBLIGATIONS OF THE MUSLIMS

These obligations are commonly described as the « five pillars of Islam ».

1. The profession of faith or *shahada,* referred to above, which believers must recite on all of the major occasions of their lives : « La illaha illa'llah wa Mohammed elrasul illah » - There is no God but Allah and Mohammed is the Prophet of God.

2. Prayer *(salah) :* from puberty onwards and satisfying many other conditions of ritual purity, the Muslim must pray daily five times while facing in the direction of Mecca. These prayers form an essential part of the Islamic liturgy. Each prayer consists of a certain number of elements repeated in turn *(rak'a)* and which are obligatory. These elements comprise the recitation of formulae, verses from the Koran and positions of deference, e.g., inclining the head and prostrations.

3. Alms Giving : called *zakat,* from the root to purify, and which is regarded as purifying those who give. This is a contribution in kind or cash given by the Muslim and destined to nourish a means of mutual assistance by charity.

4. The Fast of Ramadan : this fast takes place for all of the Muslim community in the ninth month of the lunar year *(ramadan).* It is obligatory from the age of puberty. It consists of taking neither food nor

drink from sunrise to sunset. In the evening all of the prohibitions end. This collective fast is a cause of profound joy for the community and a unifying factor.

5. The Pilgrimage : The pilgrimage is obligatory at least once in a lifetime for all adults who have the material means. It comprises two groups of ceremonies. The first consists of, primarily, making 7 ritual journeys from the Ka'aba to

The Ka'aba at Mecca

Mecca, and to cover the distance between the two sacred mounds called Safa and Marwa 4 times. The other ceremonies entail a very impressive gathering at Arafa, on the outskirts of Mecca, of a nocturnal assembly at Muzdalifa, and the sacrifice of a sheep at Mina in rememberance of the sacrifice by Abraham, and the ritual stoning of pillars representing the devil. In order to accomplish all of these rites the pilgrim must be in a state of holiness (*ihram*). For this he makes his

ablutions, wears a white habit and must refrain from all sexual relations. Numerous prayers accompany all of these rites. The pilgrimage is an occasion greatly anticipated by the people, of meetings between believers from all countries and races, of exchanges between the learned, and the beginning of commercial contacts. Those who make the pilgrimage return to their homes with the title *hagg* a term of honour through-out the Muslim world. Family feasts are organised when the pilgrim returns, his house is decorated and his friends visit.

Apart from these essential regulations for the religious life of the Muslims, the judicial manuals include a series of laws concerning prohibited foods etc., and regulations which concern even the details of personal life. However, the part of human initiative remains very great, as the studies concerning Muslim history, thought and civilisation prove.

CULT

Islam is a union of believers, not a church. There is no clergy or sacrement, but it is a practical and sober religion with a simple cult. The divine service is directed by a member of the community who has the appropriate knowledge or by a specially trained *imam*. The theologians and specialists on religious law are called *ulamas*.

In Islam the rites and cults, which correspond to the tradition of an Arab desert people, stay very simple.

There are no images which have a determined or didactic role and for good reason no images which would give rise to a cult. Also there is no place for music in the cult although it plays a great part in the daily life of all oriental people

The mosques, the houses of Islamic prayer, (Arabic : *masgid*, but the Friday mosque is called *gâmî*) are not necessarily places where God will be present. From there the *imam* (leader of the prayer) or the *khabib* (the preacher) officiates and the *muezzin* calls the faithful to prayer from the top of the minaret. On this call, the believers hurry towards the forecourt of the ablution fountain *(hanafiya)* and, after purification, enter the mosque having left their shoes at the entrance, because it can never be entered with dirt from outside (this rule applies equally to visitors). The ground is covered with carpets and the prayers are recited there ; in fact there is no furniture in a mosque, no chairs or benches, but simply the chair of the preacher and the *rahla*, a cross shaped pulpit which supports the Koran. The prayers are recited out loud by heart and some are silent ; the faithful have to alternate between kneeling, standing and squatting and must sometimes touch the ground with their foreheads.

The organisation of the interior of a mosque is as follows : the *mihrab*, which is generally opposite the entrance is the most important place. It is a niche cut in the wall and most of them are especially worked and decorated. It always gives the direction of Mecca very exactly to which the prayers are directed. The imam stands in front of the mihrab bet-

ween the two chandeliers which flank the sides of the niche and which were most often offerings of the founder of the mosque. Very near him at the right, seated on the *minbar* (large wooden chair), the preacher reads the profession of the faith. The minbar has 15, 20 or 23 steps and ends in a type of throne covered with a pointed roof. Like the mihrab, the chair is very well worked and artistically decorated (wood encrusted with mother or pearl or alabaster). Because Muslim sacred art bans images, superb faience tiles and bands of kufic or classic inscriptions cover the walls, cupola and the columns in the richest mosques. The inscriptions always consist of verses from the Koran or repeat the name and attributes of Allah, or commemorate Mohammed and the first caliphs. In the ancient mosques, there were chandeliers suspended from the cellings, consisting of innumerable small vases of glass or crystal made into oil lamps which used to illuminate the rooms before being replaced by modern and less aesthetic bulbs or neon tubes.

Islam reached its greatest strength in the first decades after the apparition of the Prophet and his death, when the Arabs were freshly converted and had conquered up to Persia and Spain. Much later, when other peoples turned towards this faith, Islam knew a new expansion towards the interior of Asia and up to China, towards the archipelago of Indonesia, towards black Africa and the Balkans. It is estimated that 350 million people profess Islam today.

Holidays in Egypt

Egypt was part of the classic tour in antiquity and it has remained so up to the present day. The monuments of a civilisation several millenia older attracted the Greek historians and geographers Herodotus and Strabo and they have never lost their strong attraction. On the contrary, the modern visitor can contemplate marvels which are in fact more numerous and more extraordinary than those seen by Strabo two thousand years ago. This is because of the results of excavations and museum objects, without counting the careful reconstructions which provide a grand panorama of ancient Egyptian civilization.

On the other hand, comfortable and fast means of transport are available for the modern visitor. In almost all the important sites, or in the very close neighbourhood, the hotels are comfortable, often air conditioned and they provide the type of accommodation that the modern tourist expects. Whereas, in antiquity, and even in the nineteenth century, visitors had to suffer hot, dusty journeys riding from site to site, the modern tourist can travel to scenic areas, monuments and towns as comfortably, even luxuriously, as his budget permits and also bathe in swimming pools or the sea.

But Egypt does not only furnish a superabundance of monuments of the pharaonic period : the buildings and the works of art of the Coptic period considerably enlarge the choice of things to visit and, in the Middle Ages it was in the Nile valley that Islam began to expand its art and civilisation. The modern tourist is able to include these aspects of the country in his programme.

The following pages give a guide for planning a stay in Egypt, from which the visitor will be able to arrange each stage according to the time and means at his disposal and also his centres of interest. This advice, as well as illustrating the way this guide book can be used, also allows the individual to visit and admire Egypt without the need to join a group.

The « classic » tour in Egypt is that which consists of following the Nile from Cairo and travelling to the south. On the other hand, for the majority of tourists, Cairo is also the point of arrival and departure and, for the visitor who arrives by boat, Alexandria is the first contact with the country.

The division of visits into « mornings » and « afternoons » fits in with local conditions and the time required which has been verified on more than one occasion. It will be understood that certain important sites may have to be omitted by those who do not wish to take that choice of excursion.

Lower Egypt

FOUR DAYS IN CAIRO

First Day : morning, visit Egyptian Museum ; afternoon, the Citadel and the Mosques of the same sector, then the Mosques of Ibn Tûlun and the adjoining quarter.

Second day : morning, the Giza Pyramids ; afternoon, the Islamic Museum.

Third Day : full day excursion to Memphis and Saqqara.

Fourth Day : morning, Old Cairo ; afternoon, the Mosque of El-Azhar and the bazaars.

EIGHT DAYS IN CAIRO

First Day : morning, Egyptian Museum ; afternoon, modern Cairo and the banks of the Nile.

Second Day : morning, the Citadel and its surroundings ; afternoon, the ramparts and the Tombs of the Mamelukes.

Third Day : morning, the Giza Pyramids ; afternoon, the Mosque of El-Azhar and the bazaars.

Fourth Day : full day excursion to Memphis and Saqqara.

Fifth Day : morning, the Islamic Museum ; afternoon, Old Cairo.

Sixth Day : full day excursion to the Fayûm.

Seventh Day : morning, the mosques situated between the Citadel and the bazaars ; afternoon, tour to Moqattam and Tombs of the Mamelukes.

Eighth Day : morning, the Zoo or a museum according to interest ; afternoon, excursion to the Nile Barrages, to Heliopolis or Helwan.

FOUR DAYS IN ALEXANDRIA

The visitor who arrives by air and who does not gain access to Egypt by the port of Alexandria may add to his stay in Cairo a visit to the Mediterranean city (by the Delta route

and the desert route) and, in spite of lack of time, he may be able to look at several sites. The time necessary for this excursion is about four days.

First Day : leave for Alexandria by the Delta route. One can take time and look at life and the country. Stop at Tanta (Mosque of Badawi) and at Kafr el-Zaiyat (finally visit a cotton factory).

Second Day : the morning at Alexandria, walk on the cornice next to the Fort of Qait Bey and to the Palace of Ras el-Tin ; afternoon : one can visit the Museum of Antiquities.

Third Day : morning, Pompey's column and the catacombs ; afternoon, visit the Palace of Montaza and the beaches (bathing according to the season).

Fourth Day : return to Cairo by the Desert route (leave early !). From the rest house at half-way, visit the convents of the Wadi Natrûn. See one or two convents (above all Deir el-Suryani). There will be enough time to stop again at Abu Roâsh.

Middle and Upper Egypt

Between Cairo and Luxor travel can be direct or with stop-overs according to the means of travel chosen. Those who travel by boat, rail or by local bus, must often put up with long periods of waiting. Plans which are always changing have their effect on the time reserved for visiting the principal sites. It must be realised that in general one must allow a minimum of three hours to visit the sites next to the banks of the Nile or the temples, tombs and monasteries situated next to the road or the rail-

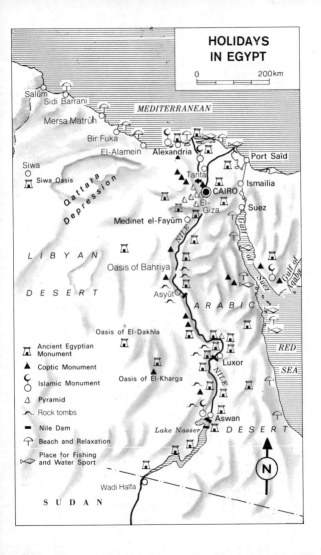

HOLIDAYS IN EGYPT

0   200km

MEDITERRANEAN

Salûm
Sidi Barrani
Mersa Matrûh
Bir Fuka
El-Alamein   Alexandria   Port Saïd
Tanta   Ismailia
Siwa
Siwa Oasis   CAIRO
El-Giza   Suez
Qattara
Depression   Medinet el-Fayûm

L I B Y A N

D E S E R T   Oasis of Bahriya

Asyût   A R A B I C

Oasis of El-Dakhla   Gulf of Suez   Gulf of ʿAqaba

Luxor   RED

Oasis of El-Kharga   SEA

Aswan
Lake Nasser   D E S E R T

Wadi Halfa

S U D A N

Ancient Egyptian Monument
Coptic Monument
Islamic Monument
Pyramid
Rock tombs
Nile Dam
Beach and Relaxation
Place for Fishing and Water Sport

N

way ; a half day is preferable however. An exception should be made for Tell el Amarna and Beni Hasan, where the tombs to be visited are numerous, as well as for Hermopolis Magna and Tûna el-Gebel which cover a very large area. Two days should be reserved for visiting all these sites.

THREE DAYS AT LUXOR

In any case, the ruins of the region of Luxor should never be seen very quickly, because they certainly constitute the most important site of Upper Egypt. The minimum time to look at them should be three days, In too short a time, the particularities and subtleties of the pharaonic monuments cannot be understood. In doubling the length of the stay an even more convenient visiting time will be achieved.

First Day : morning, the Temple of Karnak ; afternoon, the Temple of Luxor.

Second Day : full day excursion over to the left bank with a visit to the Valley of the Kings, Deir el-Bahri and the Ramesseum.

Third Day : return to the left bank and visit the Tombs of the Nobles, the Valley of the Queens, Deir el Medina and Medinet Habu.

SIX DAYS AT LUXOR

First Day : morning, the Temple of Karnak ; afternoon, the Temple of Luxor.

Second Day : the left bank with the funerary Temple of Sethos I, the Valley of the Kings (particularly the tombs numbered 8, 9, 17 and 62) ; return by the mountain track which leads to Deir el Bahri.

Third day : the left bank with a visit to the Temple of Hatshepsut and its dependencies, the Temple of Mentuhotep, the Tombs of the Nobles at Qurna (above all Nakht, Userhat, Ramose, Menna and Antefoker) and finally the Ramesseum.

Fourth Day : the left bank again, with a visit to the necropolis and Temple of Deir el Medina, the Valley of the Queens, Medinet Habu and the Colossi of Memnon on the return.

Fifth Day : full day excursion to Dendera, to Esna or to Edfu.

Sixth Day : morning : visit Medamud or Tôd in the neighbourhood of Luxor ; afternoon, return to Karnak, to the Temple of Luxor, or walk along the Nile or in the country.

FIVE DAYS AT ASWAN AND ABU SIMBEL

First Day : the Island of Elephantine and its Museum, Kitchener's Island, the modern town of Aswan.

Second Day : the Tombs of the Nobles on the west bank, the Aga Khan's Mausoleum, the Monastery of Saint Simeon.

Third Day : long tour to the south with a visit to the unfinished obelisk, the old dam, the Temple of Philae, the new dam and the reconstructed monuments in its neighbourhood (Kalabsha, Beit el-Wali).

Fourth Day : morning : sail in a feluka up to the cataracts and the Island of Sehel, then in the afternoon leave by air for Abu Simbel where you stay.

Fifth Day : visit Abu Simbel and its monuments, then return to Aswan or Cairo by air (preferably by hydrofoil for comfort).

The other regions of Egypt

THE SINAI PENINSULA

Up to 1967, the tours to Sinai were organised from Cairo ; they demanded serious organisation and a minimum of three days (five days was the ideal length of time). A single itinerary was possible with some variations.

TWO DAYS AT THE SUEZ CANAL

First Day : Cairo-Suez-Ismailia

Second Day : Ismailia-Port Said-Damietta (or Ismailia-Cairo). Possibility of a boat excursion on the canal ; length of the crossing totals 15 to 20 hours.

THE RED SEA COAST ROUTE

Like Sinai and other regions, this visit is subject to the political problems of the region and their settlement. For instance, access to the Red Sea zone is difficult and its coast and beaches are practicable in a few areas only. In normal times. it was necessary to reserve several days for the voyage (2,000 km (1,243 miles) Cairo-Mersa Alam and back) and a stay on the superb beaches.

ALEXANDRIA - EL ALAMEIN - SIWA OASIS

To completely accomplish this journey it needs at least two days to go and return and one or two days at Siwa itself.

OASES

A journey to the oasis of Kharga takes one full day, and at least two days are required to visit its monuments. From here the oasis of Dakhla can be reached in half a day, and a stay of one day is recommended. Although Farafra can be reached from Dakhla the road is very difficult, and it is better to approach it via Bahriya. A trip to these two will take three days.

Cairo

See plan pages 354-355

Cairo (Arabic : *Masr el Qahira),* the capital of Egypt has nearly eight million inhabitants and is therefore the largest African city. It is situated on both banks of the Nile, 20 km (12½ mi) from the place where the river divides into two principal arms, the *Damietta* and *Rosetta.* Today the most important quarters of the city are on the right, east bank of the Nile. The area known under the name of Old Cairo, which was the original city, is there. In the course of history this was extended to the north to the *Moqattam* hills, the modern quarter of the *sûqs.* In the XIXth and XXth centuries, the orientation changed and moved towards the west and the Nile, the islands and the west bank of the river. But in the west, as in the east, the city ends in the desert, in the western *Libyan desert* where the pyramids were constructed or in the eastern *Arabic desert* with the spurs of *Moqattam.*

Between the ancient centre of the town, the *Ezbekiya Gardens* and the new situated at *Tahrir Square,* between the ancient symbol of the town, the Citadel and the Muhammed Ali mosque and the modern Cairo Tower, an animated exuberant life prevails. For those who know the Arab world, Cairo appears as one of the most « oriental » cities of the Near East and North Africa. Cairo is also the gateway to Egypt. The Pyramids, the Egyptian Museum, the Coptic Museum and the Museum of Islamic Art allow the links which unify the different phases of the history of the country to be understood. It is

only a few hours by air to this city of marvels. And furthermore, Cairo is also a modern city with almost all the necessities of modern life and it has fully equipped hotels to satisfy the visitor.

Finally it should be noted that Cairo is the capital of the « Arab Republic of Egypt » and also the site of the famous mosque and Islamic university El-Azhar which was for a long time the centre of political, ideological and religious debate in the Arab world and now continues to be but to a lesser extent.

HISTORY

During the most ancient times a place existed without doubt on the east bank of the Nile which was known to the ancient Egyptians by the name of *Kher-Aha* or the « place of combat » because it was said that it was there the battle took place between the rival gods, Horus and Seth.

Much later, several centuries B.C., this town was also known as the *Babylon of Egypt* which depended administratively on *Heliopolis,* the sun town, the ancient *On.* Not far from Kher-Aha was *Per-Hapy* (« The house of the Nile god ») which was where the source of the Nile was reputed to exist.

But it was chiefly in the north-east of modern Cairo that an important city developed which played an immense part in the religious history of the country ; *Heliopolis,* mentioned briefly above. Site of the cult dedicated to the sun, numerous temples were erected there, consecrated to the god Re. The town corresponds to the modern quarters of *Matariya* and *Ain Shams* (which signifies the « source of the sun »). But virtually nothing remains of this important city today except the solitary obelisk of Sesotris I.

By the place where the Holy Family rested on « the Flight into Egypt » a sycamore is still shown to rare visitors (the Virgin's Tree) under which the Virgin and Child once rested. A long distance from On, on the west bank of the Nile, towards the south, the great town of *Men-nefer* was created, *Memphis* of the Greeks which was always, from the time of the legendary king Menes (about 3,000 B.C.), the political capital or in any case one of the most brilliant towns in the land. Memphis corresponds to the modern villages of Mit Rahina and Badrashein and the area stretching between Saqqara and the Giza pyramids comes under their administration.

When they arrived in the interior of the country, coming from Alexandria in 30 B.C., the legions of Augustus chose the area of Babylon and Memphis as one of their principal quartering places and the Romans fortified it.

In 640 A.D., the Arabs, acting for the caliph Omar, under the leadership of general Amr Ibn el-As, took the fortress of Babylon and a little later founded the mosque of Amr at *Fustât* which corresponds today to Old Cairo, at the actual place where the general is supposed to have pitched his tent. The legend in fact recounts that a dove made her nest under the tent of Amr and she laid her eggs. When the general decided to raise camp, he discovered the nest, refused to disturb the bird's peace and the camp remained dressed. Thus the first great Islamic city was founded which was called *Fustât* in remembrance of the tent of Amr (in Arabic the word means « tent ») ; but actually the name comes from the latin *Fossatum* which denoted the Roman entrenched camp which was installed there.

In 750, after bloody battles with the Umaiyads, the Abbasids took over the caliphate and their lieutenant, El Salah Ibn Ali extended Fustât further towards the north and constructed El-Askar where the houses of the modern inhabitants stand today. Then when Ahmed Ibn Tûlûn, the founder of the Tulunid dynasty (868-905) became sovereign of Egypt, he also extended the town towards the north and constructed the town of El-Qatai on the height where his mosque is situated.

Therefore all these towns, On, Babylon, Memphis, Fustât, El-Askar and El-Qatai, large or modest, formed the origin, directly or indirectly, of the great contemporary capital of Cairo.

The foundation of Cairo proper is owed to Gohar, the general of caliph El Muizz el-Din Allah. In 969, when he was about to lay the first stone of the new capital situated slightly north of El Qatai, the planet Mars (Arabic : *Qahir* « the Victorious ») appeared above the town, according to the chroniclers. The new foundation was also called *El-Qahira* « the Victorious ». Quite soon after, the Fatimids put into practice an active policy of construction and it is to this period that, for example, the Mosque of El-Azhar, the Mosque of El-Hakim, the Mosque of El-Aqmar and monumental gates of Babel-Futuh, Bab el-Zuweila and Bab el-Nasr are dated.

The Aiyubid dynasty which succeeded the Fatimids profoundly changed the town with their buildings that can still be admired today. Under Salâh el-Dîn the famous « Saladin » of the Christians, practically all the area of the town (El Qahira, El-Qatai, El-Askar and even Fustât) was enclosed in strong walls, which remained incomplete however. In 1176, on the other hand, the construction of the Citadel was begun.

The centuries which followed, up to the Turkish conquest and very much later up to Bonaparte's victory at the Battle of the Pyramids, consisted of a series of epidemics, internecine struggles, pillages and sometimes fires which formed the back-drop of the scene where the dramatic history of the Mamelukes unfurled. Through veneration of their God, and also through pride, they built prolifically, seeking to make the city a prestigious capital, the monuments of which would impress the population and visitors. It is to them that we owe a certain number of mosques and the superb « Town of the Dead » which made Cairo original.

The destiny of Cairo as a brilliant capital was confirmed after the victory of the Ottoman sultan Selim (1517). But in contrast to the brilliant metropolis, Cairo declined a little during the 250 following years when it was not so much the capital but an indolent province of the Turkish empire. In 1798, Bonaparte landed in Egypt, fought the Battle of the Pyramids on the 21st of July and entered Cairo as a victor. The French interlude was followed in 1805 by the reign of Muhammed Ali ; the « alabaster mosque » (Mosque of Muhammed Ali) and the Cairo barrages constitute the best architecture of his epoch.

At the end of the second half of the XIXth century, when European civilisation had made its entry, the appearance of modern Cairo, which can still be seen in parts, began to be created. Certain quarters at the foot of the Citadel were traversed or knocked down and large avenues, great squares, parks, public edifices, palaces and museums were constructed. With the development of tourism, the great modern hotels appeared, on the cornice of the Nile, for example. Today Cairo presents all the advantages and inconveniences of great modern cities.

VISITS

The ideal point of departure for excursions visiting Cairo is « Liberation Square » (Midan el-Tahrir, Arabic midan = square). It is in the centre of modern Cairo and certain large hotels, banks, the main line station and airline companies are situated there or nearby.

In order to impart a thorough knowledge of Cairo and its environs, all the monuments and excursions are divided into five itineraries, are visits to the Pyramids of Giza, Memphis and Saqqara, as well as excursions to Helwan and to the Barrages. The visitor who can only spend a few days in Cairo should try to visit : the Pyramids, the Citadel and the sûq quarter, as well as the mosques of Muhammed Ali in the Citadel, of Sultan Hassan, Ibn Tûlûn and El-Azhar, Old Cairo with the Coptic Museum, the Egyptian Museum and the Museum of Islamic Art. On the other hand, a walk can be taken on the bank of the Nile near the Andalucian Garden. A sail in a feluka on the river would complete the picture of the city and the visitor might eventually say, on his return, like the philosopher and historian of the XIVth century, Ibn Khaldun : « I have entered the metropolis of the world in the garden of Allah ! »

Itinerary n° 1 : Modern Cairo

This circular walk should give the visitor first of all an idea of the whole city. The point òf departure is

Tahrir Square [1]. In the middle is the monument commemorating liberation. The *Nile Hilton* hotel is situated on the west and the imposing building of the *Egyptian museum* is on the north. Near there, towards the south, the administrative building of *Mogamma* and the *Ministry of Foreign Affairs* can be seen. The *New Shepheards* hotel is in front of the Nile (the *Semiramis* Hotel has now been demolished). Leaving there, cross the *El-Tahrir* bridge to reach *Gezira Island*. While on this bridge looking towards the south the *El-Gamaa* bridge can be seen linking *Rôda Island* (with the *Meridien* hotel) with the quarter of Giza. Downstream to the right there is the *Hilton* Hotel and further along the curious radio and television building which took the one in Paris as its model. In front, on *Gezira Island,* the Nile flows beside the *Andalucian Gardens* and other pleasant parks and the characteristic Cairo Tower stands behind. The new *6th October bridge* links the two banks of the river Nile over *Gezira Island*. Once past the bridge you reach *Midan el-Gezira* **[2]** with a statue of *Saad Zaghlul Pasha* (founder of the nationalist *Wafd* movement) in the centre. Nearby is the entrance to *Exhibition Park* where the *Museum*

of Egyptian Civilisation will be found. From there, turn to the right towards the

Andalucian Gardens [3]. The entrance is on the square on the right in the *Sharia El-Gezira* (Arabic Sharia = street). The gardens were given this name to commemorate Alhambra of Grenada and his celebrated lion fountains. There are copies of original Egyptian monuments here, above all statues, but the principal charm of the place resides in its Moorish-Andalucian style, with pools, fountains and terraces. A bit further on towards the *Cairo Tower*, there is an obelisk of Ramesses II from *Tanis* in the Delta. So Cairo in its turn uses one of these granite needles for decoration like the world's other great capitals.

Cairo Tower [4]. It forms the symbol of the modern city, 187m high (590 ft.) and elegant in form. Constructed in concrete it has the stylised form of a lotus stem and bud, therefore recalling the favourite theme of ancient Egyptian art. The exterior of the Tower is curiously decorated with a type of trellis. At the summit (lift), there is a platform with a restaurant, a café and a superb panorama over the city and its surroundings. It is worth the trouble to go up the tower again when night falls to look at the Nile illuminated by the last rays of the sun and the city gently lit by thousands of fire-flies.

From the tower, a great circular survey of 25 km (15 mi.) can be accomplished without moving which gives an excellent opportunity to understand the orientation of the city and to get to know its environs.

At the north the *Island of Gezira* can be seen with the vast area of the *Gezira Sporting Club* (golf, tennis, swimming), the residential quarter of *Zamalek* and, further on, the river with the island of *El-Hadar* and the beginning of the Delta. Turning a little towards the right *Heliopolis* can be seen and *Cairo Airport* in the desert.

At the east, south of the airport, stand the heights of *Moqattam,* sometimes red and sometimes pale which are beginning to be covered with new quarters of habitation. Even further to the south. Old Cairo can be seen and, beyond the verdant suburb of *Maâdi,* the railway line which goes to *Helwan.*

At the south, facing the town of *Helwan,* where heavy industry has developed with its thick black smoke, the Step pyramid of *Saqqara* and the other funerary monuments of the region may be seen.

Finally, at the west stands the new quarter of *Doqqi* and towards the southwest the *University* and the *Zoological Garden.* Further on, the three pyramids of *Giza* reflect the sun and mark the beginning of the immense yellow Libyan desert. The desert routes which go to *Alexandria* and the *Fayûm* may be seen.

After this visit to the Tower, return to *El-Gezira* square [2] and turn towards the south point of the island towards

the Tahrir Gardens [5], where there are various forms of amusement and agreeable cafés on the bank of the river. From here, there is a pleasant view towards the south with a large *fountain* in the middle of the river, unfortunately often not working, and the rounded façade of the Meridien hotel which blocks *Rôda Island.*

Passing the El-Tahrir Bridge, a little further on, is *Liberty Square (1).* This square should be crossed in order to follow *El-Tahrir Street* going eastwards.

As it changes direction, the street changes its name and become the *Sharia Abd el-Aziz.* Continuing along here the

Midan Ataba el-Khadra [6] is reached. In this square is the main post office, where letters can be collected and where there are night-safes. There is also a small postal museum, whose collections illustrate the history of the Egyptian postal service etc. This square is a chief point of intersection between the « European » city and Old Cairo. It lies near the Opera Square, where the charming *Opera House* was situated. The Opera House was built in 1869, but sadly was completely destroyed by fire in October 1971. From the square there is only a short distance to go before reaching the

Ezbekîya Gardens [7]. *Muhammed Ali* constructed here around a lake, which is now silted up, a promenade in the Parisian style. In 1870 Sultan *Ismail* transformed the garden into a park in the English style and planted many rare trees and shrubs. Unfortunately these gardens are now much altered owing to the effects of modern urbanisation.

To the east of the Ezbekîya Gardens there commences the truly oriental and colourful part of Cairo. At one time this was the centre of the Moslem city and was a popular place for walking. Today a main road called the *Sharia 26th July* crosses the gardens. Along this road are the law-courts and to the left is *Sherif Street*. At n° 44 Sherif Street is the *Lehnert and Landrock Library*. Further along on the left is *Talaat Harb Street*, which was formerly *Sulîmân Pasha Street*, and which leads to a square of the same name, and then to *El-Tahrir Square*.

Itinerary n° 2 : The Citadel

From *El-Tahrir Square* (see p. 106) take a taxi, or walk if there is time, eastwards towards the *El-Qalaa*, the Citadel. The first stopping point is *Saladin Square*.

Midan Salâh ed-Dîn [8]. The huge Saladin Square lies at the foot of the Citadel and at one time was a place of joyous festivals, when the caravans of pilgrims set out or returned safely from Mecca. On the north side of the square is the *Midan Muhammed Ali*, where is situated the

Mosque of Sultan Hasan [9]. This is one of the most beautiful mosques in Cairo. It was built in the reign of *Sultan Hasan* between 1356 and 1363, almost certainly by *Ibn Bilik el-Mohsini*. It is easily recognised by its two minarets on the east. One of them is 81-6 m (285 ft.) high and is the highest of Cairo's numerous minarets. Nearby is the southern entrance to the mosque, but it is better to walk round to the main entrance [A], which is on the north side. The entrance has an arch of « stalactite » formation set into the wall, and which is decorated with inlays of green marble. The original gates are now in the Mosque of El-Muaiyad. They are made of wood and covered with bronze plates. On this north side, the exterior façade is so high that it almost resembles a rampart wall. It

has eight rows of windows and is crowned with a projecting cornice and pinnacles.

In plan, the mosque is an irregular pentagon of 7,906 m² (85,000 sq. ft.) in area. A *corridor* on the north [B] passes *a court with a fountain* [C] and the *prayer rooms*. This plan is designed to lead naturally to the mausoleum. The building was also conceived as a school-mosque, or *madrasa* mosque, for the four orthodox rites of Islam. This explains its cruciform plan with four divisions or arms around the central court for the *Hanefite, Hanbalite, Malikite* and *Shafiite* schools. Their teaching and prayer rooms are the four liwan, one for each rite of the faith. A *liwan* or *iwan* is a hall or room in a mosque which has a great door, which leads onto the court. These halls are often large and barrel-vaulted.

From the *entrance hall* or vestibule, which has a remarkable domed roof in red stone and openwork windows carved in gypsum, a cruciform *corridor* in the form of a miniature mosque [B] leads on through several corridors to the north room of the *court* [C]. This is also cruciform and open to the sky in the square centre and has arches around the four sides. In the middle of the court or *sahn* is an octagonal *fountain for ablutions*, the *hanafiya*. This fountain is supported, by columns and surmounted by a domed roof [D]. Arches and high vaulting support the ceilings of the four prayer rooms. The eastern room is the most beautiful with its walls decorated with marble and passages from the Koran in Kufic writing on a background of elegant arabesques. Enamelled lamps on metal chains formerly hung from the vaulted ceiling. Most of these can now be seen in the Islamic Museum. The *prayer-niche* or *mirhab* [E] is richly decorated in Syrian style with grape and trellis motifs.

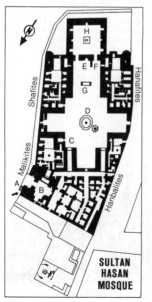

SULTAN
HASAN
MOSQUE

The *throne* or *minbar* [F] and the *pulpit* or *dikka* [G] are made of white marble, which looks like pearl. The door is of bronze and decorated with gold and silver.

Through two doors set in the wall with the mirhab is the way to the *Mausoleum of the Sultan*. In the centre of the mausoleum [H] lies the sarcophagus beneath a dome with stalactitic pendentives which are 28 m (91 ft.) high. Round the lower part of the apartment is a beautiful inscribed, polychrome frieze. It was here that in 1386 *El-Khehab Ahmed*, the son of Sultan Hasan, was buried. Originally Sultan Hasan had intended the mausoleum to be for his own burial. The visitor should also look at the ancient desk for the Koran, called a *korsi*, and the chair of the imam. The chair is the oldest of its kind in Egypt and is a masterpiece of inlaid work. It is made of pine-wood and intricately decorated with inlays of ebony and ivory. From the massive eastern grilled window there is a magnificent view over the *Citadel*, which is often seen reproduced on postcards and in guide-books.
In the immediate neighbourhood is the modern mosque of

Er-Rifâi [10], whose name is derived from the tomb of *Sheikh Er-Rifâi* which is beneath it. This mosque was completed in 1912 and is built in the Mameluke style. Its exterior is sumptuously decorated with marble, cedar wood and ivory ornamentation. It is possible to visit the cenotaph of Princess *Taufida Hanem*, the daughter of the Khedive *Ismail*. The mosque is in fact the family vault of *Ismail* and within it are buried *Princess Khoshiar*, *Ismail* himself, his wives. *Sultan Husein Kamil*, and *King Fuâd I*, who was buried here in 1936. From the architectural and artistic point of view, the mosque is not of any particular interest.

The Citadel [11] was at one time one of the strongest fortresses of the Islamic world. The construction was begun in 1176 by order of *Salâh ed-Dîn (Saladin)*. A nine-line inscription to that effect is engraved on a stone of the main entrance or gateway. The construction was completed in 1207, year 579 after the Hegira according to the Mohammedan calendar, by the minister, *Baba el-Dîne Karakosh*. It is said that the stones used to build the defences were blocks taken from the smaller pyramids and from the casings of the monuments at Giza or from buildings at Memphis.

From a strategic point of view the site chosen for the fortress on a plateau above the city is a good one. The original plan underwent many modifications. The strong walls, which have loop-holes in them, surrounded the whole complex and projecting square or round towers to the height of one or more storeys added further strength to the walls. All the main defensive installations were in the eastern part. In the western part various buildings were erected : mosques, palaces and gardens, administrative offices, barracks, kitchens, stables, etc. The Citadel became the official residence of the Sultan. However, in 1824 an explosion caused a considerable amount of damage to the fortress and its structures. *Muhammed Ali* then built here three palaces and a mosque, known as the « Alabaster Mosque ». Thus today in the Citadel there can be seen a mixture of Aiyubid, Mameluke and Neo-Ottoman architectural styles.

Today the Citadel is entered by the new gate at the side of the town (*Mîdan Muhammed Ali*), the *Bab el-Azab*. The old entrance situated between two watch-towers is now closed. The principal mosque of the Citadel is *the Muhammed Ali Mosque*, which is one of the landmarks of Cairo with its great central dome and 84 m (273 ft.) high minarets, which can be seen from several points in the city. *Muhammed Ali* employed a

The Mosque of Sultan Hasan (on the left) and the Mosque of Er-Rifai (on the right)

Greek architect from Istanbul, *Yusuf Boshna*, to build the mosque. He took as his model the Ottoman mosques in Istanbul. In any case Muhammed Ali wanted to rival the efforts of the Turkish Sultan. Boshna constructed a building with a characteristic central dome and all the necessary features. The entrance is on the north side. There is a corridor lined with columns and this leads to the court. In the centre of the court, the fountain for ablutions is covered by a projecting dome in the heavy neo-Ottoman style. Beneath the court is a large tank. The clock tower, which is 84 m (266 ft.) high, is situated on the western side and is unique. The clock itself was a gift from King Louis-Philippe to Muhammed Ali in 1845.

The interior of the building is spoilt by the heavy decoration, which has given to the building its name, « the Alabaster Mosque ». The walls are decorated with alabaster from the quarries near *Beni Suef*. Four square pillars support the central dome, which is flanked by semi-circular domes. The height of these vaulted chambers is 52 m (169 ft.) and they are 21 m (68 ft.) in diameter. They rest on four arches, and thus emulate the classic style of Byzantine domes : a central dome, four semi-circular domes, four small complete domes and four corner towers. There is also a semi-circular dome above the mirhab.

The interior decoration and its lighting have a striking impression but are not particularly interesting. The baroque Turkish style is too predominating and exaggerated, the alabaster panels are excessive and overbearing, the carpets are too gaudy and the decor is over-gilded. The great *minbar* or throne is of cedar-wood with gold-covered decoration. The small minbar is of alabaster and was a gift from king Farûk in 1939. This last Egyptian king also

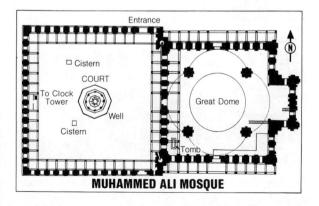

MUHAMMED ALI MOSQUE

had the *mirhab* recovered in alabaster and decorated with shells and gilded verses from the Koran. The lighting system is rather unusual. Circular lights are suspended on chains and attached to the chains are numerous glass and crystal pendant lamps.

The tomb of *Muhammed Ali* is behind a bronze grille in a corner to the right of the entrance. The marble cenotaph is decorated in relief and covered with inscriptions. On the outside of the building the two cylindrical minarets in Turkish style are fluted and adorned with circular balconies.

Near to the « Alabaster Mosque » is **the Mosque of Sultan En-Nâsir** which was built between 1318 and 1335 by *Nâsir ed-Dîn Muhammed ibn Qalâûn*, a Mameluke sultan.

The central part of the monument is its great court surrounded by four

liwans. The biggest of these is oriented towards *qibla*. *Qibla* is the direction in which the Moslem faces when praying, towards Mecca.

The interior room which measures 59 × 53 m (192 by 172 ft.) has four naves. The dome in front of the mirhab rests on ten ancient Egyptian granite columns and wooden stalactitic pendentives. In this mosque many ancient columns were reused with Roman and Byzantine capitals.

The mosque has two *minarets*. The taller one on the north has three storeys and is round but has a square base. The dome at the top is decorated with mosaics and has an inscription, which reads : « There is only one God, the Powerful, the Unique ». The minaret on the west has two storeys and is cylindrical. Its dome is similarly decorated with mosaics.

The Mosque of Sulîmân Pasha or Sidi Sariya was built in 1528 by the

The Mosque of Sultan En-Nasîr and Mûhammed Ali (on the right) in front of the Moqattam Heights.

Mameluke *Sulîmân el-Khadem Pasha*. It was the first mosque to be built in Cairo in the Turkish style. Its slender minarets soar towards the sky. The dome and the half dome above the prayer-niche are richly decorated with paintings and inscriptions from the Koran. The vault of the dome was at one time covered in green plaster. Light is admitted through twelve ogival windows.

Behind the mosque, turn towards the *Bab el-Moqattam* or *Bab el-Gebel* gate, the « mountain gate », and there is

Joseph's Well, the *Bîr Yusûf*, which is an interesting well with a spiral staircase. The well is a square shaft 80 m (290 ft.) deep with two stages and has within it a spiral staircase of 300 steps. When the well was carved out of the limestone rock, an ingenious wall with windows was also fashioned in the rock. At each stage in the well, the first being at a depth of 50.30 m (155 ft.) and the second at about 40 m (130 ft.) further down, there is a platform with a water wheel or *sâqiya*. Oxen were used at the wheels to raise the water. The well may have been constructed by *Baba el-Dîn Karakosh* to provide water for the Citadel. The connection between this well and the Biblical Patriarch, *Joseph*, is probably derived from the story of Joseph being put into a well by his brothers. Joseph has always been a popular figure in Egypt. However, it is also said that it was sultan *Saladin* who made the well as his full name was Salâh ed-Dîn Yusuf.

To the south of the « Alabaster Mosque », Muhammed Ali constructed as a residence for himself and as a guest palace,

the El-Gawhara Palace. This building was made into a museum. The interior is very interesting, but sadly it has been partially damaged by fire, and is no longer open to the public. The exterior gives some idea of the style of the neo-Ottoman palace and shows the heavy baroque and Italian influences in style, which were characteristic at the time. The palace has great historical value and preserves within it the story of an important period of Egyptian history. In the hope that one day the museum will be reconstructed and restored and open again to the public, there follows a brief description of the interior :

the *clocks room* contains all kinds of clocks around the walls. The clock which King Louis-Philippe gave to

The El-Gawhara Palace

Muhammed Ali should one day be displayed here rather than in the tower of the « Alabaster Mosque », its present resting-place. The *Alabaster room* has a floor of Egyptian alabaster and display-cases containing collections of porcelain and Bohemian glass.

The *Bathroom* is entirely faced with alabaster and contains alabaster baths. There are oval serving hatches in the wall.

The *main room* possesses a liwan. The doorway bears the inscription : « It is only God who grants success, 1229 ». The date is according to the Mohammedan calendar and marks the date when the building was completed. The *Throne room* or official reception room contains the throne of Muhammed Ali. It is grandly decorated and gilded. Two statues support the crown. One is a boatman with his oar, who symbolises the Nile, the other is a woman holding a sickle and an ear of corn, who represents the fertility of the land.

There is a magnificent view from the terrace, which is particularly impressive in the early morning and at sunset.

In 1827 *Muhammed Ali* built

the **El-Harîm Palace,** which was intended as a private residence for himself and his family. At present, it is not open to the public, but it contains a collection of militaria and Egyptian weapons of all periods. Nearby are the old *Law courts* in which is now preserved a collection of State archives. The « Son et Lumiere » spectacle, which was at one time shown in the Citadel, was discontinued some time ago.

Leaving the Citadel proper, descend to *Muhammed Ali Square* and then

go along *es-Saliba Street* in order to visit the

Ibn Tûlûn Mosque [12]. This mosque was built by *Ahmad Ibn Tûlûn,* the founder of the Tulunid dynasty, between 876 and 879. It is said to be built in imitation of the Kaaba at Mecca or the huge mosque at *Samarra* in Mesopotamia. The building is striking on account of its immense size and its sombre appearance. It occupies a total area of 26,000 m² (31,000 sq. yd), of which the mosque itself occupies 17,000 m² (20,330 sq. yd.) The building is constructed with baked brick, which is covered with stucco with incised decoration.

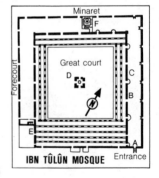

IBN TÛLÛN MOSQUE

From the *main entrance* [A] near to the south-east corner, the visitor enters an *outer court* [B], which surrounds the mosque on three sides. The court is bordered by *liwans* with two naves [C], the vaults of which are supported by strong pillars and which have decorative openings in their pointed arches. There is a frieze running round the upper parts of these. The *fountain for ablutions* [D] is situated in the centre of the square court, whose sides each measure 90 m (292 ft.) in length. The basin is octagonal and is covered by an oval dome 8 m (26 ft.) high.

The court is surrounded on each side by arcades with ogival arches. The arches are 3,70 m (12 ft) high and 4,60 m (15 ft.) wide and are the earliest examples of their kind. The capitals are fashioned in the Byzantine style, but their vine-leaf ornamentation is of Mesopotamian origin (Samarra).

The *sanctuary or prayer niche* [E] is divided into naves by five rows of columns with capitals with vine-leaf ornamentation. The interlacing designs cover the pointed arches and also surround the openwork balustrades between the columns or pillars. The pointed plaster-work windows of the sanctuary wall are covered with delicate engraved filigree decoration. There are six mirhabs or niches. The main mirhab is concave in shape and is decorated with gilded mosaics and marble. The *minbar* was erected in 1298. Most of its inlaid ebony and ivory panels are now missing. (Some of them are now in the Victoria and Albert Museum in London).

Although the mosque was built in brick, the *minaret* [F] is of limestone. It is situated almost in the centre of the western outer court. It is 40 m (131 ft.) high and has four storeys. There is an outside staircase which goes to the top of the minaret. From the second storey there is a stone bridge which leads on to the roof of the mosque. The staircase continues on to the top. The whole structure is

modelled on the spiral minaret at Samarra. There is a legend that Ibn Tûlûn was playing with a piece of paper and twisted it around his finger. He showed this to his architect and asked him to build the minaret for his mosque in the style of a similar spiral. From the top of the minaret there is a magnificent view over the old quarters of Cairo, which should not be missed.

Close to the Ibn Tûlûn Mosque is the

Gayer-Anderson Museum [13] (Beit el-Kreatlia). The Englishman, *Gayer-Anderson*, purchased two adjoining Mameluke houses dating to about 1630 and renovated them. He then furnished them with beautiful and precious things in rich Arab style. Since then other collections have been added. The visitor can see beautiful furniture, canopied beds, jewellery, textiles, china and bronzes. There is a Chinese room, antiques and a room in Queen Anne style. There is also a magnificent hanging garden with elegant trelliswork and which is full of luxuriant vegetation.

El-Maqid el-Labban Street, which is a fairly short walk, leads to *Es-Saiyida Zeinab Square*, where the

Mosque of Es-Saiyida Zeinab [14], is found, which was completed in 1803 and restored later in the nineteenth century. Inside (closed to non-Mohammedans) is the tomb of Zeinab, the daughter of *Imam Ali* and the grand-daughter of the Prophet Mohammed. At the time of Ramadan and other festivals, many believers visit this sanctuary in order to touch the bronze railing around the sarcophagus and to pray for the blessing of Zeinab. In fact, she does not lie here but rests inside a nest of three coffins in another Islamic sanctuary.

Itinerary n° 3 : The Ramparts, The Tombs of the Mamelukes (northern group), The Bazaars.

Departing from *El-Tahrir Square* (see p. 105), go along *Qasr en-Nil Street* in the modern quarter of the city, cross *Opera Square* and continue along to the *Midan el-Ataba*, then go along the *Sharia el-Gish* until the

Ancient City Walls [15] are reached. These are the second walls which were built. The first wall of Gohar, which enclosed the newly founded quarters of the city in 969, no longer survives. Of the second walls only a length of about half a kilometer (third of a mile) remains. They were built for the sultan by the vizier, *Badr el-Gamali*, between 1087 and 1092 and had about sixty gateways. Of these only three still survive, and were built very much in the Roman and Byzantine defensive style. The three architects employed by the *sultan Mustansir* to build these gates were Armenian and, like the sultan himself, came from the Turkish fortified town of *Edessa* (Urfa). The building material used for the gateways was not the usual mud-brick but stone blocks taken from the small pyramids at Giza and from ancient buildings at Memphis. Hieroglyphic inscriptions on some of the blocks can still be seen. In general style there is a great resemblance to Roman gateways.

Bab el-Futûh (16), « The Gate of Conquests », like the nearby « Gate of Victory », is a fortified gate made of solid blocks of stone embedded in the wall.

The actual gateway is nearly 4.85 m (16 ft.) wide and 6.79 m (22 ft.) high and is surmounted by a shallow dome resting on curved pendentives.

Originally the total impression was more imposing as in the eleventh century the street level was 4 m (13 ft.) below the present level. Thus the gate originally rose to a total height of 22 m. (71 ft.) In 1799 the soldiers of Napoleon Bonaparte established a strong defensive position for themselves here.

Between this gate and the next one can be seen the very old

Hakîm Mosque (17). This was completed in 1012 by the Fatimid ruler, *El-Hakîm*, the son of El-Aziz. It was later destroyed by an earthquake but was restored soon afterwards. The round south minaret was enclosed by square foundations and today only the top part is visible above the polygonal tower which protects it. The other minaret is supported and strengthened by the city wall. The top parts of the two minarets are decorated with small domes. The prayer room is in a ruinous condition. Square pillars support the modern wooden roof. The sanctuary

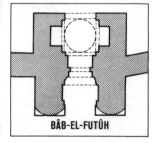

BÂB-EL-FUTÛH

imitates that in the Ibn Tûlûn Mosque. Of the three liwans only the one against the city wall is well preserved. All the exterior and interior decoration is in the Fatimid style. The projecting entrance is covered by a cradle-vault and is situated on the very ruined north-west façade. On the façade can be seen the decoration of lozenges and bands with bands of inscriptions on the uprights and in the niches. As well as the main entrance, several others can still be seen.

Bab en-Nasr (18), « The Victory Gate », was built at the same time as the Bab el-Futûh, but it is more imposing because of its austere and sober decoration. Two bastions or towers flank the vaulted gateway and the inner court has a cruciform vaulted ceiling. The structure is 24 m (78 ft.) wide, 21 m (68 ft.) high and 20 m (65 ft.) in depth. A winding staircase covered by a cradle-vault in the eastern gate-tower leads onto the top of the city wall.

The visitor can walk along the city wall to « The Gate of Conquests ». From the wall there is an interesting view over the old City and the varied activities of its inhabitants. On the front and eastern side of the Bab en-Nasr gate above the arch, there is an interesting inscription in Kufic writing, which reads : *« It is by the power of God, the Strong and All-powerful, that Islam is defended, for He was the power who built the fortifications and the walls. This work was undertaken in Muharram 480 »* (i.e. from April to May 1087). The engravings of arms, shields and rosettes are the heraldic emblems of the builder, the vizier, Badr el-Gamali.

The visitor should follow the city wall along the *Sharia el-Baghala* towards the south-east. The street ends at a cemetery area with funerary mosques dedicated to the great Egyptian rulers of the Middle Ages. These are often wrongly called « The Tombs of the Caliphs ». As it is the Circassian and Arab Mamelukes who are buried

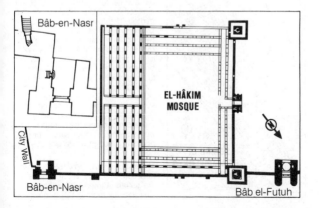

here, the more correct name is « The Tombs of the Mamelukes ».

The Tombs of the Mamelukes (Northern group) [19]. The most important funerary mosques are situated inside the cemetery. Here, the simple Mohammedan, as elsewhere in the Islamic world, is laid to rest in a grave under a tombstone. Two stones, one at the head and one at the feet, are inscribed with his dates of birth and death and with a verse from the Koran. But the sultans and dignitaries were buried in family tombs associated with houses and mosques. These buildings were intended as places for the deceased's family to stay during the feast for the dead and for the recital of the daily prayers.

The northern group of the Tombs of the Mamelukes (the other group lies

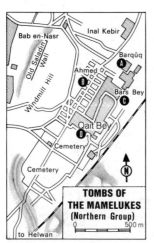

TOMBS OF THE MAMELUKES (Northern Group)

0   500 m

to Helwan

to the south of the Citadel between the Moqattam Hills and Old Cairo) is best visited by progressing from north to south.

The Mosque of Sultan Barqûq [A] is a *khanqah* or convent mosque. It was built for the first Circassian Mameluke sultan by his sons, *Abd el-Aziz* and *Farag*, between 1389 and 1411. The grandiose construction has a square ground-plan and has two minarets on the western side and domes on the other sides. The minarets are 50 m (162 ft.) high. They are square at the bottom, then become octagonal and have bell-towers at the top, which are now partly ruined. They have ornamental balconies built out over stalactitic cornices and arcades. The two main domes. rest on strong wall-blocks. Their structural mass harmonises perfectly with the imposing aspect of the exterior and the simplicity of the interior of the building. These domes were the earliest ones built in stone in Egypt and thus are of considerable architectural importance. There is another smaller dome over the mirhab. The court is surrounded by a pillared hall. The liwans have one, two or three naves. Some of the monks' cells are still well-preserved. In the principal mausoleum lies the body of Sultan Barqûq, who was laid to rest here in 1399. The other two tombs are those of his sons. A stone column or *shahid* by the side of the sultan's tomb probably indicates his high rank. Another mausoleum on the south contains the burials of two women and is noticeable for the beautiful wooden trellis-work on the doors.

The visitor should now follow a path between the funerary mosques of the sultan *Ahmed [B]*, sultan *Bars Bey* and his mother [C] and others which all date from the fifteenth century before arriving at the

Mosque of Qait Bey [D]. The sultan had this mosque built between 1472 and 1474. It is the finest example of Arab architecture dating from this period. The decoration is sober, despite the numerous stalactites. The mosque is built with clear yellow and brownish-red stone. The dome has banded decoration with circular and geometric motifs. The dome and the minaret are in fact the most interesting parts of the structure. The dome is covered on its exterior with stucco, bands carved in relief and delicate filigree tracery work. The minaret, which is 40 m (130 ft.) high, is square at the bottom, then becomes octagonal, then slender and cylindrical and has a bulbous top. It is beautifully proportioned, is ornamented with filigree designs and has three fine, distinctive stalactitic galleries or balconies. In the interior the most noticeable features are the decoration on the dome, the marble mosaic work, the engraved wood inlaid with ivory, the gilded decoration and the coloured windows. These

are all masterpieces of Islamic art. In the mausoleum by the sarcophagus of the sultan in front of a carved desk can be seen two sets of footprints impressed into stone. One set is of feet wearing sandals, the other set is of bare feet. These are said to be the footprints of the Prophet, Mohammed, which were brought from Mecca by the Sultan.

Returning towards *Salah Salem Street,* turn left into *Gohar el-Caid* Street. A short distance along on the left is the *El-Azhar Mosque,* and on the right in a square is the

Mosque of El-Hasanein [20]. The building has been completely modernised. It is dedicated to *Husein,* the son of Ali. Ali was the son-in-law of the Prophet. Husein was killed at the battle of Kerbela in Mesopotamia in 680. His friends brought back his head to Cairo wrapped in a green silk bag. The head was buried in the mosque under the dome of the mausoleum. Certain interesting features of the monument should be noted. These are the entrance, the

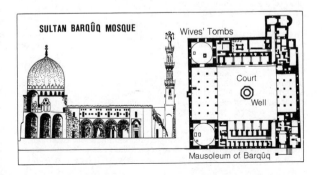

SULTAN BARQÛQ MOSQUE   Wives' Tombs

Court

Well

Mausoleum of Barqûq ►

The Mosque of Qait Bey

« green gate » on the south side, the lower part of the minaret and the dome of the mausoleum, which is profusely decorated and gilded. The cenotaph is now in the Islamic Museum. It should be noted that non-Moslems are forbidden to enter the mosque.

The visitor now finds himself in front of one of the most famous bazaars or sûqs in the Middle East, which is called

The Khân el-Khalîli. In part it dates back to the thirteenth century. Originally this quarter was part of the Mameluke cemetery and was known as the *Zaafaran* cemetery. Prince *Garkas el-Khalîli* wanted to establish a commercial centre and therefore he closed the cemetery and built in its place a large caravanserai or *khân*. This was made an endowment or *waqf* for the benefit of the poor of Mecca. In 1511, sultan *El-Ghuri* destroyed the workshops. In their place and extending over a larger

area, he set up stalls and markets. Since then, the Khân el-Khalîli has been destroyed and rebuilt several times and over the years it has expanded over a still larger area. It is worth noting that the usual Arabic word for a market is *sûq* and that the term *bazaar* is of Persian origin. However, the word bazaar is now as commonly used as the term sûq in Egypt.

It is probably wise when visiting the bazaars for the first time to follow the route which is described below. This route takes the visitor to all the main monuments in the area. When a general idea of the lay-out of the area has been gained, the visitor can then make a special visit to the Khan el-Khalili and can wander along the narrow streets and alleyways. In this way it is possible to see all the little shops and traders and to soak up the oriental atmosphere. The atmosphere is still largely oriental, although modern influences are slowly making themselves felt here. There are numerous shops and stalls, some of which are very small. The whole scene is very picturesque and particularly striking are the pervading smells of wood, tobacco, perfumes and spices all mingled together. All along the narrow streets are a wide variety of shops and trades side by side - textile and carpet shops, carvers of ebony, jewellers and trinket sellers, coppersmiths and leather workers. The visitor is made very welcome in the shops and is often offered a coffee or a soft drink. In doing this the trader is obeying the oriental customs of hospitality but of course at the same time he is capturing the attention of his client. Even if he manages to sell nothing to his client, the trader will often indicate how pleased he is to have met him and spoken with him. In fact many of the traders can make themselves understood in several languages. The visitor who wishes to buy something can try to bargain with the trader. However, this is very much a bazaar for tourists and the trader will very often refuse to haggle over the price. It is therefore often wise to pay the price asked or simply to move on to another shop.

A little to the north of the *Mosque of El-Hasanein* is the

Beit el-Qadi [21], the « House of the Judge ». The house was built in 1496 and parts of it have been preserved. The gateway with its superb stalactitic decoration can still be seen as can the veranda of five pointed arches. These once formed the façade of an inner court.

From here there is only a short distance to walk to reach the main street of the Bazaar quarter, the *Sharia el-Muiz Lidin Allah.* On the left is

The Mosque of Qalâûn [22]. The construction of this school-mosque, domed mausoleum and hospital or *muristan* was started by *Sultan El-Mansur Qalâûn* in 1284. It was

completed by his son, *En-Nasîr,* in 1293. After the sultan had allowed his Mamelukes to ravage and pillage the city, he became repentant and as a gesture of his repentance, he built a *muristan* or hospital for the inhabitants of Cairo. Today the hospital is in ruins and is no longer in use. The façade of the mausoleum which can be seen from the street is quite remarkable. It is in the Fatimid style and has high pointed arches. The pillars which separate them are massive. They rest on light columns with Corinthian capitals. A band of inscription above the first row of windows runs round the whole of the building. The minaret is situated at the northern end of the façade and is 56 m (182 ft.) high. The lower part of the minaret is square and has a squared balcony, above is an octagonal balcony and the upper part of the minaret is cylindrical in shape.

The entrance portal is constructed of black and white marble laid in alternate courses. It leads into a corridor, which separates the mausoleum on the right from the madrasa on the left. The impressive main liwan of the madrasa is divided into three naves by porphyry columns. There are gilded mosaics in the dome and in the corners. The liwans on either side and the court at the end are in a very ruinous state.

The *mausoleum* is one of the most beautiful Arab buildings in Cairo. The entrance hall in front of it on the north contains four red granite columns with Corinthian capitals, which support the arches. The masonry domes are also very impressive. The entrance façade is in the form of a wooden trellis or *masharabîya* and is 4 m (13 ft.) wide with a door in the centre. The door is surrounded by friezes and stucco orna-

The Mosque of Qalâun

mentation with a variety of motifs. The structure is 17 m (55 ft.) high. The mausoleum itself measures 21 × 23 (68 by 74 ft.) and is almost square in plan. Its dome, which imitates that in the *Mosque of Omar* in *Jerusalem,* collapsed and was reconstructed in 1903. It is now supported by pillars and granite columns and there are eight pointed arches. Eight other arches link the centre of the dome to the walls of the room and thus form rectangular or pentagonal wooden ceilings which are decorated with artistic designs. The walls are covered with marble and mother-of-pearl. The elegant mirhab is in the form of a horseshoe and is flanked and ornamented by three pairs of red porphyry columns with Persian capitals, a band of polychrome inscription, marble mosaics in a shell pattern and several kinds of arches. Beneath a canopy, surrounded by a carved and decorated wooden grille lies the sarcophagus, which is covered by hangings. Inside it, lies the body of *Sultan Qalâun* and close to him that of his son, *En-Nasîr.*

Nearby is the

Mosque of Muhammed en-Nasîr [23]. The minaret is beautifully decorated but is now partly collapsed. The building was completed in 1304. However, the sultan was not buried here but in the mausoleum of his father, *Qalâun.* Here are buried En-Nasîr's mother, *Bint Sûqbey* and his son, *Anûq.* The entrance gateway with its pointed arch is of considerable interest. When the fortified city of *Acre* in Palestine was captured in 1291, *Sultan El-Ashraf Khalîl,* the brother of En-Nasîr, brought away the gateway with its Gothic columns from the Church of St. John of Acre. He had it re-erected at the entrance of this mosque.

The third interesting building in this area is the

Barqûqîya Mosque [24], which is also a madrasa-mosque. It imitates in many ways the *Mosque of Sultan Hasan* (see p. 108). It was built in the time of *Sultan Barqûq* (see also p. 108).

The gateway with its alternate black and white marble decoration is particularly striking, as is the prayer room with its four ancient Egyptian columns. The central nave is higher like that in a basilica and the ceilings are flat. It was here that the members of *Barqûq's* family were buried. Barqûq himself was buried in his funerary mosque in the cemetery. Inside the mosque, there has been a great deal of restoration. The colours used are far too bright and gaudy and this has ruined the effect of the interior. The minaret has three storeys and is 50 m. (162 ft.) high. Its architecture and decoration, in spite of the modern balconies, conform to the Egyptian-Arab style. The middle storey is decorated with marble inlays, a feature which has been imi-

The Façade of the Mosque of El-Aqmar

tated many times in other later mosques. On the south façade of the madrasa, there are very fine windows with high pointed arches. Instead of the normal stucco trellises around the windows, the ones here are of wood. There is a stone inscription with the name of the sultan and the date of the completion of the building - 788, according to the Mohammedan calendar, i.e.1386.

Beit el-Sihaimi [25] is also situated in this area, a little further along in a small street on the right. This old Arab house dates from 1648 and was the residence of the rector or *sheikh* of the *University of El-Azhar*. Although additions were made to the house at a later date, many of the old parts of the structure have been preserved. The reception room can be visited. It contains marbles, china and wooden carvings. There are also fountains and baths and a small mosque in the house.

In the garden is an old oil-press and a *saqiya*, near to an elegant pavilion. In the street outside to the right can be seen

The Mosque of El-Aqmar [26] which dates from 1125. It has been

much added to and altered but the decoration of the façade is particularly rich. The lower part of the wall is adorned with niches and inlaid panels, one of the first of its kind in Egypt. The façade is divided into two parts by a central band of inscriptions. Another large band of inscription comes between the wall and the roof. The decoration is beautifully balanced in design, and interspersed with gilded arabesques and rosettes on the gateway. This style of decoration later became a typical feature of monuments of the Fatimid era.

This excursion ends at the town-gate, the *Bab el-Futûh* (see p. 116). In order to return to the *El-Tahrir Square*, (p. 105) it is advisable to take a taxi.

The Barqûqîya Mosque

Itinerary n° 4 : The Egyptian Museum

On *Mariette Pasha Street* to the north of *El-Tahrir Square* is the entrance to **the Egyptian Museum [27]**.

The French Egyptologist, *Auguste Mariette*, whose memorial and tomb are in the museum garden to the left of the entrance, was the founder of the *Egyptian Antiquities Service* in 1857. In the same year a museum of ancient Egyptian civilisation was also founded. This museum was initially at *Bulaq*, then at *Giza* and finally was transferred to its present building, which was designed by a French architect. The collections grew immensely as a result of the continual excavations, which took place throughout Egypt. The Museum is really crowded with objects and also has large collections in reserve or storage. There is a projected scheme for a new museum, but it is not envisaged in the near future. The Egyptian Museum has the richest collection of pharaonic antiquities in the world. The scope and interest of the collections is inexhaustible and thus visits to the Museum can be for as long and often as possible. Displays are changing and parts of the Museum are often reorganized. Therefore the guide to the Museum, which is given below, is a brief description of the main rooms. These rooms contain numerous famous and beautiful items and only some of them are listed under the room where they are at present displayed.

GROUND-FLOOR

Room 48, the Rotunda : new acquisitions ; objects from recent excavations ; temporary displays.

Monuments of the Old Kingdom

Room 47 : stone saroophagi ; group-statues or triads of King Mycerinus with the goddess, Hathor, on one side and a provincial or nome

The « Village Headman » Vth Dynasty

divinity on the other. Along the walls are stelae and false doors. In the display cases are wooden and stone sculptures. Limestone reserve heads. Royal statues in alabaster.

Rooms 46, 41, 42, 36, 37, 31 and 32 : monuments of the Third, Fourth, Fifth and Sixth Dynasties from the sites of Giza, Saqqara, Memphis, Maidum, etc.

Rooms 46 and 41 : statues and wall-paintings ; inscriptions ; mastaba doorways. These include the doorway and wall-paintings from a Fourth Dynasty tomb at Maidum.

Room 42 : The famous seated statue of King Djoser from his pyramid at Saqqara ; the magnificent diorite statue of Chephren protected by a falcon, found in his Valley Temple near to the Sphinx ; the wooden statue known as the Sheikh el-Beled ; the statue of a seated scribe ; granite palm-columns from the mortuary temples of Unas and Sahure.

Room 31 : the famous wooden relief panels from the tomb of Hesy-re at Saqqara of the Third Dynasty ; reliefs from the mortuary temple of Sahure.

Room 32 : painted limestone statues of Prince Rahotep and his wife, Nofret, from Maidum ; limestone statue

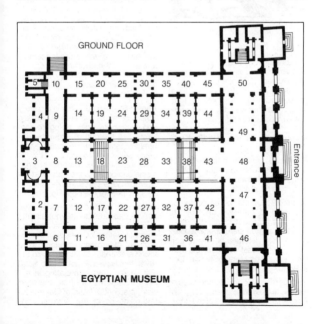

GROUND FLOOR

Entrance

EGYPTIAN MUSEUM

Rahotep and Nofret

of Ranufer from Saqqara ; statue of Ti from his famous mastaba ; statue of the dwarf, Seneb, and his family ; the rare copper statues of Pepi I and his son from Hierakonpolis ; a fragment of painted wall depicting geese from a mastaba at Maidum.

Monuments of the Middle Kingdom

Rooms 26 and 21 : sandstone statue of King Mentuhotep ; statues of the Kings Ammenemes III and Sesostris III from various sites.

Room 22 : Limestone sarcophagus and painted funerary chamber of Harhotep, Eleventh Dynasty from Thebes ; seated statues of Sesostris I from Lisht ; statues of private persons ; on the east wall is a stela from the Temple of Mentuhotep at Deir el-Bahri.

Room 16 : black granite sphinxes of exotic appearance from Tanis of Ammenemes III ; statues of the gods,

of fishing and hunting in the marshes.

Monuments of the New Kingdom

Room 11 : head of Queen Tiy ; a beautiful statue in grey-green schist of Tuthmosis III from Karnak.

Room 12 : statuary of the Eighteenth Dynasty : group statue of Tuthmosis IV and his mother from Karnak ; statue of Senenmut, the architect of Hatshepsut, with Princess Neferure ; victory stela of Tuthmosis III from Karnak ; the chapel from Deir el-Bahri with scenes of Tuthmosis III and the cow-goddess, Hathor. In front is a statue of a cow, which was found in the chapel ; statue of Amenophis, son of Hapu, the architect and high official of Amenophis III ; granite statue of the moon-god, Khonsu, with the features of Tutankhamun ; a relief from the temple at Deir el-Bahri showing the Queen of Punt, who apparently suffered from elephantiasis ; pink granite statue of Queen Hatshepsut.

Rooms 6; 7, and 8 : This is a gallery which contains numerous statues and stelae : stela describing the restoration of the cult of Amun by Horemheb ; statue of the lioness-goddess, Sekhmet ; fragments of walls of tombs of the New Kingdom ; small stelae dedicated to the Sphinx at Giza who in later times was believed to be an aspect of the god, Horus.

Room 3 : at the end of the museum is a room dedicated to the monuments of the Amarna period : the strange, colossal statues of the king, Amenophis IV-Akhenaten, which were found at Karnak ; stelae showing the royal family worshipping the solar disk, Aten. Rays terminating in human hands emanate from the solar disk ; a splendid head of Queen Nefertiti ; heads of the Amarna princesses with elongated skulls ; coffin of the king Smenkhkare (?), gilded and inlaid with glass and paste ; paintings from the palace at Amarna ; numerous small objects and amulets executed in exquisite taste ; clay tablets with inscriptions in Akkadian cuneiform, which are part of the diplomatic correspondance form Amarna ; alabaster canopic jars with lids in the form of an Amarna princess's head.

Crossing the rooms which lead to the Central Atrium, the following rooms are now visited :

Room 13 : the victory stela of Merneptah, called « the Israel Stela », because it contains the only known mention of Israel on any Egyptian monument ; at the end of the atrium is a colossal group-statue of Amenophis III and Queen Tiy.

The Seated Scribe from Saqqara in Cairo Museum

The Dwarf, Seneb, and his Family. VIth Dynasty.

Room 23 : naos or divine shrine of Ramesses II from Tanis.

Room 28 : large, painted pavement depicting birds and plants from the palace of Akhenaten at Tell el-Amarna.

Room 33 : sarcophagi of Tuthmosis I and of Hatshepsut ; sarcophagi of the Late Period ; cenotaph of Osiris from Abydos ; pyramidions from Dahshur.

Room 38 : on the staircase : sarcophagus of King Ay.

Room 43 : two wooden boats of the Middle Kingdom found at Dahshur. Returning to the north gallery, the Amarna room *(room 3)* is crossed and then the following rooms are visited :

Rooms 9 and 10 : « The Table of Saqqara » on which are listed the names of about fifty early Egyptian kings ; entrance to *Room 4,* a small room which contains a collection of Graeco-Roman coins ; group-statue representing the falcon, Horus, protecting Ramesses II, who is shown as a child.

Room 15 : numerous monuments of the Eighteenth, Nineteenth and Twentieth Dynasties.

Room 14 : statues of high-priests ; Ramesses VI seizing a Libyan ; sun-altar from Abu Simbel.

Objects of the Third Intermediate Period and the Late Period

Room 24 (naos room) : funerary reliefs imitating the style of the Old Kingdom ; great historical stelae ; head of the king Taharqa ; statue of the hippopotamus goddess Thoeris ; naos of Saft el-Hena.

Room 30 : alabaster statue of the « divine adoratrice of Amun », Amenardais ; great historical stela of the « Ethiopian » Piankhi.

Rooms 34,35,39,40 and 45 : objects of the Late Period and Greek and Roman periods : stelae, statues in pure Egyptian style, pure Greek or Roman style or of mixed style ; works of the beginning of the Byzantine period.

Room 44 : objects from Nubia ; reconstruction of a Nubian horse burial.

Rooms 49 and 50 : statues and sarcophagi of the Late Period and the Graeco-Roman period, sometimes of large size ; coffin of the dwarf Taho ; coffin of Petosiris with inlaid hieroglyphs (Tûna el-Gebel).

UPPER FLOOR

Go up by the south-east or south-west staircase.

Rooms 46,47,48,49 and 50 : in the great gallery (with busts of the first Egyptologists along the walls), royal sarcophagi and sarcophagi of the

Theban priests ; objects deposited in tombs ; tools, domestic objects and furniture ; funerary tent of queen Esiemkhebi ; reconstruction (model) of the funerary complex of Sahure ; in a case, the unique and minute statue of king Cheops (in ivory) ; head of queen Tiy ; decorated sarcophagus of the princess Kauit (XIth dynasty).

Rooms 54 and 55 : prehistoric and archaic objects, such as pottery, stone and flint tools : weapons, etc.

Room 53 : natural history collection with animal skeletons, remains of vegetation (fairly well preserved wheat, « mummified ») and mummies of sacred animals.

Rooms 43 and 42 : objects of the Archaic period, including the first

Narmer Palette (Ist Dynasty)

dynasty : funerary furniture from the tomb of Hemaka (Saqqara) ; blue faience from Djoser's pyramid ; flint knives ; slate palette of Narmer.

The long gallery comprising rooms *41, 36, 31, 26, 21, 16* and *11* in principle contains sarcophagi and coffins, but at present houses a new exhibition on the theme of War and Peace (entrance fee), which includes objects drawn from other parts of the Museum.

Room 37 : coffins and sarcophagi of the Old and Middle Kingdoms ; funerary models (in particular boats, groups of soldiers in painted wood, from Asyût).

Room 32 : funerary furniture essentially consisting of models which give an excellent idea of life in ancient Egypt in the early periods : agriculture, craftwork, temple life (slaughter), houses of distinguished people.

Room 27 : models of ancient Egyptian houses in clay or wood ; boats with their crews ; craftsmen's workshops ; scenes of daily life ; interesting group showing the counting of herds led by peasants in front of a noble assisted by scribes, characteristic of the strong administrative structure of Egypt.

Room 22 : funerary furniture of the New Kingdom, particulary small ob-

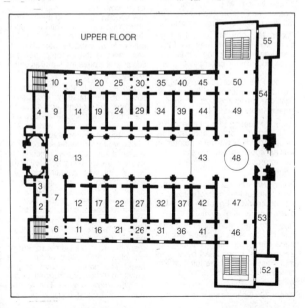

jects such as amulets, jewellery, figurines ; stelae of painted wood ; head-rests.

Room 17 : funerary equipment of the fan-bearer Mahirper of the XVIIIth dynasty in a remarkable state of preservation. Furniture from the tomb of Sennedjem, a director of works at Deir el-Medina (some of his tools were deposited in his tomb) ; some pieces are unique.

Room 12 : objects from the tombs of the Valley of the Kings (tombs of Amenophis II, Tuthmosis IV, Horemheb), often in bad condition, but sufficiently splendid to give an idea of the original furniture of these tombs which were unfortunately robbed very soon (compare also with the furniture of Tutankhamun).

Room 13 : chariots of Tutankhamun ; very beautiful funerary furniture (beads, sarcophagi, chairs) of Yuaa and Thuiu, parents of queen Tiy.

It would be better to continue the tour of the interior rooms and to postpone the visit to Tutankhamun's objects until later.

Room 14 : dating to the Graeco-Roman period, coffins and mummy masks ; mummy portraits painted in wax on wood, absolutely remarkable and approaching our conception of painting.

Room 19 : representations, in the form of statuettes (many bronzes) of the innumerable Egyptian divinities, often in the form of animals.

Room 24 : very numerous and interesting fragments of limestone ostraca with sketches of paintings or decorations, drafts used by scribes and artists (plan of the tomb of Ramesses VI, sketches, satirical drawings).

Room 29 : writing equipment ; ornamental texts on papyrus (« Book of the Dead ») ; literary texts on papyrus or ostraca ; foreign inscriptions found in Egypt.

Rooms 34, 39 and 44 : small objects, mostly textiles, objects of daily use, musical instruments, weights and measures, wooden tools (agricultural) and bronze utensils.

Objects from the Tomb of Tutankhamun

Room 8 : the four shrines which were superimposed (gilded wood). The decoration should be noticed, the door shutters, and, on the outermost shrine, the representation of the celestial cow. Equally sumptuous are the wooden shrines and the canopic chest with the four protective goddesses who guard the corners. In the interior is an alabaster box which itself contains the canopic jars, the lids of which have the features of the young king.

Room 4 : this is the most famous room of the museum because it contains the coffins and funerary mask of Tutankhamun. The layout of the funerary chamber was as follows : four superimposed shrines of gilded wood, inside the smallest was a granite sarcophagus (which is still in situ in the tomb in the Valley of the Kings) ; the latter contained successively the first mummiform coffin of gilded wood (also in the tomb with the mummy), then a second coffin of the same type and finally, inside the last, a solid gold coffin (225 Kilos (495 lbs)). The emblems of royal power, the vulture and cobra ornament the front, a false beard adorns the chin, two collars encircle the neck. The hands crossed on the chest hold the royal insignia of power, the crook and flail. The decoration on the chest consists of a representation of the protective divinities (vulture and uraeus) inlaid with multi-coloured semi-precious stones.

The face of the mummy was covered with a gold funerary mask ; the vulture and uraeus are on the wig, whilst a collar terminating in falcon heads decorated the chest. The king's features are probably fairly lifelike and convey his youth ; the eyes are of lapis-lazuli. All the coffins and also the mask are superbly sculptured and inlaid with lapis-lazuli (blue), carnelian (red) and polychrome glass.

Numerous cases hold the king's jewellery, the objects originally deposited in the mummy equipment, toilet utensils and writing instruments.

Rooms 9, 10, 15,20,25,30,35,40 and 45 : other objects of every category from the tomb of Tutankhamun ; wigs, sandals, gilded wooden beds with stylized cows or hippopotami, a gilded and a decorated handle which was once mounted with ostrich plumes as a fan ; gold trumpets ; a box with figures of the king ,chasing deer or fighting enemies, sceptres, staves, perfume vases, alabaster lamps, chairs, a box with a family scene, the king's throne splendidly decorated with his figure and his wife under the Amarna sun (in fact numerous objects date to the Amarna period of the king and have this style), large natural statues of the king which guarded the funerary chamber, a superb Anubis on a portable box, wooden shabtis, etc.
Return after this visit towards

Room 3 : very large collection of jewellery which illustrates the art of the Egyptian jewellers from the beginning of the Old Kingdom up to the Byzantine Period and shows the mastery achieved with all the techniques which were used. There are exceptional pieces of unequalled beauty and, among others, the jewellery found in the princesses' tombs of the Middle Kingdom, the treasures of Bubastis and Mendes and the jewellery of queen Tiy (XVIIIth dynasty),

Room 2 : objects from the tomb of the royal mother Hetepheres, mother of Cheops. They were found near his pyramid, at Giza : a tent, a bed, a chair, a litter, a canopic chest and funerary and cult material.

Room 2 A : here is a royal treasure almost as exceptional as that of Tutankhamun from the excavations of the royal tombs at Tanis (XXIst and XXIInd dynasties), superb silver sarcophagi, a gold mask, silver vases, various ornaments.

Room 6 : numerous amulets ; beautiful collection of collars and above all scarabs some of which have historical or artistic importance.

Mummy Room

or *Room 52 :* this re-opened exhibition of mummies (entrance fee) now includes X-rays of the bodies taken by an American research team. The mummy of Ramesses II underwent restoration in Paris in 1977 and now once again rests here with the other human remains.

During the XXth dynasty, according to papyri, the robbers of royal tombs were active in the Valley of the Kings, they were apprehended and legal action followed, then, much later, the priests gathered together the principal royal mummies of the New Kingdom and reburied them in a cache discovered only about a century ago (at Deir el-Bahri), or in the tomb of Amenophis II. These two extraordinary discoveries form essentially the contents of Room 52, but there are also more ancient remains generally very badly preserved.

A brief description of each mummy follows :

Seqenenre, height 1.70 m (5ft.7in.) ; age : about 40 ; one of the most ancient mummies in the museum ; XVIIth dynasty ; found at Deir el-Bahri ; the king died a violent death (at war) because there are traces of blood in his hair, his mouth still screams in agony, his hands are twisted in pain ; several assassins seem to have participated in his death because there are wounds on his face as well as at the back of his head.

Amosis, height : 1.64 m (5ft.5in.) ; age : about 40 ; king of the XVIIIth dynasty ; the tomb robbers damaged the nose and the head and he was re-bandaged afterwards ; his hair is curly and dark brown ; his dentition intact ; the upper jaw protrudes a little ; the surface of the body is coated with black resin.

Amenophis I, height : 1.65 m (5ft.5in.) ; king of the XVIIIth dynasty ; his mummy is not opened for study because it is entirely enveloped with floral collars which would be disturbed during unwrapping. All the species of flowers used are known.

Tuthmosis I, height : 1.55 m (5ft.1in.) ; age : about 50 ; king of the XVIIIth dynasty ; delicate features with fine wrinkles on the face ; bald head.

Tuthmosis II, height : 1.68 m (5ft.6in) ; age : less than 30 ; the head and nose are large ; good natured type ; bald head with a rim of hair ; arms crossed on the chest ; nails of the hands carefully manicu-

red ; the rest fairly badly preserved ; king of the XVIIIth dynasty.

Tuthmosis III : height :· 1.62 m (5ft.4in.) ; age : about 50 ; king of the XVIIIth dynasty ; pinched face, narrow forehead ; head almost bald with a short rim of white hair ; the body seems to have been the object of new embalming techniques (particularly concerning the abdominal incision) ; the mummy is very damaged, the tomb robbers practically tore it in three.

Amenophis II, height : 1.67 m (5ft.6in.) ; age : about 50 ; robust features (this pharaoh boasted about his physical prowess) ; brown hair ; small marks on the skin (disease ?) ; probably died a natural death.

Tuthmosis IV, height : 1.65 m (5ft.5in.) ; age : about 30 ; king of the XVIIIth dynasty ; facial features fine ; the ear lobes are pierced ; wavy brown hair ; arms crossed on the chest.

Amenophis III, age : about 50 ; king of the XVIIIth dynasty ; bald head ; bad teeth (abcesses and some teeth missing) ; the mummy was re-bandaged, it was not in its original coffin.

Pharaoh of uncertain identity, perhaps *Smenkhkare,* height : 1.65 m (5ft.5in.) ; age : about 26 ; probably of the XVIIIth dynasty ; back of the head slightly elongated (typical of the Amarna kings ?) ; mummification rapid and mediocre so that now only the skeleton is preserved. The mummy was found in a sarcophagus on which the cartouches were erased.

Sethos I, height : 1.67 m (5ft.7in.) ; king of the XIXth dynasty ; mummy very well preserved ; bald head ; face fine and noble ; arms crossed on the chest ; tomb robbers badly damaged the neck and broke open the abdomen.

Ramesses II, height : 1.73 m. (5ft:8in.) ; age : about 90 ; king of the XIXth dynasty ; bald head ; face imposing ; signs of degeneration due to advanced age ; hands and feet coloured red with henna ; hair whitish-yellow ; nails on the hands carefully manicured ; the skin colour seems to have been modified by the embalming.

Head of the mummy of Ramesses II

Merneptah, height : 1.71 m (5ft.7in.) ; age : advanced ; fairly fat ; the heart was not removed, viscera absent ; arms crossed ; this is possibly the king of the Exodus, the one who was drowned in the sea according to the Bible.

Siptah, height : 1.64 m (5ft.5in.) ; king of the XIXth dynasty ; hair reddish brown ; deformed foot ; died prematurely.

Sethos II, height : 1.64 m (5ft.5in.) ; middle aged ; king of the XIXth dy-

nasty ; arms crossed, the front right arm missing ; carefully mummified, found in the tomb of Amenophis II.

Ramesses III, height : 1.68 m (5ft.6in.) ; age : about 65 ; king of the XXth dynasty ; robust appearance but shows his age ; incision on the face (from embalming ?) ; arms crossed ; hands open ; linen in the orbits ; mummy found at Deir el-Bahri.

Ramesses IV, height : 1.60 m (5ft.3in.) ; age : about 50 ; king of the XXth dynasty ; head almost bald ; hole in the back of the head ; arms crossed.

Ramesses V, height : 1.73 m (5ft.8in.) ; age : between 45 and 50 ; king of the XXth dynasty ; hole in the head from a wound ; face covered with pock marks and pimples as is the whole body (presumably the illness which caused death, smallpox ?).

Ramesses VI, height : 1.71 m (5ft.7in.) ; middle-aged ; king of the XXth dynasty ; arms crossed ; the mummy was so damaged by the robbers when it lay in the coffin that it had to be reconstructed on a wooden tablet.

Ramesses IX or XI, height : 1.69 m (5ft.6in.) ; middle-aged ; XXth dynasty ; identification uncertain.

Nefertari, height : 1.61 m (5ft.4in.) ; advanced ·age ; very probably the wife of Amosis of the beginning of the New Kingdom ; the bald head (old age) was recovered with tresses made of knotted human hair ? the mummy was found at Deir el-Bahri.

Sitkamosi, height : 1.62 m (5ft.4in.) ; age : less than 30 ; princess of the XVIIth dynasty ; robust stature ; mummy badly damaged by the tomb robbers.

Meritamun, height : 1.55 m (5ft.1in.) ; age : about 50 ; wife of Amenophis II ; delicate appearance ; hair curly brown ; attacked twice by robbers, the mummy was reburied each time and was dressed and replaced in its coffin.

Nedjemt, height : 1.55 m (5ft.1in). middle-aged ; the wife of the priest-king Herihor of the XXIst dynasty ; curly grey hair covered with a brown wig ; artificial eyes in black and white stone ; cheeks padded out with sand ; viscera replaced in the abdomen after purification ; pearl bracelets on arm articulations (in a straight position).

Maatkare, height : 1.52 m (5ft.1in.) ;

age : young ; daughter of king Psusennes of the XXIst dynasty ; divine adoratrice of Amun ; certain parts of the body are padded with sand and linen ; artificial eyes ; jewels on the thumbs ; badly damaged by robbers.

Henuttaui, height : 1.52 m (5ft.1in.) ; age : young ; body seems badly proportioned ; padded ; artificial eyes ; wig ; coloured face ; representation of the four sons of Horus on the gold plate which covered the abdominal embalming incision.

Esiemkhebi, height : 1.59 m (5ft.3in.) ; middle-aged ; XXIst dynasty ; still enveloped in bandages ; appears to have been padded like the other mummies.

Itinerary n° 5 : Pyramids of Giza

The Giza pyramids can be reached from *el-Tahrir* square in a taxi (or even in a bus, which is less comfortable but considerably cheaper). The journey may take about 40 minutes if the traffic is congested.

Cross Rôda island by *el-Gamaa* bridge (constructed by the Krupp factory), then pass the Zoo (the University is on the right, further on), then cross the popular Giza district before taking the pyramid route *(Sharia el-Ahram)* on its most direct part and at about the level of the old *Mena House Hotel* (further along to the right is the *Oberoy* hotel), walk on foot to the desert plateau. There, it is impossible to be left alone by the invasion of tourist guides, the trash sellers and the ride hirers, but it is better to remain indifferent and to

continue the ascent to the plateau where the pyramids stand (the impression will be better at night without all these disturbances). The office of the tourist police and the stables are on the left where it is possible to return eventually after the visit to hire a camel or a horse (magnificent rides in the desert).

HISTORY

The three pyramids of Giza, those of *Cheops, Chephren* and *Mycerinus* belong to the IVth dynasty (2723-2563 B.C.). They represent the highest achievement in pyramid construction. In fact from *Abu Roash* (in the north) to the Fayûm (in the south) the pyramids extend for 100 km (62 miles), totalling more than sixty in all. Their form may vary, as well as their height and their technical character ; some are unfinished ; others are in an excellent state or even partly demolished.

All the pyramids are on the left bank of the Nile, near to the border between the cultivated land and the desert, or rather the lower or valley temple is found there, at the beginning of the desert and the kingdom of the dead. At the end of the causeway, the upper temple or actual funerary temple is built ; it is constructed on the east side of the pyramid, although the pyramid entrance is generally found on the north. The question of orientation was important from the Egyptian point of view. Although there was no systematic and obligatory lay-out, a change of direction is often observed, after entering the north entrance, in the interior of the pyramid : at the east (left) the chamber destined for the statue of the deceased is found (serdab), whereas on the right, the west, is the sarcophagus chamber ; therefore the east signi-

fies rebirth, whereas the west corresponds to the empire of the dead. Note also that speculation of every kind (« mathematical » as well as pseudo-mystical) which flourishes in the subject of pyramids is without foundation and remains pure fantasy, due to a total incomprehension of ancient Egypt and a complete misunderstanding of its civilisation. This has however nothing to do with the well known fact that all the Old Kingdom pyramids are orientated on the four cardinal points by their faces, and with very great precision : so that the Cheops pyramid only differs by 5° 30' at the most from an absolute orientation ; that of Chephren by 5° 32' at most and that of Mycerinus by 14° 30'.

The significance and meaning of the construction of the pyramids is uniquely sacred and religious. The dead king had to continue to exist in the after-life because he became divine (in part) and also had to assure the welfare and survival of his people. Death was not the only important feature in prosaic reality (the pyra-

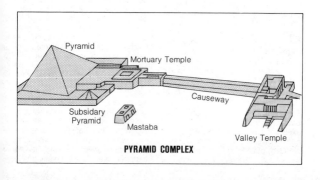

PYRAMID COMPLEX

mid, a giant simple tumulus to commemorate the memory of the dead one), the whole Egyptian mythological image counted almost as much because the two were intimately connected. That is the reason why the Old Kingdom pyramids (the most important) were not constructed, as related in a very old legend, by hordes of humiliated slaves but, a little like western cathedrals, were built by organised groups of Egyptian peasants participating in a sacred operation. No doubt, the hardships of the work did, however, cause human suffering. That is the reason why this « fatigue » was only practical during the time of inundation when field work was stopped (and when the water came up to the desert and allowed the transportation of the blocks of stone almost to the place of work). When it is realised that almost 100,000 men worked for twenty years on the construction of Cheops' pyramid, the exceptional system of provisioning, which must have been put in motion for such an army of workers and which allowed the porterage of water, food, materials, and necessary tools so that the planned programme for Cheops could be finished in time, must be admired. Almost 2 1/2 million blocks of lime-stone, 2 1/2 tons (each block more than a cubic metre) were piled up, several monoliths in the interior weigh more than 200 tons. The lower courses can reach 1.50 m (5ft.) in height, the upper courses are only 50 to 60 cm. (1ft.8in.-2ft.).

The diorite pounders, quartzite for polishing, the flint drills, the copper axes and saws and the ramps of baked bricks on which the wooden sledges pulled by men or beasts were slid, formed the principal means employed in construction, because the wheel, lever, block and tackle and iron tools were as yet unknown. Nevertheless, the construction was so precise in certain cases (at Giza) that the level of the courses for a length of 200 m (636 ft.) does not vary more than 2 cm (1in.).

The organisation of the work was inspired by the same simplicity. First of all, the rock platform was levelled, then the first layer was set down, the lower layer which formed a square stone foundation. Then, a brick or mud ramp was installed on which it was possible to take up the necessary material to the second layer as well as the blocks themselves (on wooden sledges). The ramp was built up and lengthened for the third course and the following courses, so that the ramps became progressively longer and higher. The necessary interstices for corridors and chambers were evidently arranged according to the architect's plans. Finally, when the apex was reached, the courses had the appearance of an immense staircase (something like their present state). Then, going from top to bottom, the already conveniently cut casing blocks were added, which were finally carefully polished, course by course, so that the ramps were simultaneously demolished. The immense mass of material which must have been used merely for the construction of the ramps, of which nothing remains today, can be imagined.

The building material used for the body of the pyramid was chiefly lime-stone found at the site, although for the casing blocks, the fine, white nummulitic limestone from the quarries of *Tura,* facing Memphis, was used (making the maximum use of the Nile in flood). The greater part of the casing blocks was removed in the Middle Ages and re-used as cheap building material in the Citadel and monuments of Cairo, but there is a little remaining on the three pyramids. The innumerable steps of the pyramids can therefore be climbed today, particularly those of Cheops. This is a fairly difficult exercise which is justified by the exceptional view from the summit, the ascent is often forbidden or permitted only with a guide and the greatest prudence is recommended (guard against vertigo).

The Pyramid of Cheops [28], also known under the name of *Akhet Khufu*, « Horizon of Cheops ». The pharaoh *Cheops*, the second king of the IVth dynasty constructed it about 2690 B.C. Its base forms a square of 440 Egyptian cubits on each side, which is 23,038 m² (75,587 sq. ft.) with the casing and now only 22,750 m² (74,642 sq. ft.). It originally rose to 146.6 m (481½ ft.) (the peak was still present) ; now it is more than 137 m (449½ ft.) from the platform to the summit (10 m (31 ft.) less). The greatest height measured on the inclined plane of the face was 186 m (610 ft.) and today, without the casing, it is 173 m (567 ft.) (with a slope forming an angle of 51°52', which is a little less than that of Chephren). The siting of the pyramid of Chephren is such that its diagonal is a projection of that of Cheops, which is not the case for the pyramid of Mycerinus in relation to the other two. The volume of material used for Cheops (body and casing) reached 2.5 million cubic metres (today a little less than 2.34 million cubic metres (3,400,000 cu.yd.) remains).

The ancient entrance, on the north side, was blocked and was fairly high (it can be distinguished very well). Today, a much lower hole pierced by tomb robbers 15 m (49 ft.) below the rock plateau is used ; it penetrates into a passage only 1.20 m (4 ft.) high and narrow which descends for less than 20 m (65 ft.) to a fork. In the first plan, the original, the passage which descends another 80 m (260 ft.) and ends in a subterranean funerary chamber situated under the projection of the central axis of the pyramid was without doubt intended to be enlarged and embellished.

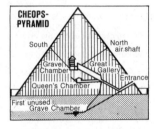

CHEOPS-PYRAMID

South   North air shaft

Gravel Chamber   Great Gallery

Queen's Chamber   Entrance

First unused Grave Chamber

But the passage that is followed today corresponds to an alteration of the plan and ascends, after the fork, for 38 m (125 ft.). Then the great gallery is reached, 8.5 m (28 ft.) high, the sides of which are formed of seven corbelled courses, and which ends in a horizontal section once closed by granite portcullises. An ingenious system of wooden props held the portcullises up in special grooves during the time needed for work. Once the burial was finished, the props were released so that the enormous portcullises slid into the passage and closed it, in principle, for eternity.

In a type of ante-chamber, one of the granite port-cullises may still be seen in situ in its run-way. The antechamber is followed by the king's chamber or funerary cham-ber, the construc-tion of which is so perfect that it is almost impossible to slide even a sheet of paper between the blocks.

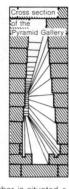

Cross section of the Pyramid Gallery

The funerary chamber is situated a little off the axis of the pyramid, at 42.30 m (138 ft.) above the level of the plateau. It is 5.80 m (19 ft.) high and forms a rectangle of 10.45 × 5.20 m (34 × 17 ft.). It is entirely lined in granite and the ceiling is formed of nine monolithic blocks of granite, 5.65 m (18 ft.) long. Because of architectural wisdom, five discharging chambers were built to support the enormous mass of the pyramid which would otherwise have threatened the roof (the last has a chevroned ceiling) and it is only there that a mention of the name of the king, in red, is found. At 1 m (3 ft.) above the floor of the funerary chamber there are two air vents which lead to the exterior and turn to the north and south through angles of 31° and 45°. These vents are not intended for ventilation but have rather a symbolic role ; they permit the soul to come and go after the funeral.

The lower part of Cheops' sarcophagus is still preserved ; it is a granite tank 1 m (3 ft.) high, 2.30 m (7½ ft.) long and 0.89 m (2 ¾ ft.) wide.

The sarcophagus was empty when the pyramid was penetrated and the royal mummy had been destroyed. On the way back, in descending, it is possible to see, under the funerary chamber, the so-called « Queen's Chamber » (in fact the result of another modification of the plan of the pyramid).

Before visiting the temples and the two other pyramids, those who had the courage and the physical ability and had obtained an authorisation, could recently undertake the ascent of the pyramid. But this ascent is at the moment forbidden. The best way to take was near the north-east edge. The panorama from the platform is one of the most striking spectacles that it is possible to see in Egypt ; the Nilotic oasis between the two deserts, the green of the cultivation in the middle of the yellow ochre of the sand, the city of Cairo with its dozens of minarets in a sort of violet vapour, the line of pyramids stretching south, the funerary temples, the small pyramids and mastabas at the foot of the Great Pyramid, the Sphinx near to the Arab cemetery and the last dunes of sand beside the first irrigation canals.

From on high a good idea of the area and plan of the pyramids can be gained. Around the pharaoh's tomb there were cult buildings. On the east side of the pyramid there was a funerary temple, destined for the eternal prayers and offerings, in which there was a group of chapels, courts and porticos. A covered way (usually described as the « causeway ») connected the funerary temple with a massive lower temple at the edge of the cultivated land and the flood waters. It was the entrance to the after-life and it was there that purification ceremonies took place, opening of the mouth and also mummification ; the area was therefore only accessible to priests. The plan and the pavement of the temple of Cheops still exists. Three Queens' pyramids stand in front of the Great Pyramid and there the necropolis area for the king's relatives, great people of the court and funerary priests extends towards the south. Finally, five barques are associated with the Cheops pyramid, solar barques rather than funerary barques. There are three on the east side cut in the stone, while two others of wood were discovered only in 1954 on the south.

The south barques were found in trenches 31 m (100 ft.) long, 3.50 m (11 ft.) deep and covered by a pavement of 18 tons, the joins of which were so well fitted that the cedar wood below hardly appeared 5,000 years old. Only one boat has been taken from its pit and remounted (the shelter where it is housed will soon be accessible to the public). The barque was made of about 600 pieces, and includes accessories like an oar 12 m (39 ft) long and an elegant cabin with a canopy supported by papyriform poles. The planks were assembled only with cords and a very efficient system of knots. In water, moisture did the rest and tightened the cords. The significance of these boats is still slightly problematical ; it is generally thought that they

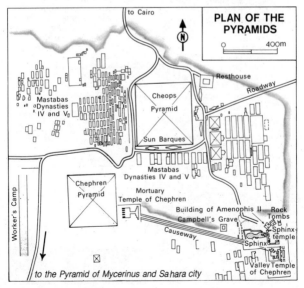

PLAN OF THE PYRAMIDS

0   400m

to Cairo

N

Resthouse

Roadway

Mastabas
Dynasties
IV and V

Cheops
Pyramid

Sun Barques

Mastabas
Dynasties IV and V

Chephren
Pyramid

Mortuary
Temple of Chephren

Building of Amenophis II

Campbell's Grave

Causeway

Rock
Tombs

Sphinx-
temple

Sphinx

Worker's Camp

Valley Temple
of Chephren

to the Pyramid of Mycerinus and Sahara city

are meant to represent the solar barque in which the king could sail after his death, rather than barques involved in carrying him to the realm of the dead.

The building which is called the *Pyramid Rest House* (essentially a café) was originally a villa which king Farûk built at the foot of Cheops'pyramid. Everything there imitates or plagiarizes-pharaonic style, and the architecture, decoration and furniture are inspired by that of Tutankhamun. It is not in very good taste.

The Pyramid of Chephren [29] is the second pyramid of the Giza necropolis ; it is also of the IVth dynasty. In general the pyramid seems higher and more imposing than that of Cheops, and if it gives this impression it is only because the plateau on which it stands is slightly higher at this point. Built on a square of 210 × 210 m (689 × 689 ft.), its apex today reaches 136.5 m (448 ft.), but was originally 143.5 m (470 ft.). At the summit (limestone) as well as the base (granite), the casing is still very well preserved (the incline is 52°20').

The plan of the complex is identical to that of Cheops. The foundations of the funerary temple at the east are preserved as well as the elements of the funerary causeway which leads to the valley temple. The emplacement of the funerary chamber posed similar problems to those of Cheops. But whereas with the latter, it was the third change which proved the best, here with Chephren it was the second which became definitive when the installation of a subterranean funerary chamber was planned. Today an entrance near the ground at the north leads to a descent of 32 m (105 ft.) and, after a fork, the corridor continues horizontally to the funerary chamber, built almost on the axis of the pyramid. It is a chamber cut in the rock and covered with a limestone ceiling. The king's sarcophagus is sunk in the floor, its cover was broken and there was no trace of the royal mummy.

The Pyramid of Mycerinus [30]. The third pyramid of Giza, also of the IVth dynasty, was only 66.5 m (218 ft.) high (today (62 m 203 ft.)). The base formed a square of 108.5 m (355 ft.). Partly dispersed around the pyramid and partly still in place, the beautiful blocks of Aswan granite which formed the lower part of the casing can be seen, the upper part was built of limestone. The interior which is to be opened to the public can be visited. There are also three small pyramids at the foot of the large one, on the south side ; they were reserved for the close relatives of the king, and the queen. The usual complex is found next to the pyramid : valley temple, causeway and funerary temple where the very beautiful groups of Mycerinus were found (Cairo Museum Room 47 on the ground floor). Very recently, in 1973-74, a village was discovered in the desert to the south-east ; it probably housed the workers who built the funerary complex.

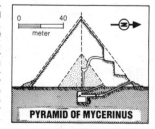

0   40
meter

PYRAMID OF MYCERINUS

The Lower Temple of Chephren [31] is one of the most beautifully preserved examples of this type of Old Kingdom building (the roof and some parts are missing). It is a splendid, very simple and strong construction in granite in the very geometric style of this period. In front of the east façade, there are two entrances, once flanked by small sphinxes ; a vestibule, a large room with a transverse and a longitudinal nave. In the first, superb granite monolithic architraves are supported on six pillars and in the second nave there are lines of five pillars (also granite monoliths). Between these pillars there were once

Chephren-Pyramid

Valley Temple of Chephren

Facade (Reconstruction)

diorite statues of the king in twenty niches cut in the walls (some are partly preserved, the finest of which is in the Egyptian Museum). Further chambers are cut on one side whilst on the other a ramp is cut in the stone mass which rises towards the temple roof and allows access to the once covered causeway which leads to the funerary temple.

The valley temple of Chephren is situated very near the famous **Sphinx [32].** It is a couchant lion with a human head (more precisely a royal head). It wears the nemes' headdress and the forehead was formerly ornamented with a uraeus (the hole in the forehead where it was attached can still be seen). The beard and the nose have disappeared (fragments in Cairo Museum) because the monument served as a target for a Mameluke sultan.

The quarrymen and the architects of king Chephren used a spur of rock as their base which was perhaps exposed when Cheops' blocks were extracted. The measurements are as follows : height 20 m (65½ ft.) ; length 73 m (239½ ft.) ; face width 4.15 m (13½1 ft.) ; width of mouth alone 2.32 m (7½ ft.)

The sphinx (the Egyptian sphinx is masculine whereas the Theban sphinx of the Greek legend is feminine) is considered as an effigy of king Chephren in monumental form, and also as an image of the sun god Re-Harakhty : Harmarchis. But its prestige became such that other divinities were assimilated with it and it rapidly received its own important cult (there is nothing left to see of the temple buildings connected with it). An important event connected with it is commemorated on a stela set-up by Tuthmosis IV between the lion's paws. This stela tells how one day the king was hunting in the neighbourhood and he rested at the foot of the statue, embedded in sand at that time. The god then appeared to him in a dream and asked him to clear away the sand in exchange for which he assured him the kingship of Egypt ; this was effectively accomplished. Several times the Sphinx had to be cleared of invading sand, during the Roman period for example (an altar of this period was also found between the paws). Furthermore, not all visitors spoke of this statue in classical times, proving that the sand may have encroached again then. Finally the Arabs called the Sphinx *Abul Hol* « Father of Terror ». In the neighbourhood of the statue, there are the remains of the *Temple of the Sphinx*, and a little to the north, rock tombs, (in the direction of the rest house).

There is a daily performance of « Son et Lumière » at the pyramids which takes place early or late in the evening according to the season. Finally, after visiting the site, it is possible to take a horseback or camel ride around the site or towards *Sahara City*, several kilometres to the south where there is a splendid view of all the monuments. There, under a Bedouin tent, Egyptian cuisine can be tasted and the evening passed watching varied folk performances.

Itinerary n° 6 : Museum of Islamic Art and El-Azhar Mosque

From *El-Tahrir* square, follow *Sharia el-Tahrir* once more up to Midan el-*Gumhuriya* (Square of the Republic).

Abdine Palace [33] is found there, which takes its name from *Abdine Pasha,* from whom the khedive Ismail bought it. Ismail made it luxurious until 1873 so that it could be the viceroy's residence and attest to the oriental magnificence of that time and the extravagances of Egyptian sovereigns. One wing is composed of a great number of rooms which are still used by the presidency. In another part of the palace, there is the *Military Museum* (previously in the Citadel) with an interesting retrospective of the whole of Egyptian military history.

Among the show rooms of the palace, the reception salons in the Egyptian-Italian style of the XIXth century can be visited, the festival rooms, the princely rooms, the salon of Ismail and the *red gallery*. The queens and princesses' suites are full of alabaster, Venetian glass and pseudo-Renaissance decor, particularly in the bedrooms, the dining rooms and the baths. The throne room is similarly styled. In the *Byzantine Hall* there is an abundance of marble, mosaics and furniture of Arab or Byzantine style, creating a pompous and ostentatiously decorated gallery. Finally, there is a small gallery of portraits of Muhammed Ali's family.

In the adjacent square, *Ahmed Maher* (behind the palace) the

Museum of Islamic Art [34] is situated, just beside the National Library, with a rich and famous collection of important Arab works of different periods and styles. It merits a separate visit because of this exceptional collection of Islamic art, classified and exhibited in 23 rooms (all on the ground floor) according to the category of objects, materials and chronological order. It is the richest collection of its kind with more than 60,000 pieces. The brief description here has to be limited to the objects which are considered the most significant.

Entrance Hall and Room 1 : plan of the collection and chronological table of the Islamic dynasties in Egypt. Temporary exhibitions of new acquisitions, jewels and medals.

Room 2 : Umaiyad Period (661-750,

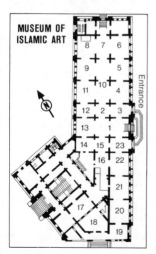

fusion of Arab, ancient eastern, Hellenistic and naturalistic elements) : wooden and glass objects, pottery, bronze ewer with geometric and floral decoration which belonged to Marwan II the last Umaiyad caliph.

Room 3 : Abbasid Period (750-867, beginning of stylisation and abstraction, Sassanid decoration) : vases, ornaments with light relief. Tulunid period (868-905, arabesques, jewels, representations of men and animals, chandeliers) : stucco arabesques from houses, tomb stones with kufic inscriptions, pottery, lustrous faience, metal objects.

Room 4 : Fatimid Period (969-1171, particular decorative style, predominance of moving forms, calligraphy and arabesques) : objects in rock crystal with jewelled decoration, sculptured or painted panels (eg. those from Qalaûn hospital), mashrabiya doors, pottery and coloured tiles, wooden objects, ivory objects, bronzes, embroidered textiles.

Room 5 : Mameluke Period (1250-1517, artistic renewal, Turkish and Moorish elements and forms, elegant and rich in detailed decoration) : mosaics, particularly on a fountain with geometric decoration, bronze lamps with several tiers, copper with arabesques, images of gold and silver, enamel.

Room 6 : works in wood ; doors and mihrabs, including an element from El-Azhar mosque (XIIth century), a delicately worked mihrab ; engraved frieze from the Qalâun hospital, cenotaph of El-Hussein decorated with verses from the Koran in kufic.

Room 7 : cenotaph of Suliman el-Kasim, 1433, numerous mashrabiyas of exceptional quality.

Room 8 : elements of the cenotaph of the Aiyubid Mansur Ismail (XIIth century), decorated wooden panel from the mausoleum of Shafei, pulpits for the Koran, chests, various wooden utensils with ivory inlay (Mameluke).

Room 9 : numerous panels and benches with geometric inlays (XIVth century), objects in red and yellow copper.

Room 10 : very instructive reconstruction of an Arab room with its fountain and beautiful wooden ceiling (XVIIth century).

Room 11 : bronze work, chiefly the panels of the door of the Salih Talai mosque (1160) ; other furniture and instruments of the XIVth century ; hangings of the Mameluke period.

Room 12 : weapons, many with marquetry inlays, others with the names of Islamic sovereigns ; carpets.

Room 13 : very important collection of ceramics of every period ; particularly the ancient periods ; numerous imports alongside the Egyptian pieces.

Room 14 : terracottas, mural tiles of Persia, Syria, Tunisia and Turkey, lustrous tiles.

Room 15 : collection of ceramics from foreign lands, collection of foreign faience and porcelain vases found at Fustât, Persian ceramics (IXth to XIVth centuries).

Room 16 : Iznik faience, Persian relief tiles, Andalucian and Syrian pottery, Chinese porcelain. Reconstruction of a school room from Rosetta with wooden panelling.

Room 17 : textiles from the Yemen, Turkey, Iran and Egypt. A résumé of cloth work showing clearly that two qualities were produced : one was destined for the caliph, his family and the upper classes, the other for the common people. The two qualities were controlled by the authorities. The varied and particular decoration should be noticed.

Room 18 : Capitals and tomb stones (with kufic inscriptions). The latter clearly show the evolution of Arab calligraphy with its different stages. Marble mosaics from the floors of mosques and palaces ; marble sun-dials and other stone objects.

Room 19 : examples of pronounced Muslim style for book miniatures ; calligraphy ; copies of the Koran ; bindings ; miniatures, particularly those originating in Persia, India or Egypt.

Room 20 : examples of Turkish minor art ; ceramics from Kutahia and Iznik ; Chinese porcelain ; carpets of the XVIIth to XIXth centuries ; horse trappings of Bursa (XVIth century) ; silver objects from Constantinople.

Room 21 : glass vases and fragments, chiefly the unique collection (of its type) of 70 mishkats (lamps from mosques artistically made from enamelled glass) exhibited in chronological order. Carpets of Ispahan and other origins in wool and silk (chiefly XVIth century).

Room 22 : works of art from Persia, chiefly a very instructive collection of ceramics. The variations of colours and forms, base material and decoration should be noticed this time and also the painted representations on numerous faience tiles ; carpets of the XVIIth and XVIIIth centuries.

Room 23 : objects of different periods and places ; such as carpets. The Museum is justly proud of its important collection of carpets which decorate the walls of numerous exhibition rooms.

The *Arab Library* is situated on the first floor of the Museum (entrance by El-Qalaa street) : manuscripts of the whole Islamic world and various documents, such as Korans (nearly 2,700, the most ancient dating to the VIIIth century). Papyrus was fairly rapidly replaced by paper. Original Korans which belonged to various sultans, including a very large example which belonged to Qait Bey (1.15 × 0.90 m (44 ¾ × 35 in.)). Persian manuscripts and miniatures, particularly poetry such as that of Saadi (XVIth century), or historical works.

Rare Turkish books (Korans and manuscripts) among them the first work written in the Arab language in Turkey, and the *Qudatku Biliq*, written in 1350 in Cairo. As well as these, Turkish and Persian bindings which denote an advanced technique, and a collection of historical Arab money and medallions (more than 5,000 items).

From the Midan *Ahmed Mahir*, following *Ahmed Mahir* street,

Bab Zuweila [35] (or *Bab el-Mitwalli*) is reached, a remarkable collection of cut stones (1091) with semi-cylindrical columns and the two minarets of *El-Muaiyad Mosque*, which at the level of the gate, project above the towers with their 50 metres (165 ft.). Essentially, the gate resembles that of *Bab el-Futûh* : between two semi-cylindrical towers, there is a large passage 4,84 m (16 ft.) wide, which is covered by a smooth dome. The loggia and the platform above the door are provided with loop-holes. For a long time there were gibbets on the gate terrace and it was from the loop-holes that the heads of Christians killed at *Mansûra* were exposed. There are stone balls visible on the west tower

dating from the period of the Mameluke quarrels, and it was here that on 15th April, 1517, the last Circassian sultan of Egypt, *Tuman Bey* was hanged. In the square in front of the gate, there is the fountain of sultan Farag, enclosed by bronze railings. Down to the XIXth century, executions by strangulation took place there. The name of *El-Mitwalli* gate and the pieces of cloth, teeth and other marks of devotion hanging from the gate, are connected with the saint *Qûtb el-Mitwalli*, who is reputed to appear sometimes near here. The

El-Muaiyad Mosque [36], also known as the « red mosque », was meant to be the most notable and elegant Cairo mosque according to the pretensions of *Selim I.* The gate is remarkable in itself ; the lime wood swing doors are 5.50 m (18 ft.) high and studded with bronze plaques ornamented with rosettes. They came from the principal entrance of the *Sultan Hasan* Mosque, were purchased in 1410 for 500 dinars and have sultan Hasan's name. A band of marble, alternating black and white and a stalactite arch surround the door, which is the entrance to the domed vestibule (cruciform arches),

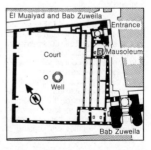

El Muaiyad and Bab Zuweila

Entrance

Mausoleum

Court

Well

Bab Zuweila

then to the court with its fountain as well as the sultan's mausoleum. Only part of the original porch remains standing on the east side. There, behind a graceful railing of the XIXth century, various forms of columns divide the prayer room into three naves, above which slim pointed arches 14 m (46 ft.) carry a ceiling decorated with wooden framework and boxes decorated with gold and silver. Deserving attention is the mihrab wall with its seven niches : inlays of marble, columns, stalactite domes, plaster work and glass inlays, friezes of gilded and arabesque writing are present in all the empty spaces and on all the wooden parts ; also here and in the prayer room are elegant inlays of ivory. The sultan's mausoleum is surmounted by a high dome with stalactite pendentives. The white marble sarcophagus of *El-Muaiyad el-Mahmudi* is decorated with a band of kufic inscriptions. Near his catafalque is the tomb of his son, *Ibrahim* ; behind, the doors give access to the mausoleum of the sultan's wives, which has now lost its dome.

Those who are interested in Islamic art and architecture may take *Darb el-Ahmar* and *Bab el-Wazir* streets and visit two other interesting monuments :

El-Mardani Mosque [37], on the right of the street, mosque and tomb of the emir *Mardani*, cup bearer of sultan Nasi. It was finished in 1340, and consists of a porticoed mosque. After being reconstructed in the XIXth century (modern dome, etc.,), the most remarkable features are the beautiful columns of the Ptolemaic period in the liwan and the small antique columns under the dome, the mihrab, minbar and casing of polychrome wood, the fountain in

the court (it comes from the *Sultan Hassan Mosque*) and the *maksura* with its incised frieze.

A little further on, on the left of *Sharia el-Tabbana*, there is the

Aqsûnqûr Mosque [38] also called the *Mosque of Ibrahim Agha* or the « blue mosque » *(El-Azraq)* because many of the walls are cased in brilliant blue-green tiles in Persian style (intertwined floral motifs like on a carpet), as for example, around the tomb of *Aqsûnqûr*, the founder of the mosque (1346) or *Ibrahim Agha* (he undertook the restoration of the monument in 1651, after an earth tremor), both beside the south liwan. A third tomb, near the entrance of the mosque, is that of sultan *Allah el-Din Qutshuk* who died in 1351. *Aqsûnqûr* married the sultan's daughter and was covered with honour, then he fell into disgrace and, in 1347, was imprisoned and beheaded.

Returning towards *Bab Zuweila* and turning now towards the north (to the right for those who come from Aqsunqur mosque), enter the small *Muizz el-Din Allah* street. Passing in front of *El-Faqahami Mosque* (stalactite arch and portal with exaggerated arches, porticoed mosque, walls of mihrab lined with blue Turkish tiles) and, for particularly interested visitors, the nearby *House of Gamal el-Din Sahabi* (old merchant's house of 1627, with a fountain in the court and an interesting wooden dome above the great room). Here is the *El-Ghûri* quarter and the

El-Ghûri Mosque [39] stands here which was constructed in 1504 and has the mausoleum in which the Circassian Mameluke sultan, *El-Ghûri*, who fell on the plain of Merj Dâbiq near Aleppo, was supposed to be interred (he was never brought back) ; members of his family lie in his vault. Note particularly the square minaret 65 m (213 ft.) high with its two balconies set on stalactite cornices, and the five small domes which surmount it. The mausoleum and the funerary monument are accessible by an exterior marble staircase. Contrary to the tradition according to which such monuments have to have a sober appearance, the architect of the mosque decorated it richly like a reception room and gave it, internally and externally, a deliberately symmetrical appearance. The master-pieces are the dome which surmounts the sultan's mausoleum and all the marquetries and inlays of the prayer room and liwan.

The same master was responsible for the neighbouring building of Wakalet el-Ghûri, once a commercial and caravan centre with boutiques, shops and guest rooms for merchants and their clients from the provinces. Note especially the windows ornamented with beautiful mashrabiyas which encircle the great court at this place.

El-Azhar street is now reached and it is only a few paces on (to the right) for the mosque and the university, situated on the new El-Azhar square.

El-Azhar [40]. It is one of the oldest Islamic universities, one of the largest and the most important of all, and also a mosque, Furthermore it houses administrative buildings and student lodgings. It is a type of world centre of Islamic tradition. Gohar, the founder of Cairo, began the construction of the mosque, « The Most Blooming » in 359 of Hegira (970 A.D.), in the month of Gumada el-Wala ; in his mind he meant this

mosque to be the great municipal mosque of the newly founded town of Cairo ; it was inside the ramparts and near the palace.

He undertook the construction one year after the Fatimids took power and this new stone building was finished on the 7th of Ramadan, 361 years after the Hegira (22nd June, 972) ; the caliph El-Muizz directed the first service there. According to his wishes, this mosque became the symbol of the Shiite doctrine of the Fatimids and of their judicial domination. When the well-read vizier Yakub Ibn Killis delivered a lecture on a book which he had written on the Shiite law there, it came to be realised that henceforth academic and theological study could also be dealt with. In 988, El-Azhar was officially proclaimed a university by the Caliph El-Aziz and began with a law faculty, then a theological faculty. Consequently, in the course of the following centuries, the building was constantly enlarged, up to the destruction caused by an earth tremor in 1303 which led to the total reconstruction of numerous parts. The sultans Hasan and Qait Bey worked intensively on these tasks during the XIVth and XVth centuries and Abd el-Rahman Kikhya enlarged the prayer room in the XVIIth century by adding four new aisles. Even although the XIX and XXth centuries (and also more recently) have witnessed other enlargements and restorations, the character of the whole monument has remained virtually the same.

From El-Azhar square, turn towards the north-west side of the building and enter by the principal entrance of Bab el-Muzaiyinin, « Gate of the Barbers » [A]. It was there in the passage where the students were once shaved.

From the small corridor [b] one may go towards the left to the offices of the steward (in the ancient mausoleum) and the library [c], which is housed in the ancient *Madrasa el-Aqbughawiya*. The mihrab with its fine miniature arcades and glass mosaics of Byzantine style should be noticed. Nearly 80,000 volumes, of which 20,000 are precious manuscripts, are put at the disposal of students.

On the right of the corridor the *Madrasa el-Taibarsiya* can be entered [d] where the elegant mihrab, dating to 1310, should be admired. Small antique porphyry columns and glass mosaics of Byzantine style flank it and beautifully cut miniature arches constitute its decoration. The portal and the adjacent minaret [e] were constructed by Qait Bey in the XVth century. The mosque has five minarets altogether, most of which were erected by different sultans. Through the portal, the great interior court, the *Sahn el-Gami*, 90 × 40 m (295 × 152 ft) is entirely enclosed by a columned arcade. This is decorated with keel-arches, ornaments, niches, medallions and has a frieze

above. The 375 marble columns of the arcades probably came from the Tulunid residence at *El-Qatai*. On the north and south sides, the arcades with double columns form the *riwaqs* [f] with triple naves, which are lodging rooms for poor students, divided by province or country. There are up to 38 *riwaqs*, for the Turks, Maghrebians, East Africans, men of Upper and Lower Egypt, Sudanese, Syrians, Indians, those from Mecca, the Hanifites, etc.

El-Azhar Mosque

The area reserved for ablutions (court for ritual ablutions) [g] is not in the principal court, but in one of the neighbouring rooms specially reserved for this purpose. At the south-east, a little like a type of transept, with its aisles of columns aligned perpendicularly to the wall of the qibla, the great prayer room with nine naves [h] is found, almost 3,000 m² (9,845 sq.ft.). Originally, there were only five naves. At the place where an aisle of columns is inter-

rupted there is a central nave in front of a mihrab [i] capped with cupolas at the entrance and above the mihrab ; these were the first cupolas to surmount an Islamic religious edifice in Egypt. The development of the « transept » follows the example of the *Sidi Oqba* at Qairawan (Tunisia), the point of departure of the Fatimids when they entered Egypt. The decoration which covers the first ancient mihrab [i] must be the most ancient example known in Egypt.

A framing arcade rests on the marble columns with bell-form capitals surrounding the circular niche and its half-cupola. Vertical bands of black and white marble complete the decoration.

In the course of the enlarging process, aisles of columns forming four new naves were entirely built, the ground and the ceiling were raised and the new mihrab [j] was placed towards the north, towards the new centre, but the original plan was virtually maintained. Of the total of 140 marble columns, there are about 100 which are of antique origin ; they support the ceiling of the principal court which is also the sanctuary of the mosque. Carpets mark the limits of the different classes where the students customarily sit in a circle around their master.

Near to the chair, a staircase leads to the upper floor and near that is the prayer niche of *Abd el-Rahman*. This generous, pious and rich man is interred on the south side of the building, of which he was the principal benefactor, in a small mausoleum [k].

On the opposite north side, the charming *Madrasa el-Gohariya* [l] can be visited, which dates to 1440, a small meditation room from which the prayer room can be seen through a window.

Six doors lead into the university of El-Azhar, some have significant names : « Gate of the Barbers » (*Bab el-Muzaiyinin*), « Gate of the North-West Africans » (*Bab el-Magharba*), « Gate of the Syrians » (*Bab el-Shauwam*), « Gate of the Upper Egyptians » (*Bab el-Saaida*), « Soup Gate » (*Bab el-Shorba* because it was there that the poor students ate), « Gate Goharija » (*Bab el-Goharija*). A minaret can be seen from afar as an emblem of El-Azhar, completely exceptional with two points, at the south of the « Gate of the Barbers » ; it is one of the monument's five minarets.

Today, as before, students come from more than 30 Islamic countries to study at El Azhar University ; there are a little less than 20,000 who are taught by 2,000 professors. The University depends partly on the Ministry of religious endowments (*waqfs*). It is directed by an administrative committee of five members and the *Sheikh el-Islam* (rector). For 1,000 years, they have worn almost exactly the same costume : white turbans and brown sombre *galabiyas*. They take their courses in the *riwaqs* (rooms) and also in their neighbourhood, in front of the students seated on carpets. The end of studies at El-Azhar is reached after a long stay which may reach up to 17 years. The average age of entry is between 12 and 15 years. The entrance requirement is the ability to recite the entire Koran. Theology and law, logic, rhetoric, poetry and composition were once the obligatory subjects until a short time ago, but today all disciplines are taught at El-Azhar, and beside the traditional Islamic university, there is a modern university with its laboratories and usual structures. After having taken the final examination of the traditional university successfully, the laureats, having gained an academic honour, return to the country or province of their origin in all parts of the Islamic world where they represent the official position of Islam. They become scholars (*ulamas* or doctors of law), professors (*mudares*), judges (*qadis*) or simply religious men.

To return to *el-Tahrir square* follow *Muski* street; one of the most animated commercial streets of Cairo, where not only typical oriental products can be bought, but also merchandise of every kind. This is one of the principal streets of the *sûqs*, next to the bazaar of *Khân el-Khalîli* and its picturesque animation amazes visitors. In the direction of *Ataba square*, a passage is passed where there was once a canal and there is a bridge which was built by Musk, a successor of *Saladin,* which is often known under the name of *Muski bridge* from which the street took its name. At *Khân el-Khalîli, Muski* opens onto *Sagha*, the *sûq* of the jewellers.

Itinerary n° 7 : Moqattam - Petrified Forest-Tombs of the Mamelukes (south group)

The local mountain of Cairo, *Moqattam*, can be visited most easily by leaving from the *Citadel* (inquire about freedom of access which is often suspended). Take a taxi which goes straight to the new residential quarter of the *City of Moqattam*. Then the route follows hairpin bends across the ancient pharaonic quarries, to climb up to the citadel which is 200 m (762 ft.) high ; the old casino is transferred to the town.

Moqattam [41]. From the terrace of the casino there is a very beautiful view over the Nile valley and the city with the green strip of alluvial earth which separates the two deserts in the distance. Whereas the *Libyan desert* consists of a limestone plateau with sandstone strata and sand dunes, the *Arabic desert* is formed of granite, diorite, gneiss and schist, and the mountains which bord the latter, such as Moqattam, are conglomerates of pebbles, marl, sand and the remains of fossil wood.

From Moqattam a good car can take the visitor (if he has permission) several kilometres into the east desert to the small *petrified forest*. There the so-called « Spring of Moses » is found which trickles from a cleft in the rock and a little further on the remains of tree trunks « petrified » (more exactly silicified) ; there are palms, acacias and bamboos which date to the Tertiary period. From there, one can return to *Maâdi*.

In the *Great Petrified Forest* (four hours on foot) similar plant remains are found which are yellow-red, brown and black (iron oxide) in colour and which have been polished like mirrors by the sand. From here also an excursion across the *Wadi el-Tih* up to *Maâdi* is possible. In any case neither excursion should be undertaken without a guide who knows the region perfectly.

From the summit of Moqattam, a tarred road is followed, then it turns to the left and the

Mosque of Giyushi [42] is reached by a footpath. It is the funerary mosque of a great vizier of the caliph *El-Mustansir* ; which was constructed by *Badr el-Gamali* (called the « Giyushi » or military chief) in 1085 and it is one of the most ancient mosques of the city with its minaret of archaic type. It is visible from afar and is situated on a hill of the Moqattam chain, the *Gebel Giyushi*, altitude 200 m (525 ft.). Legend says that the emir could see his favourite wives again after his death because they were buried in seven mausolea situated in the necropolis below. It was for this reason that he had chosen this site to build his mosque.

The plan is clear and the lay-out is symmetrical : a corridor [a] with a cistern [b] at the left and facing it a staircase which leads onto the roof [c], then a small *sahn* flanked by rooms [d]. The prayer room [e] is entered through a portal of three ogival arches and is entirely decorated in Persian and Byzantine style. The mihrab [f] is situated under the dome in a half-niche ; it is a work of art with Fatimid stucco decoration. All the parts are covered with barrel or cross vaults. The minaret is 20 m (64 ft.) high and is composed of a square element with friezes and sta-

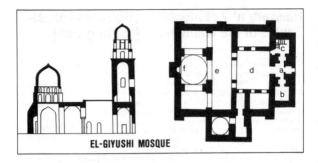

EL-GIYUSHI MOSQUE

lactites and then an upper octagonal section with eight arches crowned by a cupola. The *Aga Khan's* mausoleum at Aswan (see p. 252) took this mosque as a model. The view over the Citadel from on high is impressive ; the city can also be seen, *Muhammed Ali's Fort* and, further down towards the south, the southern necropolis of the Mamelukes to which you descend.

The Tombs of the Mamelukes (south group) [43]. This area, south of the town of the dead, is more destroyed than the northern area which is described on pages 116 to 123. Many of the funerary mosques are at least partially ruined and their origin is still unknown. The only one worth drawing attention to is the mosque of

Imam el-Shafii situated in the street of the same name. Shafii founded the very orthodox rite of the *Shafiites* (he died in 819). The mosque was only remodelled in the XIXth century and only the mausoleum survives as an example of the ancient buildings (1211) and surprises the visitor with its vast size.

The dome is 26.5 m (87 ft.) high. It is made of wood and rests on a very rare device by means of intermediate wooden pendentives : three series of superimposed niches. The cupola is illuminated by fourteen windows and it can be seen fairly precisely how it was made in wood. The summit of the dome is capped by a copper nave in which food and water are placed for the birds.

The great room of the mausoleum is high ; it is lined with marble and its balconies are sculptured and painted. The four finely carved wooden sarcophagi are found here ; in the north corner, that of the imam, and in another corner those of his mother, the *Sultan el-Kamil* and another person. The carvings and inlay of wood on the sarcophagi should be noted, as well as the geometric designs, the arabesques, the inscriptions and the leaf decoration. The most ancient Arab writing attested in Egypt, *nasqi*, was used to write the artist's signature on the sarcophagus of imam el-Shafii (summit of façade). The tomb screen (maqsûra), made of turned wood, is modern (1911). Up to this day, this sepulchre, is visited by pious Muslims as a place of pilgrimage.

In the neighbourhood is the *Hoch el-Pasha*, the family tomb of Muhammed Ali and his relatives. The domed rooms containing the sarcophagi are placed one against the other in an extraordinarily confined manner. The Mamelukes killed by Muhammed Ali also found their last repose here, under tomb stones crowned with turbans.

Return towards *Midan Muhammed Ali*.

Itinerary n° 8 : Old Cairo - The Coptic Museum - The Nilometer

Old Cairo can be reached from *el-Tahrir* square by taking a taxi (ask for Mari Girgis) ; outside peak hours a train can be taken in the direction of Helwan (to *Bab el-Lûq* station) descending at St.George / Mari Girgis station.

Near the station, you will notice at once two round towers which mark the entrance to the Coptic quarter of *Qasr el-Shamah* and further to the right, the Coptic Museum. These towers date to the time of Trajan and Hadrian and no doubt served as watch-towers (among many others) of the Roman fortress of Babylon, which, at that time, as the Nile flowed further east, had a water gate. The train station is situated very near to *Mari Girgis* street, where there is a small narrow staircase which leads to the Coptic quarter. There

St. George's is found, a Coptic orthodox church including a monastery. Only a room of the primitive church survives ; the modern church offers little of interest (*iconostasis* or screen of separation between the public and the sanctuary decorated with icons). Going along the narrow streets with old houses, sometimes ruined (notice

the numerous crosses on the doors and windows) you then come to

St. Sergius Church (Arabic : *Abu Sarga*) with a basilical plan, a triple nave and a raised transept, a narthex (vestibule) and a covered pulpit. The church was rebuilt in the Xth-XIth centuries and is dedicated to the martyrs Sergius and Bacchus. It only measures 27 × 17 m (88 × 56 ft.) ; today it is sunk deeply below present ground level ; its ogival arches are supported by antique columns. The marble pulpit should be noticed and in the narthex, in front of the central nave, a basin which is used at the festival of Epiphany.

But the really notable curiosities are the wooden and ivory sculptures consecrated to the Nativity and the Last Supper which can be seen on the panels on the entrance to the side chapels (XIth century).

The other chapels are dedicated to St.George and St.Michael. The crypt is 10 m (33 ft.) below the church and it measures only 5 × 6 m (16 × 19 ft.). Its arches are supported by antique columns. According to tradition, this was the place where the Holy Family stayed for a month during the Flight into Egypt, because

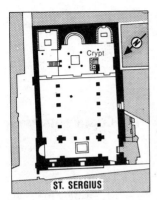

ST. SERGIUS

Joseph had found work in the Roman fortress (interesting annual commemorative mass, 1st June). From August to October (the time of the inundation), the chapel can become almost flooded by the infiltrating water.

Several streets further on, towards the west, the

Church of St. Barbara *(Sitt Burbâra)* can be visited, which dates originally to the VIIth century. As well as *Saint Barbara*, it is also dedicated to *St. John* and *St. Cyr*. The iconostasis (icon panel) is worth noting with its ivory sections as well as the very sober baptistry next to the sanctuaries consecrated to the saints. The precious church furniture, such as carved wood, was transported to the Coptic Museum where it can be admired (Room XIV, see p. 155).

Ben Ezra Synagogue is near St. Barbara's church. It was originally a Coptic church constructed on the site of a synagogue of earlier date, whence its basilical plan with three naves. Extremely ancient and beautiful manuscripts of the *Torah* can be seen there. Here in the *geniza* there were once thousands of manuscripts in Hebrew script some of which had a great documentary value. The Jewish quarter behind the synagogue is now uninhabited.

Returning to *St. Sergius* and passing the Coptic Museum, you can go to one of the most ancient churches of the Coptic quarter,

El-Muallaqa Church, that is « resting upon columns ». It has a possible origin in the IVth-Vth centuries, but in fact it was reconstructed in the decades which followed its destruction in the IXth century. It then began to serve as the seat of the Coptic patriarch. The interesting façade of the church has an almost « baroque » aspect ; the western side is richly decorated with stucco arabesques. The ogival arches supported on antique columns divide the interior of the church into five unequal naves. The marble pulpit and the high reliefs date to about 1100. In front of the three eastern chapels stands the iconostasis with wood and ivory elements and representations of saints on a gilded background (XIIIth century). The stained glass windows are modern, Finally, in front of the west façade of the church, there are ruins of two bastions of the Roman gate.

Coptic Museum. This museum (founded in 1908) began as a private collection which was nationalised in 1931. It is a unique museum which holds the richest collection of Coptic objects and works of art in the world. The exhibits cover nearly a thousand years and are displayed in 29 rooms arranged around a court. The museum also conserves Coptic houses with their doors, their windows, their

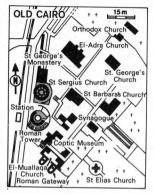

OLD CAIRO — 15 m
Orthodox Church
El-Adra Church
St George's Monastery
St. George's Church
St Sergius Church
St Barbara's Church
Station
Synagogue
Roman Tower
Coptic Museum
El-Muallaqa Church
Roman Gateway
St Elias Church

balconies and their woodwork as well as elements from churches. A brief description has been given here, but the museum has been undergoing re-arrangement for some time and this description may no longer correspond to the present situation.

Rooms I to VIII : architectural fragments such as bases, columns, pilasters, capitals, friezes, windows, door lintels, to which the remains of friezes from monasteries of Upper and Lower Egypt must be added.

Room IX : frescoes, note particularly the fresco from Umm el-Breigat in the Fayûm, representing the « Fall » (Adam and Eve before and after sin) with a naive character and unequal proportions.

Rooms X, XI and XII : Coptic textiles ; note the representations of figures which decorate some cloths or scraps ; many have mythological themes, but also animals, soldiers and Christian symbols.

Room XIII : Coptic ivories and paintings. Remains of frescoes from

churches and funerary chapels of Upper and Lower Egypt, generally with brown figures with emphasized contours and surrounded by floral friezes. Attention should be drawn to the importance of icons, with themes taken from the Bible or figures taken from the history of the Church, all produced first as painted bas-relief, then as panels of sculptured wood.

These frescoes mostly decorated the cupolas which surmounted the high altar ; they were precise in detail, beautifully coloured and very thoughtful in their composition. Even although Coptic painting was subject to outside influence (Byzantine), its representations (on frescoes, as well as wooden panels and parchment and paper manuscripts) are characterised by a sense of life peculiar to them ; they also have great humility. As regards the ivory representations which can be seen in the cases, they took Hellenistic motifs as a model.

Room XIV : Coptic woodwork. Numerous examples attest to a unique mastery of woodwork, particularly in turning, sculpture and inlay destined for doors, screens, etc., but also for furniture, cult instruments, boxes, chairs and episcopal thrones which often had inlays of wood or ivory.

Rooms XV and XVI : Coptic metalwork. Note chiefly the sacred objects which are decorated with finely cut or chiselled Christian motifs.

Room XVII : Collections of manuscripts dating to the period from the IVth to XIIIth centuries ; many come from Coptic monasteries and are enhanced with coloured miniatures ; the Gospel written in Arabic can also be seen. The codex of a Gnostic library of the II-IIIrd century should be noted particularly ; it has contributed much to knowledge of the origins of Christianity (it was found in 1945).

Room XVIII : works in stone and marble, fragments, capitals, columns, etc.

Court : funerary stelae, some very simple with an inscription, others more refined with the appearance of funerary chapels with a stylised temple façade, rarely decorated with representations. All the stelae date to a long period between the IVth and the XVIIIth centuries. The stairs leading to the upper floor are in the court.

In the rooms of the *upper floor* there are more wood carvings, chiefly from churches and monasteries, admirable pieces because of the rare character of their sculptured decoration.

Room XXVI : pretty collection of toys often ingeniously designed, many pieces are coloured in a lively manner.

Rooms XXVII and XXVIII : glass and pottery.

The visit to this museum shows clearly that Coptic art is chiefly popular art ; and also that it is very difficult to ascertain the names of the artists who created the works.

After the museum, turn to the right to follow *Mari Girgis* street which leads directly to

Amr Mosque, the most ancient and in fact the first mosque of Cairo, founded in 642 by *Amr Ibn el-As*, the general-in-chief of the caliph Omar. After that, it was the subject of numerous enlargements, and it was ravaged in 1169 by a fire and the sultan Saladin reconstructed it. A century later, it was an earth tremor which destroyed the monument again. The mosque was once again

restored and enlarged and, up to the XVIIIth century, it was preserved in a good state, but since then it has fallen into disrepair and it is only used once a year, on the last Friday of Ramadan, for a divine service. Important restoration work is however in progress. The entrance is near the minaret. Among the liwans

which surround the court ; the one at the east, with its side naves is the best preserved. There were 365 columns in the prayer room of which nearly 200 are preserved ; they gain attention because they come from Roman, Byzantine or Coptic buildings. All the columns reach the height of the prayer room because of different base heights. Two column bases with deep crevices are found near the tomb of the son of Amr, Abdullah. Legend tells that the fervent abasings of gravely ill believers marked these columns. Near the minbar, a column of white veined marble is surrounded by a metal railing. According to a story, it was supposed to have been miraculously transported from Medina where the caliph Omar ordained it with the cut of a whip ; the white veins in the stone are the imprints of Omar's whip and they indicate the names of Allah, Mohammed and Suliman. In the western liwan a double column stands. Only those who creep past them will one day go to heaven. It is also said that the very deep well in the court is connected underground to the sacred Zem-Zem fountain in Mecca. These are popular beliefs and legends such as may be found in all the mosques.

Towards the east of the mosque the

Ruins of Fustât are situated, which was once the « most beautiful town in Egypt » with its gardens, terraces, suspended gardens, markets, monuments and public baths. Its tall houses, sometimes with seven floors, formed an urban unity which was reinforced by thick walls and fortified gates. In 1168, when the Christians led by king *Amalric I* advanced up to the town from Jerusalem, the great vizier Shawar ordered the town to be burnt rather than have it fall intact into the hands of the Christians ; the fire lasted 54 days. For fifty years, the ruins of the town have been the subject of archaeological excavation. Now, the plans of some roads and monuments can be easily restored. All the important works of art have been transferred to the Museum of Islamic Art and the Coptic Museum (sometimes Fustât is called the « Arab Pompeii » with, however, some exaggeration).

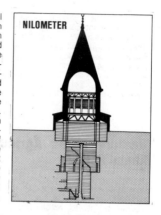

NILOMETER

In returning towards the Nile, in the quarter situated between Fustât and the Mosque of Amr, note particularly the pottery in the potters' quarter called *el-Qulla*. Long necked vases are made there besides water-jars with bulbous shapes. For these, about 60 kilns are in use (5,000 pots per kiln) and they are fuelled with wood, maize waste or cane sugar remnants. The ashes which are mixed with the clay serve to produce the required porosity which allows water to be kept fresh in the vessel (the potteries can be visited and examples purchased).

Now you return towards the Nile and there you hire a boat or take a ferry to reach the south point of *Rôda* island and

The Nilometer [44]. Before the construction of the Great Aswan dam which has modified the hydrology of the river, when the waters of the Nile attained their greatest height (second half of August), the Nilometer was used to measure the flood

and it was accomplished there with very ancient rites (now fallen into disuse). A decorated boat carrying important dignitaries arrived there. A doll was thrown into the river, called the « fiancée of the Nile » in order to render the inundation propitious.

The priests of ancient Egypt had measured the height of the Nile with various instruments and by means of fixed nilometers constructed on the banks of the river. The normal height of the water for agricultural work had to be 14 *cubits*, but it could reach 18 cubits at high water. In their turn, the Arabs installed several nilometers because, as previously, tax was calcutated partly after the rise of the water. *Amr Ibn el-As* constructed three nilometers at Aswan, Dendera and Helwan.

When the nilometer at Helwan fell into ruin, a new one was built on Rôda island.

This nilometer is formed of a square well in which three openings let in the water. The octagonal column which rises in the centre is graduated and is 9.18 m (30 ft.) high. Kufic inscriptions permitted the levels to be read. It is possible to go down into the well by means of steps. The water ducts are now sealed ; the well is covered with a cupola of Arab style. Now the exact level of the water is

read on the exterior of the nilometer on a scale on which however the former graduations are used.

In the small *El-Monasterli palace,* constructed in the Turkish rococo style of the XIXth century, an instructive exhibition on the theme of the Nile flood can be visited (inquire about conditions of entry).

Itinerary n° 9 : Agricultural Museum-Zoo - Manial Palace

From *Tahrir* square, cross the south point of *Gezira island* and go over *el-Galaa* bridge to reach *Doqqi* quarter ; then turn to the right by *Kassab* street up to the

Agricultural Museum [45] which, standing in a pretty park, exhibits a rich collection divided in several buildings. The objects are classified under a *pharaonic section* (agriculture, surveying, hunting weapons, tools, etc.), *Sudanese rooms* (weapons, tools, objects of copper and ivory, etc.) and in a section concerned with statistics and graphs where models show the improvement of the soil, means of irrigation and the development of the cultivation of cotton and cane sugar. A fairly communicative group of objects is formed by the life size models which reconstitute certain scenes of peasant life (village life, weddings, markets, cafés) ; all these scenes are composed of authentic pieces and the costumes are those of different parts of the country. Twelve other rooms are devoted to agriculture and domestic animals, but also to wild animals, reptiles, insects, butterflies and fish of the Mediterranean and the Red

Sea. A very comprehensive library completes the collection.

Now returning to the south, cross *Tharuart* street and enter the area of the University, continuing to the

Zoological Garden [46]. This zoo contains almost the largest collection of African animals (among others) ; it was installed in a part of the gardens of *Ismail.* The scene there is characterised by grottos, benches of petrified wood (from the eastern desert) and paths made of coloured pebbles. On the *tea* island *(Gezira el-Shai),* there is a pleasant cafeteria. Metal bridges give access to the artificial hills.

On leaving the zoo, turn towards the *University bridge (Kubri el-Gamaa).* Before crossing over it, you can visit the *Papyrus Institute* on the left bank, where papyrus is still made according to the techniques of the ancient Egyptians (samples can be purchased, with or without decoration, and they can be inscribed with the text of your choice). After having crossed the bridge onto *Rôda* island again, continue right up to

Manial Palace [47], constructed from 1805-1818 by *Muhammed Ali* and occupied up to the Revolution by members of the royal family. The architecture and the interior installations give a good idea of the luxury which was admired by the Egyptian notables during the XIXth century. The palace also offers rich examples of the neo-Ottoman art-work of the period. It also houses a museum containing interesting pieces of pottery as well as objects of wood from Asia Minor dating to the XIVth-XVth centuries. The numerous ceilings of wood or stucco should be mentioned, a niche of Moroccan style in the reception room (XIXth century), another decorated with columns in the Blue Room and chiefly a ceiling of Byzantine-Turkish style in the Gilded Salon (private entry) with wooden decoration and gilded stucco. Several beautiful eastern carpets can also be seen. Other than its museum, the Manial Palace houses a French holiday club in the middle of its superb gardens ; entry is reserved to members.

Leaving *Rôda* island by *Manial* bridge, take the Nile cornice, on the east bank of the river, which leads to *el-Tahrir square* (very beautiful view over the Nile and the modern city, also over the islands).

ENVIRONS OF CAIRO

Excursion n° 1 : Heliopolis

(see map p. 160)

From *el-Tahrir square*, take a taxi up to Matariya (the train line called « metro » also goes there, but the service is infrequent).

At the west of the railway line, near a canal, stands the solitary obelisk of Sesostris I. It marks the emplacement of the temple of the sun god of *Heliopolis*, famous in antiquity. In this city, from the Ist dynasty, the sun cult of *Re* took on considerable importance, alongside that of the god *Atum.* The sun could also take the form of *Re-Harakhty* (Re-Horus of the horizon), or of *Khepri* (in the aspect of a scarab). At Heliopolis, Re could also be incarnate in the phoenix or in the Mnevis bull. Different forms of goddesses related to Hathor were also the object of cults. The city marked the site of the creation of the world according to a very well known tradition which in fact has very ancient origins ; it played a special role in the idea of monarchy. These reasons explain why many of the gods of other towns were associated with Re (such as Amun-Re). It was at Heliopolis that the divine college of the *ennead* was particularly worshipped.

Of the great sun temple dating to the Middle Kingdom, practically nothing remains beside the obelisk of Sesostris I, some blocks of granite and mounds of rubbish. Everything was taken down and destroyed (often some time later) and the stones were re-used elsewhere. There is still much to be excavated however. There is reason to believe that the site of a great city may be found here and above all a great intellectual and religious centre (the greatest Greek thinkers went to stay there, attracted

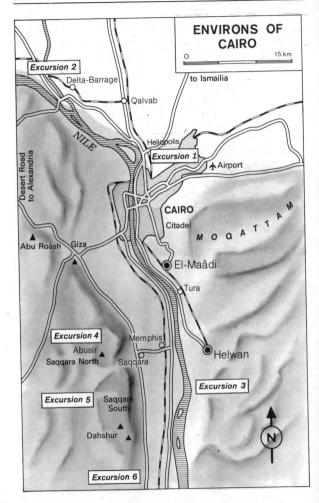

ENVIRONS OF CAIRO

0 ⊢——————————⊣ 15 km

Excursion 2

Delta-Barrage

to Ismailia

Qalvab

NILE

Heliopolis

Excursion 1

Desert Road to Alexandria

✈ Airport

CAIRO

Citadel

M O Q A T T A M

Abu Roâsh ▲

Giza

▲

◉ El-Maâdi

Tura

Excursion 4

Memphis

Abusir ▲

Saqqara North   Saqqara

◉ Helwan

Excursion 5

Saqqara South ▲

Excursion 3

Dahshur ▲   ▲

N

Excursion 6

by the prestige of the Heliopolitan priesthood).

The obelisk still in place (it has simply been better mounted recently) is a monolith of pink granite (mounted on a modern concrete stand) which came from Aswan. It is a little less than 20 m (65½ ft.) high and its point, the pyramidion, was once, without doubt, capped with gold. On its four faces, similar inscriptions mention royal titles and protocol and record the jubilee at which the monument was erected. It was only a few centuries ago that the obelisk was still standing and the ruins of the temple were still impressive. It is possible on the other hand that some obelisks from Heliopolis were transported to Rome during antiquity, because the town served as a quarry for the Roman emperors.

The town of Heliopolis was called *Iwnw* in Egyptian (and *On* in the Bible where it is mentioned several times) and it extended over a wide area. Only a few sparse ruins are left to testify to its grandeur. An enclosure containing an old dead tree can be seen at Matariya, a more or less lively site. It is called the *Virgin's Tree*. Indeed in this place there seems to have always been a tree (sycamore) which was always the object of a cult. With Christianity, this tree became the object of specific legends according to which the Holy Family rested under its shade. The tree which is there now dates to the XVIIth century ; it succeeded another, more ancient tree. The site was once a place of pilgrimage, but it is visited much less today.

In the neighbourhood of Matariya, the new town of Heliopolis is found, which was founded by Baron Empain and a Belgian company in 1905. It has undergone a rapid enlargement and now it is really only a residential district of Cairo. The international airport and the university of *Ain Shams* are in the immediate vicinity.

Excursion n° 2 : Nile Barrage

(See map p. 160)

This excursion can be accomplished in several ways. The most simple is to take a taxi from the centre of town to reach the site of the barrage directly going along the right bank of the river towards the north, (as if you were departing for Alexandria by the « agricultural route »). The journey is about 25 km (15½ mi.). A more pleasant, but less simple way of access, is obviously to go by boat. Steamships leave regularly from *Embabah bridge* in the *Rôd el-Farag*

quarter (timetables available in the principal tourist agencies). It is also possible to get there by making an arrangement with the owner of a feluka (from in front of *Shepheard's Hotel* for example) and sail there with him.

The *barrage*, a strong device which once served as a retainer and lock gate, is situated at the place where the Nile divides in two branches and it was used to regularise the level of the flood up stream and so irrigate the Delta more efficiently. The construction was started about 1835 under *Muhammed Ali* and it was finished in 1861. Various technical reasons made it necessary to use reinforcements and consolidate it from 1885 to 1890, and again in 1909. A second barrage was constructed to the north of the first. The whole structure allowed different canals to be filled. The barrage is double. The one which bars the *eastern arm*, the *Damietta*, is the longest, it measures 522 m (1712 ft.) and has 68 arches. The barrage of the *Rosetta arm* is 452 m (1483 ft.) and has 58 arches. With the aid of this Delta barrage it is possible to irrigate an area of about 35 million feddans.

On the island which separates the two parts of the barrage, pleasant gardens were installed (cafés). A small museum relating to irrigation and the barrages can be visited.

Excursion n° 3 : Helwan.

(See map p. 160)

You can reach Helwan most comfortably by taking a taxi. If you wish to travel in the most economic way, it is still possible to take a train (30 minutes) which leaves regularly from *Bab el-Lûq* station, very near *el-Tahrir* square. It is absolutely imperative to avoid the rush hours. Whatever means of transport is used, the itinerary remains virtually the same (with a taxi however you travel along the east bank of the Nile where there is a magnificent view). *Maâdi* is at about 12 km (8 miles). It is a very pleasant, residential suburb because the houses are fairly isolated in the middle of magnificent gardens full of plants. A walk in the calm of Maâdi is the perfect solution to forget the noise of Cairo for a time. Further to the east, there is the desert of Moqattam with its *wadis* (dry river beds). Very important Egyptian prehistoric remains were found at Maâdi. After Maâdi, you arrive at *Tura*. It is in the great cliffs which border the village that the limestone quarries are found where the Egyptians extracted the blocks which were used, among other things, for the casing of the pyramids. Soon after, the black smoke of the industrial complex of Helwan can be seen.

Helwan (60,000 inhabitants). In 968, the governor *Abd el-Aziz Ibn Marun* took the waters here for his health. The town had received its name from another *Helwan*, in Iraq, where sulphur waters also gush. The ferruginous quality of the water had no doubt caused the re-naming of the site at the end of antiquity, as well as the dry and healthy nature of its climate.

The town lies at an altitude of 85 m (278 ft.), at some distance from the Nile on the desert plateau. The khedive *Ismail* and particularly his son, *Taufiq*, established its status and encouraged its construction. By means of transported soil, a type of oasis and a town of rectilinear roads and numerous parks were created. The thermal bath-house was built in 1899 in Moorish style. With the development of the town, hospitals, hotels, baths and a casino were built and a *Japanese garden* was arranged. But Helwan suffered a progressive decline which accelerated as time passed and the town has lost much of its thermal and holiday character. It must be stated that since 1950, a very heavy industrial complex has been developed near Helwan, unique in Egypt as well as in the Near-East. The steelworks are particularly important. The town therefore has a new destiny, very different to the old one.

From *Helwan observatory* situated on the mountain chain which dominates the town (inquire about the possibilities of access), there is a very good view over the site and its surroundings and, further on, over the Nile up to Saqqara and Memphis which are opposite on the other bank of the river.

There is also a small *waxworks museum* in the town with dolls from every province.

From *Helwan*, it is possible to go (perhaps on horseback) up to *Wadi Gerraui* (11 km (7 mi.) to the south-east) where the remains of an ancient retaining barrage can be visited dating to antiquity (Old Kingdom) which was used to retain the water necessary to the quarry workers (discovered by G. Schweinfurth).

Excursion n° 4 : Memphis and North Saqqara

(See map p. 160)

There are several ways of visiting the sites of Memphis and Saqqara according to taste and possibility. The area can be reached by train and then a mount can be hired ; the whole journey can be made in a taxi or a car ; finally the enthusiast may like to make this excursion from Giza by horse or camel. The complete tour with the return to Cairo is about 50 km (31 mi.) with the various visits, a whole day must be taken to complete it (take a packed meal).

A : By train
Cairo is soon left by the principal station situated in *Ramesses square*. A statue of Ramesses II stands in the centre of the square which came from Memphis ; it is 10 m (33 ft.) high and is carved in Aswan granite. The king's name is incised on the shoulder and on the girdle in a cartouche. The train crosses the Nile on *Embaba bridge*, then crosses the suburb of the same name where Bonaparte vanquished the Mamelukes on the 21st of July, 1798 at the « Battle of the Pyramids ». After *Giza* station, you will see the pyramids on the right and, on the opposite bank, *Moqattam*. A little further on, at the edge of the desert, are the pyramids of *Abusir*. Opposite is *Gebel Tura*, and further on, the site of *Helwan*. Leave the train at *El-Badrashein*. It is possible to obtain a taxi in front of the station or a mount (donkey or horse). An ascending route is then followed to reach the palm groves of *Memphis* which will take less than half an hour.

B : By car
If you do not take a bus excursion or an organised tour, the best way by

car is to follow the Pyramid road up to *Giza*. When the last canal is reached, cross over a bridge and turn left, or better still, follow the last but one canal (pleasant and well asphalted road) and reach *El-Badrashein* or *Saqqara* (best way of reaching the site). Once there you can hire a mount, but a visit combining a car and walking will ensure that no delight is missed.

C : Horseback across the desert

Preference is given to this itinerary (which demands however good physical condition and no fear of fatigue) because for the tourist it forms a permanent memory and because it

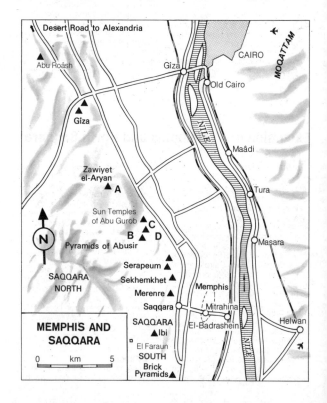

Desert Road to Alexandria

CAIRO

MOQATTAM

Abu Roâsh

Gîza

Old Cairo

Gîza

NILE

Maâdi

Zawiyet
el-Aryan
A

Tura

Sun Temples
of Abu Gurob
C
B
D

N

Masara

Pyramids of Abusir

Serapeum

SAQQARA
NORTH

Sekhemkhet

Memphis

Merenre

Saqqara
Mitrahina
El-Badrashein

Helwan

SAQQARA
Ibi
SOUTH
El Faraun

**MEMPHIS AND
SAQQARA**

NILE

Brick
Pyramids

0   km   5

permits a certain number of pyramids and temples to be seen where access would otherwise be difficult (but it is also possible to make an extensive tour of these from Memphis).

In the caravanserai situated near to *Mena House Hotel*, hire a camel, or rather a horse, or even a donkey, and get a guide to accompany you (one who shows his licence beforehand). The guide will be able to look after the animals when you visit the monuments. It will cost at least £3 E per person (without counting the tip). As it is necessary to anticipate having food and drink at *Mariette's House* at Saqqara, independence may be more expensive than with an organised tour by bus ; but the increased pleasure which will be gained will amply compensate for the difference.

In fact, it should be stressed that a long tour on camel-back may be very tiring because the animal's walk is extremely supple and it produces a type of pitch and roll. Finally, you do not sit on a camel as on a horse, but place your feet on the camel's neck. If the camel proves to be too painful, you can always borrow the guide's horse or donkey to return. Besides this, do not forget to take with you a good torch which you will certainly have need of in the temples and tombs which are not always well lit.

From *Giza*, you follow the border of the desert with your mount and catch sight of the villages which border the left side of the neighbouring canal. After a ride of less than an hour across the desert, the mound of debris which is the pyramid of

Zawiyet el-Aryan [A] is reached, the remains of the stone pyramid of Khaba of the IIIrd dynasty. There is

nothing particular to see here ; the area is often forbidden for military reasons (in that case, make a diversion around it with your mount).

After about 30 minutes more,

Abu Gurob [B] is reached, the solar temple of *Nyuserre* of the Vth dynasty. There is not very much left of the valley temple, the rising causeway, the walls, the doors and the barque. But in the vast court of 100 × 75 m (328 × 246 ft.) is the central element of the cult : the solar obelisk of masonry (the lower part of

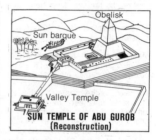

SUN TEMPLE OF ABU GUROB (Reconstruction)

the construction is partly preserved), as well as a large alabaster altar of 5,5 × 6 m (18 × 19 ½ ft.). From the place where the animals were offered in sacrifice, channels took the blood away to ten alabaster tanks, nine of which are preserved. The reliefs which decorated the monument are found in Cairo Museum and chiefly in Berlin.

A little further south (500 m = 547 yd.) there is the solar temple of

Userkaf [C] also of the Vth dynasty and originally almost identical to that of *Nyuserre*, but little can be recognised now from its miserable ruins. A portrait of the king in black stone found here is exhibited in the Egyptian Museum (ground floor).

Abusir [D]. A group of pyramids stand here dating to the Vth dynasty, belonging to the kings *Sahure, Nyuserre, Neferirkare,* and *Neferefre* (in that order from north to south). All the pyramids are enormous mounds of debris, desolate and badly invaded by sand ; the interior chambers cannot be visited. It should be noted that the pyramid of *Neferirkare* was once the highest of all with its height of 70 m (230 ft.) and that *Neferirkare's* causeway was curved in and annexed by the later king *Nyuserre* to his own pyramid.

Between the pyramids of *Sahure* and *Nyuserre* the

Mastaba of Ptahshepses is situated, also of the Vth dynasty ; it is still being excavated by a Czechoslovakian mission. Twenty pillars support the ceiling of the great hall ; behind, in a small chamber, there are columns with lotiform capitals. In the chamber there are different reliefs on which can be seen scenes of a market, craftsmen at work and the dead man accompanied by his wife.

For all those who take this excursion by train or by car, the visit begins at *Memphis.* From there, it is usual to visit *Saqqara* and the necropolis area up to the Serapeum − clockwise − in such a way that the rider will find easy to reconcile with our description ; or even, and this is perhaps more advantageous, ride up to *Saqqara* and there commence, after a short rest, a complete tour such as is described here : Memphis-Step Pyramid-Pyramid of Unas-Unfinished Pyramid-Mastaba of Ptahhotep-Serapeum-Mastaba of Ti-Mastaba of Mereruka-Mastabas situated in the northern necropolis.

MEMPHIS

At the division between Upper and Lower Egypt, the brilliant town of Memphis was formerly situated, for a long time the capital of Egypt and always one of its principal cities. Only an immense field of debris and a few glorious ruins of some buildings remain. Everything was demolished and destroyed in the later centuries. But the present impression should not induce misunderstanding. This once gigantic field of debris was, throughout the centuries, a heavily spoiled quarry which was used to construct palaces, mosques, houses and public walls in Cairo. Then, what remained began to be eroded by the infiltration waters and to be engulfed by the inhabited area. Archaeological research in the region has allowed the grandeur of ancient Memphis to be reconstructed in theory from the existing ruins ; they have enabled its evolution to be traced from the legendary Menes, the founder of the 1st dynasty, from Thinis near to Abydos, who united Upper and Lower Egypt under his rule and made Memphis his residence, excellently situated at « the balance of the two lands ». The principal temple was that of Ptah, in the neighbourhood in which the pharaoh resided ; this fortress was commonly called the « White Wall ».

During the Old Kingdom (2780-2270 B.C.), when the pharaohs of the third to fourth dynasties reigned, Memphis knew one of its principal periods of glory. It was both the economic and political centre. Most of the social and moral currents spread from there through the country, as well as some abstract and strongly advanced religious ideas. Therefore the town of *Men-nefer* became more

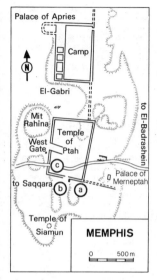

Palace of Apries

Camp

El-Gabri

Mit Rahina

Temple of Ptah

West Gate

to Saqqara

ⓒ

ⓑ ⓐ

Palace of Merneptah

Temple of Siamun

to El-Badrashein

MEMPHIS

0   500 m

and more celebrated, to the extent that its reputation was to pass into the Greek world under the name of *Memphis*.

The very favourable position of the town from a strategic point of view ensured that it would always remain the most important garrison centre in Egypt, even when the kings of the Middle Kingdom and New Kingdom took their residence elsewhere to the south, or even to the north. This was the reason why, in spite of the fame of Thebes, Amarna or Pi-Ramesses, Memphis never ceased to be a city of the first importance. And also, in the Late Period, under the Greeks as well as the Romans,

it remained the heart of Egypt (beside Greek Alexandria). It is not surprising, in these conditions, that so many foreigners took Memphis, even for a short period, (Hyksos, Assyrians, Persians, Greeks) when they coveted Egypt. And Herodotus in his History tells of Phoenician merchants, Carian and Greek soldiers and other foreigners whom he had met in the streets of the town; in the religious sphere, although Ptah remained the principal god, Syrian divinities such as Baal and Astarte also had their cult places there.

Even if this capital which was almost indestructible has perished, the dead remain in their necropolises to continue to tell of its glory; because there, in the Memphite funerary area, particularly of Saqqara, several kings and innumerable inhabitants of the town found their last resting places.

On the left of the route from *Badrashein,* in a palm grove and a little before the village of *Mit Rahina,* the

Alabaster sphinx [a] is found. It was discovered in 1912. Its right side, on which it lay for more than a thousand years in the wet earth, exhibits a certain state of disintegration. But the nobility of the portrait and its very suggestive smile have not suffered through the passing of time, or through the destructive hand of man. It is generally thought that the sphinx represents a king of the XVIIIth dynasty (perhaps Amenophis II). It is 8 m (26 ft.) long, 4,25 m (14 ft.) high and weighs about 80 tons. Once it stood in front of the south entrance of the *temple of Ptah.* A stone stela with a decree of the king *Apries* of the XXVIth dynasty was found here according to which the temple was free of certain obligations.

In a special building lies a statue commonly called

colossal [b] ; it is a powerful limestone statue representing *Ramesses II* which once certainly stood in front of the temple entrance between the sphinxes of the avenue. An example of the taste of this king for monumental expression is shown here. The statue was originally 13.5 m (42 ft.) high, but it is only 10.30 m (34 ft) high now because the legs and the crown are missing. There are royal cartouches incised on the chest and girdle ; in the girdle there is a dagger with two finely carved falcon heads. Another colossal statue of Ramesses II in granite, found in the area, was taken to Cairo in 1954 and exhibited in the station square (see p. 163). Between the legs of that statue, a relief of Ramesses' wife *Bent-Anath* is carved.

To end the tour, a little further along to the right on the road which leads to Saqqara, visit the ruins where several

embalming tables [c] are found, one of which is very well preserved and is situated at the north-east angle of the walls. This table, used for the embalming of the Apis bulls, is carved from a beautiful block of alabaster, and has the following dimensions : 5.40 × 3.07 × 1.!0 m (18 × 10 × 4 ft.). It is decorated with lion heads and a deep channel allowed the body fluids to be collected and allowed them to flow out below. It weighs about 50 tons. It probably dates to the XXVIth dynasty.

There is practically nothing else to see of ancient Memphis. Only very ruined accumulations of stones give an idea of the site of *the temple of Ptah, the temple of the Apis, the royal palace of Merneptah* and that

of *Apries*, all situated more or less north of the sphinx and the colossal statue.

Follow the route again and cross the last canal to reach the limit of the cultivated land and enter the desert to come to the plateau of Saqqara, the principal necropolis of Memphis.

NORTH SAQQARA

In the larger sense, the name of the village of *Saqqara* in fact designates the vast necropolis, almost 7 km (4½ mi.) long, of ancient Memphis. The name has an origin which is still a little obscure. It is admitted now that, as well as recalling the name of the god of the dead, *Sokaris*, the name comes from a tribe which was once installed there. All periods of Egyptian history are represented at the site, from the most ancient periods

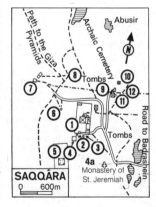

SAQQÂRA
0   600m

up to the Greeks and Romans and even later with the ruins of the *Coptic Monastery of St. Jeremiah*, therefore offering a complete view of the history of Egyptian art. The monuments of *south Saqqara* are described in our excursion n° 5 (see p. 177 on).

Today, the central point of the necropolis and at the same time the first monument to be visited is the

Step Pyramid of Djoser [1]. It dates to about 2,700 B.C., to the time of the IIIrd dynasty, and was constructed for the king *Djoser*.

The architect and the master of the work was the king's famous vizier, the sage, *Imhotep* who was afterwards deified ; with this monument he became the instigator of stone building in Egypt. Throughout Egyptian history, Imhotep was renowned for his divine wisdom. Unfortunately his writings are lost and his tomb, searched for actively for several years, has still not been found. In the Late Period he became a god of healing and was assimilated with the Greek Asklepios. Throughout Egypt, chapels were built in his honour.

The tomb of king Djoser was originally conceived as one of the bench-form mastaba tombs in use up until then. This was enlarged three times, over the mastaba, and it eventually became a square four-sided pyramid. Finally, this construction was extended to become a mastaba with six steps, the « step pyramid », the base of which was rectangular. All the stones form layers, inclined at certain places. But, at the same time, it is possible to see the different building stages on the southern and eastern faces. With this construction, Imhotep abandoned the ancient wooden buildings and techniques based on the use of simple bricks. But details in the stone recall, in a very stylized way, constructions in brick and wood, or rush and reed buildings.

The pyramid complex is larger here than anywhere else. The pyramid stands almost in the centre of a rectangle of 555 × 278 m (607 × 304 yd.) which is surrounded by an enclosure wall 10 m (33 ft.) high. It is decorated with recesses and fourteen false doors. The entrance is on the south of the east wall. There, the vast court of the pyramid is entered by passing through a colonnade. An immense work of restoration has been going on for many years under the direction of the French architect of the Egyptian Antiquities Service, J. Ph. Lauer, and this has given the whole complex the appearance which can be seen today.

On the south side of the court, a masonry building is supported by the enclosure wall which is a type of *ka tomb* [a] which protects certain elements essential to the king's personality. It is a mastaba with a sarcophagus ; the funerary chamber is in pink granite, 2.5 m (8 ft.) square at the bottom of a vertical shaft 28 m (92 ft.) deep. A group of buildings fill the court and the space between the pyramid and the wall (the right = the east), beyond the entrance colonnade. There are three interior courts ; one with chapels for the celebration of the royal jubilee (the festival of *heb-sed*), the two others with religious buildings consisting of the « House of the South » [b] (for Upper Egypt) and the « House of the North » [c] (for Lower Egypt) ; these are symbolic buildings, of solid masonry, originally covered and supported by fine gracious columns.

The *pyramid* itself has a rectangular plan (109 × 121 m (357½ × 397 ft.). Each « step » is 2 m (6½ ft.) wide and the height varies between 8.40 m (27½ ft.) to 10.10 m (33 ft.). All the stones are laid horizontally (layers sometimes inclined) ; they are restrained in size as if they were bricks, with a height of about 25 cm (10 in.). It is only in the subsequent constructions that the larger sizes known elsewhere were attained.

In front of the north face, the ruins of the funerary temple can be seen, destined for the actual ritual cult [d].

By means of three holes cut in the stone it is possible to see the representation of the pharaoh's *ka* in the form of a very beautiful limestone statue ; the closed structure in which it was found is the *serdab*. The original statue is in the Egyptian Museum (see p. 125) (a replica sits in the serdab), as well as all the finds from the complex corridors of the subterranean tomb and from the chambers situated 32 m (105 ft.) deep. Some chambers of the south tomb were partly cased in tiles of blue faience imitating mural hangings made of reeds, sometimes in patterns.

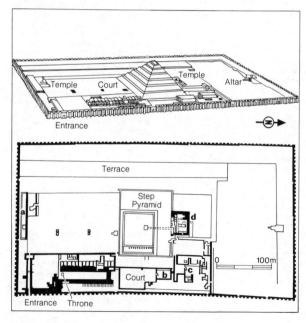

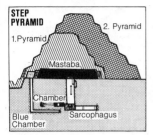

In this complex, the enclosure wall is equally remarkable with its different and numerous features which recall ancient architecture in wood and brick. Also, on the *House of the North,* the fluted columns imitating wood and the stone ceilings carved to resemble log rafters may be´mentioned ; and the engaged columns of the *House of the South ;* on the outer walls of the mass of the south tomb, notice the beautiful wall with a *frieze of cobras.*

From this wall with cobras and turning towards the south, the

Persian tombs [2] can now be visited. They are 25 m (82 ft.) deep. The sarcophagi were found at the bottom of a very deep shaft (descend by an iron staircase). The three tombs are those of important people of the Persian period (XXVIIth dynasty) ; they communicated with one another. Their decoration recalls that of the Old Kingdom.

North of the Persian tombs is the

Mastaba of Princess Idut [3]. This mastaba was originally constructed for a vizier of the end of the Vth dynasty, but it was then re-used for the princess *Seshseshet,* also called *Idut* (the first inscriptions were not always corrected). Five of the ten chambers are decorated with pain-

ted reliefs in lively colours. Idut is represented during a sail on a boat in the Nile marshes, accompanied by fishermen and harpooners ; the usual scene is depicted with the presence of fish, crocodiles, hippopotami, etc., in the river.

Very near, at the east, is the *mastaba of Mekhu* which merits a visit because of its well preserved paintings. But it is generally only opened for specialists.

The Pyramid of Unas [4]. The funerary monument of the last king of the Vth dynasty was originally 44 m (144 ft.) high ; its plan was a square of 67 m (220 ft) each side. In contrast to the Step Pyramid, a visit to the funerary chamber is possible here. From the entrance, situated on the north, a corridor is followed, which was blocked by means of three granite portcullises, and an antechamber is reached, on the left side of which is the statue room or serdab (three niches, flat ceiling) and, on the right, the sarcophagus chamber. The latter has a ceiling with two points which surmounts the granite sarcophagus. The rooms are completely covered in hieroglyphic texts arranged in columns and painted blue. These constitute the first appearance of the « Pyramid Texts », a collection of funerary texts which were supposed to allow the dead pharaoh to face the after-life and to triumphantly rejoin heaven

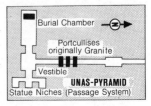

and the sun. This result is attained by the collection of religious or magic formulae on the walls. These texts were to know a great use during the VIth dynasty. In leaving the pyramid, the complex of the associated buildings can still be seen. These include some reliefs from the lateral walls of the causeway (only 2.60 m (8 ½ ft.) wide) which connected the valley temple (destroyed) to the funerary temple ; they have been discovered and partly replaced on the walls. Notice the very lifelike scene of the transport of great stone columns for temple decoration by boat, or the market scene, craftsmen at work, soldiers, hunting scenes, etc.

Tomb of Horemhed [4a]. Rediscovered in 1975, this is the Memphite tomb of the general Horemheb, who became king at the end of Dynasty XVIII (the tomb may not yet be visited). The royal tomb of Horemheb s in the Valley of the Kings at Thebes (see p. 230).

Pyramid of Sekhemkhet [5]. This is on the south-west of the Pyramid of Unas and is generally described as the « unfinished pyramid », because the building was apparently abandoned when it was only a few metres (yards) high. It was destined for *Sekhemkhet,* without doubt a successor of king Djoser. It is not surprising that the general plan is fairly close to that of the Step Pyramid. This is also the case for the great wall which encloses the pyramid complex, but with differences in the masonry and in the use of limestone ; it is to some extent an imitation, but much poorer than the original. At the end of a long descent of 75 m (246 ft.), at a depth of about thirty metres (98 ft.), there is the sarcophagus chamber where an empty alabaster sarcophagus was found. A small collection of jewellery found in

a gallery is now in the Egyptian Museum.

At the north of this complex, at a fair distance, almost on the axis of the pyramid court, there is the

Mastaba of Ptahhotep [6] of the VIth dynasty. The noble *Akhtihotep* built this structure for himself and his son, *Ptahhotep.* It is given the name of the « mastaba of Ptahhotep » however because the part reserved for the latter surpasses the other's part in its beauty and decoration. Cross the antechamber (reliefs finish half way) and enter the pillared hall and, in continuing, the chapel of Akhtihotep. On the west wall, two false doors can be seen with an offering table : on the east wall, scenes in the papyrus thickets : Akhtihotep is seen engaged in various activities ; on the side walls, the dead man assists at the presentation of offerings.

The chapel of *Ptahhotep* is found in the south part of the mastaba. The reliefs exhibit a remarkable technique and their colours are still very well preserved. On the *west wall,* Ptahhotep is seated between two

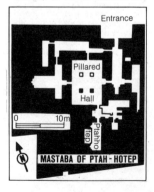

MASTABA OF PTAH-HOTEP

false doors ; in front is a richly furnished table of offerings with every type of victual ; servants carry offerings. *East wall :* Ptahhotep assists at the activities of daily life which take place before him (the representations are arranged in seven horizontal registers). *North wall* (around the door) : Ptahhotep listens to musicians play while seated at his morning toilet. *South wall :* various activities (representations of animals, wrestling, etc.).

Passing the vast tent where refreshments can be ordered, turn towards the north-west (you will see a modern wall built on the site of the old « Mariette's House ») and reach the

Serapeum [7]. In 1850-1, Mariette discovered the subterranean galleries with the sarcophagi of the sacred Apis bulls. Indeed, in Egypt, sacred animals were mummified and buried like men. Originally, Apis, who was the focus of a cult at Memphis, was the sacred animal of the god Ptah, the patron of the city ; he was then assimilated with the god Re and the solar disk was placed between his horns. As he was also quickly connected with Osiris, he also became a funerary god.

The death of an Apis was the occasion of great ceremonies ; he was mummified and interred with solemnity ; first placed in a wooden coffin, then in a voluminous granite sarcophagus. Shortly after the funeral, the priests found a young black bull among the herds with a white patch on its forehead, a white cross on its neck and flanks and a knot on its tongue, then Apis was reborn in his mortal form : celebrations took place. From that time, the bull lived with its mother and the other animals in the sacred enclosure of Memphis ; it was fed with care and drank only pure water.

Only the subterranean corridors of the *Serapeum* are preserved ; all the walls of the superstructure, temples, palaces are virtually all destroyed. Once an avenue of sphinxes led from the cultivated land to the funerary temple of the Serapeum. In the Ptolemaic period (Ptolemy I was particularly responsible for developing the cult of Serapis), a semi-circle was installed with statues of poets and Greek philosophers (*It is very cool in the corridors ; be careful about getting cold ; take a pocket torch*).

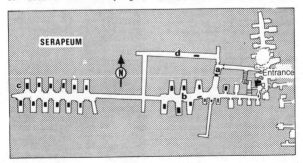

The subterranean galleries are entered today from the east ; the *stelae room [a]* is reached and there on the left the *great gallery [B].* is entered, which is lined in limestone and has a vaulted roof ; measurements : 3 m (9 ½ ft.) wide by 8 m (26 ft.) high and 340 m (372 yd.) long. The sarcophagi stand in large niches to the right and left, most of them are of Aswan granite, pink or black, several are of limestone ; all are very well polished. Each of the 24 sarcophagi is carved from a single monolithic block. The average measurements are : 4 m (13 ft.) long, 2,30 m (7 ft.) wide and 3,30 m (11 ft.) high, each sarcophagus weighs between 65 and 70 tons. Virtually all of them have plain exteriors without decoration ; the last sarcophagus is unique (in black granite) in the gallery on the right [c] because it is decorated and has inscriptions (« Apis son of Osiris ») ; on three others there are names of kings : Amasis, Cambyses and Shabaka. In the *parallel gallery* [d] a unique black granite sarcophagus practically obstructs the passage. Its lid lies on the ground a little further on. All the sarcophagi were broken and robbed ; some objects were however found between them.

From the *rest-house* (refreshments, souvenirs, parking) turn towards the west to the

Mastaba of Ti [8]. This high court official, Ti, lived about 2,500 B.C., under the Vth dynasty, and he held, among other titles, that of administrator of the royal funerary temples. This great personage owes his renown partly to the artists who decorated his mastaba. The reliefs give us a glimpse of the civilisation of the Old Kingdom, full of detail, which are arranged in an intelligible manner ac-

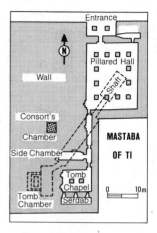

cording to fairly clear guide lines. It is particularly in the well known chapel that all the representations are centred on manifestations of the cult and where all that is profane has a religious meaning.

The best way to visit the tomb is with the two schemes here. Without losing time, the visitor will be able to appreciate the finesse and the delicacy of the detail in spite of the lay-out which is perhaps sometimes a little difficult.

Enter the *pillared court* through the vestibule which, like the entrance, is situated on the north ; the pillars and the wooden ceilings are a modern restoration. This is the place of funerary offerings from which a passage descends obliquely down to the sarcophagus chamber containing the empty sarcophagus of Ti. Notice the opening to the *serdab* on the north wall of the court. The *bas-reliefs* of the pillared court are

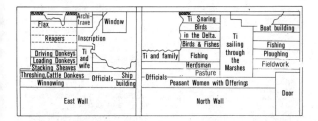

badly obliterated and have partially disappeared. On the right in the vestibule which leads to the chapel, is a false door with Ti and his wife Neferhotep ; in the vestibule there are representations of porters bringing offerings into the deceased's tomb ; further on, sacrificed animals ; then Ti inspects his domain.

In the *side chamber,* the bas-reliefs are also devoted to representations of food offerings. Their permanent presence is explained by the ancient Egyptian conception that the dead depended essentially on the living ; also that their actions in favour of the dead had to be placed in a prominent position for them on all the bas-reliefs. Death was always understood as a prolonging in eternity of life, and that is the reason why the life of the

dead was not to be endangered in his tomb. As in other mastabas, representations are found here of the lively scenes of life, of constantly renewed offerings and opulent feasts.

The *chapel* measures 5 × 7.20 m (16 × 23 ½ ft.) and is 4.50 m (14 ½ ft.) high. Two pillars support it. In the north wall there is a narrow gap which allows light to pass into the serdab : it is the passage for the ka.

Representations appearing on the bas-reliefs :

North : Life in the Delta, peasants, livestock, the daily life of the master, Ti.

East : Ti, feudal noble and his domains.

South : Preparations of the offerings and the offerings themselves.

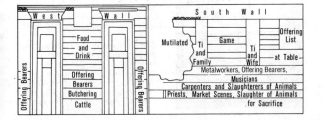

West : Ti in the after-life ; two false doors : the doors which led to life in eternity, orientated towards the subterranean funerary chamber.

Mastaba of Mereruka [9]. This is situated on the east of the *rest-house* near the collapsed pyramid of Teti. The minister *Mereruka* constructed it in the course of the VIth dynasty for himself, his wife, and his son. He is represented immediately at the entrance with his wife, his son and his servants. On the opposite wall, the minister Mereruka traces the deities representing the three seasons on an easel with his palette and colours. The scenes are for the most part the same as in the mastaba of Ti. The variety in the details is surprising, Mereruka is represented throughout with his wife, particularly in the pilla-

MERERUKA
Rooms
of Mereruka
of his wife
of his sons
0   10 m

Store Chambers

Sacrificial Chapel

Shaft to
Tomb Chamber

Pillared Room

Mummy Shaft

Entrance

red room where harem scenes are also found. In the pillared hall (six pillars), notice the stone ring fixed to the floor where the animals for sacrifice were tied to cords. In a niche above the offering table, there is a striding statue of the dead man, the left foot advanced, ready to receive the offerings after the funeral which is represented on the lateral walls with a wealth of detail.

As in the mastabas already visited all the representations are organized in almost the same way in the following adjacent mastabas (at the east), such as the

Mastaba of Kagemni [10], belonging to a minister of the VIth dynasty. It consists of 10 chambers in all, all with bas-reliefs ; the best executed are those in the chamber with three pillars. On the roof of this mastaba (ascending staircase) there were formerly two long chambers (11 m (36 ft.)) for Kagemni's solar barques.

Mastaba of Ankhmahor [11]. In the « tomb of the Physician », named on account of the representations of a scene of circumcision and an orthopaedic operation, notice the difference to the other mastabas ; bloody scenes of butchery, evisceration ; the stone cutters and other craftsmen. The mastaba also dates to the VIth dynasty and was constructed by the minister Ankhmahor.

The Mastaba of Nefersesshem-ptah [12]. This is the tomb of an official of the Fourth Dynasty. He appears frequently in the reliefs on the walls of his tomb. In the last room the deceased is depicted twice in the false doorway and his bust is seen looking out of the window above.

Excursion n° 5 : South Saqqara and Dahshur

(See map p. 178)
A complete description of both these sites is given below in order to mention the important monuments of the area. However, it should be noted that access to both South Saqqara and Dahshur is strictly regulated and it is difficult to obtain permission to visit this restricted zone. It is necessary to apply in Cairo for a permit.

The visit begins at Memphis and Saqqara as for excursion, n° 4 (see p. 163)

On leaving Saqqara, it is best to follow the last canal on the desert edge travelling towards the south. On the west lie the ruins of the pyramids of Pepi, Merenre and Djedkare Isesi, and a little further to the south those of Ibi and Pepi II. By making a short detour of 250 m. (273 yds) the visitor will arrive at the tomb of Shepseskaf, which is known as the

Mastabat Faraûn [1], the « Grave of Pharaoh ». The tomb is constructed in the form of an immense sar-

cophagus with barrel-vaulting and its outward appearance is particularly striking to the visitor. Although it is similar to the royal tombs of the First and Second Dynasties, it was built by Shepseskaf, the last king of the Fourth Dynasty. It is 18 m. (59 ft.) high and covers an area of 100 × 72 m. (109 × 79 yds.). A causeway led from the valley temple to the entrance in the north face. This no longer exists. From the entrance a horizontal passage leads to the burial chamber and to several storerooms. The walls of these inner chambers are faced with large blocks of granite and are good examples of the architecture of the Fourth Dynasty.

Further to the south on the right are the five pyramids of Dahshur. Three of them are situated at the edge of the desert and the other two lie beyond.

The North Brick pyramid [2],

which is also known as a « Black Pyramid », dates from the Twelfth Dynasty. It was built of bricks made of the black Nile mud. Here was buried Sesostris III, who according to the records and texts was one of the greatest pharaohs in Egyptian history. His empire extended from Nubia to Asia and it was said of him that he « could destroy men without touching them with his scimitar and could fire an arrow without drawing his bow ». His pyramid, which was approximately 65 m. (213 ft.) high when built, was originally faced with limestone from Tura. At the base each side is 105 m. (344 ft.) in length. In the burial chamber and not lying on the main axis of the pyramid was found the huge granite sarcophagus of the King. The vaulted bu-

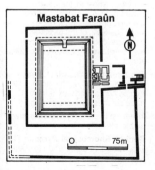

Mastabat Faraûn

N

0   75m.

rial chamber was also constructed of granite. Sesostris III also built himself a cenotaph at Abydos.

The Pyramid of Ammenemes II [3]. This was constructed with blocks of Tura limestone, from which it derived its name — « the White Pyramid », laid over a core of bricks and sand. The royal sarcophagus made of sandstone was found in the burial chamber. This chamber was oriented on an east-west axis and had four niches, two on the south side, one on the east and one on the west. The sarcophagus lay in the western niche. The pyramid is now in a very ruined state.

The South Brick Pyramid [4]. Like the North Brick Pyramid this is constructed of bricks of black Nile mud and is called a « Black Pyramid ». It was the tomb of King Ammenemes III of the Twelfth Dynasty.

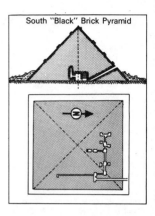

South "Black" Brick Pyramid

At the base each side is almost 105 m. (344 ft.) in length. It was originally faced with blocks of Tura limestone and was 80 m. (262 ft.) high. The entrance was on the east side. Inside a system of passages branches out in different directions. The western passage leads to a small chapel dedicated to Anubis. Eventually the burial chamber is reached. This is situated almost in the centre of the pyramid. In the burial chamber lay the pink granite sarcophagus of the king. The walls of the passages were probably faced with limestone as they were partly blocked with fallen stones.

The three pyramids which have just been described each had a valley temple and a mortuary temple. Only traces of these structures remain.

The most interesting of the pyramids at this site is the

Bent or Rhomboidal Pyramid [5]. This is built of stone and is situated about 1 km. (just over half a mile) to

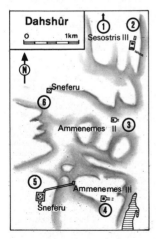

Dahshûr

0   1km

N

Sesostris III ① ②

Sneferu ⊠
⑥

Ammenemes II ⊡ ③

⑤
Ammenemes III
Sneferu ⊠   ⊡ ④

the south of the South Brick Pyramid of Ammenemes III. Neither a sarcophagus nor any other equipment were found in the pyramid. Nevertheless it seems certain that this pyramid, the northern stone pyramid at Dahshur (see p. 180) and the unfinished pyramid at Maidum were all built by King Sneferu of the Fourth Dynasty. The pyramid is called rhomboidal or bent on account of the change in its angle of incline about half way up. The angle of incline decreases from 54° 31' to 43° 21'. It has been suggested that the pyramid was originally planned as a true pyramid, but that it was finished hastily by the height being reduced by the expedient of altering the angle, which also reduced the weight of the upper part.

This suggestion is confirmed by the fact that the stone blocks in the upper part of the pyramid are laid with less care than the lower ones. Much of its outer casing of Tura limestone is well preserved. It is possible to climb up the south-western side. From the top there is a magnificent view of the remains of the causeway and the valley temple and over the pyramid field of Dahshur. This pyramid is unique in that it has two entrances, one on the north and one on the west. These are at different heights in the superstructure and lead to central burial chambers. The passage in the north side starts from 11 m. (36 ft.) above ground-level and leads to two chambers, one below the other. The lower chamber is below ground-level in the rock. It has a magnificent corbelled roof. Below the lower chamber is a vertical blind shaft and, above it is a passage, which is at first horizontal and then ascends to link with the upper chamber and the other passages. The roof of the upper chamber is also corbelled. The plan of the interior was probably intended as a system of protection for the tomb. Stone portcullis blocks were used to seal the access to the passages. These were slid into position as the last workmen left the upper chamber along the passage to the ceiling of the lower chamber.

The other passage starts from the west face at a height of about 34 m. (111 ft.) above ground-level. It descends through the pyramid to ground level and then continues horizontally for a short distance before reaching the upper chamber. The corbelled roof of projecting stone and the framework of cedar wood around the room, imported from Lebanon by Sneferu, are truly remarkable. The total height of the pyramid is 97 m. (318 ft.) and each side of its base measures 189 m. (620 ft.) In front of the east side of the pyramid stood an offering table and two limestone stelae bearing the king's names and titles. To the south of the pyramid, within the stone enclosure wall, stands the subsidiary pyramid. This was 32 m. (105 ft.) high and its sides at the base each measure 55 m. (180 ft.). It has an entrance in the

Place of worship

Subsidiary Pyramid

←Ⓢ→

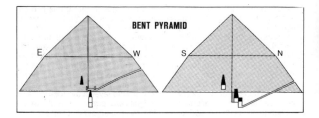

north side, a chapel and a central burial chamber. It was intended as 'the house of eternity' for the *ka* of the king.

The causeway ascended from the valley temple to the northern side of the pyramid enclosure wall. The valley temple is striking on account of its immense size and the superb quality of its reliefs (nearly all of these are now in the Egyptian Museum in Cairo). In plan the building comprises an entrance hall, an open court, a pillared portico and six shrines. Two limestone stelae bearing the names and titles of the king stand on either side of the entrance to a narrow court in front of the entrance to the temple. The temple is not situated in the valley but well into the desert, and therefore its identification as the valley temple cannot be regarded as absolutely certain.

The Northern Stone Pyramid [6]. This is also known as « the Red Pyramid ». It was built by king Sneferu after the Bent Pyramid (see p. 178) and the unfinished pyramid at Mai-

dum (see p. 182) and was therefore his third pyramid. The stones are laid in level courses in the construction, as they were in the later pyramids at Giza. Each side at the base measures 220 m. (722 ft.). It rises to a height of 102 m. (335 ft.) and its angle of incline is 43°40'. It is possible to climb the pyramid, but as the limestone is friable and liable to crumble, this should be done carefully.

From the entrance on the north side which is 28 m. (92 ft.) above ground-level, a passage 60 m. (197 ft.) long descends to ground-level and then runs horizontally for 7 m. (23 ft.) before reaching the three chambers. These all have corbelled roofs and resemble the chambers in the Bent Pyramid. Two of the chambers measure 9.30 m. × 3.60 m. (30 × 12 ft.). The third which is at a higher level is 9 m. (29 ft.) long by 4.50 m. (14 ft.) wide by 15 m. (49 ft.) high. It remains doubtful whether the king was ever buried in this pyramid and it seems likely that he was in fact laid to rest in the Bent Pyramid.

Excursion n° 6 : The Pyramids of Lisht and Maidum

The visit to the cemeteries of Lisht and Maidum is described separately below. However, it is possible to combine such a visit with the excursion to the pyramids at Dahshur (see p. 177), or to make the visit during the journey in Middle and Upper Egypt, or even to make this trip as part of the excursion to the Fayum (see p. 262).

If travelling by train, the visitor should journey to the station at *El-Matanya*. If travelling by car it is best to leave it at El-Matanya, because beyond here the road is very rough. It is advisable to hire a donkey or a carriage, for the distance to be travelled is about 5 km. (3 miles).

The Pyramid of Ammenemes I. This is the northern pyramid at *Lisht* and like the southern one it dates to the Twelfth Dynasty. King *Ammenemes I* and his son, *Sesostris I*, built their tombs in the traditional form of a pyramid. At this time, at the beginning of the Middle Kingdom, the kings of Egypt resided at Thebes. However, in order to strengthen his authority over the rebellious *nomarchs* or provincial nobles of the north, Ammenemes moved his residence northwards to a site to the south of and not far from Memphis. His new capital was called It-tawy, « Seizer of the Two Lands », which is now known as Lisht. From here he directed the affairs of state, at first as sole ruler and later with his son, Sesostris, as co-regent.

His funerary monument shows certain similarities in design with the temple of Mentuhotep at Deir el-Bahri (see p. 46). The mortuary temple stands on a low terrace to the east of the pyramid. Inside the enclosure wall nearby are the tombs of the minister and chief inspector of the necropolis, Antefoker, princesses and close relatives. Outside the enclosure wall, all around the pyramid, were more than a hundred mastabas of nobles and officials of the king. From the entrance on the north side a corridor leads towards the burial chamber. For most of the time this chamber is flooded by water owing to a rise in the level of the Nile bed since it was built. It should be mentioned that for the construction of the pyramid, Ammenemes I reused many blocks of stone taken from the pyramids and tombs at Giza and Saqqara. The remains of a construction ramp on the north of the mortuary temple can still be clearly seen. The pyramid has suffered from the ravages of time and today is only 20 m. (65 ft.) high. Originally it was at least 58 m. (190 ft.) high. At the base the sides each measure 84 m. (275 ft.) in length.

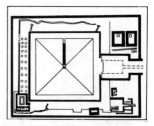

Pyramid of Ammenemes I

The Pyramid of Sesostris I. 2 km. (just over one mile) away to the south stands the funerary complex of the son of Ammenemes I. His complex is very similar to that of his father. On the east side of the pyramid is the mortuary temple. Within the outer enclosure wall are nine small pyramids which contained the burials of members of the royal family. Around the pyramid outside the outer enclosure wall were the mastaba tombs of the king's officials. Each side of the pyramid at the base measured 105 m. (344 ft.) in length, and originally it rose to a height of about 60 m. (197 ft). The superstructure of the pyramid had a framework of eight massive stone walls radiating out from the centre. The compartments in between were filled with rough pieces of limestone and sand, probably for reasons of economy. The valley temple has now disappeared but remains of the causeway and the mortuary temple are preserved. In the mortuary temple close to the walls were found painted low-reliefs, statues of Osiris, and standing and seated statues of the king. Jewels, toilet articles, vases and

other funerary items of the lady, Senebtisi, were found in her tomb near here. All of these finds are now in the Egyptian Museum in Cairo and in the Metropolitan Museum in New York. The Metropolitan Museum directed the excavation of the pyramids at Lisht between 1908 and 1934.

From here, clearly visible in the distance 20 km. (12½ miles) away to the south, rises the interesting shape of the Pyramid of Maidum. The visitor should leave the train at the station at El-Wasta and hire a donkey or carriage to make the journey to this monument.

The Pyramid of Maidum. This is one of the three pyramids built by the king Sneferu. The other two are the Bent Pyramid (see p. 178), and the Northern Stone Pyramid at Dahshur (see p. 180). It is certain that Sneferu was not buried in this pyramid at Maidum. The evidence indicates that Sneferu finished this pyramid for his predecessor, Huni. Huni had died young and before he was able to finish the pyramid. The initial building erected here was in the style of a traditional mastaba. There were several alterations in plan of which the result was a seven-stepped pyramid, built up with thick coatings of masonry on all four sides. A new coating of masonry was then added to make the structure an eight-stepped pyramid and the whole of the exterior was faced with dressed blocks of Tura limestone.

The present damaged condition of the monument makes it possible to see the different stages in the construction. At the base the lowest part of the eight-stepped pyramid lies surrounded by sand and stones. Further up can be seen the casing of the seven-stepped pyramid, then the

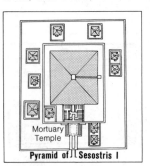

Mortuary Temple

Pyramid of Sesostris I

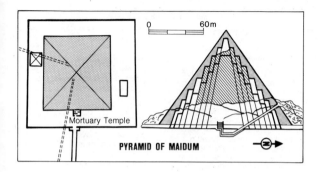

PYRAMID OF MAIDUM

core without its facing and at the top the lower part of the top of the pyramid when completed with eight steps. Originally each side of the pyramid at the base measured 144 m. (472 ft.) in length and it rose to a height of 92 m. (302 ft.).

The entrance is on the north side at 30 m. (98 ft.) above ground level. From here a passage 57 m. (187 ft.) in length descends obliquely through the superstructure and into the underlying rock. It then runs horizontally for a short distance before coming to an end. From the end of the passage a vertical shaft ascends to the burial chamber. The floor of the chamber is cut out of the rock, the walls and the ceiling are of limestone and the chamber has a corbelled vaulted ceiling. The chamber measures 5.90 m. (19 ft.) by 2.65 m. (8½ ft.). As in the Bent Pyramid, a framework of cedar wood baulks was found in the chamber and also in the shaft and probably was used as a supporting structure by the builders.

The mortuary temple stands against the east side of the pyramid and is in a good state of preservation. The entrance leads into a passage. Behind this there is a chamber and then an open court. In the court is a low limestone altar and two large limestone stelae which are uninscribed. On the walls are various graffiti carved by visitors in the Eighteenth Dynasty. One of these dates to year 14 of Tuthmosis III, and was carved by a man called Akheperkare-Seneb who had come here to see the famous tomb of king Sneferu. At the end of the text he offers a prayer for the *ka* of Sneferu and for queen Meresankh, who was the mother of the king.

In the vicinity of the pyramid, in a mastaba tomb, Mariette found the famous painted limestone statue of the general Rahotep and his wife, Nofret. This statue dates to the beginning of the Fourth Dynasty and to the reign of Sneferu. It is now preserved in the Egyptian Museum in Cairo (see p. 126).

Alexandria

(see plan, p. 187)

Alexandria, in Arabic *El-Iskandariya*, is the second largest city in Egypt and has a population of 2.2 million. It is one of the most important ports on the Mediterranean. It has interesting ancient sites, beaches, a warm, sunny and healthy climate, gardens, clubs, luxury hotels, museums and palaces. The city is often referred to as « the pearl of the Mediterranean », and although much of it was formerly very European in character, the oriental part of the city is preserved in the area between the two harbours and in the narrow streets of the sûqs or bazaars. Alexandria is situated on the narrow isthmus between the Mediterranean and *Lake Mareotis*. The old harbour is now used only by fishing boats, whereas the large modern harbour with a total area of 900 hectares (2,224 acres) is used by commercial and passenger ships. This modern harbour is protected by the nearby Island of *Pharos* and a mole or pier which juts out for 4,000 m. (nearly 2½ miles) into the sea. Alexandria has thus become a major commercial centre between the East and the West. At one time the price of cotton, the chief export, was fixed by the stock exchange in Alexandria. In the city itself are established several of Egypt's most important industries. These include factories engaged in the weaving of cotton and in metallurgy as well as plants for the preservation of food, principally fish, and a petrol refinery.

HISTORY OF ALEXANDRIA

Originally Alexandria was scarcely larger than the Island of Pharos, which was linked to the land by a causeway 7 stadia (1,300 m. or 1,422 yds.) long, known as the *Heptastadium*. Today the quarter of *Ras et-Tin* is all that remains of this early part of the city. The lighthouse of *Pharos*, which was considered to be one of the wonders of the ancient world, was destroyed by a tidal wave after an earthquake. The Eastern Harbour is today a wide open bay and the Western Harbour, which was named Eunostos in ancient times, is now the large modern harbour.

In 332 B.C. Alexander the Great founded the city here, which was named after him, near to the small ancient Egyptian village of Rhakotis. His intention was to build here a new city which would replace and be far grander than Naucratis, the ancient commercial centre for the Greeks in Egypt. It was essential that this city should be situated on the Egyptian coast and yet not be exposed to the danger of its harbour being choked by alluvial deposits of Nile mud. The western side of the Delta was an ideal site and the harbour would be sheltered by the island of Pharos. Alexander conquered the island of Pharos and instructed his architect, Deinocrates, to build on the mainland opposite the island a city, which was to be enclosed by walls and which was to be planned with streets crossing each other at right angles. Several months later Alexander left Egypt for the East, never to return to see « his city ». However, Alexander's body was apparently brought back to Alexandria for burial. His governor, Cleomenes, ensured that work on the city was continued. Within a very short time Alexandria became one of the great commercial centres of antiquity, taking the place of the then ruined city of Tyre. In less than a century Alexandria became a greater and more brilliant city than Carthage and was considered the greatest city after Rome.

Under the rule of the Ptolemies from the reign of Ptolemy I Soter, Alexandria became a centre for Greek culture and learning on account of its famous *Museum* or academy. The cult and worship of Serapis were introduced by the Ptolemies and a great temple called the *Serapeum* was built to the new god. Celebrated men of learning came to Alexandria from all over the known world. Among them were Euclid, Zenon, Plotinus, Erasistratus, Herophilus, Antiphilus and Lucian. Demetrius Phalereus founded the famous Library of Alexandria, which contained a million manuscripts. Unfortunately

it was destroyed by fire during the time of Caesar. In the reign of Ptolemy II Philadelphus the architect, Sostratus, the Cnidian, built the lighthouse of Pharos on a site where today stands the Fort Qait Bey, which dates from the 15th century. The lighthouse was constructed of white limestone and was 140 m. (459 ft.) high. As the tallest building in the world it was admired for more than a thousand years. It was built in 280 B.C. for a cost of 800 talents. Caesar sought to conquer it and Cleopatra, the Emperor Anastasius I and Ibn Tûlûn all repaired and restored it at various times. It finally collapsed and was destroyed in the 14th century.

It was in Alexandria that Cleopatra was crowned as queen, here that she met Antony and here that they lived together and met their tragic deaths. On the site of the modern Missalla Street in the district of

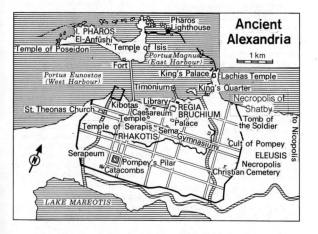

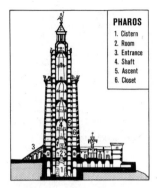

PHAROS
1. Cistern
2. Room
3. Entrance
4. Shaft
5. Ascent
6. Closet

Ramleh, Cleopatra built a temple, called the Caesareum, in Antony's honour. Two obelisks, known as « Cleopatra's Needles », stood at the entrance to the temple. Today one of them stands in New York and the other in London.

In 30 B.C. Egypt became a province of the Roman Empire. However, Alexandria retained its importance as a city. Vespasian was proclaimed as emperor here in 69 A.D. Hadrian and Marcus Aurelius visited the city several times. The decline of Alexandria began in the 3rd century under Caracalla and resulted in the destruction of the city by Diocletian. Christianity began to spread very quickly in the area.

It appears that the evangelist Mark preached the new religion of Christianity in Alexandria and that from here it spread throughout Egypt. Much later during the debates on dogma within the Christian church, Athanasius triumphed over the heretics in asserting that « God, the Father, and God, the Son, were of the same nature ». When Christianity became the State religion, those who were still pagans were persecuted by the emperor Theodosius I. He authorised Theophilus, the patriarch of Alexandria, to destroy all the pagan temples including the Serapeum and many other monuments.

The Persians conquered the city in 619. In 642 the general of Omar, Amr ibn el-As, entered Alexandria and it became an Islamic city. It began to decline rapidly as the Moslem headquarters and capital of the area were established at Fustât and Rosetta became the new commercial centre. Alexandria became nothing more than a large provincial village and remained as such for about a thousand years.

After many centuries had passed, Napoleon Bonaparte set foot on Egyptian soil near Alexandria and it was here that Nelson defeated the French fleet. It was not until 1820, under the rule of Muhammed Ali, that the Mahmudiya Canal was constructed which once again linked Alexandria with the Nile and the rest of Egypt. From this time Alexandria entered the modern age and began to re-establish its importance. During the Second World War, the city was a prime objective for Rommel's forces, who sought to capture it. The decisive battle for Alexandria took place very close to the city gates at El-Alamein and was a victory for the Allied Forces. Alexandria stands at the crossroads of the commercial routes between Africa, Asia and Europe and occupies a strategic position at the eastern end of the Mediterranean. The city remains today a very important commercial centre.

TOUR OF THE CITY

The tour starts from the centre of the city in « Liberty Square » or the

Midan el-Tahrir [1]. This was formerly known as « Muhammed Ali Square » and is a long, rectangular square, which contains an equestrian statue of Muhammed Ali. Around the square are situated St. Mark's Church, the Law Courts and the Stock Exchange. Going towards the Eastern Harbour, the visitor crosses the *Midan Ahmed Orabi*, where there is a monument to Ismail Pasha, and then comes to the superb *avenue* which runs along the edge of the Eastern Harbour. Turn right onto the avenue and walk along to

Ramleh Station [2], which is near to *El-Qaid-Ibrahim* Mosque with its slender minaret. From the station trains run to the resorts on the coast. Continue along the *avenue* and then turn right into the *Sharia Champollion* and walk down to

The Museum of Graeco-Roman Antiquities [3]. The Museum houses a collection of about 4,000 objects of art, which illustrate the art history of nearly six centuries from 300 B.C. to 300 A.D. Most of the items come from Alexandria and the area around the city.

The visitor should preferably begin his tour of the Museum in Room 7 and finish by looking at Rooms 1 - 6 and the Museum garden. In the guide to the Museum given below only the most important and interesting items are mentioned. As the displays are being redone, it is possible that the description given below may soon become out-of-date in some respects.

Entrance Hall : flint tools of the Prehistoric period ; limestone statue of Victory of the 2nd century ; cast of

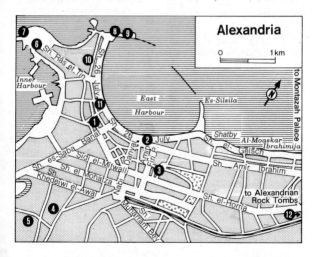

the Rosetta Stone with its bilingual inscription, which provided the key for the decipherment of the hieroglyphs. (The original is in the British Museum in London).

Turn to the left and cross Room 6 in order to visit

Room 7 : colossal pink granite statue of Ramesses II ; royal heads of the Late Period, various fragments of sculpture.

Room 8 : capital of a Hathor column in black basalt ; wooden and limestone coffins ; mummies ; a fine low-relief of the Saite Period depicting musicians and dancers.

Room 9 : devoted to objects from the Fayum ; mummy of a crocodile on a bier and stand ; remains from a chapel to the crocodile god ; wooden door with a Ptolemaic inscription.

Room 10 : this room contains the collection of John Antoniadis, which he bequeathed to the Museum. It comprises numerous Egyptian items, sculptures, faience objects, funerary masks, jewellery, canopic jars, a hawk from the Serapeum and vases.

Room 11 : examples of items made in a partly Graeco-Roman and partly Egyptian style including small objects, wall paintings, votive objects dedicated to Isis and Serapis, a statue of Horus, low-reliefs from temples.

Room 12 : statues and busts of the Ptolemaic and Roman periods, white marble statue of Serapis found near the Serapeum, statuette of Venus, head of Pan, colossal statue of the emperor Marcus-Aurelius found in the theatre - the eagle on his armour was replaced in the Christian period by the monogram of Christ, head of the emperor Hadrian.

Rooms 13 and 14 : architectural fragments, statues, sphinxes, mosaic depicting a Medusa from Gabbari.

Room 15 : architectural fragments, pieces from several statues, capitals of Graeco-Egyptian style, small funerary altars and frescoes.

Rooms 16 and 16 a : colossal statue of Serapis, statue of the Nile god in the form of an old man, small sculptures including the « Antoniadis » head of queen Arsinoe II, marble head of Alexander, statue of a woman and her young daughter dated to the reign of Ptolemy III, torsos of men and women from statues of the 2nd and 3rd centuries which came from a monument in the royal quarter of the city.

Room 17 : marble sarcophagi decorated with garlands and medusas, reused as troughs or baths, head of the emperor Vespasian, colossal porphyry statue of a Roman emperor of the 4th century (the largest known statue carved from a monolithic block of porphyry) ; at the door leading to the garden is an Alexandrian sarcophagus bearing mythological reliefs of Ariadne and which dates to the beginning of the 2nd century.

Room 18 : funerary items : glass flasks, jewellery, urns, terracottas, engraved bronze cups, mummy masks and portraits, terracotta lamps, ivory objects, faience items.

Room 18 a : painted terracotta statuettes made in wooden moulds and only found in the tombs of children and adolescents ; terracottas of which some are extremely delicate and fine and rival the best Tanagra figurines and others which are grotesque.

Room 19 : terracottas, urns, various

vessels and vases, mosaics and plaster models.

Room 20 : urns and funerary items, terracottas, group statue of Dionysos and the Faun of the school of the sculptor, Praxiteles.

Rooms 21 : funerary items, urns and clay figurines.

Room 22 : objects of daily life, mosaics, finds from Abuqir, inscriptions of the 1st to the 3rd centuries.

Room 22 a : gold and silver objects : coins, amulets, gilded silver cups, a silvered torso of Venus, an engraved silver peg, funerary material from the Serapeum dating to the reign of Ptolemy III comprising gold, silver and bronze plaques bearing inscribed dedications - this was the main find which established the position of the ancient site of the Serapeum.

Return to Room 17 and walk across to the Entrance Hall from where Rooms 1 - 6 may be visited.

Room 6 : in the centre of the room is a life-size granite statue of the Apis bull dating to the time of Hadrian ; Greek and Latin inscriptions of the Ptolemaic and Roman periods, which are arranged in chronological order - these represent an important body of evidence on all aspects of life and interesting sources' for the history and religion of these periods.

Room 1 : Christian antiquities, oil-flasks said to be from the tomb of St. Menas, the martyr (see p. 195), tombstones bearing pious inscriptions, objects carved in ivory, Coptic textiles, clay lamps, a marble relief of St. Menas between two kneeling camels, a sarcophagus-lid in porphyry of the 4th century.

Room 2 : coin collections, including several hundred Ptolemaic and Roman coins of which some are extremely rare examples.

Room 3 : wall-paintings and tools and implements of the Coptic period.

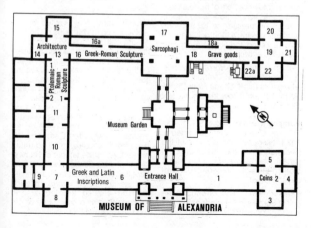

Room 4 : Coptic funerary material, textiles, terracottas.

Room 5 : tombstones, stelae, numerous utensils of which many are brightly painted, St. Menas flasks, clay lamps.

Garden, northern part : Reconstruction of the chapel of the crocodile-god, Pnepheros (the original contents of the chapel are on display in Room 9), sphinxes, sculptured lions, stone sarcophagi, colossal head of Antony as Osiris, statue of Ramesses II and his daughter.

Garden, southern part : sarcophagus decorated with garlands, architectural fragments from buildings of the Roman, Coptic and Arab periods, reconstruction of two rock-cut tombs with a sarcophagus of the 3rd century B.C., an antechamber and an atrium.

Near to the Museum at *Kom el-Dik* a small Roman theatre was discovered in 1964. It has 12 semi-circular stepped rows or tiers of marble seats and could accommodate 800 spectators. At present it is the only example of such a theatre in Egypt. It can be visited and tickets are available at the entrance.

Return towards *El-Horreya Avenue*, turn right onto the avenue and go along it as far as *Sharia Nebi Daniel*. At the station follow the *Sharia Bab Sidra* to

Pompey's Pillar [4], which marks the site of the ancient Serapeum. The present erroneous name of the pillar dates from the time of the Crusades, when it was believed that it marked the site of the tomb of Pompey the Great.

It was Ptolemy I who introduced the cult of Serapis in Alexandria. Serapis was a syncretic divinity associated with the ancient Egyptian gods, Osiris and Apis, and also with Zeus, Dionysos and Asklepios. It was in honour of Serapis that the Serapeum was constructed and the building achieved great fame throughout the

Pompey's Pillar

ancient world. It was sited on an eminence on the outskirts of the city. A flight of 100 steps led up to it and the temple was surrounded by open courts. The statue of Serapis, carved by the sculptor Bryaxis, depicted the god seated on a throne wearing a long garment. His hair and beard were curled and he wore a calathos head-dress (a calathos being a type of vase). In his left hand he held a long sceptre. His right hand rested on the triple-headed Cerberus, the dog of hell, who lay stretched out at his feet. As in the temple of Ramesses II at Abu Simbel, the architect here had constructed the building so that the rays of the sun in the early morning entered the temple and touched the lips of the statue of Serapis and bathed them with light.

This Ptolemaic sanctuary of Serapis was destroyed in 391 A.D. by the bishop Theophilus acting on the orders of the emperor Theodosius I. Little now remains of the sanctuary except for this pillar of pink Aswan granite. The diameter of the pillar is about 2.70 m (9 ft.) at the base and about 2.30 m (7½ ft.) at the top. The total height including the Corinthian capital is 27 m (88 ft.).

It is possible that the pillar was erected in 302 A.D. in honour of the emperor Diocletian. After the siege of the city, he had distributed bread to the starving populace. In the foundations a number of blocks were found, one with an inscription in honour of Diocletian, and others with the cartouches of Sethos I of the Nineteenth Dynasty and with the name of Arsinoe Philadelphos.

Other remains come from the library which stood near the Serapeum (this was not the great Imperial library, which was situated elsewhere). These include two pink granite sphinxes, a headless sphinx of Horemheb, a headless seated statue of Ramesses II, a scarabaeus of pink Aswan granite, and several shafts of granite columns. The visitor should also note the ancient water-basin to the north of the pillar.

Cross the *Sharia el-Nasriya* on the path leading to « the hill of potsherds » or

Kôm esh-Shuqâfa [5]. Here lie the catacombs of the 1st and 2nd centuries A.D. and which are the most remarkable Roman tombs in Egypt. The chambers are situated in three stories one above another which are linked by flights of steps. Here the typical Alexandrian fusion of Egyptian and Graeco-Roman styles can be clearly seen.

From the entrance the visitor enters an interior court with a winding staircase and then a rotunda. To the right are rooms with loculi and niches [a] and [b], which contain sarcophagi and funerary urns. On the left is the Triclinium Funebre [c], a large room where the funeral feast took place. The room has four pillars and benches carved out of the rock. Descend the staircase to reach the vestibule [d], which has elements of Egyptian style. The antechamber [f] is completely decorated in the Egyptian style and has on the right and left deep niches containing the limestone statues of the deceased and his wife in Egyptian dress. The burial chamber [g] has three niches guarded by a jackal-headed Anubis and a deity with a serpent's body and dog's head. In the niches stand the

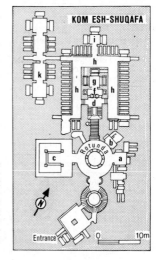

KOM ESH-SHUQAFA

sarcopnagı, which are hewn out of the solid rock. The walls of the niches are decorated with scenes : Central niche : Horus, Anubis and Thoth performing the funerary rites around the bier of the deceased ; the deceased offering prayers ; priests reading ritual texts and making offerings to Isis. Lateral niches : king offering a collar to an Apis bull ; Isis acting as protector-goddess and two figures of the god of the dead, on the right shown as human-headed and on the left as dog-headed. In the corridor which surrounds the burial chamber on three sides are 91 loculi or shelf-tombs arranged in two rows [h]. Each loculus contains three or four bodies. On the slabs sealing the tombs were painted in red the names of the dead and some of these inscriptions can still be seen. To the west of the corridor is another gallery [k] with niches and loculi for sarcophagi and funerary urns.

After leaving the catacombs go down one of the streets which leads to the Mahmudiya Canal. Turn right onto the road by the canal and follow it until the installations and docks of the Western Harbour are nearly reached. Continue along following the course of the Western Harbour in the direction going towards the palace of Ras et-Tin. Before reaching this the visitor will come to :

The Necropolis of Anfushi [6]. These Greek rock-cut tombs of the 2nd century B.C. are fine and characteristic examples of the Graeco-Egyptian styles of the Ptolemaic period. Their lay-out is in some ways similar to that of the tombs at Kôm esh-Shuqâfa and in particular with regard to the decoration of the burial chambers. Here are seen representations of Egyptian gods taking part in the funerary rites with Egyptian

decorative details side by side with motifs and mythological scenes which are purely Graeco-Roman.

The Palace of Ras et-Tin [7]. This palace, which was built by Muhammed Ali, was the official residence of the Egyptian king in Alexandria. The interior furnishings are somewhat pompous in style but good examples of 19th century taste. The best rooms are the Gothic room, the marble room and the throne room, where king Farûk signed his document of abdication on July 16th, 1952.

An avenue 25 km (15 miles) long goes from the palace and follows the seashore. It is perhaps the most beautiful avenue in the Eastern Mediterranean area. It goes to the Montaza Palace to the east of Alexandria.

Behind the palace of Ras et-Tin stands the Muhammed Karim Mosque, built in the Turkish style.

The visitor now turns to the right into the Sharia Kasr Ras et-Tin and passes the front of the Yacht Club before reaching

The Museum of Hydro-biology [8], which contains a fine aquarium. There are about fifty tanks containing varieties of fish, shell fish, sponges and corals from the Nile, Mediterranean and Red Sea. There are also models of boats, fishing implements and the skeleton of a whale nearly 17 m (55 ft.) long, which was stranded near Rosetta in 1936.

Fort Qait Bey [9]. The fortress was built in the 15th century on the site of and with stones from the lighthouse of Pharos, one of the wonders of the ancient world, by the sultan Asraf Qait Bey. The massive square enclosure of the fortress has round towers at the four corners and is surrounded by an outer wall, protected by semi-circular towers against it. The fortress is a good example of secular Islamic architecture. From the Fort Qait Bey there is a good view over the bay and the port.

The visitor should now go southwards along the *avenue* round the Eastern Harbour to the

Mosque of Abul Abbas [10]. This mosque was built in 1767 over the tomb of Abul Abbas, a pious Andalusian of Mursi who lived in *Alexandria* in the 13th century. The building has been beautifully restored and today can be considered as a masterpiece of Islamic architecture. Of particular note are the decorations on the exterior walls, the entrance façades, and the exterior decoration on the domes. Inside, the four cupolas are decorated with fine geometric ornamentation and the minbar has a square base surmounted by a round dais and wooden carvings.

The Ibrahim Terbana Mosque [11], further to the south, was built in 1684. It is not particularly famous but a number of ancient columns were re-used in its construction.

The tour of the city finishes in the *Midan Ahmed Orabi.*

The Alexandrian Hypogeum of Shatby [12]. This is situated in the eastern part of the city, not far from the sea, in the new Catholic cemetery. The monument comprises one room in a good state of preservation, which lies between the vestibule and burial chamber of a sepulchre. There is no indication as to who was the owner of the tomb. From the remains the tomb can be dated to the 3rd to 1st centuries B.C. It has been suggested that this was the Nemesion of Caesar where the head of Pompey was buried or that it was part of Se-

ma, the family sepulchre of the Ptolemies, where Alexander the Great was laid to rest. However, there is no proof that either of these suggestions is correct. The room which remains today is about 3.50 m (11 ft.) long and 2.65 m (8½ ft.) wide. The walls, ceiling and floor are faced with blocks of alabaster and the doorway is constructed with monolithic blocks of stone. This room is the most well-known and most beautiful of the remains of the Ptolemaic tombs of Alexandria.

EXCURSIONS

Montaza Palace

Montaza Palace is 17 km (10½ miles) from *El-Tahrir Square.* Bus nº 20 leaves from the square, goes along the *avenue* and then right to the palace.

The original building which dates from 1892 was altered several times in an indifferent and tasteless way. Finally it was reconstructed by the Italian architect Verrucci as a

Montaza Palace

three-storeyed residence in Neo-Byzantine style. The outbuildings, estate enclosure walls and even the small private railway station were built in the same style. The decoration of the interior and the furnishings are in the somewhat bombastic and pompous style of the 19th century. Much of it was copied from other sources like the large frescoes which imitate paintings in the Vatican. Here, however, the wings on the angels are omitted for religious reasons. The private royal apartments have now been opened as a museum.

From the terrace there is a good view of the hanging gardens and of the sea. The great park covers an area of 150 hectares (370 acres) and has various sports facilities and a very good restaurant. Near the palace is a luxury hotel, the « Palestine ».

Beaches

The nearby beaches, situated on the southern coast of the Mediterranean, have a constant, sunny and temperate climate. It is never too cold to go on the beaches in winter and because of the refreshing cool breeze it is never too hot even at the height of summer. The gently curving bays and fine white sandy beaches stretch out for 30 km (18 miles) along the coast. All the beaches on the eastern side of the city are on the n° 20 bus-route. The beaches situated in the city and nearest to it are the most popular. The best beaches are those outside the city. On the eastern side these are *Stanley Beach*, *Sidi Bishr*, *Glim*, *Cleopatra* and best of all *Montaza* and *Mamura* beaches and on the western side the beaches at *Agami* and *Hanoville*. Nearly all of them have cafés and clubs.

The ruins of Abu Mena (a distance of about 100 km (62 miles) for the journey there and back to Alexandria).

The ruins of the city of *Abu Mena* (City of St. Menas) lie to the south-west of Alexandria on the road to Mersa Matruh in the Mareotic Desert. Whether travelling by car or by train, the visitor should go as far as Bahig. From here a guide will take him to the ruins which are difficult to find.

At this site are the most important Coptic ruins which have so far been discovered. In 1905 the German Karl Maria Kaufmann discovered here the tomb of St. Menas and a church. After 1905 excavations took place over many years, except during the years of the two world wars, under the direction of the German Institute of Archaeology and the Coptic Museum in Cairo. Most of the finds are displayed in the museums in Cairo and Alexandria.

Abu Mena or St. Menas was an Egyptian or Libyan soldier who served in the Phrygian army. He became a Christian and was martyred in 296 A.D. in the reign of Diocletian. His last wish was to be buried in his own country. According to legend the camels carrying his body stopped at a certain place and refused to go any further. When they were replaced with other camels, the same thing happened - they also refused to move. This was considered as a miracle and as the wish of St. Menas. Consequently he was buried at that spot. Later a church was built here to mark the place. A number of hermits came to live here. The abundant water supplies in the area from about 90 sources meant that men and animals could live here without any difficulty. A century after the death of

St. Menas, the village of Abu Mena had become a place of pilgrimage, very similar to modern Lourdes.

The different stages in the construction of the sanctuaries here are now known, and particularly those relating to the Burial Church of St. Menas and the *Basilica of Arcadius*. The tomb-chapel of St. Menas was built in 297 A.D. This is a crypt 8 m (26 ft.) below the church. The Burial Church itself was built over the crypt in 365 A.D. Next to it, is the Basilica of Arcadius built between 395 and 408 A.D. This basilica was the central monument of the ancient city and the largest church in Egypt, being 67 m (220 ft.) in length and 32 m (105 ft.) in width. Most of the building materials, the marble, the wood, the mosaics and the painting materials, were brought from Europe. It is said that the emperor Arcadius built this church when his wish was granted by the saint and his son was cured of a serious illness.

The cruciform baptismal fonts in the rectangular baptistry are well preserved. Opposite, to the north of the Burial Church, Kaufmann found some tanks and a bathing pool, which probably contained the wonder-working waters. Some of the tanks were for the ordinary pilgrims, while others were baths for those of importance. Pilgrims also took away with them flasks filled with the miraculous waters. These vessels were specially made for this purpose and are known as St. Menas flasks. Examples in clay and pottery have been found. They are decorated in a very characteristic way with a scene of St. Menas dressed as a Roman soldier with a halo praying between two camels, which are usually shown as kneeling. Examples of these flasks can be found in many museums and particularly in the Museum of Graeco-Roman Antiquities in Alexandria (Room 1, see p. 189)

Pilgrim's Flask from Abu Mena

At Abu Mena four churches have been discovered and also two baptistries, two catacombs, baths, piping, reservoirs, and round these lie the remains of the city with its houses and streets. Abu Mena flourished between the 5th and 8th centuries. Coptic and Greek texts of the period relate the established itinerary of the pilgrims who came to the Church of St. Menas to pray at the tomb of the saint and to drink the waters. Recent analysis has shown that this water, which contains certain minerals, did have a definite therapeutic effect.

Luxor

Luxor and Karnak with their celebrated temples are two complexes situated on the east bank of the river Nile on the site of Thebes, the ancient capital of united Egypt.

During his stay at Luxor, the tourist can visit the tombs and temples of the necropolis of Western Thebes on the opposite bank of the river, which are not far from the Valley of the Kings (see p. 215). He can also visit the temple of Deir el-Bahri (see p. 223), the private tombs situated in five different areas, the Ramesseum (see p. 231), the temple of Deir el-Medina (see p. 232), the Valley of the Queens (see p. 235), the temple of Medinet Habu (see p. 236), and the Colossi of Memnon (see p. 239). In order to visit all the monuments just mentioned, the visitor should plan to stay for at least three days. This allows one day for the visit to the two temples of Luxor and Karnak, and the other two days for visiting the monuments on the West Bank. The visitor can travel to Luxor to see the remains of ancient Thebes and its necropolis either by air (p. 394), or by Nile cruiser (p. 394), or by train (p. 394). If travelling by car, follow route 3 (Cairo to Asyût) and route 4 (Asyût to Luxor) (p. 287).

Ancient Thebes (Luxor and Karnak)

Luxor has a population of 30,000 and is an ideal place to spend a winter holiday as the dry and healthy climate is particularly pleasant in the winter months. It is situated on the site of the southern part of the city or the « Southern Harem » of ancient *Thebes*, the capital of the Egyptian empire. Homer described Thebes as the hundred-gated city and from the time of the Middle Kingdom all the wealth of Egypt came to Thebes to be dedicated to *Amun*, the powerful state-god. From Thebes, Egypt's power extended to the Sudan, to the Mediterranean coast, across to the Red Sea, to the borders of Libya and as far as the Land of Punt.

The real development of the city began after the unification of Upper and Lower Egypt under Ammenemes I and reached its apogee during the Eighteenth, Nineteenth and Twentieth Dynasties, when it was one of the greatest cities of the ancient world. It was here that the Pharaohs built their great royal monuments. Even today, the Twentieth Century visitor will be impressed by the grandeur of these monuments and by the technological skills of the Egyptians who built them.

The temples of the principal gods and the royal palaces were situated on the right bank of the Nile. The tombs and mortuary temples were on the left bank further back from the river in the desert cliffs, which was the land of the dead in the west.

The power of Thebes declined after the Royal Residence was moved to the Delta and the city suffered during the Assyrian invasion and under the rule of the Ptolemies. The province of Thebes was heavily taxed by the Roman governor, Cornelius Gallus, and in 30-29 B.C. rose in revolt against the excessive taxes. The Romans suppressed the revolt, defeated the rebels and destroyed the town of Thebes. During the Christian period many of its buildings were altered and used as churches and monasteries. Many works of art were destroyed. Some were burnt to make lime and others were moved elsewhere. Peasants moved into the ruins to live with their animals. Until relatively recent times collectors, supposedly acting in the interests of archaeology, were able to either damage through ignorance a great number of objects or to take ancient items away for museum and private collections all over the world. The name « Luxor » is derived from the Arabic *El-Qûsûr*, which means « the castles ».

The Temple of Luxor

(see plan, p. 199) Amenophis III of the Eighteenth Dynasty probably built this temple on the site of a more ancient sanctuary. He dedicated the temple to the divine triad of Amun, Mut, and their son, Khonsu, the moon-god. The original building, which was 150 m. (492 ft.) long and 50 m. (164 ft.) wide, had an open court with a double colonnade, a hypostyle hall, chapels for the gods, a sanctuary, adjoining rooms, and a hall with a colonnade at the front of the temple, which was only half-finished. Akhenaten, the heretic king, ordered the representations and names of Amun in the temple to be erased. He built a sanctuary dedicated to Aten beside the temple and

moved the seat of government from Thebes to his new capital, Tell el-Amarna. Tutankhamun moved the Royal Residence back to Thebes, finished the hall with the colonnade at Luxor and had its walls decorated with reliefs. The temple of Aten was destroyed. Ramesses II added to the temple of Luxor by building in front of the original structure a great court with a double colonnade, in front of which he erected a great pylon gateway. In so doing he extended the temple to a length of 260 m. (853 ft.). In later times the Christians used part of the temple as a church and the Moslems built the mosque of Abu 'l-Haggag in the great court of Ramesses II.

The *entrance of the temple* is on the north facing in the direction of the south gate of the temple of Karnak. The two temples were at one time linked by an avenue of sphinxes 2.5 km. (1 ½ mile) long, parts of which are preserved. The holes dug for the trees, which were planted between the sphinxes, have been found.

The Great Pylon [1]. The entrance of this monumental gateway lies between two great towers with slanting walls, which are decorated with reliefs. The gateway symbolises a valley between two high mountains, the horizon over which the sun rises, the throne of the gods and of the king and at the same time an impregnable fortress, which defended the entrance of the sanctuary against any powerful enemy. In front of the pylon there were originally *six colossal statues of Ramesses II*, two sitting and four standing statues. Of these two sitting and two standing statues remain. In front of the statues and flanking the entrance were two obelisks of pink Aswan granite. The obelisk on the left remains in situ.

The one which stood on the right is now in the Place de la Concorde in Paris. It was a gift from Muhammed Ali to king Charles X of France. The obelisk at Luxor is 24 m. (79 ft.) high, that in Paris is 26 m. (85 ft.) high and they weigh approximately 230 metric tons (226 tons).

At the front of each tower of the pylon can be seen the vertical grooves in which the flagstaffs were placed. There were two flags in front of each tower, which flew above the towers at a great height. The *reliefs* on the exterior walls of the pylon illustrate the campaign which Ramesses II conducted against the Hittites and the Battle of Kadesh in 1285 B.C.

On the right tower : Ramesses II holds a council of war with his generals. The Egyptian camp is attacked by the Hittites. Ramesses II in his chariot attacks the enemy.

On the left tower : The king shoots his arrows ; the Hittites flee into the fortress of Kadesh ; the king of the Hittites flees in his chariot. On both towers there is a long inscription describing the Battle of Kadesh. At the back of the pylon on its inner walls are religious cult scenes and scenes of the festival of the god, Min. The festival with its solemn processions took place at the beginning of the harvest season. Min, the god of fertility receives offerings of lettuces, the symbol of his power of fecundity.

The Great Court of Ramesses II [2]. This was entirely surrounded by a double colonnade of 74 papyriform columns with closed bud-capitals. In the north-west corner is a small granite chapel built by Tuthmosis III.

Between some of the columns stand statues of Amenophis III, which were usurped by Ramesses II. Their average height is 7 m. (23 ft.). The walls

of the court are covered with relief scenes and inscriptions. Among the *reliefs* here are sacrificial scenes and scenes of the presentation of tribute.

The Great Court of Ramesses II

In the western corner is a representation of the temple as it was in ancient times with its pylon, flagstaffs, statues and obelisks and a procession approaching from the right. The scene is an interesting and important historical document. The axis of this great court of Ramesses II differs from that of the original construction of Amenophis III as it was added at a later date and had to surround the chapel of Tuthmosis III which stood in front of the original temple.

The Colonnade [3]. This has 14 columns with open papyriform capitals which are 16 m. (52 ft.) high and which support heavy architraves. This hall was the processional way leading to the temple of Amenophis III and was flanked at a later date with the statues of Ramesses II. The walls

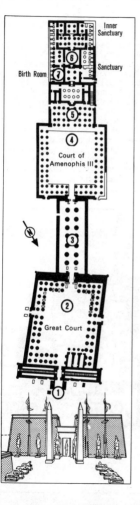

were decorated with fine *low-reliefs* by Tutankhamun. The detailed scenes depict the Festival of Opet which took place every year. The god Amun leaves Karnak and is brought to the temple at Luxor for the festival and then returns in his sacred boat to Karnak. Musicians and dancers accompany the crowds who follow the festival procession. The festivities lasted for twenty-four days and were enjoyed by everyone, including foreigners, as is shown by the detailed reliefs. The series of scenes begins in the north-west corner of the colonnade.

The Court of Amenophis III [4]. This is surrounded on three sides by a double colonnade of columns. On the east and west sides the architraves are well preserved, the colours are still fresh and bright and indicate how impressive this court must have been in ancient times.

The Hypostyle Hall [5]. The roof was supported by 32 papyrus columns arranged in four rows of eight. The walls are decorated with reliefs which include scenes of Amenophis III before the gods of Thebes, personifications of the Egyptian nomes bearing gifts and the coronation of Amenophis by the gods. At the back of the Hypostyle Hall is a *small hall,* which originally had eight columns. This was converted into a church at the end of the 4th century. The walls were plastered and painted with Christian decoration. Some parts of the Christian paintings have now fallen away exposing the original reliefs of Amenophis III.

The Sanctuary [6]. From the small hall the visitor passes into a square hall supported by 4 columns, which was an *offering room,* and then into the sanctuary or holy of holies of the temple.

This sanctuary for the sacred boat of Amun was originally square in plan and had four columns supporting the roof in the centre of the room. The room was altered and rebuilt in the reign of Alexander the Great. The sanctuary is now a chapel open at both ends and contains a granite pedestal for the sacred boat. The exterior and interior walls of the chapel and the walls of the chamber are decorated with reliefs. On the entrance wall : the King arriving in the sanctuary.

On the far wall : the solemn coronation of the king who kneels before Amun and receives the double crown in the presence of the ennead of gods.

On the side walls are representations of the king offering before the sacred boat of Amun. The scenes on the chapel walls are of Alexander the Great, those on the walls of the chamber are of Amenophis III.

Behind the sanctuary is a room supported by twelve columns, which was the second offering room. At the back of this are three chapels, of which the central one supported by four columns is decorated with reliefs of religious scenes. There are other rooms, mostly store rooms at the sides of the sanctuary, among which is :

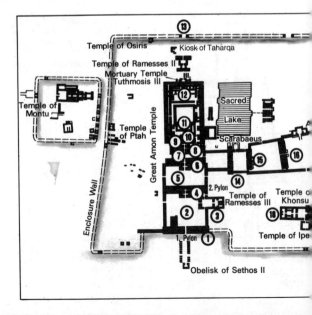

The Birth Room (mammisi) [7]. On the west wall are scenes of the story of the divine birth. Hathor embraces the mother of Amenophis III in the presence of Amun. Amun converses with Thoth. The union of Amun and the queen seated on a bed. Khnum, the creator-god, fashions Amenophis III and his ka on his potter's wheel in the presence of Hathor.

Thoth announces to Mut-em-weya that she will be the mother of a royal son, Amenophis. The pregnant Mut-em-weya is taken to the birth room. The prince is born. Amun receives the child in his arms from Hathor in the presence of Mut. The young prince and his ka are suckled by two divine nurses and by two cows. The ennead of gods take the infant prince and his ka before the Nile god. Horus presents the child and his ka to Amun. Amenophis and his ka before Seshat, the goddess of writing who registers all the coronation scenes in the Egyptian temples.

The exterior walls of the temple : these are decorated with reliefs of the campaigns of Ramesses II against the Hittites. The best preserved reliefs are those on the west wall of the court of Amenophis III, on the colonnade and on the Great Court of Ramesses II up to the Pylon.

KARNAK

0   150 m

The Luxor Museum

Situated on the bank of the Nile near to the Antiquities Service, the Museum was opened in 1977. The objects are artistically displayed and range in date from the Predynastic to Islamic periods. There is a fine collection of sculpture, some from the Karnak cache. Particularly noteworthy are statues of the vizier Montuhotep. Sesostris III, an outstanding statue of Tuthmosis III, a group of Amenophis III with the god Sobek, and the famous Amenophis, son of Hapu, as a seated scribe. A restoration of part of a wall from one of Akhenaten's temples provides a unique opportunity to view the decoration of these temples. Also included are objects from the tomb of Tutankhamun and statues of the boy-king. Most of the objects originate from the Theban area. Guide books are available.

The Temple of Karnak

(see plan, pp. 200-201). The visitor can hire a donkey, a cab or a bicycle for the journey from *Luxor* to *Karnak*, a distance of nearly 3 km. (1 3/4 ml). The best route is the road along the bank of the Nile. A turning to the right, which is clearly marked, leads to the *Great Temple of Amun*. On the return journey the *Temples of Khonsu* and *Mut* can be visited.

The construction of the Great Temple of Amun was started at the beginning of the Twelfth Dynasty. Over many years the temple grew in size until, by the time it was completed, it had enclosed a number of sanctuaries originally outside the complex. These were those of Ptah on the north and Khonsu to the south. The plan of the temple complex was never static in ancient times, additions and alterations were continually taking place. Today the monuments provide a wide spectrum of Egyptian art. The buildings date mainly to the reigns of Tuthmosis III, Amenophis III, Ramesses I, Sethos I, Ramesses II, Sethos II, Ramesses III, the Twenty-second or Bubastite Dynasty, Taharqa and the Ptolemies.

At first the monumental character and complex plan of the temple seems very confusing to the visitor and difficult to understand. For this reason it is probably best to follow the itinerary for the visit which is given below. This itinerary is designed so that the visitor can see everything of importance and understand clearly the lay-out of the temple. The itinerary for the visit begins near to the two obelisks of Sethos II, at the quay where in ancient times boats could moor up to take on board the statues of the gods. From here an *avenue of ram-headed sphinxes* leads to the First Pylon, the main entrance of the temple. After passing through the gate, turn to the left to the staircase which goes to the top of the north tower of the Pylon. From the top there is a superb view over the Nile Valley and over the temple itself. By looking at the plan on pages 200 and 201 it is easy to get some idea of the total plan of the temple : the First Pylon opens onto the *Great Court [2]*, which encloses on the right the *temple of Ramesses III [3]* and on the left the *temple of Sethos II* ; then follows the *Second Pylon [4]* which leads into the *Great Hypostyle [5]* ; further away lies the *Third Pylon [6]*, an obelisk in the *Court [7]* and then the *Fourth Pylon [8]* ; beyond this is a hall and the *obelisk of Hatshepsut [9]*. Small rooms and halls lie behind the *Fifth Pylon* before reaching the final *Sixth Pylon [10]*. Behind this,

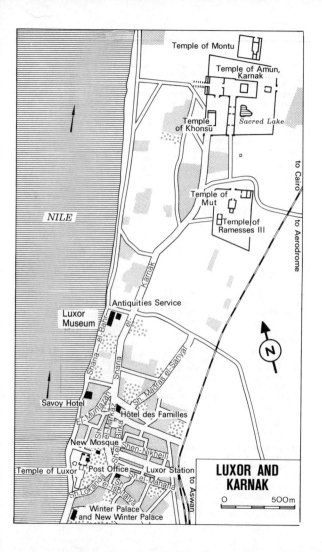

Temple of Montu

Temple of Amun,
Karnak

Sacred Lake

Temple
of Khonsu

to Cairo

to Aerodrome

Temple of
Mut

Temple of
Ramesses III

NILE

Karnak

Antiquities Service

Luxor
Museum

Sharia el-Bahr

Sharia el-Sanya

N

Savoy Hotel

El-Muntazah

Sh. Mahras el-Sanya

Hôtel des Familles

El-Markaz

Sh. Birka

New Mosque

Shen-Nikheili

Temple of Luxor

Post Office

Sh. el-Mahatta

Luxor Station

to Aswan

Sh. Lokanda

Sh. el-Isbitalya

Winter Palace
and New Winter Palace

**LUXOR AND
KARNAK**

0   500m

there are halls and the *sanctuary of the sacred barques [11]*. Beyond lies the oldest part of the temple and the *Festival Hall [12]* with its adjoining rooms and chapels. At the end is the *East Gateway [13]*. To the right of the temple is the *Sacred Lake* and in front of it the processional avenue with the *Seventh Pylon [14]*, the *Eighth Pylon [15]*, the *Ninth Pylon [16]*, and finally the *Tenth Pylon [17]*. To the west is the Temple of Khonsu [18] and to the south in their own enclosures the temples of Mut and Ramesses III.

THE GREAT TEMPLE OF AMUN

First Pylon [1] : This was built towards the end of the Ethiopian period in Dynasty XXV. It is the most recent in date of the pylons of the temple and also the largest one as the temple expanded in size by the addition of new structures in front of the more ancient ones. The pylon was never completed and parts of the scaffolding made of rough bricks are still visible in the corner of the court on the right. The measurements of the pylon are surprisingly colossal. The walls are 15 m. (49 ft.) thick. the height is 43 m. (141 ft.) and the width of the pylon is 115 m. (377 ft.). In the gateway itself high up on the right-hand wall is an inscription which was placed there by the French scholars who accompanied Napoleon's expedition to Egypt in 1799 in order to record the monuments of the country.

Great Court [2] : This is the largest of all the Egyptian temple courts with an area of over 8,000 sq. metres (c. 10,327 sq.yds. = 2 acres) being 84 m. (275 ft) long and 103 m. (338 ft.) wide. It was built by the kings of the Twenty-second Dynasty. It has a row of columns on each side with two rows of ram-headed sphinxes. The

ram was the sacred animal of Amun. These sphinxes were part of a processional avenue of sphinxes which were placed here long before the court was built. In the corner of the court on the left is the small temple of Sethos II, which was dedicated to the divine triad of Amun, Mut and Khonsu. In the middle of the court there remains one complete column out of the ten which once supported the kiosk of Taharqa of the Twenty-fifth Dynasty. The column is 21 m. (69 ft.) high and is constructed of 25 courses of stone for the shaft and five more for the capital, which is 5 m. (16 ft.) in breadth.

In the right-hand corner of the court and partially enclosed within it is

The Temple of Ramesses III [3], which was dedicated to Amun. The pylon of the temple stands in the Great Court.

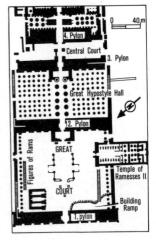

Eight Osiride pillars flank the court of the temple on the sides. On the exterior of the pylon are scenes of the king conquering foreign peoples in the presence of Amun to whom the temple is consecrated. The walls of the court are decorated with reliefs depicting the procession of the god, Amun. Behind the court is a vestibule supported by four pillars and four columns and behind this the Hypostyle Hall, which has eight columns.

At the back are three chapels. The middle one is dedicated to Amun, the one on the right to Khonsu and that on the left to Mut. This temple exhibits the classic plan of the Egyptian temple which evolved in the Middle Kingdom and which was the basic design for all temples from that period onwards.

Second Pylon [4]: Two statues of Ramesses II flank the entrance to the vestibule in front of the pylon. In the vestibule is a standing colossal figure in granite of Pinudjem, son of the high-priest. The second pylon measures 98 m. (321 ft.) by 14 m. (46 ft.). It dates from the time of Horemheb and Ramesses I but was completed by Sethos I. The blocks which formed the foundations and the core of the pylon bore the name of Akhenaten and came from his destroyed monuments (see p. 202). Beyond the pylon is the Great Hypostyle Hall.

Great Hypostyle Hall [5]: Even in antiquity this hall was considered as an architectural wonder and indeed the scale of the project and the perfection of its realisation are worthy of admiration. The area of the hall is 5,356 sq. metres (6,400 sq. yds). The Great Cathedral at Cologne covers an area of 6,166 sq. m. (7,375 sq. yds), which gives the visitor some idea of the massive size of the hall here. The roof was supported by 134 columns in 16 rows which were papyriform columns in limestone. Of these 122 have closed capitals and the 12 higher and larger columns in the centre have open capitals. The columns are built of courses of stone 1.10 m (3 ½ ft.) high laid one on top of another. The shafts of the central columns are 21 m. (69 ft.) high and 10 m. (33 ft.) in circumference and therefore are as thick as the Vendôme Column in Paris. The majestic capitals of the central columns are 3 m. (c.10 ft.) high and thus the total height of the columns in the central nave is 24 m. (79 ft.). On top of these were laid the roofing blocks. The smaller columns at the sides are 13 m. (42 ½ ft.) high and were similarly constructed in courses of stone 1.10 m. (3 ½ ft.) high. During the building of the hall it was probably filled with mud bricks, mud and gravel as the work progressed up to the height of the architrave. The cutting of the relief decoration started at the top and continued downwards as the filling material was slowly removed.

The different heights of the architraves in the hall meant that the hall could be lighted at the top. Above the architrave over the first rows of side columns there were stone grilles which rose to join the extended architrave over the higher central columns. Through these windows or *claustra* light streamed downwards into the hall, and penetrated parts of the interior. At various places the ancient colours of the reliefs are still visible, particularly on the shafts and capitals of the columns and on the architraves. Most of the columns on the left of the hall to the north which date to the reign of Sethos I are decorated with fine low-reliefs. But on the right side to the south it can be seen that Ramesses II and other Ramesside kings preferred sunk-relief decoration. All the walls of the hall are decorated with reliefs and inscriptions which show the Pharaoh before the gods. On the left is Sethos I and on the right Ramesses. There are similar scenes on the two *exterior walls* of the Hypostyle Hall.

North wall : between the 2nd and 3rd pylons : the inhabitants of Lebanon cut cedar trees for Sethos ; battle against the Bedouins in front of a fortress in Canaan : the besieged demand mercy ; attack on the fortress of Yenoam, which is surrounded by water ; Sethos binding captured Syrians ; the king leads rows of prisoners before the divine triad ; the triumphal march of the king through Palestine ; battle against the Asiatics near a canal infested with crocodiles which marks the frontier between Egypt and Asia ; the returning king is presented with bouquets of flowers ; he presents the captured booty to Amun. Near the door on the east part of the wall : Amun presents the curved sword of victory to Sethos. On the west part of the wall : storming of the fortress of Kadesh ; Libyans with their pigtails and feathers ; battle with the Hittites ; Sethos presents the captives of war to the gods.

South wall : the famous triumphal inscription of Sheshonq I, commemorating his victory over Rehoboam, the son of Solomon which is mentioned in the Old Testament, I Kings, 14 and II Chronicles, 12. ; Semitic prisoners ; five rows of conquered towns, each of which is represented by a fortress wall enclosing its name ; below, Waset, the goddess of the Theban nome, leads five rows of captives ; Sheshonq smites Asiatics with his club ; in the corner of the wall, behind the court and in front of the 7th Pylon, is inscribed a copy of

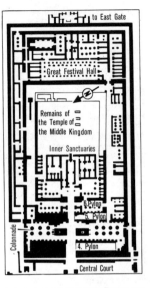

the peace treaty between Ramesses II and the Hittites and various scenes of the wars of Ramesses II.

Third Pylon [6] : From the inscriptions found on the core and foundation blocks of this pylon, it is clear that it was built by Amenophis III from stone taken from earlier buildings of Sesostris I, Amenophis I and Hatshepsut. Some of the superb reliefs can still be seen : on the left, there are two ships, sacred barques of Amun, which were used in the celebrations of the Festival of Opet at Luxor.

Central Court [7] : This lies between the Third and the Fourth Pylons and, in ancient times, four slender obelisks stood here. Two of them were erected by Tuthmosis III. The other two were placed here by Tuthmosis I and marked the entrance to the temple during his reign. In the court, today, one obelisk of Tuthmosis I remains. It is about 23 m. (75 ft.) high and weighs nearly 130 metric tons (128 tons). It stands on a base 2 m. (6 ½ ft.) square. On each face of the obelisk, in the centre, is a vertical dedicatory inscription of Tuthmosis I. The vertical inscriptions on either side of the central one are later additions by Ramesses IV and Ramesses VI.

Walk past the processional avenue which leads off on the right and continue to follow the main axis of the temple which lies straight ahead.

Fourth Pylon [8] : This is inscribed with the name of Tuthmosis I, but is today in a fairly poor state of preservation. Two slender flagstaffs of cedar wood with gilded tips towered above the pylon in ancient times but all trace of these has now disappeared.

Small Hall [9] : There are Osiride pillars on each side of the hall. In the centre were two great monolithic obelisks in pink granite which were erected by Queen Hatshepsut to celebrate her jubilee. Relief scenes showing the transport of two such obelisks can be seen in the Queen's temple at Deir el-Bahri on the left bank of the Nile (see p. 223). Of the obelisks which she placed in this small hall, the one on the left still stands. The one on the right has fallen and fragments from it can be seen scattered on the ground. The inscription on the left obelisk records that the quarrying and making of the two obelisks from Aswan granite took only seven months. They were

nearly 30 m. (98 ft.) high and the tips were covered with sheets of electrum, a natural alloy of gold and silver, which caught and reflected the rays of the sun.

The obelisk which still stands, weighs 320 metric tons (315 tons) and is nearly as tall as the Lateran Obelisk in Rome, which is the highest ancient obelisk known. On the four faces of the obelisk are vertical inscriptions and reliefs, some of which relate the quarrying and transport of the monument. The figures and names of Amun were erased by Akhenaten and later restored by Sethos I. The erasures and the restoration can still be clearly seen. Tuthmosis III enclosed the obelisks of Hatshepsut behind a sandstone structure so that only the tips of them could be seen. Traces of this structure still remain. On a fragment of the fallen obelisk can be seen a superb relief of Hatshepsut being crowned by Amun. In the hall there was a beautiful low-relief of Amenophis II firing an arrow at a target, which came from the filling of the 3rd Pylon and is now preserved in the Luxor Museum.

Fifth and Sixth Pylons [10] : These were built by Tuthmosis I and Tuthmosis III respectively. The two pylons and the rooms in between them are now in a very poor state of preservation. Between the pylons on the right and left are two small hypostyle halls with Osiride pillars. Beyond the 6th Pylon is a court, the Hall of Records, of Tuthmosis III. In it are two granite heraldic pillars, that on the south bearing the lotus of Upper Egypt, and that on the north the papyrus of Lower Egypt. Standing as they do in front of the entrance to the sanctuary of the barques, they sym-

bolise the establishment of the kingdom by the union of the Two Lands
before the god of the empire, Amun.
Here also are two colossal statues in
red sandstone of Amun and the
goddess Amunet which were erected here by Tutankhamun after his
return from Amarna to Thebes.

**Sanctuary of the sacred barques
[11] :** The granite chapel is divided
into two chambers, one being open
at the east end, where the sun rises
and the other being open at the west
end where the sun sets. Thus the
light of the sun-god in the morning
and evening could rest upon the sacred barques of Amun and on his
divine effigy on its pedestal. The
chapel was built on the site of an
earlier one around 320 B.C. by *Philip
Arrhidaeus,* the brother and successor of Alexander the Great, who was
recognised as legitimate king of
Egypt. All of the interior and exterior
walls of the chapel are decorated
with reliefs. On the interior walls are
scenes of the king offering sacrifices
and performing religious rites. On
the exterior walls are scenes of more
religious ceremonies. The walls
which surround the chapel are those
of the second Hall of Records of
Tuthmosis III and bear long inscriptions describing his military achievements. In the adjoining rooms, several of which were storerooms, are
small granite altars of Tuthmosis III.
On the walls the names and figures
of Hatshepsut were replaced after
her death with those of Tuthmosis III.
This occurs in several places in the
Temple of Karnak, and also in the
Theban necropolis. When Tuthmosis
III came to the throne after Hatshepsut, he only preserved intact her two
obelisks at Karnak and even these
he enclosed so as to hide them from
view.

Behind the sanctuary of the sacred
barques lay the early Temple of the
Middle Kingdom. The site is now an
open, empty court with very few remains. At the back of this is the

**Great Festival Hall of Tuthmosis III
[12].** Tuthmosis III built this hall
transversely to the main axis of the
temple and thus its entrance is at the
south-west corner. The building was
used for the celebration of the rites
of the royal ancestors. 20 columns
with bell-shaped capitals imitating
tent poles, and 32 smaller pillars
supported the roof. The hall is 44 m.
(144 ft) in length and 16 m. (52 ft.) in
breadth and has five aisles. The
three central aisles are higher than
the side-aisles. On the inner side of
the centre aisle the bases of the columns have been cut straight to allow
the processions to pass easily along
the aisle. There are a number of
rooms adjoining the hall. One of
them on the south-west contained
the famous Karnak Table of kings, an
important historical relief, on which
Tuthmosis III made offerings to 57 of
his royal ancestors, the kings of
Egypt from earliest times down to the
Eighteenth Dynasty. This monument
was removed from the temple in
1843 and is now preserved in the
Louvre, in Paris.

On the east side of the hall is a small
room with four columns with closed
papyrus capitals, which is known as
the *Botanical Garden.* The walls are
decorated with detailed representations of plants and animals which
were collected on one of Tuthmosis
III's expeditions to Syria and brought
back to Egypt.

Behind the Festival Hall there lies an
area of remains which stretches as
far as the East Gateway. The scattered blocks which lie here come from

a small temple which in ancient times had some obelisks before it. The building was commenced by Tuthmosis III, continued by Ramesses II and later altered by Taharqa. The Lateran Obelisk, which is 30.8 m. (101 ft.) high, once stood here. It was moved to the Circus Maximus in 357 A.D. by the emperor Constantine, and to the Lateran Square by Pope Sixtus V in 1587.

The East Gateway [13]. This gateway is in the great brick enclosure wall which surrounds the temple area. The wall is 19 m. (62 ft.) high. Its purpose was to fortify and enclose the domain of Amun. It was begun by Nectanebo I in the 4th century B.C. and finished by the Ptolemies. It is not possible to ascend to the top of the gateway. The distance from the First Pylon of the temple to the East Gateway is about 450 m. (492 yards). After leaving the gateway return to the Central Court between the 3rd and 4th Pylons. Leading off from the Central Court is

The Processional Avenue

The 7th, 8th, 9th and 10th pylons form part of the processional avenue. Beyond the 10th Pylon is an avenue of ram-headed sphinxes which leads to the Temple of Mut. Both the Temple of Amun at Karnak and the Temple of Mut each had a *sacred lake*. The lake of the Temple of Karnak is roughly rectangular in shape and is fed with water from the underground water-table. Between the south wall of the temple and the sacred lake, are the ruins of a structure built by Taharqa, which was like an Osireion. On the bank of the lake is a large granite scarabaeus on a pedestal. It was dedicated to the sun-god, Atum-Khepri by Amenophis III.

On the west side of the court which lies in front of the 7th Pylon in a pit 14 m. (46 ft.) deep, known as the Karnak Cachette, was found a collection of over 20,000 stone and bronze objects. These had been removed from the rooms of the temple in the Twenty-fifth Dynasty as they were no longer needed and had been buried here. Most of the objects are now in the Egyptian Museum in Cairo.

In front of the north façade of the **7th Pylon [14]** are seven colossal red granite statues of kings of the Middle and New Kingdoms. On the south side are two red granite statues of Tuthmosis III. On the side of the east wall of the court, between the 7th and 8th Pylons, is a small ruined chapel of Tuthmosis III and further along on the wall is an interesting relief of the high-priest Amenhotep in the presence of Ramesses IX. The **8th Pylon [15]** was built by Hatshepsut. The religious and cult scenes on the pylon are well preserved as is a scene on the south side of Amenophis II smiting his enemies. Six royal statues once stood on the south side of the 8th Pylon. Four of these remain. They are 4 m. (13 ft.) high and that of Amenophis I is well preserved.

Between the **9th Pylon [16]** and the **10th Pylon [17]** is a court with a small Temple of Amenophis II on the east side. The reliefs of the temple are well preserved and much of the colouring can still be seen. The two pylons were built by Horemheb with blocks from the demolished temples of Akhenaten. In front of the north side of the 10th Pylon are the remains of statues of Ramesses II and his wife, Nefertari. On the south side of the pylon are the remains of colossal statues of Amenophis III and Horemheb.

THE TEMPLE OF KHONSU

To the west of the Temple of Amun and at the south gateway of the brick enclosure wall of the Karnak temple complex is the *Temple of Khonsu [18]*. Khonsu was the Theban moon-god and the son of Amun and Mut. Ramesses III began the temple and it was completed by Ramesses IV, Ramesses XI, and Herihor. In plan it is a typical example of a New Kingdom temple and has an avenue of sphinxes, a pylon, a court, a vestibule, a hypostyle hall, sanctuary and adjoining rooms. The reliefs on the east wall of the colonnaded court are particularly interesting. On the left the priest-king, Herihor, offers incense before the sacred barques of Amun, Mut and Khonsu.

The *Pylon* which marks the entrance to the temple, extends across the front of the court. It is 18 m. (59 ft.) high, 10 m. (33 ft.) thick and 32 m. (105 ft.) wide. In ancient times it had four flagstaffs in front of it. The court is surrounded on three sides by a double row of a papyriform columns with closed capitals. A ramp leads up

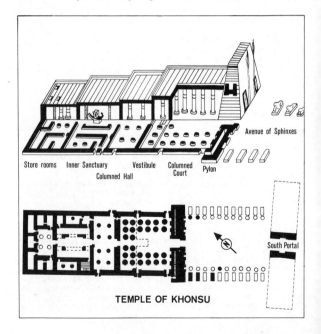

Store rooms   Inner Sanctuary   Vestibule   Columned   Pylon
                                               Court
               Columned Hall

Avenue of Sphinxes

South Portal

TEMPLE OF KHONSU

to the colonnade on the north side which is on a higher level and which is the vestibule or pronaos of the temple. Behind this is a hypostyle hall, greater in breadth than in length. It has 12 columns. The four columns, 2 each side of the central aisle, are papyriform with open capitals. The side columns are lower in height. Windows above the central aisle admit light into the hall. Behind lies the sanctuary which contains a pedestal for the sacred barque of Khonsu and for the cult statue of the god.

A statue of Khonsu dating to the reign of Tutankhamun was found in the sanctuary, where it had been buried by the Ramessides. It is now in the Egyptian Museum in Cairo. Of the rooms which lie on either side of and behind the sanctuary, the most interesting is a room which was dedicated to the worship of Osiris. Here there is a representation of the dead Osiris on his bier with the goddesses Isis and Nephthys watching over him.

The scenes in the temple and in the subsidiary rooms are nearly all religious and ritual representations.

Immediately to the west of the Pylon and adjoining the Temple of Khonsu is a small *temple of the goddess, Opet [19]*, who was a hippopotamus goddess. The temple was built by Euergetes II.

THE TEMPLE OF MUT

The Eastern Avenue of ram-headed sphinxes leads to the Temple of Mut, the wife of Amun and mother of Khonsu. The temple was surrounded by a brick enclosure wall and forms the second largest temple complex at Thebes after the Great Temple of Amun.

The basic plan of the temple is similar to that of Khonsu, although there are certain differences between the two temples. In the first and second courts of the Temple of Mut there are numerous seated and standing granite statues of Sekhmet. Sekhmet was a violent goddess, who was connected with wars, plagues and diseases and who was depicted as a woman with the head of a lioness. A great number of her statues were found in this temple. Many of them remain in situ and the rest are now in museum collections all over the world. The temple itself is in a very ruined condition. The remains of two other *temples*, of *Amenophis III* and of *Ramesses III* lie respectively to the north-east and to the south-west of the sacred lake of the Temple of Mut. This lake is shaped like a horseshoe and lies behind the Temple of Mut.

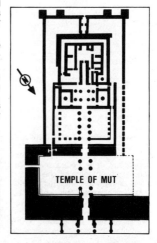

TEMPLE OF MUT

As the visitor has already seen, *the Eastern Avenue of ram-headed sphinxes* starts from the 10th Pylon of the Great Temple of Amun and links that complex with that of the Temple of Mut. After leaving the Temple of Mut a short distance along

The Barque of Amun (on an ostracon)

the Eastern Avenue of sphinxes another *avenue of sphinxes* leads off to the left to join the road back to Luxor. This was the route between the temples of Luxor and Karnak which was followed by the procession of the Festival of Opet. W. Wolf in « Die Kunst Agyptens » says that « the temples were completely organized so that they could control and isolate the masses of people who came from outside to take part in the festival, make them submit to the divine presence and inspire in them a state of religious fear and piety. In order to sense this impression today, it is necessary to reconstruct by imagination the painted reliefs on the walls and their inscriptions which were richly underlined with gold and silver, the festival robes of the numerous religious and civil dignitaries, the golden divine barques which swayed as they were

carried amid clouds of burning incense on the shoulders of the priests above the heads of the faithful and the crowd following behind inspired with religious fervour. »

THE TEMPLE OF PTAH

To the north of the Great Temple of Amun are the temples of Montu and Ptah. The temple of Ptah is certainly worth visiting if this proves possible. To reach the temple, go to the north side-door of the Great Hypostyle Hall of the Great Temple of Amun. From here, an ancient paved road leads to the north-east directly to the temple. Tuthmosis III built and dedicated this temple to Ptah, the god of Memphis. In later times it was enlarged by Shabaka, the Ethiopian king of Egypt and by several of the Ptolemies. Ptah was a creator god, who was believed to have created the world and like Amun was one of the great gods of the Egyptian pantheon. Five successive gateways lead to a colonnade supported by four columns, a small pylon and then a court. The portico at the back of the court is supported by two sixteen-sided columns. There are niches in the walls and a staircase leading to an upper storey. Immediately behind the court are the three chapels of the sanctuary. The central chapel contains a headless seated cult-statue of the god, Ptah. The chapel on the right contains a statue of the goddess, Sekhmet. The statues are illuminated by narrow apertures in the ceiling, which gives them a weird and striking effect, and recreates the mysterious atmosphere which reigned in the temple in ancient times.

Near the Temple of Ptah, the North gateway of the enclosure wall of the Great Temple of Amun leads to the

North Temple precincts, surrounded by a brick wall, and to

THE TEMPLE OF MONTU

The temple is now very ruined. It was built by Amenophis III and dedicated to the god, Montu, who originally was the principal deity of Thebes and who had become a war-god. He is depicted as falcon-headed. An access ramp leads to a colonnaded court with payriform columns, a hypostyle hall, a sanctuary for the sacred barques and the inner sanctuary. Outside the Temple of Montu are the remains of several small adjoining chapels of the Ethiopian and Saite periods, a temple dedicated to the goddess, Maat, and finally the great Ptolemaic gateway on the north.

Further away to the north but not far from the temple are the remains of a quay, which was situated on a canal which in ancient times went to the Temple of Montu at Medamud.

West Thebes

It is recommended that a collective ticket for all the visits is obtained from the Antiquities Service before the excursion to the left bank because tickets are not sold on the sites. This ticket can also be purchased near the landing-stage on the left bank of the Nile. Hire a vehicle, a taxi, a bicycle or even a donkey (for prices see p. 394). At least a whole day needs to be taken for the visit to the necropolis ; that is the minimum time to see the most important things superficially. Stay two days for a little more detailed visit. Remember that all the kings' tombs close at one o'clock ; the private tombs close later, at five o'clock.

By car, you are confined to the roads and will therefore follow the same route several times ; conversely, with a donkey, there will be the opportunity to follow the magnificent mountain path which connects the *Valley of the Kings* to the temple of *Deir el-Bahri* or to tomb no. 16 at *Deir el-Medina*. To take the path on foot requires no fear of heights, heat (no shade) or long distances. It is not possible to visit all the known royal tombs, some may be closed at the time of your visit.

After inhumation in mastabas in the Archaic period, the most common form of royal funeral had the following schedule from the end of the Third Dynasty : from the valley temple, to the causeway, the funerary temple and finally the pyramid. With the beginning of the Eighteenth Dynasty a new scheme developed which was to be maintained throughout the next few centuries, with the exception of Akhenaten who excavated his tomb at *Tell el-Amarna,* all the other pharaohs of the XVIIIth, XIXth, and XXth dynasties were interred at *Biban el-Mûlûk,* the Valley of the Kings.

In the flanks of the Libyan desert wadis which constitute this valley with limestone peaks about 300 m (985 ft.) high, the kings excavated systems of galleries which reached 200 m (655 ft.) in length and a great depth ; the rock tombs were organised and planned according to an established plan. The most usual was of three corridors extending one after the other with annexes for the first, niches for the funerary material in the second and third ; then an antechamber, the vault with a hollow for the sarcophagus and annexes for the precious funerary furniture. The walls were decorated with litanies and representations from the funerary books and the very necessary instructions and provisions which would be needed on the way to the after-life in order to overcome danger.

From *Luxor*, cross the Nile in a moter-boat. Then the route leads right towards the west in the direction of the red tinted mountain chain. At *el-Fadlya* canal turn to the right, reach the village of *Qurna* and enter to the left into the village street. The

village well at the cross-roads is just in front of the funerary temple of king Sethos I.

The Funerary Temple of Sethos I

Sethos I undertook this edifice which was to be a funerary temple for his father Ramesses I and himself, but he was not able to finish it. It was left to Ramesses II to finish and decorate it. Only a third of the original temple exists today and it is entered directly by the colonnade, the nine clustered papyrus bud columns (once ten) of which formed the façade. The middle door leads directly to the beautiful *hypostyle hall* (6 papyriform columns with closed capitals) ; the ceiling is decorated with cartouches

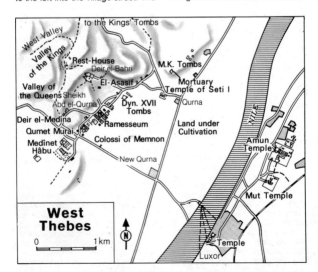

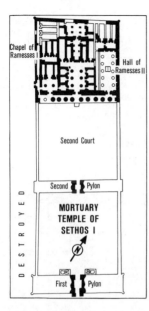

Chapel of Ramesses I

Hall of Ramesses II

Second Court

Second Pylon

MORTUARY TEMPLE OF SETHOS I

First Pylon

DESTROYED

of Sethos I surrounded by vultures, serpents and winged solar disks.

Bas-reliefs : (on the left) Sethos and Ramesses II making offerings ; Mut suckles Sethos ; (on the right) Hathor suckles Sethos. In three lateral chambers on the right and left, finely executed bas-reliefs reproduce cult scenes and the king presenting offerings in front of the sacred barque ; he is dressed as a priest or even as Osiris in front of Amun and Mut of Thebes and Ptah and Sekhmet of Memphis.

The *sanctuary* is situated in the centre in the middle of various chambers ; at the right is the hall of the cult

of Ramesses II ; at the left is that of Ramesses I. Now deprived of its columns, the solar court of Ramesses II is complete on the right with its solar altar of Re ; notice the reliefs of the chapels on the other side, in the west wing of the temple. Sethos censes the barque of Amun and anoints the statue of his father ; a representation of the king's Osiris coffin with Isis seated in the form of a falcon.

From the temple of Sethos I, take the route to the Valley of the Kings, a route which has been followed for 500 years, and several millenia ago there were funeral processions to inter the dead sovereigns in the valley. The path at the bottom of the valley winds between the limestone mountains and ends in the gorge called *Biban el-Mûlûk* by the Arabs « the doors of the kings », and also the « Valley of the Dead ».

The Valley of the Kings

The most interesting tombs for the tourist are described here, grouped

BIBAN EL MÛLÛK
"VALLEY OF THE KINGS"

simply according to their site and in the order which will be followed on the visit. These are the tombs numbered 6, 8, 9, 62, 35, 34, 11, 16, 17 (22, 23) ; the official numbers of the tombs are used to identify them.

Tomb of Ramesses IX, XXth dynasty (n° 6). Staircase entry with a ramp ; the first corridor has four lateral chambers, the second and third corridors have two niches ; the antechamber is a hall of four pillars ; then follows the sarcophagus chamber. It is excavated into the rock for a distance of 82 m (270 ft.). *Paintings* on the walls : the corridor walls have texts taken from the *Book of the Dead* ; the king in front of the gods (third chamber on the right) ; representations of the king's mummy, a scarabaeus with solar disc. Walls of the sarcophagus chamber : divinities and genii of the after-life. On the ceiling : the sky goddess Nut represented twice as the symbol of the morning sky and evening sky : constellations and barques which cross the heavens.

Tomb of Merneptah, XIXth dynasty (n° 8). Very long corridor with landings ; on the walls there are litanies of Re, texts from the *Book of the Gates* and representations of divinities ; in the antechamber the granite cover of the exterior sarcophagus, in the sarcophagus chamber, which has pillars and a vaulted roof, the interior sarcophagus lid with a representation of the pharaoh ; the bottom of the sarcophagus is in place. Total length of tomb : 110 m (361 ft.)

Tomb of Ramesses VI, XXth dynasty (n° 9). It consists of three corridors, a vestibule, an antechamber, two corridors, a second vestibule, and the sarcophagus chamber. *Wall paintings in the corridors* : scenes

and texts from the *Book of the Gates* and the *Book of that which is in the Underworld* ; the navigation of the sun. *Hall with four pillars* : set of astronomical `representations. Third corridor : on the ceiling there are numerous constellations. *Sarcophagus chamber* : remains of the granite sarcophagus ; on the ceiling two representations of the sky goddess Nut which correspond to the day and night sky ; astronomical figures : on the walls, texts from the *Book of the Dead*, Greek and Coptic graffiti.

The tomb was started for Ramesses V. The debris from this tomb covered the entrance to the tomb of Tutank-

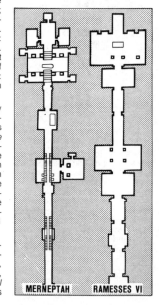

MERNEPTAH   RAMESSES VI

hamun up to 1922. This tomb had been violated after the burial of the king and then resealed. From then it remained unknown and intact, unlike the other royal tombs.

Tomb of Tutankhamun, XVIIIth dynasty (n° 62). This hypogeum of the late eighteenth dynasty is in fact the smallest, but certainly the most celebrated of the tombs in the Valley of the Kings. The treasures which were found there have so far never been surpassed, either in quantity nor in quality. After a staircase and a corridor, the antechamber is entered where a step leads into the sarcophagus chamber (6,50 m × 4 m (21½ ft. × 13 ft.)) ; the wall which originally closed the entrance has been removed. The two statues of the king which guarded this door are now in the Egyptian Museum in Cairo. The shrines which enclosed the king's coffin are also in Cairo. The exterior sarcophagus of yellow quartzite, now covered with glass, is still in place with a gilded wooden coffin which still contains the mummy of the young king. The other coffins, as well as all the rest of the objects, have also been transported to Cairo Museum. The wall paintings, of mediocre quality, but interesting because of their themes, are fairly well preserved. Only the sarcophagus chamber was decorated ; on the east wall is a representation of the king's funeral, with the coffin on a sledge. The north and west walls show king Ay, the successor of Tutankhamun, performing the rite of « opening the mouth » for the dead king ; Tutankhamun makes a sacrifice to the gods ; he stands with his ka before Osiris.

The Englishman, *Howard Carter*, who was commissioned by Lord Carnavon to explore the valleys of the Theban desert, discovered the tomb in 1922. By chance it had been forgotten and the tomb robbers (except those in antiquity) had missed it. The young king Tutankhamun had been virtually unknown in Egyptian history up to the discovery of his tomb. Carter must be thanked for his perspicacity because, thanks to him, all the riches of Tutankhamun's tomb can be admired today *in situ* and in Cairo Museum. Carter had the fortune to find a seal, a cup and a wooden box with the name of Tutankhamun and he concluded that the tomb of this little known king must be somewhere in the area he was searching. After several seasons of research he finally found the entrance to the tomb.

The story of the work and the opening of the chambers, the shrines and the sarcophagus and coffins, the discovery of the well preserved treasures and jewels, furniture and tomb paintings reads like a romantic novel, yet it only relates the truth. Its hero, a young pharaoh, became at one stroke one of the most celebrated Egyptian kings. Furthermore, after the excavation of the tomb of Tutankhamun, it is possible to deduce what the extent of royal possessions was which had hitherto only been imagined, but of which there is now concrete proof.

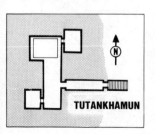

TUTANKHAMUN

« Opening the Mouth »
(Tutankhamun)

If such treasures were deposited in the tomb of such an insignificant and inglorious king as Tutankhamun and if he could command gold and semi-precious stones in his coffin, what sumptuous treasures must have been contained in the tombs of the great kings such as Sethos I or Ramesses II ! The supposition that a single chamber of the tomb of a celebrated king would have contained more treasures than the entire tomb of Tutankhamun revealed is without doubt true. They must be counted among the inestimable riches which have fallen into the hands of tomb robbers. It is improbable that anymore intact tombs will be found in the Valley of the Kings.

Tomb of Amenophis II, XVIIIth dynasty (n° 35). The plan of this tomb shows how the tomb robbers, who almost always arrived after the tombs were closed, were feared.

The intent was to build a vast and « secure » sepulchre. Therefore the

principal corridor ends in front of a pit ; in it, the entrance to the first chamber was carefully walled up. In the right corner, a staircase and sloping passage lead finally to the sarcophagus chamber. The ceiling represents the blue coloured night sky decorated with many yellow stars which constitute the constellations and the astronomical figures of the decans.

The pillars and walls are decorated with painted representations, here above all are found, on a beige background, rapidly outlined figures, cursive hieroglyphs, in some ways an imitation of unrolled papyrus ; on the pillars, representations of the king in front of the funerary gods. The sandstone sarcophagus in the small chamber with a sunken floor contained the royal mummy of the king until 1934 ; it it is now in Cairo. As well as the mummy of Amenophis, in 1898 nine other royal mummies were found in the tomb which were carried here during the Twenty-first dynasty for reasons of security.

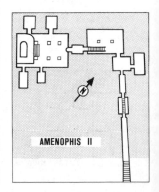

AMENOPHIS II

In turning towards tomb 34, the tomb of king Horemheb is passed (n° 57, on the left). If possible, the unfinished sketches of the Egyptian pantheon can be admired there in passing and some representations with very well preserved colours. The granite sarcophagus is still in the funerary chamber.

Tomb of Tuthmosis III, XVIIIth dynasty (n° 34). By the choice of the siting of the tomb and the construction itself, it is the first tentative step, before even that of Amenophis II (see tomb n° 35, p. 218) to prevent robbers gaining entry to the tomb.

TUTHMOSIS III

The entrance is situated about 10 m (33 ft.) below the ground level. A descending corridor, barred by a pit, leads up to a chamber supported by two square pillars. White stars are sprinkled over the blue ceiling as in the preceding corridor. The walls are entirely covered with very dense representations of genii and divinities.

From there a staircase leads to the sarcophagus chamber which takes the form of an immense royal cartouche. Two pillars support the ceiling which is also blue with yellow constellations. On the walls, figures and texts and cursive hieroglyphs taken from the *Book of that which is in the Underworld* are painted in red on a grey background. On the pillars, there are representations of Tuthmosis III and his family. The sarcophagus is carved of sandstone, its decoration of funerary texts and representations was painted in red. The king's mummy is now in Cairo Museum ; it was found with others in the « royal cache » and not in the tomb.

Returning to the neighbourhood of the tomb of Tutankhamun, and, immediately at the cross-roads, there is the

Tomb of Ramesses III, XXth dynasty (n° 11). The entrance corridor has five niches on each side. The funerary material they must have contained has disappeared. Then the direction of the tomb is changed by a right angle after which a straight line is followed to the chamber with four pillars with an annexe on the right. Two successive vestibules lead to the sarcophagus chamber with eight pillars and four lateral chambers ; further on there is another corridor divided into three parts ; the tomb is 125 m (410 ft.) long.

The decoration is particularly remarkable in the ten lateral chambers or niches of the first corridor ; niches on the left : artisans at work ; the Nile god offers his gifts to the gods of the fields ; scenes of offerings ; sacred animals ; the *ka* of Ramesses ; two harpists, those who were responsible for the tomb being called « the Harper's tomb ». Niches on the right : two sailing boats ; king's armoury with representations of armour and weapons of war ; treasure chamber with representations of jewels and furniture ; scenes of ploughing ; representations of twelve forms of Osiris.

In the corridors and chambers which follow, there are scenes from the *Book of the Dead* ; representations of divinities, etc. In the chamber with four pillars, the four human races. The base of the sarcophagus is in Paris, the lid in Cambridge, although the king's mummy is preserved in Cairo.

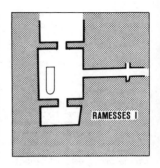

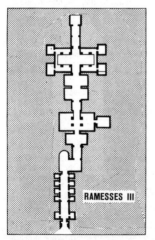

Tomb of Ramesses I, XIXth dynasty (n° 16). The small tomb (Ramesses I reigned only two years and was not able to cut a very important hypogeum) resembles that of Tutankha-

mun ; after a staircase and a corridor, another steep flight of stairs leads to the sarcophagus chamber flanked by two rooms. The walls are decorated with texts from the *Book of the Dead* and representations of the king in front of various divinities on a grey background ; also the goddesses personifying the hours of the night. The sarcophagus is granite with scenes and inscriptions from the *Book of the Dead* painted in yellow.

Tomb of Sethos I, XIXth dynasty (n° 17). If the tomb of Tutankhamun has become the most celebrated in the Valley of the Kings because of its treasures, the tomb of Sethos I is without doubt the most interesting for its plan and its decoration. Time should be taken to visit it calmly.

First corridor : on the walls the god Re and the *Sun Litanies* ; on the ceiling, vultures with outspread wings.

Second corridor (with staircase) : on the walls, representations of the 75 transformations of Re, and texts from the *Book of that which is in the Underworld* ; at the foot of the stairs, on either side, Isis and Nepthys.

Third corridor : on the walls, the voyage of the sun during the hours of the night ; in the small square room which follows, Sethos I before different gods. In continuing to descend, a deep pit is met with. By a wooden foot-bridge and stairs, a room with four pillars is reached ; once again with representations of the sun's transformations in the course of the hours of the night. Also Horus and the four human races : Egyptians, Asiatics with tapered beards, Negroes, Libyans with a feather on their heads. Horus leads the king in front of Osiris and Hathor. On the pillars : the king and divinities. In the lateral annexe room, interesting paintings remain unfinished and are only sketches representing the sun in the course of the hours of the night ; representations of the damned. The king in front of the gods of the dead. Representations of the *Book of the Opening of the Mouth.*

Sarcophagus chamber : in two parts ; at the front it is supported by six pillars, at the back, vaulted. The alabaster sarcophagus which was found there was taken to London (Soanes Museum) ; the king's mummy is in Cairo Museum. The wall paintings reproduce scenes taken from the *Book of the Gates* and the *Book of that which is in the Underworld.* At the left, Anubis performs the ceremony of opening the mouth for the god of the dead, Osiris. In the lateral chamber, on the right, Shu, the god of air, supports the cow of heaven, Nut. The solar barques are represented on her body. Myth of « the destruction of men » by the gods. Re annihilates the guilty humans and only saves a few men. In the left lateral chamber, there are themes taken from the *Book of the Dead.*

The great left *lateral room* with two pillars was probably a chamber consecrated for offerings, which were no doubt deposited on the stone bench which runs around the walls ; on the walls : themes of the *Book of that which is in the Underworld.* Opposite is a small chamber of the resurrection of Osiris, neither this nor the chamber with four pillars at the end is decorated.

If there is time and if the rocky austere paths of the desert appeal, the valley on the west of Biban el-Muluk can also be visited. The tomb of Amenophis III, of the XVIIIth dynasty (n° 22) is found there and the **Tomb of Ay,** XVIIIth dynasty (n° 23). Ay reigned between Tutankhamun and Horemheb. His hypogeum is al-

The Constellations on the Ceiling of the Tomb of Sethos I

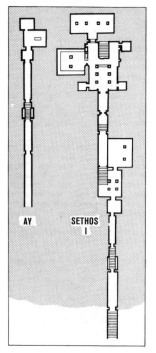

AY   SETHOS I

From the tomb of Sethos I, follow the path which rises to the

Tomb of Hatshepsut, XVIIIth dynasty (n° 20). This is the second tomb of the queen, more than 200 m (700 ft.) long and it goes down almost 100 m (318 ft.) deep. A long corridor with several series of staircases describes an arc and leads to the deep funerary chamber with three pillars. Hatshepsut's sarcophagus (now is Cairo) and that of her father, Tuthmosis I (now in Boston), were found there. Three small annexes open off the sarcophagus chamber. The tomb is unfinished and does not have any decoration.

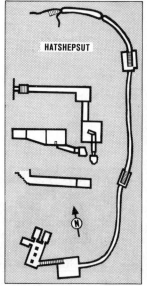

HATSHEPSUT

so called the « tomb of the apes » because twelve cynocephalic baboons are represented on the walls beside funeral scenes, sacrifices and the opening of the mouth. The plan of the tomb is simple ; the style is like that of Tutankhamun, still with Amarnan influences. It is composed of a long descending corridor, a vestibule, the sarcophagus chamber and another small room behind it.

A steep path winds above the Valley of the Kings. From on high, there is a good viewpoint over the whole of the valley and the numerous tomb entrances. Soon the crest is passed over and the Nile valley is seen below with Luxor and Karnak on the other bank. Perpendicularly, at the foot of the cliff, is the cirque of Deir el-Bahri with the ruins of the temple of Mentuhotep on the right and those of the temple of Hatshepsut on the left. Following a large curve, the valley is reached near the rest-house (refreshments) in front of the nobles' tombs of the XIth dynasty.

The Temples of Deir el-Bahri

TEMPLE OF HATSHEPSUT

History : King Mentuhotep of the XIth dynasty had already built his funerary temple in terraces. Hatshepsut's architects and favourites, Senmut and Dedia, were also masters of the work at the temple of Amun at Karnak, and they revived the idea, about 500 years later, of a terraced temple, and erected this unique edifice in Egyptian architecture for the queen. It is situated next to the temple of Mentuhotep, in a semi-circle of rock, dominating the monument with its height of 300 m (984 ft.), at the end of a deep and grandiose valley.

Makare Hatshepsut, daughter of Tuthmosis I and Ahmosi, married her halfbrother, Tuthmosis II, son of princess Mutnefert, who reigned only for a short time. At his death, putting aside her nephew and stepson, the young Tuthmosis III, son of a concubine, she took power and became queen ; finally Tuthmosis III succeeded her and sought to efface her memory. The funerary temple of Hatshepsut was consecrated to Amun with chapels dedicated to Hathor and Anubis. Tuthmosis III erased the figure and the name of Hatshepsut to replace them with his own ; Akhenaten erased the name of Amun in the temple, which was partially restored later by Ramesses II.

Visit : an avenue of sphinxes with portrait heads of the queen formerly led from the temple at the border of the cultivated land and the desert up to a pylon which is now destroyed. In front of the pylon of the funerary temple, two persea trees were planted in square holes in the masonry, the roots of which have been preserved until today. From this point the plan of the temple appears distinct to visitors with its three terraces ; at the front of the upper terrace with lateral sanctuaries, a court opens which gives access to the holy of holies, with three rooms in a row cut deeply into the rock.

A first ramp rises to the lower terrace ; on each side of the ramp, T-shaped pools were used for ritual navigation. The base of the parapets was decorated with recumbent lions. The ramp divides the lower terrace into two colonnades, north on the right, south at the left. Notice the very beautiful bas-reliefs ; south colonnade : the famous representation of the transport and dedication of a temple obelisk of queen Hatshepsut. It has been believed for a long time that it is the obelisk which still stands in the court between the third and fourth pylons of the temple of Karnak (see p. 206). North colonnade : scenes of royal ritual hunting and fishing in a pool.

As on the lower terrace, a ramp separates the intermediate terrace into two parts : at the left the *Punt colonnade*, at the right, the *Birth colonnade*, both admirably decorated with

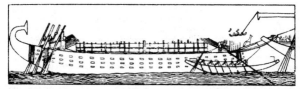

Transport of the Hatshepsut Obelisk

very interesting reliefs and each supported by twenty-two square pillars. The pillars have the same representation on each of their four sides : Amun blessing Hatshepsut (mutilated) or Tuthmosis III by putting his hands on his/her shoulders.

Punt Colonnade : the reliefs record the queen's expedition to Punt (starting on the left). Notice the village of the country with its pointed huts ; the prince of Punt greets the Egyptians ; presents are offered to them ; ivory, gold, incense, ebony, etc. Arrival of the queen of Punt, afflicted by elephantiasis ; myrrh bushes in pots are loaded onto the Egyptian boats ; representations of Red Sea fish ; boats with apes in the rigging ; the return of the Egyptian boats to their land ; Hatshepsut represented as a pharaoh and accompanied by her *ka* dedicates the foreign produce to Amun ; everything is weighed and measured by Thoth ; other gods register the inestimable quantity of precious produce ; the goddess of writing, Seshat, keeps a register. Tuthmosis III censes the barque of Amun ; the queen speaks to Amun ; Hatshepsut seated under a canopy accompanied by her *ka*. Some fragments which are in the Museum at Cairo have been replaced on the walls by casts.

At the extreme south (on the left) there is a chapel of Hathor, protecti-

ve goddess of the necropolis ; the level of the different rooms continues to rise as the temple is penetrated further. The first hypostyle hall is supported by proto-doric columns and Hathor pillars ; the second by sixteen-sided columns. The representations are interesting, although very badly preserved : the queen appears in the form of a young boy suckled by the Hathor cow ; Hatshepsut makes an offering to the Hathor cow in her barque. Notice a very discreet representation, behind a door, of the architect Senmut who wished to be represented in the temple which he had built.

At the right, the north part of the intermediate terrace, is the

Birth Colonnade. Reliefs : Amun engenders Hatshepsut ; the queen Ahmosi hears the news from the mouth of Thoth ; Khnum and the frog-headed goddess Heqet conduct the pregnant Ahmosi to her confinement ; the infant is born ; Amun carries it ; the royal wet-nurses suckle the infant, etc. The various themes of this relief correspond exactly to those represented in the royal birth scenes in the temple of Luxor (see p. 201).

On the right, at the north of the Birth Colonnade, a few steps are climbed to the small chapel of Anubis. It consists of a small *hypostyle hall* (twelve columns) with representations of Hatshepsut in front of various divinities ; then three vaulted chambers which form the sanctuary. On the walls, there are beautiful reliefs which have kept their colours : the queen or Tuthmosis III makes offerings to Anubis and Amun.

The second ramp now leads to the *upper terrace* (important Polish restoration work in progress ; entry forbidden), the Osiris pillars of which are all destroyed except one at the south end. The great hypostyle hall is then entered, now completely destroyed. The representations on the walls, in particular the geographical procession, are very mutilated. The

Sanctuary is composed of a suite of three chambers and different annexe rooms cut in the rock. The first vaulted room is the sanctuary of the

barque ; the second chamber is also vaulted ; the third was not cut until the Ptolemaic period by Euergetes II ; the cults of important gods, Imhotep and Amenhotep, son of Hapu, were evoked there. The chapel became a place of pilgrimage because Imhotep was considered as a god of healing.

On both sides of the central hypostyle hall, there are two symmetrical groups of rooms. On the left, the royal funerary ensemble destined for Tuthmosis I and Hatshepsut with an offering room ; on the walls there are representations of the sacrifice of cattle and antelope ; the reliefs are fine and well preserved. On the other side, there is a solar shrine dedicated to Re-Harakhty with a sun altar in an open court ; small chapel dedicated to Tuthmosis I.

Up to the present, the inventory of

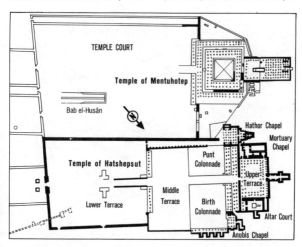

finds from the temple of Hatshepsut includes numerous granite statues of the queen, more than 100 painted sandstone sphinxes, 22 granite sphinxes and more than 40 statues of Osiris in limestone. Fragments of these statues were discovered in the temple, but also in the nearby quarry where Tuthmosis III had transported pieces of statues which he had destroyed. He also erected a shrine above the chapel of Hathor. Recently the remains of a hypostyle hall with bas-reliefs depicting the king's coronation have been discovered, and several colossal statues, one of which represents Senmut.

Under the north angle of the intermediate terrace is the now concealed tomb of *queen Nofru* of the XIth dynasty. At the north of the first terrace, the entrance to the *tomb of Senmut* opens in a quarry. As the architect, he obviously knew this quarry and was allowed to build his tomb there. Later, he fell into disgrace and was buried in his second tomb (n° 71). Under the temple terrace, a corridor about 100 m (328 ft.) long which turns to the west leads to a burial vault through two chambers. Notice a very interesting astronomical ceiling in the second small room.

At the south of the temple of Hatshepsut, the fellahîn discovered, in 1875, a pit where most of the mummies of the pharaohs of the XVIIIth-XXth dynasties had been re-buried together, through fear of robbers, in the XXIst dynasty (the others were put in the tomb of Amenophis II). The robber of Qurna, Abd el-Rassul, must have plundered the royal cache for almost six years up to the time the mummies were transported to Cairo in 1881 by Maspero.

They can be seen today in the mummy room of the Museum (see, p. 131). In the neighbourhood, another common sepulchre with more than 100 coffins of Theban priests was found.

FUNERARY TEMPLE OF MENTU-HOTEP

The temple dates to the XIth dynasty, its construction was finished after the unification of the country. In the courtyard in front, note the descent to the first tomb known as the Bab el-Husan which was never finished ; a royal statue and some furniture were found there however. The funerary temple itself is constructed in terraces above the burial vault. A ramp, flanked on each side by a set of square pillars, leads to the temple terrace. One hundred and forty octagonal columns support a large hall (40 × 42 m (132 × 137 ft.)) above which stands a *pyramid* ; the architecture of this temple is still the same type as in the Old Kingdom. In the burial vault, under the pyramid, the sarcophagus was unexpectedly found. The temple terminates with a large hall supported by 80 octagonal pillars, of which only the bases remain, and the sanctuary cut in the rock. The chapels of the princesses of the royal family were found chiefly in the west part of the enclosure of the funerary temple of Mentuhotep. At the north-west of the temple, a small Hathor shrine was found cut in the rock, dating without doubt to the Middle Kingdom, then perhaps re-decorated by Tuthmosis III and later embellished by Amenophis II. The reliefs represent the Hathor cow ; there was also a statue of the goddess in the form of a cow which is now in the Museum at Cairo (see p. 126).

The Tombs of the Nobles

More than 500 « private tombs » of which 464 are numbered, are known up to the present in the area of the Theban necropolis. Most of the tombs and their chapels belonged to dignitaries and nobles of the New Kingdom (XVIIIth-XXth dynasties), but also the XXVth and XXVIth dynasties. They show us the daily life of the Egyptians as it was almost 4,000 years ago through their freshly coloured paintings. According to the time available, a certain number of these tombs could be visited.

After the vestibule, they have, for the most part, a reversed T-shaped plan. After a court or terrace, the vestibule is entered which is wider than it is long, sometimes supported by pillars, then the chapel is reached with a niche cut in the wall at the back to shelter the statue of the deceased, his wife and sometimes other members of his family. The themes represented on the walls are generally the following : daily life, agricultural work, and the professional occupations of the deceased which permit him to recover in the after-life the occupations and pleasures of his life

to Deir el Bahri Temple
Horemheb
Ineni   Antefoker
     Amenemhat
Amenemhab   Menena   Nakht
Rekhmire

                    Userhat
                    Neferhotep
        Ramose

SHEIKH ABD EL-QURNA   Ramesseum

Ladies at a Feast (from the Tomb of Nakht)

on earth ; representations of the funeral are also found with cult scenes ; frequent representations of funerary banquets appear with musicians and dancers. In the private tombs, few reliefs will be seen, but on the other hand there are many paintings on the walls which were plastered with mud and then whitewashed before being painted light blue or ochre.

From the north to the south, five different areas are known : at the north *Dra Abu el-Naga*, then *Asasif, Sheikh abd el-Qurna*, the most interesting for tourists, *Deir el-Medina* and *Qurnet Marai*. Here the tombs of *Qurna* are described in detail where the visitor, if pressed for time, may stop, Unfortunately, for the other areas only the most important tombs can be enumerated here for reasons of space.

AREA OF ASASIF

Around the excavation house of the *Metropolitan Museum*, at the south of the path which leads to the temple of Hatshepsut, interesting tombs are found, some of which date to the XXVth and XXVth or Saite dynasties : n° 33, Tomb of *Pedamenopet*, one of the largest Theban tombs with numerous mythological scenes ; n° 34, Tomb of *Mentuemhet* ; n° 36, Tomb of *Ibi* ; n° 39, Tomb of *Puimre*, XVIIIth dynasty ; n° 181, Tomb of *Nebamun*, XVIIIth dynasty ; n° 192, Tomb of *Kharuef*, XVIIIth dynasty, very large with columns and pillars and fine reliefs ; n° 279, Tomb of *Pabasa*, deep pit, high brick wall with a very classic plan.

AREA OF SHEIKH ABD EL-QURNA

It is preferable to commence the visit in the north part of this area, at the south of the path which leads from the *Ramesseum* to *Deir el-Bahri*.

Tomb of Nakht (n° 52) astronomer of Amun and royal scribe under Tuthmosis IV. It is perhaps the most beautiful tomb of the necropolis. The paintings are very fresh and well preserved : the dead man and his wife make offerings ; ploughing, sowing, harvesting with a gleaner, flax gathering, measuring and winnowing of the corn ; these agricultural scenes set out in four registers take place in the presence of Nakht ; banquet scenes in the presence of Nakht and his wife ; under her chair, a cat eats a fish ; musicians, dancers, guests ; a blind harpist ; a servant hastens to a guest. Nakht and his wife in a garden ; servants bring birds and fish, capture of the birds ; wine-harvest ; the pitchers are filled. Nakht hunting and fishing in the papyrus thickets. The meal of the deceased and his wife ; offerings.

Tomb of Userhat (n° 51), prophet of the *ka* of Tuthmosis I. Beautiful paintings characteristic of the beginning of the Ramesside period. Paintings : Userhat and his wife and his mother near a pool, under a tree. Their souls are represented in the form of birds drinking the water which is given by the goddess of the sycamore. Amenophis I painted black, Ahmes, Nefertari and Osiris receive the offerings of Userhat, his wife, his mother and his son.

Tomb of Neferhotep (n° 50). Beautiful paintings on the ceiling, but badly preserved. On the walls : king Horemheb presents Neferhotep with a gold collar as a reward. Neferhotep's son offers a sacrifice to the deceased and his wife ; musicians ; pilgrimage to Abydos ; different versions of the « harpist's song » ; festival calendar. At the back of the tomb, five niches with the cult statues of Neferhotep and his family.

Tomb of Ramose (n° 55), vizier under Amenophis III and Amenophis IV (= Akhenaten). Plan : court, hypostyle room with 32 columns, long

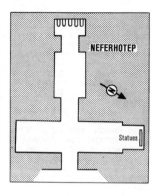

chamber supported by columns. The tomb was not entirely decorated (only sketches in some places and note the change of style which intervened with the Amarna period). *Hypostyle hall* (Amarnan style) : offerings in front of the deceased and his wife ; three beautiful young girls ;

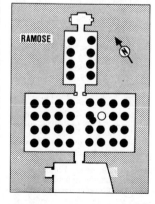

incense is burned on an altar ; Ramose is purified ; group of the dead man's friends ; banquet scene ; priest wearing a panther skin ; parents and friends. The funeral with mourners ; servants bring the funerary presents ; mummies in front of the tomb. Ramose and his wife adore Osiris (classic style). Ramose represented four times offering bouquets to Akhenaten seated under a canopy and accompanied by the goddess Maat ; Ramose rewarded by Akhenaten ; Ramose pays homage to Akhenaten and Nefertiti while the people shout joyfully (compare with the reliefs at Amarna which have the same themes depicted in the same style, p. 283)

Tomb of Menna (n° 69), surveyor and scribe of the cadastral survey under Tuthmosis IV. Paintings : accumulated offerings in front of Menna and his wife, seated ; scene of surveying with the surveying cord ; scenes of agricultural work ; Menna's chair ; the corn is carried and measured ; winnowing, threshing and transport of the corn ; the master surveys the harvest ; young girls quarrel and pull each other's hair ; a peasant plays on the flûte ; ploughing ; harvesting of flax. Menna and his wife adore Osiris. The offering bearers bring various products to them. Scenes of prayers and offerings. Funerary banquet. Funeral procession ; funerary furniture and transport of the coffin ; scene of adoration in front of a stela ; judgement in front of Osiris, Thoth and Horus ; Menna's heart is placed on the balance ; pilgrimage to Abydos. Menna hunting and fishing. Offerings for the dead ; double seated statue of Menna and his wife. The tomb was probably usurped later.

Tomb of Antefoker (n° 60), governor under Sesostris I. It is the most ancient tomb of the necropolis, the only one of the XIIth dynasty. It is composed of a long corridor and a square funerary chamber with a niche which contains a statue of Senet, wife of Antefoker. The paintings are in a rigid style ; hunting with a net ; hunting in the desert ; butchery ; baking ; cooking ; brewing ; the deceased and his wife receive New Year presents ; pilgrimage to Abydos ; funeral procession on the Nile and on the land ; dance of the priestesses of Hathor ; musicians ; harpists ; stelae dedicated to Senet.

Tomb of Horemheb (n° 73), royal scribe under Tuthmosis III, Amenophis II, Tuthmosis IV and Amenophis III. Paintings : banquet with musicians and dancers ; recruiting and supplying of soldiers. Nubians and Syrians carry tribute to king Tuthmosis IV. Funeral ; funerary furniture ; judgement in front of Osiris ; Thoth and Maat ; offerings to the dead man. Horemheb hunts birds and fishes in the marshes.

Tomb of Ineni (n°81), inspector of the granaries of Amun. Paintings : Ineni at work ; treasures of the temple of Amun ; Nubian and Syrian tributes destined for the temple. Ineni hunts in the Nile marshes and in the desert. House, garden, pool and granaries of the deceased ; agricultural scenes ; harvests. Funeral convoy ; pilgrimage to Abydos ; scenes of offerings ; Seated statues : Ineni and his wife, his parents.

Tomb of Amenemhet (n° 82), scribe and superintendent of the granaries of Amun. Paintings ; banquet at the New Year festival with music and singing. Bull fight. Funeral ; pilgrimage of the deceased to Abydos ;

scenes of a banquet with musicians ; offerings ; festival of Hathor with singers.

Tomb of Amenemhab (n° 85), commander of the troops under Tuthmosis III and Amenophis II. Paintings on the walls and on the pillars ; the dead man and his wife. Supplying of the troops. Autobiography of the dead man in front of king Tuthmosis IV. Syrians bring tribute ; Amenemhab inspects the tomb equipment. Banquet. Funeral ; funerary banquet with numerous musicians ; procession to the tomb ; offerings. Fish pond in the garden ; hyaena hunt. The gods Anubis and Osiris.

Tomb of Rekhmire (n° 100), governor of Thebes and vizier under Tuthmosis III and Amenophis II. Paintings : audiences ; collection of taxes ; text concerning the installation and the duties of the vizier ; presentation of foreign tribute ; gifts from Somalia, Crete, Nubia and Syria ; temple workshops. Hunting in the marshes and the desert. The dead man inspects the work of the craftsmen. Funeral ; banquet with musicians ; offerings to Rekhmire, his wife and his mother ; pilgrimage to Abydos.

The Ramesseum

This funerary temple of Ramesses II was dedicated to the dynastic god, Amun. Beside the actual temple, the scribes and artists were organised into a type of temple school. The centre of an important installation was there surrounded with a brick enclosure (270 × 175 m (885 × 574 ft.) which contained a palace of Ramesses II, a small temple of Sethos I, magazines, stables, granaries

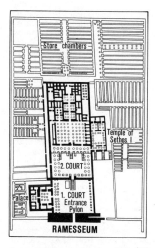

RAMESSEUM

and houses of the personnel. All the brick buildings are very ruined. The funerary temple itself has suffered a lot ; nevertheless it is one of the most interesting and monumental groups of ruins of west Thebes. The plan of the temple is still recognisable : entrance pylon, first and second courts, vestibule, great hypostyle hall, two vestibules and the sanctuary.

The *pylon* at the entrance is 67 m (220 ft.) wide. On the interior face, notice the great reliefs with scenes of war against the Hittites. In the first court, almost entirely destroyed, lie the remains of a pink granite statue of Ramesses II ; it was destroyed by the Persian Cambyses. When it was standing, this statue was 18 m (60 ft.) high, 23 m (75½ ft.) with the crown and it weighed almost 1,000 tons (Shelley's « Ozymandias »).

Only four Osiris pillars remain in the second court which was once enclosed by a double colonnade on each side. Behind this, on the interior face of the second pylon, are scenes of war against the Hittites (battle of Kadesh) and above them, a representation of the festivals of the god Min. The central staircase which leads to the vestibule was flanked by two colossal statues of the king in black granite, partially preserved.

Notice three registers of interesting representations on the walls of the vestibule ; from base to top : the eleven sons of Ramesses II ; Atum and the war god Montu escorting the king into the temple ; Montu presents the sign of life to the king ; Ramesses II venerating the Theban triad, makes offerings to Ptah and offers incense to Min.

The great *hypostyle hall* is composed of three high naves (papyrus columns with open capitals) and three lower ambulatories on each side (papyrus columns with closed capitals), as in the temple of Karnak, and it is illuminated in the same fashion by stone grilles. Reliefs : storming of the Hittite fortress of Dapur ; exploits of the sons of Ramesses II. At the back of the hall, on each side of the door, Ramesses II and his sons in front of different divinities. On the column shafts, Ramesses II makes offerings to the Theban gods.

Eight papyriform columns with closed capitals support the ceiling of the first *vestibule*. Between the columns, on the ceiling, are astronomical representations, circumpolar stars, phases of the moon. On the walls, on the left and right of the entrance, a procession of the barques of Amun, Mut and Khonsu carried by priests ; on the west wall the persea,

the sacred tree of Heliopolis ; Atum, Seshat and Thoth write the name of Ramesses on the leaves in his presence.

In the *second antechamber*, once the temple library, only four pillars of the original eight remain ; on the walls, representations of cult scenes ; the king offers to Ptah and Re. The sanctuary and the annexe chamber at the back are completely destroyed.

Deir el-Medina

The path which leads from the Ramesseum to the « Valley of the Queens » allows a visit to be made to the

Temple of Deir el-Medina, as it passes the mountain (about 1 km (½ mi.) from the Ramesseum). Ptolemy III Philopator began the construction of this sanctuary which was completed by Ptolemy VIII Euergetes II (145-116 B.C.). It is dedicated to the goddess of the necropolis, Hathor, and to Maat, goddess of truth. The plan is as follows : court, small hypostyle hall, pronaos and three small chapels. Two flower capital columns elegantly support the ceiling of the hypostyle. Notice the representations of royal sacrifices in the pronaos, the four winds on the architrave : the north wind in the form of a ram with four heads and two wings ; the south wind, a lion with four wings ; the east wind, a scarab with four wings with the head of a ram ; the west wind, a bird with four wings and the head of a ram. The reliefs of the three chapels are very interesting ; right chapel : Ptolemy IV and Ptolemy VII before the gods ; central chapel : Ptolemy IV and his sister Arsinoe ; Ptolemy VI and VII make offerings to the gods ;

left chapel : the judgement of the dead ; the goddesses of justice with feathers on their heads lead the deceased to the tribunal of the after-life ; Thoth records the verdict ; at the back, Osiris separates the good from the sinners with the four sons of Horus on a lotus flower on one side, the « Great Devourer » on the other in the form of a hippopotamus. On the door lintel is a representation of Osiris in the form of a ram with four heads.

THE VILLAGE OF THE NECROPOLIS WORKERS

At the south east of the temple, at the end of a small valley, the long rectangular plan of the *village of the necropolis workers* can be distinguished (entrance at the north). This village is surrounded with an enclosure wall and existed separately from the rest of the region. This is the reason why the inhabitants were supplied directly from the royal administration. The necropolis workers

lived there ; quarrymen, stone-workers, engravers, painters and officials in the administration of west Thebes ; the exact location where they worked as well as the reason for their work remained fairly secret. The thousands of ostraca (pottery or stone) with figures or inscriptions, inform us of the daily life of the village in its smallest detail and of the social problems of the workers. The small buildings were very narrow ; traces of the principal village streets have been found. The houses had an upper floor, sometimes with a store-room and a terrace ; the illustration shows the plan and section of the house-type of Deir el-Medina.

TOMBS OF THE NECROPOLIS WORKERS

They were constructed and decorated by specialised necropolis workers who had the opportunity to build their personal tombs in the style of their period ; the most remarkable can be visited. Notice the

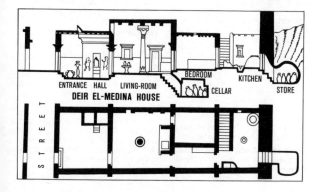

ENTRANCE   HALL   LIVING-ROOM   BEDROOM   KITCHEN   STORE   CELLAR
DEIR EL-MEDINA HOUSE

STREET

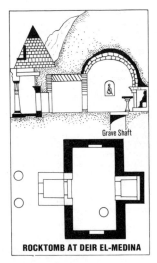

Grave Shaft

ROCKTOMB AT DEIR EL-MEDINA

small pointed pyramids which surmount the entrances of the tombs (XIXth and XXth dynasties) ; see the plan and section of a classic tomb. The visit commences on the side of the hill with tomb n° 217, then tomb n° 3 and finally tomb n° 1 (tourists pressed for time should content themselves with tomb n° 1).

Tomb of Ipuy (n° 217), engraver under the reign of Ramesses II. Paintings : daily life of Ipuy ; preparation of the funerary furniture ; funeral procession ; Ipuy's house and garden ; a shaduf ; agricultural scenes ; fishing ; prayers and offerings. Two statues : Ipuy and his wife.

Tomb of Pashedu (n° 3). Paintings in the tomb chamber. Pashedu kneeling drinks at the water's edge in the after-life ; members of the fa-

mily of the owner of the tomb ; pilgrimage to Abydos ; chapter of the *Book of the Dead* and negative confession on the limestone sarcophagus which has now disappeared ; Pashedu with his wife and child in a boat ; Osiris and Horus ; different divinities on the ceiling.

Tomb of Sennedjem (n° 1). Paintings : the sons of the deceased make an offering to the mummy accompanied by Isis and Nepthys. Sennedjem and his wife in adoration ; Anubis embalms the mummy ; Anubis leads the dead man in front of Osiris for the judgement of his soul ; the fields of the underworld full of fruit-laden trees ; Sennedjem and his wife working in the fields ; the couple adore the guardians of the ten gates. Paintings on the ceiling : the goddess of the sycamore presents food and water to the dead ; the dead man opens the doors to the after-life.

The area of the hill of Qurnet Murai has a series of interesting tombs which date from the XVIIIth and XIXth dynasties. The most beautiful is without doubt that of the viceroy of Kush, Amenhotep called Huy (n° 40) ; a visit is recommended if there is enough time.

The Valley of the Queens

A track about 1 km (½ mi.) long connects *Deir el-Medina* to the *Valley of the Queens*, Arabic : *Biban el-Harem*, which the Egyptians called « The Place of Perfection » (*ta set neferu*). It is there that the queens, princes and princesses were laid to rest. There are more than 70 tombs of the XVIIIth, XIXth and XXth dynasties. Without always having the quality, these tombs resemble however those in the Valley of the kings. No reliefs are found here, but paintings on a layer of Nile mud, smoothed, then whitewashed. Our brief circuit (5 tombs) includes the tomb of queen Nefertari ; it is certainly the most beautiful in the valley, but entry is difficult (special authorisation is required from the Antiquities Service because of its state of decay).

Tomb of queen Nefertari (n° 66), wife of Ramesses II. Unfortunately, the tomb is continually decaying (subsidence of the earth and progressive deterioration of the colours). Paintings : the queen seated under a canopy plays draughts ; the queen's *ka* in the form of a bird ; Nefertari adores different divinities ; the mummy on its funeral bier ; ritual scenes accompanied by texts from the *Book of the Dead* ; the queen before Osiris, she adores Harakhty and other gods ; Nefertari, sacred animals, different gods (Khnum, Isis and Nephthys) ; Thoth receives writing materials. Stair walls : Nefertari adores Isis and Nephthys ; Maat with large wings. The queen's sarcophagus in a very bad condition was found in the chamber with four pillars. Starry sky on the ceiling of the funeral chamber.

Tomb of Amenherkhopshef (n° 55), son of Ramesses II, commander of troops. Paintings : Isis embraces Ramesses III ; the king offers incense to Ptah ; the prince in front of divinities and his father, scenes taken from the *Book of the Gates*. The annexe rooms were not decorated. The prince's granite sarcophagus is still in place.

Tomb of queen Tyti (n° 52), wife of a Ramesses (XXth dynasty). Paintings in the corridor and the sarcophagus chamber ; the goddess Maat kneels with open winged arms to receive the queen. Tyti adores several divinities, the scorpion goddess Selkis and Neith ; gods, demons, Hathor in her human form and in the form of a cow, Osiris, Selkis, Neith, Nephthys, Thoth and Isis ; various offerings ; the queen in adoration.

Tomb of prince Khaemwese (n° 44), son of Ramesses III, high-priest

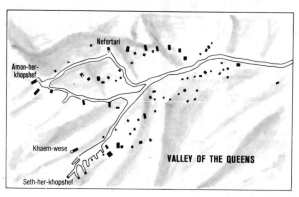

Nefertari

Amon-her-khopshef

Khaem-wese

Seth-her-khopshef

VALLEY OF THE QUEENS

of Ptah at Memphis. There are abundant paintings of the prince and his father before various gods in the process of presenting offerings and adoring them and numerous texts from the *Book of the Dead*.

The Tomb of prince Seth-her-khopshef (n° 43), the son of Ramesses III. The paintings are now very blackened by smoke, but are similar to those in tomb n° 44.

Medinet Habu

Here is situated the *Mortuary Temple of Ramesses III*, which is similar in its general plan to the *Ramesseum* (see p. 231) and which is one of the last great buildings of the Egyptian monumental architecture of the New

Kingdom. The Mortuary Temple itself is built of sandstone and lies in the centre of an enclosure, which also contained the King's palace. The brick enclosure wall is more than 10 m (33 ft.) thick and 18 m (59 ft.) high. The High Gate, or migdol, on the east and the West Gateway, which opens onto the desert behind the temple, are in line with the axis of the temple which was east-west. Still in line with the axis but outside the enclosure were a quay and an artificial lake at the end of a canal, which led from the temple to the Nile. To the north the earlier temples of *Ay* and *Horemheb* lie against the side of the enclosure wall. To the south of the main temple and on a slightly different axis is a small temple of the Eighteenth Dynasty dating to the reigns of Hatshepsut and Tuthmosis III, which was considerably enlarged in the Ptolemaic and Roman periods.

From the Twenty-third Dynasty small funerary chapels of the God's Wives of Amun were built inside the enclosure and not far from the Eighteenth Dynasty temple. In later times the Romans started building near to the storerooms, the priests' houses and the administrative offices. The Copts converted the second court of the Eighteenth Dynasty temple into a church dedicated to St. Menas in the 7th century. The temple was cleared during excavations in the 19th century, its ground-plan was revealed and can be seen today in a good state of preservation.

THE EASTERN HIGH GATE

The High Gate [A], which is 22 m (72 ft.) high, is situated behind the quay and the gate with porter's lodges [B]. It was the main entrance to the enclosure and was built like a fortress

TEMPLE OF MEDINET HABU

Great Temple of Ramesses III

Enclosure Wall of Ramesses III

King's Palace

Nilometer

Pavilion of Ramesses III

C   D

A   E

Outer Wall   B

Sacred Lake

gateway in the Syrian architectural style. The reliefs on the façades of the towers of the gateway show the king in victorious combat against his enemies in the presence of Re-Ha-rakhty. Below are seven bound prisoners who symbolise the conquered peoples : a Hittite, an Amorite, a Libyan, a Sherden, a Bedouin, a Tyrrhenian, and a Philistine. The king kills with his own hand a Libyan and a Nubian in the presence of Amun. Between the towers on the walls between the first and second stories are consoles' or brackets which are decorated with the busts of prisoners-of-war. The upper storey was used as a harem on occasions and is decorated accordingly. One such interior scene of the king being served by young maidens can be seen from below in the gateway to the left of the west upper window. A modern staircase in the south tower ascends to the upper apartments. Through the windows there is a good view over the surrounding area.

Beyond the *migdol* or High Gate on the left are the small *funerary chapels of the God's Wives of Amun* [C] dating to the Twenty-fourth, Twen-ty-fifth and Twenty-sixth Dynasties of Shepenupet I, Amenirdis I, She-penupet II, Nitocris and Mehten-weskhet. Opposite the chapels is the *Gateway of Nectanebo I* [D] beyond which is situated the small *Temple of the Eighteenth Dynasty* [E], which lies on a slanting axis in comparison with the High Gate and the main temple of Ramesses III. The temple was begun by Hatshepsut, conti-nued by Tuthmosis III and then partly destroyed by Akhenaten. It was restored by Horemheb and Sethos I. In later times it was progressively en-larged until the Roman period. The large first pylon was built in the late Ptolemaic period.

THE MORTUARY TEMPLE OF RAMESSES III

The temple was dedicated to Amun and according to Egyptian theology stood on the site of Djamy, the pri-mordial hill, the sacred place of the eight primordial gods. In the Twen-tieth Dynasty, the temple was the administrative centre of the Theban necropolis. In plan it exhibits all the

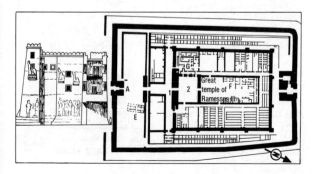

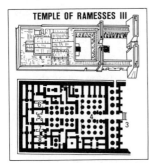

TEMPLE OF RAMESSES III

king does homage to the gods ; he leads a row of bound Syrian captives ; he storms a fortress carrying his bow and arrows ; the return of the triumphant expedition ; the king leads the captives before the Theban triad and offers them to the gods. On the wall of the *Second Pylon* is a long inscription describing the King's victory over « the Sea-peoples » in the 8th year of the reign ; the king leads the captives before Amun and Mut.

The south or left colonnade of the court forms the façade of the palace of Ramesses III. Three doors in the wall lead into the palace. Above the doors, in the middle of the wall, there was a balcony window or « window of appearances » from where the king could watch the ceremonies and festivals in the court and from where he could throw rewards to the favoured. On either side of the window are scenes of the king in battle and parading in his chariot with a lion running by the side of the horses.

elements of the classic Egyptian temple : first pylon, first court, second pylon, second court, hypostyle hall, two small columned vestibules or halls, the sanctuary and adjoining rooms.

First Pylon [1]. Except for the grooves for the flagstaffs the exterior façades are covered with reliefs. The king triumphs over his enemies in the presence of Amun-Re-Harakhty. The conquered peoples are listed. Ptah inscribes the years of the king's reign on a palm-branch. On the inner side of the First Pylon are scenes from the Libyan campaign of Ramesses. The king in his chariot pursues the fleeing Libyans. Ramesses receives the Libyan captives and the spoils of war. A long inscription describes the military expedition and campaign. The severed hands and penises of the dead enemies are counted.

First Court [2]. The court is more than 30 m (98 ft.) long and about 40 m. (131 ft.) wide. The colonnade on the right (north) is supported by seven Osiride pillars. The scenes on the walls are of great interest : the

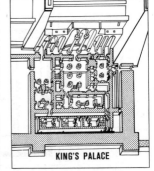

KING'S PALACE

The Royal Palace [G]. Parts of the palace have been restored and some of the rooms now give an impression of their former grandeur. These are the central audience room with a pedestal on which stood the throne, a bedroom, a bathroom, a wardrobe room, the queen's apartments and the rooms for the ladies of the harem.

Second Court [3]. This is surrounded by colonnades. On the north and south are columns with bud-capitals, on the east are Osiride pillars and on the west there is a terrace with eight Osiride pillars in front of eight columns. The court is about 40 m. square (125 × 138 ft.) in size. During the Christian period the court was converted into a church but the reliefs on the walls were not damaged. On the north and north-east colonnades are scenes from the festival of Min, the god of fertility, which show : the arrival of the king ; the presentation of offerings ; the procession of the white bull, the sacred animal of Min ; the flight of four pigeons towards the four cardinal points ; the king cutting a symbolic ear of corn ; offerings being made. Below, are scenes of the procession of the three sacred barques of Amun, Mut and Khonsu of Thebes. On the south and south-east colonnades are scenes from the festival of Ptah-Seker, and from the campaign against the Libyans with a long inscription describing the war. On the west colonnade are scenes of Ramesses and various members of his family before the gods.

The Great Hypostyle Hall [4]. The eight papyriform columns with open capitals along the central aisle were much higher than the sixteen columns with closed capitals of the four lateral aisles, two on each side of the central aisle. On the north-east side of the hall are small chapels dedicated to Ptah, Osiris, Ramesses III and Re, which contain various religious scenes. Opposite on the south-west side of the hall are the treasure rooms, which still retain their original roofing. The scenes here show the treasures of the temple : sacks of gold, ingots, precious stones, gold objects and plaques, jewels and musical instruments.

The Sanctuary [5]. There are two small halls or vestibules, each supported by eight columns between the Hypostyle Hall and the sanctuary. Four columns supported the roof of the sanctuary for the sacred barque of Amun. To the right is the sanctury of Khonsu [6] and to the left that of Mut [7]. A small room nearby [8], dedicated to the gods of the dead and in particular to Osiris, has an astronomical ceiling.

In the Eighteenth Dynasty, Ay and Horemheb had built their temples to the north. They had a similar plan to the later temple of Ramesses III. The plan included three pylons, a palace, storerooms, houses, administrative buildings and a temple at the centre with beautiful papyriform columns with open capitals in the hypostyle hall. Today only the buried ruins of these buildings remain.

The Colossi of Memnon

On the way back to the Nile the visitor passes two colossal seated statues of Amenophis III. Originally they stood in front of the pylon of his mortuary temple, which has now completely disappeared. Only a few scattered blocks of it remain. Even in antiquity, the fame of these statues

Amenophis III, an alabaster statue, a sphinx with the body of a crocodile and a large royal quartzite statue.

The two monolithic colossi were carved out of sandstone from Aswan. The name of « the Colossi of Memnon » comes from the Greek (Memnon, son of Aurore). The statues became famous in antiquity at the beginning of the Roman Empire when the north colossus after it had been broken began to emit a musical note at sunrise. Today we know that these sounds were produced by the effect of a sudden change in temperature and humidity which split the surface of the stone. After a visit to Thebes, the emperor Septimus Severus ordered the statue to be repaired in 199 B.C. and after this it was silent. Today on the colossus on the right (south) can be seen the names and dedications inscribed in Greek and Latin by numerous visitors to the monument in antiquity. There is only one inscription in demotic. The earliest inscription dates from the reign of Nero, a great number of inscriptions date to the reign of Hadrian and the latest ones date to the reigns of Septimus Severus and Caracalla.

had spread beyond the frontiers of Egypt. They are about 18 m (59 ft.) high and would have been more than 20 m (66 ft) high with their crowns, which have now disappeared. The colossus on the left (north) is flanked on the right by Amenophis's wife Tiy, and on the left by his mother, Mut-em-weya. Between the legs is another figure, which is no longer recognisable. On each side of the throne is a symbolic representation of the union of Upper and Lower Egypt — two Nile gods entwine the sedge and the papyrus, the floral symbols of the Two Lands. Aside from the colossi, the other relics which have been found of the great mortuary temple which stood here, include a large dedicatory stela of

After leaving the Colossi of Memnon, the visitor passes the modern village of Qurna and crosses the sugar cane fields in order to reach the landing-stage to catch a ferry-boat across the Nile.

Aswan

(See plan, p. 358). *Aswan*, the capital of the southernmost province of Upper Egypt, can be reached either by air (see p. 395), by river-boat (see p. 395), by train (see p. 395) or by road (see p. 297). If travelling by road, follow routes n°3 (Cairo to Asyût, see p. 274), n°4 (Asyût to Luxor, see p. 287), and n°5 (Luxor to Aswan, see p. 297). Aswan is also the departure point for route n°6, which crosses Egyptian Nubia and goes to Abu Simbel (see p. 303).

Aswan has a population of 200,000 and is the capital of the province in the area of the First Cataract. The town is situated on the east bank between the river and the eastern desert hills which here rise to a height of 100 m (328 ft.). In antiquity Aswan, called *Sunu* by the ancient Egyptians and *Syene* by the Greeks, was the gateway to the interior of Africa and an important centre of trade. All the main trading routes and caravan trails converged on the town. The stone quarries in the area around the town provided the pharaohs with grey and pink granite for their buildings and statues. The Greek geographer, Eratosthenes, (276-196 B.C.) used the geographical position of the town in order to calculate the circumference of the earth, as at that time Aswan lay on the latitude of the Tropic of Cancer. In the Christian period the town was the seat of a bishop. The town enjoyed periods of prosperity under the domination of the Caliphs, but also suffered severely from the plundering raids of Bedouin Arabs from the

nearby desert regions. These raids were ended in 1517 when the Sultan Selim stationed a garrison in the town.

Aswan

For a long time Aswan has been a popular winter holiday resort as the climate here is dry, the air is pure and the sky is always blue and clear. The climate is particularly beneficial to those who suffer from asthma and also for certain skin diseases as the sands here are slightly radioactive. But it is difficult to say whether the past history of the town as a popular holiday resort can remain compatible with its new role as an industrial centre. Today in the town there are many industrial complexes such as nitrate fertilizer factories and foundries, which are among the most important in Africa, and above all there is the new high dam across the

Nile. The dam has completely changed the town and the environment
of the area around it. In fact, as the
reservoir created by the dam is filling, the climate here is also undergoing a change and becoming
much more humid.

However, in spite of this, Aswan is
still a pleasant place to visit and the
visitor can enjoy the sights of the
bazaar quarter in the centre of the
town, the ancient fort, the avenue
along the Nile, the island of Elephantine nearby and the other islands stretched out among the rocks
of the cataract. Below are described
the principal sights of interest in the
town and in the surrounding region,
which is rich in ancient monuments.

Right Bank (east bank of the Nile)

THE QUARRIES [1]

The ancient granite quarries are
reached after a fairly short walk to
the south of the ruins of the Ptolemaic temple of Isis and of the fort of
Sidi Harun. In the north quarry is the
famous unfinished obelisk, the lower
face of which was never detached
from the rock. It is 41.75 m (137 ft.)
long and thus if completed would
have been higher than any other
obelisk known. Its weight is 1170
metric tons (1152 tons). The monument was not completed as cracks
began to appear in the stone and this
indicated to the workmen that it was
faulty and therefore could not be
raised successfully.

However, this obelisk gives much
useful information on the working
techniques of the ancient Egyptian
stone cutters and stone masons. The
upper face of the obelisk was mar-

ked out, cut and roughly dressed,
friction and applications of water ai-
ding the slow process. Then the lines
of the monument were marked out
and along them holes were made at
intervals of 0.75 m (2½ ft.) with a
diorite hammer. Gradually the two
sides and the tip of the obelisk were
partially detached from the surrounding stone. The underside of the
whole obelisk had then to be split
away and the whole structure raised.
This was done by placing wooden
wedges and baulks into the holes
already made and wetting them to
make the wood expand and to split
the stone away from the rock around
and under it. In spite of the precise
calculations which had been made
by the craftsmen, slight errors often
occurred during the difficult work.
These can be seen on many obelisks. Thus sometimes the tip of the
pyramidion at the top of the obelisk is
not exactly in line with the centre of
the base, or a slight bulging may be
evident in the centre of the structure,
or the lines of the monument may be
slightly out of true to its axis.

A completed obelisk was rolled on its
sides out of the trench and then pulled along on slides with the aid of
rollers, wooden baulks or on sledges, and taken to the river's edge.
Here it was slid transversely across a
boat at the water's edge which was
laden with ballast and lying conveniently low in the water. The ballast
was then removed and the boat rose
in the water carrying the obelisk. The
same manœuvre could be accomplished by raising the level of a canal
or waiting for the inundation instead
of using a boat weighted down with
ballast. The last stage in the operation was to move the obelisk around
on the boat so that it lay along it
lengthways. The transport of the
obelisks of Hatshepsut is depicted on

her reliefs at Deir el-Bahri (see p, 224) and shows the two obelisks lying one behind the other on two boats 82 m (269 ft.) long which had been roped together for the journey.

Further to the south in the direction of the island of *Philae* there are the south granite quarries. Here can be seen an unfinished sarcophagus and a colossal statue of Ramesses II, which was also never finished. A little further on, is a statue of Osiris similarly abandoned. The stone blocks were quarried out, roughly fashioned into sarcophagi, architraves or statues etc., and then transported to the craft workshops, where the work on them was completed.

THE ASWAN DAM OR BARRAGE [2]

The Old Dam at Aswan was built between 1898 and 1902 and was for many years admired as the largest

The Old Dam at Aswan

dam in the world. It has now lost much of its fame and importance due to the construction of a new High Dam across the Nile. Never-

theless the Old Dam is well worth seeing, although visitors should not that it is forbidden to take photographs of it. It was built of gra and after the original construct was raised twice more in 191 1934 to attain a final height 50 m (164 ft.). The dam 2,000 m (2,187 yards or long and is 30 m (98 ft.) base and 11 m (36 ft.) top. The flow of the w ted by 180 sluice ga ginning of the inun of June all the ga and the water f When the inun side, the gate sed and the l slowly filled than 5 thou of water or c.110 ter). He been High

H DAM AT ASWAN [3]

uary 9th 1960 at a site 6 km. (iles) to the south of the Old Dam the construction of the *Sadd el-Ali* or High Dam was begun. The new dam was ceremonially opened by President Sadat on January 15th 1971. The plans for the dam had been drawn up by West German firms and then taken over and modified by the U.S.S.R. The water-level was raised from 121 m. (397 ft.) to more than 183 m. (600 ft.) above the level of the river and this meant that all the Nubian inhabitants in the affected area due to be submerged had to be moved further to the north (see Kom Ombo, p. 301). UNESCO inaugurated a massive campaign to save the most important monuments of Nubia dating to various periods of

Egyptian history and as a result these monuments were dismantled in pieces, moved and re-erected in places well out of the reach of the rising waters. Many monuments could not be saved and were submerged under the waters of the lake. However, these sites and monuments were surveyed and/or excavated before they were lost for ever.

The High Dam, a great artificial mountain, is 3,600 m. (2¼ miles) long across the top and its base is 980 m. (3,215 ft.) thick. The dam is 111 m. (364 ft.) high. The top of the dam is 40 m.(131 ft.) thick. When the *Nasser* Lake behind the dam is completely filled, the water will be 183 m. (600 ft.) deep. The lake will be 500 km. (310 miles) long and have a maximum width of 10 km. (6 miles). For the necessary construction work, a total of 42.7 million cubic metres (55.8 million cubic yards) of various building materials will have been used.

The dam will increase the area of land which can be cultivated by about a third and will ensure a constant supply of irrigation water to all the cultivated areas to the north of it. The industrialisation of Egypt will be greatly accelerated by the electric power which the dam will produce, which will reach a total of 10 thousand million hourly kilowatts per year. The dam will protect Egypt against very high inundations, which would excessively flood the land. However, on the other hand, the dam and the lake behind it will retain certain materials carried down by the river. The great masses of silt which fertilized the Egyptian fields will be held back by the dam. The deposits of silt in the Delta are already decreasing and therefore diminishing the fertility of the arable land there. The pottery and brick industries are thus losing their manufacturing material- the Nile mud. The pessimists have also pointed out that if the dam should burst, 157,000 million cubic metres (5,544,455 million cubic feet) of water would be released and would constitute a serious danger to life and property throughout Egypt.

The Islands
ELEPHANTINE [4]
The *Island of Elephantine* can be reached by hiring a boat at the avenue or opposite the *Cataract Hotel*, or by taking a local ferry-boat, which leaves from half-way along the avenue.

The island and the area nearby were the cult centre of the ram-headed god, Khnum. According to Egyptian tradition a little further to the south at the cataract was the grotto between two rocks, from which the Nile inundation issued every year. The important fortified town on the island was the capital of a province and its princes and dignitaries were buried in rock-cut tombs in the necropolis to the north on the west bank of the river (see p. 249). The town of Elephantine was situated in the south part of the island and here stood the sacred temple and its enclosure. The temple was built on a huge terrace, part of which can still be seen. The great temple to Khnum, which once existed here, was enlarged and embellished by the last native pharaohs, the Ptolemies and the Romans. In the Persian period, Jewish soldiers, who were garrisoned here, erected a sanctuary to their God but this was destroyed on the orders of the priests of Khnum. Today all the town buildings and the temples are in a very ruined state. Of the great temple, there only remains a gateway built by Ptolemy XI - Alexander II, which bears some relief scenes. Some fragments of the buildings of New Kingdom pharaohs can be seen scattered on the ground.

Near to the landing-stage on the east side of the island is the nilometer. This is a large well made of solid blocks of stone in the river. The regular steps of the staircase indicate the height reached by the water. Thus the height of the inundation could be calculated from readings of the water-level. The Greek geographer, Strabo, described this nilometer in detail.

The Aswan Museum. This is near to the ruins in a pleasant garden. At the entrance are statues, stelae and sarcophagi. The *entrance hall* contains numerous fragments, granite statues of Khema and Sirenput, granite offering tables, a black granite statue of Heka-ib and a gilded sarcophagus containing the mummy of a sacred ram from the necropolis of the rams. The ram was the sacred animal of the creator Khnum.

Room 1 : Prehistoric antiquities dating from 4,000 B.C. : amulets, scarabs, cylinder seals, tools and weapons, stone vases and cosmetic palettes.

Room 2 : Old Kingdom material : tools and weapons, leather items, ostrich eggs, vases, jewellery.

Room 3 : Middle and New Kingdom material : tools and weapons, pottery, plaster mummy masks, mirrors, stelae, scarabs and amulets.

Room 4 : Late Period and Graeco-Roman material : vases, jewellery, glass, pottery, a Christian incense-burner, mummies.

Garden and Courtyard : architectural fragments of earlier periods found in the late temple. Late Period sarcophagi.

KITCHENER'S ISLAND [5]

This island, which is also called *El-Atrun*, has been made into a wonderful garden and is in effect an open-air museum of all kinds of rare and exotic plants. It was once the property of Lord Kitchener but was afterwards maintained by the government. The trees and flowers are magnificent and it is an ideal place for walking in a really beautiful setting.

PHILAE [6] (AEGILKA)

The Temple of Philae, which was threatened with total submersion beneath the waters of Lake Nasser, has now been completely re-erected on the island of Aegilka, and so for the first time since the beginning of the century the entire complex can be visited. The island of Aegilka was landscaped to recreate the topography of Philae. An enclosing dam was built around the island of Philae, the water was pumped out, and the blocks of the monuments were then moved to their new site. The temple was ceremonially opened by Mrs. Anwar Sadat, the President's wife, in March 1980.

The Temple of Isis at Philae

Hathor Capitals at Philae

For the present it is possible to obtain a good general view of the island from the top of the quay wall, which once surrounded it.

The monuments on the island are all late in date but nevertheless are very

fine. In ancient times the island was considered as the gateway and pearl of Egypt and was an oasis of verdant vegetation in comparison with the desert around it. The area was only slowly and with difficulty converted to Christianity from its local pagan cults. Even in the 5th century A.D. the Nubian tribes came to Philae to worship the ancient Pharaonic divinities. Near to one of the landing-points on the south is

The Porch of Nectanebo. The capitals of the columns are extremely interesting. Each column has a floral capital and a second capital above that, which bears on each of the four sides a head of Hathor with cow's ears. The head and its crown represent at the same time the favourite instrument or symbol of the goddess, the sistrum. Hathor was the wife of the god, Horus, and was closely associated with Isis.

The Temple of Isis [A]. This was the main temple on the island and lies at the centre of it. It was dedica-

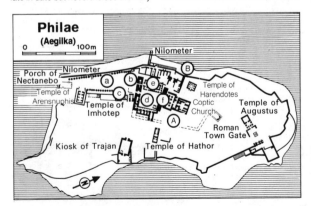

ted to the mother-goddess, Isis, and to her son, Harpocrates, « Horus, the child », The statue of Isis was regularly carried in procession out of her temple at Philae and taken in a sacred boat to the nearby island of *Bigga*. Here she visited her husband, Osiris, who according to tradition was buried in the *Abaton* on this island. Osiris was supposed to lie buried in a shady grove. Around it was the sacred enclosure of the Abaton, which none could enter except the appointed priests. Many Egyptian towns claimed the honour of being the burial place of Osiris or at least of being the burial place of a part of his body. However, the two most famous tombs of the god were at Abydos and at Bigga.

The essential plan of the temple can be dated to the Ptolemaic Period, but its lay-out is rather more complex than that of the other temples of this period. Some parts of the temple are well preserved, but others have now disappeared.

Vast walls with colonnades lead the way to the first pylon, beyond which lies a court with a *mammisi* and colonnades, a second pylon, and then the temple of Isis proper, which contained an open court, a vestibule or hall, antechambers, the sanctuary and adjoining rooms.

The colonnades [a] formed an avenue leading to the temple. The columns have elaborate floral capitals, although it should be noted that the east colonnade was never finished.

First Pylon [b]. Two obelisks once stood in front of the pylon. Two granite lions still remain in situ. This first gateway is 18 m. (59 ft.) high and 45.5 m. (149 ft.) wide, and lies across the front of the court. It is possible to ascend to the top of the

pylon by a staircase. On the right of the east tower are the remains of a gateway erected by Ptolemy II Philadelphus [c]. The scenes on the front of the east tower on the right show Ptolemy XIII at the top receiving from the gods the crowns of Upper and Lower Egypt. He offers incense to Isis and to the child Horus or Harpocrates. Below, the king is shown triumphing over his enemies. There are similar scenes of the victorious king on the west tower on the left. On the inner wall of the pylon facing onto the court are scenes of the King carrying incense followed by priests bearing the sacred barque of Isis.

Central Court [d]. This has interesting columns with floral and sistrum capitals. To the right or east is a colonnade, behind which lies a series of rooms. On the left or west is the

«Mammisi or Birth House [e], which is similar to the mammisi at Edfu (see p. 299) and at Dendera (see p. 294). The mammisi has a forecourt and two vestibules in front of the sanctuary. The scenes on the walls of the sanctuary depict episodes from the early life of *Horus*. They show the child Horus in the form of a falcon in the marshes of the Delta hiding from the evil intentions of the wicked Seth. Horus is suckled by his mother Isis. There are scenes of his birth and of Khnum fashioning him on his potter's wheel. Horus is recognized as a god in the sky and musicians celebrate his birth.

Second Pylon [f]. This is not in line with the First Pylon and alters the axis of the temple which in fact follows that of the Second Pylon. It is 12 m. (39 ft.) high and 32 m. (105 ft.) wide and thus is somewhat smaller than the First Pylon. An inner staircase goes to the top of the west tower. The scenes show king Ptolemy XIII making offerings to the divinities of the temple.

The Interior of the Temple. Behind the Second Pylon is a small court and then the vestibule or hypostyle hall of the temple, which has eight columns. This hall was converted into a church in 557 A.D. in the reign of Justinian. In 550 A. D. Justinian had given orders for all the pagan Egyptian temples to be closed. Greek inscriptions and Coptic crosses carved on the walls and columns bear witness to the use of the hall as a church. The sanctuary is surrounded by mainly dark and sombre rooms. In the sanctuary there remains the pedestal for a sacred barque. The scenes here are largely obscured by a coating of slimy Nile mud. From a lateral room on the left there is access to a staircase which leads onto the roof of the temple and to the Osiris chambers. The reliefs on the walls like those at Edfu and Dendera, show the death of Osiris, his mummification, his burial and his resurrection.

Hadrian's Gateway [B]. The gateway which lies to the west of the Second Pylon was built by Hadrian and completed by Marcus Aurelius. It dates to the 2nd century A.D. and was dedicated to Osiris. All of the relief scenes refer to the cult of Osiris. One of the scenes shows the Egyptian idea and explanation of the source of the Nile. This is on the north wall and depicts a rocky island on which stand a vulture and a falcon. The Nile-god, Hapy, who has a masculine face and an effeminate body, stands in a grotto cut in the rock protected by a serpent and pours out water from two vases. To the right is a human-headed bird, the soul of Osiris, who is worshipped by

Hathor on the left and by Isis, Nephthys, Horus and Amun on the right.

To the north are the remains of the *Temple of Harendotes* and further to the north the ruined *Temple of Augustus*. At the extreme north-east of the island is the large Roman Town Gate. By following the remains of the enclosure wall, which once surrounded the island, towards the south the visitor will come to

the Temple of Hathor. According to Egyptian tradition it was here that the goddess set foot on Egyptian soil again after her flight into the desert. On the shafts of the columns in the temple there are beautiful representations of musicians, flute-players

The source of the Nile

and the god of joy and dancing, Bes, playing a lute and dancing. The temple was built by Ptolemy VI Philometor and the decoration was completed by Ptolemy IX Euergetes II. Augustus added to the temple and his reliefs show him making offerings to Hathor. There is also a cartouche here bearing the name of the famous queen Cleopatra, the last of the Ptolemies.

Trajan's Kiosk is one of the most elegant and finest monuments on the island. It is a small building supported by fourteen beautiful floral capitals. The religious processions which came to the island landed in front of the kiosk and passed through it on their way to the temple.

The work of moving and saving the Temple of Philae was undertaken by the Egyptian Government with the help of UNESCO and carried out by Italian engineers. Trajan's Kiosk, which was totally submerged, was rescued block by block with the aid of British Navy divers. To reach the new site of Philae, follow the route towards the old dam from Aswan, then bear left and take a path on the right, which leads to a quay, where a motor-boat is available to transport visitors to the island.

Left Bank (west bank of the Nile)

QUBBET EL-HAWA [7]

On the summit of this hill is the tomb of a sheikh. From here there is a really superb view down the hill with its rock-cut tombs and across the Nile Valley, the region of the cataracts and the desert. However, the climb up the hill is quite difficult and very tiring. It is best to travel up here by donkey, which can be hired the day before in Aswan. It is also best to combine this visit with those to the tombs, the monastery of St. Simeon and to the mausoleum of the Aga Khan.

THE ROCK TOMBS [8]

The Tombs are set on several levels or terraces in the side of the hill and are the burial places of the princes and dignitaries of the town of Elephantine. They date from the Old and Middle Kingdoms. They are reached by flights of steps carved in the rock with a ramp between the steps up which the sarcophagi and funerary equipment were pulled. The tombs are similar to those at Beni Hasan (see p. 276) and some of them date from the same period. Below are described the best preserved tombs from north to south following the path along the middle terrace.

Tomb of Sirenput I (no. 36). He was a prince of Elephantine during the Twelfth Dynasty. The colonnade or vestibule has six pillars. The ceiling which they once supported has collapsed. The shafts of the pillars are decorated with figures of the deceased and with biographical texts. On the walls are various scenes : Sirenput, his sandal-bearer and two dogs ; cattle being led before the tomb-owner ; the deceased fishing ; Sirenput, a servant carrying his bow, his sons and a dog ; the deceased sitting in a garden pavilion with his wife, his mother, his two daughters and three kneeling singers. Beyond lies an almost square hall supported by four pillars with scenes of daily life on the walls. A corridor leads to a chapel supported by two pillars and which contains a niche. To the left is the way to the burial chamber. The rest of the tomb is in a very ruined state.

After leaving this tomb, the visitor should see the tombs of *Sabni, Heka-ib* (several objects from this tomb are now in the Museum at Elephantine), *Pepinakht* (on the façade of this tomb is an inscription recounting his expedition into the Nubian desert), *Harkhuf* (who was a great explorer and travelled far to the south. On the walls is a description of his voyage into Africa. He brought back a pygmy to the king. The text of the King's letter to him about the pygmy is inscribed in the tomb.), *Khunes* and *Aku* (which contains a well-decorated cult niche).

Tomb of Sirenput II (no. 31). He was a local prince during the Twelfth Dynasty. His tomb is one of the largest and best preserved in the cemetery. It has a vestibule with six pillars, a corridor with three niches on each side, each of which

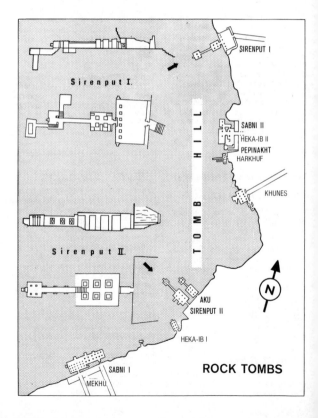

contains a statue of Sirenput as a mummiform Osiris, a chapel and a niche. At the end of the corridor is the chapel and on the walls of the niche at the back are some beautiful scenes which show the deceased at his funerary banquet accompanied by his mother, his wife and his sons.

After leaving this tomb, the visitor passes the tomb of *Heka-ib*. This has a vestibule supported by six pillars. The central part of the ceiling is vaulted. The cult niche is decorated with representations of papyrus. Nearby are two small obelisks in front of the tomb of

Sabni I, the son of *Mekhu*, who held high offices and had great power in the south. His tomb has a large vestibule supported by fourteen pillars. On the rear wall are scenes of fishing and fowling. On the façade is engraved an account of the expedition which was undertaken by Sabni to a far distant part of Nubia. He went there with a group of soldiers and royal embalmers to recover the body of his father, Mekhu, who had been killed there and to punish the tribesmen who had murdered him. Afterwards Sabni made a special journey to Memphis to thank the king for the services of the royal embalmers.
Next to Sabni's tomb is the tomb of his father,

Mekhu. The vestibule has eighteen pillars in three rows which have been very crudely and roughly carved. Between two of the columns is a stone altar on three legs and on the rear wall of the vestibule is a niche with a false-door. The mural decorations are not of very high quality. The scenes show the deceased receiving various offerings and there are also agricultural scenes in which Mekhu figures.

THE MONASTERY OF ST. SIMEON [9]

This monastery is called *Amba Samaan* after a local saint and is one of the best preserved Coptic monasteries in Egypt. It was built in the 6th - 7th centuries A.D., enlarged and restored in the 10th century and then abandoned in the 13th century. The monastery is built on the side of a hill on two terraces of rock and is surrounded by an enclosure wall 7 m. (23 ft.) high. The church, the pilgrims' court and various rooms and outbuildings are built on the lower terrace. The monastery itself is on the upper terrace. The church is a basilica with three aisles. The central aisle once had a domed ceiling. The apse has three niches and in the central niche are the remains of frescoes depicting the victorious Christ with angels and saints. Beyond the apse lies the baptistry. Behind the church can be seen some caves cut out of the rock. These were probably the original dwelling-places of the monks. In the caves many of the ceilings still retain their decoration of geometric motifs. To the north-west of the church a flight of stone steps leads up to the second terrace. Here stands the monastery, which was once a three storied building. It contains cells. which were the sleeping quarters for the monks, refectories and various utilitarian quarters - kitchens, a bakehouse, a mill, oil and wine presses and stables. In the refectory are circular pits cut out in the stone floor. The monks sat round these when taking their meals.

THE QUARRIES [10]

The excursion to the quarries in the western desert to the north of the Monastery of St. Simeon takes 2 hours by donkey for the return journey. In the large quarries cut out in the hill of St. Simeon can be seen the tracks along which the blocks of stone were pulled. The tracks are made of laid blocks of sandstone and are up to 10 m. (33 ft.) wide. The pyramidion of an obelisk of Sethos I can also be seen here. Its inscriptions and reliefs were carved on it in the quarry. The whole obelisk was intended to be 12 m. (39 ft.) high. Carved on some stone in the quarry there are prehistoric graffiti.

THE MAUSOLEUM OF THE AGA KHAN [11]

From the Monastery of St. Simeon a stone path leads to the Mausoleum

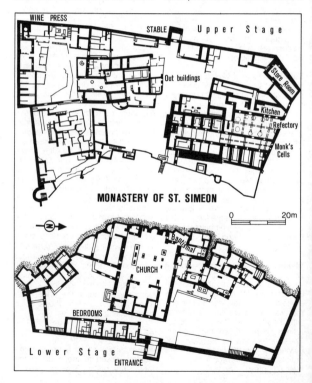

WINE PRESS

STABLE   Upper Stage

Out buildings   Store Room

Kitchen

Refectory

Monk's Cells

MONASTERY OF ST. SIMEON

0   20m

Baptismal

CHURCH

BEDROOMS

Lower Stage   ENTRANCE

In the Mausoleum of the Aga Khan

day be engraved next to the names and dates of birth and death of the Aga Khan, those of the Begum. In accordance with the wish of the deceased a fresh red rose is placed on the sarcophagus every day.

Aga Sir Sultan Muhammed Shah lived from 1877 - 1957 and was the leader of the Ismailite sect of the *Hodshahs*. His body was buried here on February 20th 1959. He had himself chosen the town of Aswan for his final resting-place. The Ismailites follow the Shiite rite of Islam like the Fatimids, who were independent Islamic rulers of Egypt, and hence the building of the Mausoleum in the Fatimid style.

THE TEMPLE OF KALABSHA [12]

of the Aga Khan. The journey takes 15-20 minutes. If coming directly from the landing-stage the visitor passes in front of the lovely white house of the Begum and after a ten minute climb up the staircase reaches the funerary monument of the Imam.

The imposing mausoleum was built in the Neo-Fatimid style. In both style and plan it imitates the *Mosque of Giyushi*, the funerary monument of the vizier Badr el-Gamali, which was built in the Moqattam Hills at Cairo (see p. 151). An impressive staircase leads to the domed chamber which contains the sarcophagus. There is a fine contrast between the fittings made of heavy granite from Aswan and the carved white marble sarcophagus. Delicately carved inscriptions of texts from the Koran decorate the sides of the sarcophagus and are ornamented with ivory inlays. There is only one plain area on the sarcophagus on which will one

Today the Temple of Kalabsha is situated 14 km. (8½ miles) to the south of Aswan and about 10 km. (6 miles) from the High Dam on a dark granite promontory which dominates the small port of *Khor Ingi*. When the Nasser Lake is full the promontory will stand out above the waters as a narrow tongue of land, almost like an island. This was the first Nubian temple to be moved. It was brought from its ancient site at *Talmis-Kalabsha*, near to *Bab el-Kalabsha* 40 km. (25 miles) away to the north. The

The Court of the Temple of Kalabsha

dismantling and moving of this colossal monument, the most important one after *Abu Simbel*, were undertaken by a technical team of the G.F.R. in collaboration with the Egyptian government. The specialised personnel, the technical equipment and the finance for this work were provided by West Germany. The work of dismantling the monument started at the end of the summer of 1961. 16,000 blocks of sandstone weighing up to 20 tons each were numbered and taken up river on about one hundred river barges. During the winter of 1963-64 the blocks were re-erected on their new site and some of the previously fallen blocks were restored to their original position in the temple. Palm-trees were planted around the temple and when these have grown they will provide a wonderful natural setting around it. Today the visitor arrives by motor-boat and lands near to the quay where the sacred boats used to moor up.

The Temple of Kalabsha held an important position in the religious life of the « land of the twelve thousand » (*Dodekaschoeni*), which was mentioned by Herodotus in 450 B.C. The temple was dedicated to the Nubian god, *Mandulis*, a Nubian form of the god, Horus, but the cult of Isis was also celebrated here and was of great importance. There are close links between this temple and the temples of Philae. From the quay at the river a causeway nearly 40 m. (131 ft.) long and steps lead to the temple. The temple complex is 150 m. (492 ft.) long and nearly 60 m. (197 ft.) wide and stands against the side of a desert plateau. The dimensions of the building are quite remarkable. The plan includes the following elements : a pylon, a great court, a hypostyle hall, a sanctuary

with three chapels, an inner passage, an outer passage, and a mammisi in the south-west corner of the complex.

The Pylon. This stands at a slight angle to the axis of the temple and the causeway. This appears to be an error made by the builders rather than a deliberate part of the plan. The pylon is 14 m. (46 ft.) high and about 28 m. (92 ft.) wide and stretches across the total width of the front of the temple. The gateway of the pylon lies on the axis of the temple but is slightly angled to the south to follow the lines of the pylon itself. Except for a rainspout on each side of the entrance gateway, the pylon bears no decoration nor reliefs on the outer façade nor on its inner side. There are only two figures of gods carved in the entrance gateway. There is a staircase which goes up onto the roof of the pylon, from where there is a very good view over the Nile Valley, the High Dam, and the Nasser Lake. There is a passage over the gateway which links the two towers and thus it is possible to walk across from one to the other.

The Court was surrounded by colonnades on three sides. Of these only four columns on each side to the north and south still stand. The columns are late in date and have richly carved composite foliage capitals. It should be noticed here that in order to correct the error of placing the pylon at a slight angle to the axis of the temple, the architect placed the columns on the south side of the court closer together. On each side of the court behind the columns are four small, narrow rooms in the walls. A door in the north colonnade opens into a passage which leads to the outer passage and to a small

Ptolemaic chapel in the north-east corner of the complex.

The Hypostyle Hall or vestibule is separated from the court by a stone screen wall built between the columns with a gateway in the centre. The *scenes* on the screen wall from left to right are : the ibis-headed Thoth and the falcon-headed Horus pour purified water on the king, the water being represented by the hieroglypic signs for « life » and « purity » ; behind sits the god Horus in his form as Harsiesis or Horus, son of Isis ; Greek commemorative inscrip-

tions dedicated to Mandulis, which name the Nubian Kings, Tamalas, Ismen and Degu ; a decree in Greek of the military governor of Ombos and Elephantine, Aurelius Besarion, which was issued in 249 A.D. The decree forbids the swineherds to come near to the temple with their pigs ; on the far right in the corner is the memorial inscription of the Nubian king, *Silko*, dating to the 5th century A.D. The inscription celebrates his victory over the Blemmyes, a fairly powerful people in the nearby area ; representation of a horseman in Roman costume, which

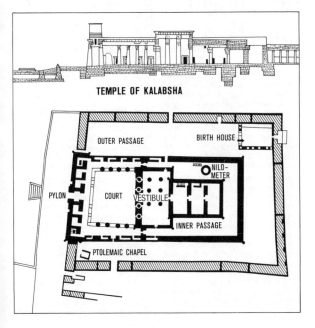

TEMPLE OF KALABSHA

OUTER PASSAGE

BIRTH HOUSE

NILO-METER

PYLON

COURT VESTIBULE

INNER PASSAGE

PTOLEMAIC CHAPEL

PORTALS OF KALABSHA TEMPLE

is perhaps Silko, receiving a crown from a war goddess. There are areas on the inner side of the gateway where the decorations were never finished.

It appears that the craftsmen were interrupted in their work and that they finished the scenes on the screen wall after the whole of the temple had been built.

The roof of the hypostyle hall was supported by 12 columns with elaborate composite floral capitals. The reliefs depict various kings in the presence of the gods ; Isis, Horus and Mandulis receive an offering of land from a Ptolemaic king ; the builder of the original temple, Amenophis II, offers wine to Min and Mandulis ; there is also a later painting of the Christian period of the three men in the fiery furnace. Work on the decoration of the temple was continued until the time of Trajan and of Antoninus Pius but the work

was never completely finished. Those scenes that were finished are large in size but rather crudely done.

The Sanctuary comprises three chambers roughly equal in size which lie one behind the other. The height of the rooms and the size of the doorways decrease, those of the first room being the largest and those of the third room the smallest.

In the *first chamber* or *pronaos* there are four registers of reliefs on the walls : from the bottom to the top : a long procession of divinities, representing the Egyptian nomes, is led by the king. The nome of Nubia is the first one, followed by the 22 nomes of Upper Egypt, the nome of Memphis and three nomes of Lower Egypt. The rest are missing. Following after from left to right round the walls : various personnages are shown looking towards the door which leads to the second chamber ; Osiris, Isis, Horus, Mandulis and the

cobra goddess welcome the king ;
Horus and Thoth purify the Pharaoh
with libations of lustral water ; the
goddesses of Upper and Lower
Egypt stand on either side of the
king ; the king is shown in the presence of the gods, in particular
Amun-Min of Thebes and the god,
Ptah of Memphis, seated in his shrine.
From this first chamber to the left is
a staircase which leads onto the roof
of the temple. A few steps along the
roof the visitor goes down a few
steps into a chapel set in the wall. In
the first room there are the remains
of a statue. Behind is a passageway
leading into a crypt large enough to
contain a seated statue. These two
rooms were probably a small Osirian
cult chapel of the type found in other
temples of this period.
In the *second chamber* or *naos* there
are only three registers of reliefs.
Here nearly all the decoration comes
to an end and it seems that this hap-

pened in the time of Augustus as his
name is carved in several places.
The quality of the reliefs is quite
good, but the colours no longer survive. From the bottom to the top : a
procession of Nile gods shown as
men with feminine characteristics
and wearing a head-dress composed of the hieroglyphic sign denoting
a marshy area ; the king presents
offerings to Osiris, Isis and Mandulis ; the king is shown in the presence of seated and standing divinities,
among whom are the lion-headed
Nubian god, *Dedwen*, and Imhotep
from Saqqara ; representations of
Amun and Khnum.

In the *third chamber* or *adyton* once
stood the cult statue of Mandulis.
The reliefs are partly preserved but
have now lost all their colour. The
reliefs are arranged in three registers. From the bottom to the top :
rows of 15 and 16 Nile gods follow
the king who leads them in proces-

Relief of Mandulis on the West Exterior Wall

sion. The king brings to Osiris and Mandulis a vase of water and a bouquet of flowers, the symbols of the inundation and of the fertility of the land ; the emperor with the gods ; the pharaoh and his wife with a horned crown and holding a flower in her hand ; on the wall at the end of the room, on the left is the king in the presence of Isis, Horus and Mandulis and on the right the king is shown with Osiris, Isis and Mandulis. The figure of Isis on the left is extremely fine.

Opposite this wall can be seen on the exterior wall of the complex the large relief measuring 1.80×1.80 m (6×6 ft.) depicting Mandulis, the god of the temple. The relief was originally protected by a wooden chapel and the holes in the wall which held the supports for this can still be seen. On the relief Mandulis is shown twice : on the right Mandulis is shown in his *royal form* wearing a pharaonic crown and holding a

sceptre and an *ankh* sign ; on the left he is shown in his *divine form* wearing a headdress of ram's horns, a uraeus, a solar disk and ostrich plumes. His cloak is made from the feathers of a vulture with the wings crossed and entwined across his body. Between the two figures of Mandulis is an altar loaded with bread and flowers.

The Inner Passage of the Temple has a nilometer near to the south corner. Only part of it is original. On the walls there are reliefs of which some are fairly well preserved, particularly the wall at the end of the sanctuary. Here are scenes of the emperor Augustus as an Egyptian pharaoh presenting offerings to Osiris, Isis and Horus on the right and to Isis, Horus and Mandulis on the left.

The Mammisi. This is situated in the south-west corner of the outer passage of the temple. The original rock-cut room which was at the back

The Mammisi after its Reconstruction

of the Birth House was not moved to this new site with the temple. Plaster casts of the remains of the reliefs which it contained have been made and are displayed here in their correct place and order. The small sanctuary was probably originally complete but over the course of the centuries various elements and blocks from it were probably taken away to be reused as building material in neighbouring villages. The small temple had an open court with a colonnade measuring 17 × 11 m (55 × 36 ft.) and colummns with composite and Hathor capitals. The columns had stone screen walls built between them. The original rock chamber at the back was a narrow room and went back 5 m (16 ft.) into the rock.

The Ptolemaic Chapel. At the north-east corner of the outer passage is the small so-called « Ptolemaic » chapel. It lies at an angle to the main axis of the temple and probably its pylon also lay at an angle to the main temple axis. This chapel was constructed with the blocks from a much earlier temple as early blocks were found in the foundations when the chapel was moved to its new site. All the sides of the chapel are decorated with reliefs, some of which were never finished. The walls on either side of the entrance are decorated with four scenes showing king Ptolemy V Epiphanes presenting offerings to the gods, Arensnuphis, Thoth and Mandulis.

※

For the modern traveller, visiting the *Temple of Kalabsha* is like visiting an open-air museum of a unique type. All of the monuments here have been resited and are thus preserved as though they were in a museum. When the plans for the High Dam were drawn up it became clear that the area to the south of Aswan for a distance of more than 320 km (198 miles) right up to the frontier and beyond it into the Sudan itself was in great danger of total destruction. Nubia and its temples, its chapels, its towns and its fortresses, its churches, cemeteries and so on would be covered by a huge artificial lake created by the dam. Consequently the Egyptian government with the collaboration of UNESCO and with the participation of a great number of countries formulated a scheme to save the threatened monuments of Nubia. More than 40 archaeological expeditions excavated and photographed, at many sites for the first time, the remains of Nubia's ancient civilisation. As soon as it proved possible, the remains of temples or whole buildings were made as safe as they could be and some monuments and remains of monuments were taken to the island of *Elephantine.* Some of these remains were offered to the countries who had contributed the most to save them. This was the case with the temples of *Debod, Tafa, Dendur* and *Elleisiya.* With regard to the other temples, once they had been dismantled and moved from their original sites, it was decided for practical reasons to re-erect them and group them in four « open-air museums » prepared for the purpose. The four sites chosen were :

The granite promontory above the bay of *Khor Ingi,* several kilometers (6 miles) to the south of the High Dam, where would stand the *Temple of Kalabsha,* the *rock temple of Beit el-Wali* (see below), and the *kiosk of Qertassi* (see below, p. 261) ;

the area containing the temples of *Wadi Es-Sebua* (see p. 304), *Dakka* (see p. 305) and *Maharraqa* (see p. 306).

The temples of *Amada* and of *Derr* (see p. 306 and 307), as well as the rock tomb of *Pennet* from *Aniba* (see p. 308) ;

The two temples of *Abu Simbel* (see p. 311), which have been moved onto higher ground not far from their original site, and also the rock temples of *Abahuda* (see p. 314) and *Gebel el-Shams* (see p. 260).

In the garden of the museum at *Khartum* in the Sudan some monuments from Sudanese Nubia have been re-erected ; these are reliefs from *Aksha, Semna east* and *Semna west*, the temple of *Buhen*, the tomb of *Djhutihotep* and from the colonnade at *Faras*.

ROCK TEMPLE OF BEIT EL-WALI

0   5m

*

A short distance to the south of the temple of Kalabsha is the **Rock Temple of Beit el-Wali.** It was moved here from its original site in the area of *Talmis / Abu Hor*. Ramesses II built this narrow rock-cut temple. The plan is roughly cruciform in shape as the temple has a long vestibule, a transverse hypostyle hall and a small sanctuary. The vestibule was converted into a church in the Christian period and was given a vaulted roof. There are remarkable reliefs of artistic and historical interest, which are delicately carved in the sandstone all along the walls of the vestibule. On the right are scenes of the war against the Syrians and the Libyans, and on the left scenes of the war against the Ethiopians.

Description of the scenes : on the right are five large scenes : a prince leads Syrian and Libyan captives before the king, the king stands upon two Syrians and holds three others by their hair ; scenes of battle around a Syrian fortress, men and women cry for mercy ; a prince hits the door with an axe ; Ramesses seizes a Syrian by his hair in order to kill him ; battle with the enemy, the king chases his fleeing foes, he kills two men and binds two others to the wheels of his chariot ; Ramesses smites a Libyan, whom his dog seizes ; the victorious king sits upon a throne beneath a canopy with a lion at his feet and a table laden with offerings in front of him ; the royal prince, Amun-her-wenemef, leads Syrian prisoners before the king.

On the left wall are two scenes : the king and two of his sons in their chariots wage battle against the Ethiopians ; the enemies flee to their village which is surrounded by palm-trees ; a woman crouches over a fire cooking a meal ; two men lead a wounded man ; the victorious king sits on his throne beneath a canopy ; servants announce the arrival of the Ethiopians who bring their tribute to the king ; the viceroy, Amenemope, carries a silver tablet from which hang rings and skins ; the Ethiopians, two of whom are bound as captives, carry offerings of leopards, giraffe, ostrich, monkeys and cattle ; the silver tablet is placed before the king ; other tribute brought to the king includes elephant tusks, leopard skins, bows, shields, ostrich feather fans and jewellery and also lions, antelopes and cattle.

The ceiling of the transverse hypostyle hall is supported by two « proto-Doric » columns. The four sides of each column bear bands of inscriptions. The reliefs on the walls show Ramesses II in the presence of the gods, and in particular before Isis, Horus, Khnum and Anukis. There are also scenes of the king smiting his enemies. Against the rear wall of the sanctuary stood three statues, one of the king and the other two of gods. The reliefs on the walls of the sanctuary show Ramesses and various divinities, in particular the goddesses Isis and Anukis.

Near to the temple of Kalabsha, about 50 m (just over 50 yards) to the south is the

Kiosk of Qertassi, which was originally situated between *Debod* and *Tafa.* This small and charming building is very similar to Trajan's Kiosk at *Philae* (see p. 248). Columns with composite capitals, of which four remain standing, supported heavy architraves and the roof, which has now disappeared. Of the gateway and the constructions in front of it there only remain now two large columns with Hathor/sistrum capitals. The columns inside the kiosk were once linked by stone screen walls. An interesting scene on one of the north columns shows the king in the company of the gods. This elegant kiosk presents a pleasant contrast to the sombre masses of the Temple of Kalabsha nearby.

Capital of a Hathor Column at Qertassi

Eleven routes through Egypt

The eleven routes which are descri-bed below include visits to all the important sites which can be seen in Egypt, namely in the Fayûm, the Delta, the Nile Valley, around the Suez Canal, in the Peninsula of Si-nai, and on the Red Sea and Medi-terranean coasts. The Libyan Desert oases are described in a separate chapter (see p. 350).

The eleven routes are planned so that each starts from and ends at a principal town or tourist centre in Egypt.

Route n° 1 : The Fayûm

(see plan page 359)

The fertile oasis of the Fayûm, which lies a short distance to the west of the Nile Valley, is easily reached from Cairo. From Cairo the railway follows the course of the Nile Valley to *El-Wasta* and then leaves the river valley and goes to *Medinet el-Fayûm,* which is the terminus for this line. From Medinet el-Fayûm a small railway goes to *Sinnuris* and to *Abuksah.*

Several *buses* per day leave from the *Midan el-Tahrir* in Cairo and go to *Medinet el-Fayûm* and then on to the *Lake Hotel* (Auberge du Lac).

For those travelling by *car* there are two possible routes : either follow the course of the Nile Valley to *Beni Suef,* and from there make various visits in different directions into the Fayûm and then return to Cairo by the desert route ; or follow the desert road which starts from near the *Giza pyramids* behind the *Mena House Hotel,* which leads directly to the *Fayum* and the *Lake Hotel* and from there visit the sites in the Fayum and return to Cairo along the Nile Valley road or continue southwards for vi-sits into Middle and Uiper Egypt. If the visitor intends to stay for more than one day in the Fayûm, the *Lake Hotel* and the *Hunting Pavilion,* both on the shores of *Lake Qârûn,* can be recommended as good and relative-ly comfortable hotels.

*

The *Fayûm* lies to the north-west of Middle Egypt. Although it has many similarities with an oasis, it is unlike a true oasis in that it is linked to the Nile Valley and to the Nile, the vital artery of Egypt, by a natural stream called the *Bahr Yûsuf* or « canal of Joseph ». The waters of this stream divide into many branches and flow across the Fayum basin and into *Lake Qârûn.* The water level of the lake is continually falling. During the Prehistoric period, it is calculated that the lake was 22 m (72 ft.) above sea-level, whereas today it is 44 m (144 ft.) below sea-level.

The existence of this lake or sea in the middle of the desert naturally gave rise to various myths concerning it in antiquity. The ancient Egyptians considered the lake as the mythical primeval ocean. The aged sun-god, Re, hid himself here and took the form of a crocodile and cut himself off from men and gods.

When he was rejuvenated, he left the lake on the back of a cow. Herodotus recounts that Lake Qârûn, which the Greeks and Romans called *Lake Moeris*, was an artificial lake or basin constructed by King Moeris and that in the middle of the lake were two pyramids with statues of the king. In actual fact the lake constitutes the remains of an inland sea, which in prehistoric times covered a far greater area and grew smaller over the centuries. The waters of the lake made the Fayûm a very fertile province. By the Middle Kingdom the lake lay at 50 m (164 ft.) below sea-level and around it was a very marshy area, which was called *Phiom*, or « the Lake », from which the name Fayûm is derived. The Pharaohs hunted here for pleasure as there were many crocodiles in the area. Sobek, who took the form of a crocodile, was the god and patron of the Fayûm, and thus the Greeks called the capital of the province *Crocodilopolis*. Today the rational organization of irrigation in the area makes the land so rich and fertile that the Fayum has become the garden of Egypt. Peaches, mandarins, oranges, olives, prickly pears, grapes and pomegranates all grow here in abundance. Palm-trees, tamarisks, acacia and eucalyptus trees line the roads and paths. The abundant fertility of the province was well-known in antiquity and was particularly mentioned by the Greek travellers.

However, the marshy areas of the province were only gradually transformed into arable land. It was during the Twelfth Dynasty in the reign of Ammenemes III that the draining of the marshes to reclaim the land was started. The flow of the *Bahr Yûsuf* was regulated by dams and lock-gates, which were later described by the Greek geographer, Strabo. The famous *Labyrinth* was built, which became renowned in antiquity. A temple was constructed at Medinet Maadi which was dedicated to the serpent goddess, Renenutet. During the Middle Kingdom the capital of Egypt was in the Fayum province. Under the Ptolemies, Macedonian veterans settled in this area and extensive irrigation and agricultural works were undertaken. Crocodilopolis was renamed Arsinoe.

Today the Fayum has a population of more than a million people who are mostly Bedouin, peasants or *fellahîn* and fishermen. Medinet el-Fayûm, which lies almost at the centre of the province, is its capital. Railways and a good road system provide excellent communication networks throughout the province. The lake, the *Birket el-Qârûn* is nearly 50 km (31 miles) long and about 12 km (7½ miles) wide. Its depth varies between 4 m (13 ft.) and 18 m (59 ft.). Although the water is only slightly salty, the lake is full of fish. As well as the sites of archaeological interest in the Fayûm, the landscape is full of interest and very attractive. The province is verdant and has lush vegetation and many streams and waterfalls. Lake Qârûn is a lovely greyblue in colour and behind it rise the golden sand dunes of the desert.

The Fayûm is famous for its dark-red round pots, which are made here and used for general domestic purposes throughout the province. So that the pots can be carried more easily there are several handles around the neck. These vessels are not made on a potter's wheel. Layers of clay are built up round a complete pot making two halves which are then removed and joined together to make another pot. The neck is then added on and the handles are applied to it.

The pigeon-houses or dovecotes in the Fayûm are different to those in the rest of Egypt. Here they are made of clay pots stacked up like a great bee-hive in the form of a kind of stepped pyramid. The clay pots make good nests for the pigeons and help to keep them cool during the heat of summer.

Saqiyas are used for irrigation purposes in the Fayûm. These are large wheels to which clay pots are tied with string.

Water wheels in the Fayûm

The wheel pushes round the water like a paddle-wheel. A buffalo, donkey or camel is attached to a horizontal spar on the wheel and is made to walk round thus turning the wheel and raising water in the clay pots tied onto it. The *shaduf* operates in a more simple way as a lever to raise

water. Enormous water wheels in the Fayum raise water from the principal canals and pour it into the smaller canals to irrigate the land. These types of wheels are only to be seen in the Fayum and not elsewhere in Egypt.

The most interesting archaeological sites and monuments in the Fayûm are described below from north to south. Thus the visitor, whatever his means of transport, can work out a route and plan his visits to suit his own convenience.

Karanis [A]. This site lies to the left of the desert road coming from the direction of Cairo and on the edge of the cultivated land. The town was founded in the Ptolemaic period. The Ptolemaic temple, which was completed by Nero and later restored by Commodus, is well preserved. It was dedicated to two local gods, Petesuchos and Pnepheros. The northern temple was dedicated to the crocodile god, Sobek, to Serapis and to Zeus-Amun or Jupiter-Amun.

Dîme [B]. The ruins of this town are situated at a fairly short distance from the northern shore of *Lake Qârûn* on the top of a small peninsula. A boat leaves from near the Lake Hotel and crosses to the northern shore of the lake, from where it takes about 30 minutes to walk to Dîme. The town was founded by the Ptolemies and was called *Sobknopaiou Nesos* or « island of Sobknopaios ». The main temple was dedicated to Sobknopaios, a form of the god, Sobek. From the houses a processional avenue flanked by lion statues and 370 m (404 yards) long led to the temple. The town was the point of departure for the caravan route to the Libyan

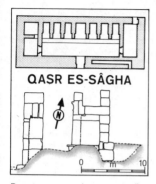

QASR ES-SÂGHA

Desert oases and was a trading centre. Among the remains here can be seen some of the houses of the town, parts of the temple and some fragments of reliefs.

Qasr es-Sagha [C]. This small temple lies about 8 km (5 miles) to the north of Dîme. It is not certain whether it is a temple dedicated to Sobek or a mortuary temple. The building is small and of limestone and has a vestibule with seven niches and two side-rooms. The vestibule measures 12×3 m (39×9 ft.). A wall faced with large blocks surrounded the building, which was apparently never completed. The blocks of stone on the inside walls of the temple were carefully polished but were never carved with reliefs or inscriptions. Some of the details of the building are very similar to those of the temple of Medinet Maadi (see p. 268) and thus it is probably to be dated to the Middle Kingdom. It is possible that this temple was built by Ammenemes III or Ammenemes IV.

Qasr Qârûn [D], known anciently as *Dionysias*, lay at the border of

the Roman province of Egypt and at that time was situated on the shore of the lake. The water-level of the lake has since fallen and the site is now nearly 2 km (1 1/4 mile) from the shore. There is a good view over the remains of the site, the lake and the desert from the top of the terrace of the Late Ptolemaic small temple, which was dedicated to Sobek and to the ram-headed god, Amun-Khnum. Above all the gateways of the temple is a representation of a winged sun-disk and above some of the doorways there are friezes of uraeus snakes. To the east of the temple is a kiosk which closely resembles that at Philae (see p. 248). Near to the kiosk is a fortress built of burnt brick, which measures 90 m (295 ft.) by 80 m (262 ft.) and which has one gateway with limestone surrounds. The building has nine towers as defences around the walls, placed at the corners and on the walls between them.

Biahmu [E]. By the railway embankment near the village of Biahmu, which is 7 km (4 miles) to

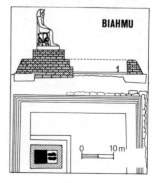

BIAHMU

the north of Medinet el-Fayûm, are two large limestone pedestals more than 6 m (19 Ft.) high, which look rather like two ruined pyramids. These were the pedestals on which once stood two colossal sandstone seated statues of Ammenemes III. They probably stood on the embankment by the side of the road which linked Lake Qârûn and the capital. According to Herodotus the pedestals of the statues were submerged by the waters of the lake at least during the inundation and only the colossi themselves could be seen.

Crocodilopolis [F]. When Ptolemy II Philadelphus made his wife the protector goddess of the *Fayûm* he renamed the capital *Arsinoe* after the queen and in her honour. The vast ruins of the ancient city stretch out to the north of Medinet el-Fayûm. Among the scattered remains can be seen limestone blocks and granite architraves, some of which bear inscriptions.

Hawara [G]. Near to the village of Hawaret el-Maqta stands the pyramid built by Ammenemes III. He also built another pyramid at Dahshur, a little to the south of his father's pyramid. His pyramid at Hawara in the Fayûm was built of sun-dried mudbrick and faced with blocks of limestone. It was built on a natural mass of rock 12 m (39 ft.) high. When complete the pyramid was 58 m (190 ft.) high but the summit is now very ruined. At the base each side measured about 100 m (328 ft.). The entrance to the pyramid is unusual in that it is on the south side. Inside, an intricate series of passages which were blocked by portcullis stones eventually lead to the burial chamber, which the king had prepared for his own burial and that of his daughter, Neferu-Ptah. She was bu-

ried here some time after the king and some remains were found in the burial chamber. The floor and walls of the burial chamber were carved from a monolithic block of yellow quartzite measuring 7 m (22 ft.) long by 2.5 m (8 ft.) wide and 2 m (6 ft.) high and weighing about 110 tons. Two uninscribed quartzite sarcophagi, one larger than the other, were placed in the chamber to contain the burials. In 1974 near to the pyramid in a tomb 15 m (49 ft.) deep a sarcophagus was found, which contained the mummy of a prince of the Middle Kingdom.

On the south of the pyramid stood the famous

Labyrinth, which was in fact the mortuary temple of Ammenemes III. After the Roman period the site was used as a quarry for many centuries and much of the building was thus demolished and removed. However, fragments of walls, architraves, columns and statues have been found here. The building was probably finished by the daughter of Ammenemes, Sebekneferu, who succeeded him and was the last ruler of the Twelfth Dynasty. The huge temple was more than 300 m (984 ft.) long and about 250 m (820 ft.) wide. He-

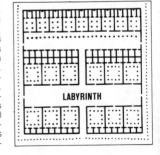

LABYRINTH

Mummy portraits

construct an exact plan of the building.

It was in the *Fayûm*, and particularly in the area around *Hawara*, that the Viennese merchant, Theodore Graf acquired some 300 *mummy portraits* painted on wood, which he afterwards took to Europe and America. The interest created by these portraits led to a systematic search for more of them and Petrie found a further 100 portraits. These paintings represent a late development in the ancient Egyptian cult of the dead and funerary customs. In early times the deceased was placed in his tomb with a « reserve head » made of stone to preserve his identity in case anything happened to his body. Later on the deceased had a gilded wood or gold funerary mask. In late times a portrait painted on wood was placed over the face and held in place by the mummy wrappings. All the portraits are painted with astonishing realism. The Pharaonic style which tended towards idealism of human features had disappeared. Here the individual features of the deceased are represented in a realistic way. The ravages of sickness and disease as well as ugliness are shown in the faces. The portraits express the mortal aspect of man. All of the portraits show the dead in the same attitude, staring out with a distant look which has no feeling or passion. The expression of their large eyes mirrors the calm and peace of the life-after-death. Many of these portraits can be seen and admired in the collections of the museums in Cairo, Paris, London and Berlin.

rodotus describes it as having twelve roofed courts and being two storeys high with numerous rooms and with a pyramid surmounting the whole structure. Strabo surmised that a stranger would be unable to find either the entrance or the exit of the building among its many colonnades and numerous rooms.

Like the Colossi of Memnon (see p. 239) and the Theban temples (see p. 196), the Labyrinth was a great tourist attraction in ancient times. It was visited in 112 B.C. by the Roman praetor, Lucius Memmius, and 300 years later by the emperor Septimus Severus. Strabo thought that there was a striking resemblance between the Labyrinth and the Temple of Sethos I at Abydos. It is possible that the complex plan of Sethos's temple might give the impression that it had certain similarities with the Labyrinth. However, it should be noted that few excavations have taken place at the site of the Labyrinth and ancient descriptions of the monument are not very precise and therefore it has not been possible to re-

Illahun [H]. The pyramid of Illahun was the tomb of King Sesostris II. It was built in the same way as the pyramids of Sesostris I (see p. 182) and Ammenemes II (see p. 181).

The framework of the pyramid consists of low limestone walls which radiate out from the centre in a star shape, five of them going north-south and five east-west. The empty spaces between the walls were filled with rubble and mud-bricks. The pyramid was built on a rocky outcrop and each side of the base was nearly 106 m (347 ft.) long. The pyramid was about 50 m (164 ft.) high. Like the pyramid of Hawara this one is unusual in that the entrance to it is on the south side. A passage inside led by a devious route to the burial chamber, which had a vaulted ceiling. The red granite sarcophagus of the king lay against the west wall on a north-south axis, in the same position as that of Cheops in his pyramid.

The mortuary temple lay on the east side of the pyramid. To the north were found eight rock tombs and a small pyramid for the queen and to the south were found shaft tombs of royal relatives. One of the shaft tombs held the burial of Princess Sit-Hathor-Yunet and here was found her magnificent jewellery, which is now in the Cairo Museum and the Metropolitan Museum in New York. Beyond the outer enclosure wall on the west, south and east sides of the pyramid were circular pits dug in the rock. These had been filled with soil and trees had been planted in them.

Medinet Mâadi [I]. This interesting small temple was built by Ammenemes III and completed by his son, Ammenemes IV. It was dedicated to Sebek, the god of the Fayum, to Horus and to the local divinity, Renenutet. It is a charming building and very original in plan. It has a portico with side-walls and a sanctuary with three niches. In many ways it resembles the chapel of Sesostris at Karnak and the temple of Qasr es-Sagha (see p. 265). In later times Greek hymns were inscribed on the pillars in honour of Isis. (These are now preserved in the Museum at Alexandria).

The columns of the portico are clustered papyrus columns. Between the columns and the architrave which supported the roof is an abacus about 20 cm. (about 8 inches) high, which adds a sense of lightness to the architecture of the whole building. Inside the temple are two standing statues of the king which stand on either side of a seated statue of the goddess, Renenutet. An avenue of lions and sphinxes links the temple with the town.

In the ruins of Medinet Mâadi were found papyri, Coptic portraits and various small wooden objects. Most of these are now in the Museum at Alexandria.

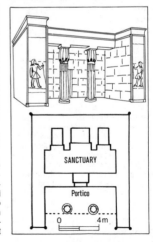

SANCTUARY

Portico

0   4 m

Route n° 2 : A. Cairo - Alexandria (Delta route, 218 km (135 mi.)

B. Alexandria - Cairo (desert route, 225 km (139 mi.)

A : DELTA ROUTE

Leave Cairo by the north road, the *Sharia Shubra*, which follows the course of the river Nile. The traffic on this road is often heavy, sometimes dangerously so, and therefore great care should be taken. Outside the city the road follows fairly closely the line of the railway between Cairo and Alexandria. At *Benha* the traveller crosses the eastern or Damietta branch of the Nile. Further on, at Kafr ez-Zaiyat, the western or Rosetta branch of the Nile is crossed.

Herodotus mentions seven branches of the Nile. Today there are only two main branches. They irrigate the Delta, which in antiquity as today was a vital and important area of Egypt. In the Delta there were many towns and cities with monuments and temples but today only a small proportion of these are preserved.

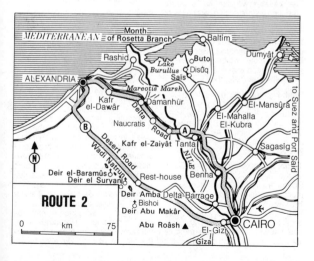

Those sites and monuments which escaped the destructive attentions of the modern inhabitants have fallen into ruins and have suffered from the devastating effects of the Delta's humid climate and from the rise in the underlying water-table and the salty water. The increasing extent of land under cultivation and the deposits of silt over the centuries have in many cases made it impossible for archaeologists to conduct excavations. Thus, except for some of the large sites, the ancient towns of the Delta have for the most part been reduced to miserable ruins, which are only of interest to the specialist scholar. In the route below only the most interesting sites are described (see also Route n° 7).

Outside Cairo the road runs north-westwards across agricultural land, which is intensively cultivated. The traveller will see fields where cereal crops are grown, orchards of citrus fruit trees, - oranges, lemons and mandarins, vineyards and fig trees. Just outside the capital of the province of Qalyubiya, Benha, are fields of roses which are used to make the rose essence perfume for which the town is famous.

Benha is 44 km (27 miles) from Cairo. To the north-east of the town lie the ruins of *Kom el-Atrib* or Tell Atrib, the ancient *Athribis* of Pharaonic and Roman times. At Benha the eastern or Damietta branch of the Nile is crossed.

Tanta, 88 km (54 miles) from Cairo, is the capital of the province of Gharbiya. In the town stands the mosque of *Saiyid Ahmed el-Badawi*. He was a Morrocan pilgrim from Fez, who in the 12th century on his way back from Mecca, settled at Tanta and became a saint. The mosque was rebuilt in the 19th century in the

Turkish style with two minarets and three domes. The mausoleum of the saint is surrounded by a bronze grille and stands beneath the central dome. Popular festivals or *mulids* are held each year in April and August to commemorate the saint. In Tanta there are several other mosques, a royal palace and sûqs or bazaars, which are colourful and interesting.

Kafr ez-Zaiyat, 108 km (67 miles) from Cairo, is an important local market town for cereals and cotton. The surrounding region is a mainly cotton-growing area. There is a small textile industry which flourishes in the town and which is particularly concerned with ginning or the separation of the cotton from the seeds. It is here that the Rosetta branch leads off from the right bank of the Nile towards Sais, which is 14 km (8½ miles) further on.

Sais. The site is very ruined and has never been systematically excavated. The finds which have been made here were distributed among various museums. Psammetichus I, the ruler of the Kingdom of Sais, defeated the Assyrians and the Ethiopians and drove them out of Egypt. He then conquered the other Egyptian kingdoms and united Egypt under his rule and established a strong government throughout the land. During his reign and those that followed in the Twenty-sixth Dynasty, Egypt enjoyed a period of order and prosperity. Many important monuments and cult-buildings were built in the towns of the Delta. The capital was Sais and the whole of this period is known as the *Saite* Period. It was a period of restoration for Egypt and there was a resurgence of nationalism. According to Herodotus all of the Saite kings were buried in Sais in the temple of the town's goddess,

Neith. Neith was a demiurge, creator of all beings, the mother of the sun, the protector of sarcophagi, coffins and canopic jars, the goddess of spinning, weaving and textiles and the personification of the Red Crown of Lower Egypt.

15 km (9 miles) further to the north, to the east of *Desuq*, on the bank of the Nile, lie the ruins of *Tell el-Farain*, the ancient

Buto. This very ancient town is frequently mentioned in the *Pyramid Texts*. It was the ancient capital of Lower Egypt and its divinity was the cobra goddess, Wadjet, who like Neith personified the Red Crown of Lower Egypt. The remains of the early town here are very ruined, but are nevertheless extremely interesting.

Just after *Kafr ez-Zaiyat* the traveller crosses the *Rosetta branch* of the Nile, which was known in antiquity as the *Canopic branch* of the Nile.

Naucratis. The Greeks founded a commercial centre and colony here in the 7th century B.C. during the reign of Psammetichus I. The town quickly became prosperous and the Pharaoh Amasis allowed the colonists to levy customs duties on imports and exports. Herodotus mentions at least three temples which were built in the town and which were dedicated to Greek gods. Naucratis was famous for its faiences and its pottery, which were exported throughout the Mediterranean area. Even before the Ptolemaic period, the town struck its own bronze and silver coinage. To the south of the town stood the *Hellenion*, which was built with the participation of all the Greek cities. Today very little remains to be seen of this ancient city.

Damanhur, 159 km (99 miles) from Cairo, is the capital of the province of *Beheira*. It stands on the site of the ancient « city of Horus », *Time-en-Hor* or Behdet, which the Romans called *Hermopolis Parva*. The town lies at the centre of a particularly fertile area. The surrounding countryside is typical of the Delta with little market towns with small fields around them.

Beyond Damanhur the traveller soon sees on the left *Lake Mareotis*. The lake lies at 2.5 m (8 ft.) below sea-level. This stretch of water became gradually filled with silt and sand and dried up during the Middle Ages. In 1801 the British cut canals through the sand dunes, the lake was once again filled with water and provided the water supply for a great number of villages. The visitor then comes to

Alexandria, 218 km (135 miles) from Cairo (see p. 184 ff.), entering the city along the course of the railway line along *Suez Canal Street*, *El-Horreya Avenue* and then reaching the main station.

B : DESERT ROUTE

The traveller should leave *Alexandria* along *Canal Street* and follow the eastern bank of the canal and go along part of the south shore of *Lake Mareotis*. On the right are the salt-works of *Mex*, which is an important industrial zone. The road then turns slightly to the left and goes up a hill, beyond which lies the desert. 15 km (9 miles) from Alexandria there is a patrol post on the road. The road then crosses the *Libyan Desert* and is very straight. Although there is not much traffic, it is necessary to keep an eye open for other vehicles, camels, etc. on the road.

Rest-house, 130 km (80 miles) from Alexandria. Here there is a petrol station and food and drink can be bought. This is the departure point for excursions to the oasis of *Wadi Natrun*. The way to the oasis is by a tarmac road, which further along becomes an earth track. It is possible to hire a vehicle for the journey from the Rest-house. Of the four monasteries at the oasis, the most important is that of *Deir Suryani*. In order to visit these places it is advisable to first obtain an authorisation permit from the office of the Coptic Patriarchate in Cairo (at *El-Esbuiya Church, 1 Atfet el-Ezba, Clot Bey Street, tel : 57 161*).

WADI NATRUN

The *Wadi Natrun* is a long depression in the Libyan desert, which is below sea-level and about 40 km (25 miles) in length. In ancient times there were about a dozen small salty lakes in the depression, which are now dried up, from which natron and salt were extracted and which gave the oasis its name. Modern methods of fertilising the soil and of providing permanent irrigation have brought changes to the oasis. It has now become possible to cultivate cereals, citrus fruits and vines here. Small manufacturing industries making glass, carpets and furniture have been established here and today nearly 10,000 people live in the oasis.

Christian monasticism was founded in Egypt towards the end of the 3rd century under the direction of Saint Anthony. Macarius and Amun, two disciples of Saint Anthony, a little later in the 4th century introduced a life of asceticism to the Wadi Natrun. At first there were only a few hermi-

tages but by about the year 1,000 A.D. there were a great number of monasteries here. In later times the buildings were fortified and defended by towers and enclosure walls and they therefore have the appearance of fortresses.

The new road goes from the Rest-house to the monastery of

Deir Amba Bishoi, which was founded in the 4th century and restored in the 14th century. A little further on is the monastery of

Deir Suryani, which is about 1 km (just over half a mile) to the west of Deir Amba Bishoi. Deir Suryani is the most important of the four monasteries here and in plan it is characteristic of Egyptian monastic architecture. Above the main gate, which is on the north side of the enclosure wall, there is an opening through which the watchman could see who was approaching the monastery. Gifts of food could also be thrown out of this opening to beggars. The

The Chapel of Mary at Deir Suryani

Bedouin in particular frequently came to monasteries to ask for food. The clock-tower of one of the churches resembles a castle keep.

To the south-west stands the church dedicated to the Mother of God (*Theotokos*). It is a basilica church with a central nave, two chancels and three chapels. It is a fine example of Coptic art and is very colourful with plaster decoration ornamented with Christian symbols. The *rood-screen* has folding doors of carved wood with ivory inlays and decoration of Christian motifs and is particularly fine. It dates from the 10th century when Gabriel of Alexandria was the Coptic patriarch. Above the vaulted doorway of the first chancel and on the south dome is a beautiful scene of the Annunciation with an inscription in Greek of the salutation spoken by the angel to Mary and the words of the heavenly host according to the gospel of St. Luke : « Glory to God in the highest and on earth peace, good will toward men ».

On the south half-dome is a fresco depicting the burial of the Virgin. The second chancel is separated from the first by a stone grille. In it are preserved relics of saints. On the west half-dome is a fresco with a scene of the Resurrection.

A passage leads from the main nave to the hermitage of Saint Bishoi, which originally was probably linked to the monastery by an underground tunnel. The chain with which the saint bound himself during his hours of meditation and prayer still hangs from the ceiling. The tables and desks in the refectory are remarkably well preserved. The three other churches of the monastery are dedicated to the *forty martyrs of Sebastian*, to the Virgin Mary (this is

also known as the « church of the grotto ») and to the saints *Hinnes* and *Marotha*. The visitor can also see the tamarisk of St. Ephraim, which grew at the spot where the saint touched the ground with his pilgrim's stick. In more recent times a *library* was established at the monastery, which contained a superb collection of precious manuscripts. Some of these are now in the British Museum in London. The small *museum* at the monastery is very interesting. It contains a collection of Coptic and Bedouin material and some very good icons.

Deir el-Barâmûs, the northernmost of the four monasteries, is also known as the « Roman » or *Romeus* monastery. It was apparently founded by Maximus and Domitius, the sons of the Emperor Valentinian, who had become monks. The monastery was destroyed by the Berbers in the 5th century and it was rebuilt in the 9th century. Inside, the pulpits and iconostasis which date to the 13th century are particularly striking.

Deir Abu Maqâr, the southernmost of the monasteries of the Wadi Natrun, is 5 km (3 miles) to the south-east of Deir Amba Bishoi. In the 4th century the hermit, Macarius the Great, lived here. Two hundred years later the Patriarch Theodosius I of Alexandria took refuge here and was appointed as Patriarch for the second time. He was buried in the *church of St. Macarius,* a three-storied building, which contains the chapel of the Patriarch and the chapel of his successor. In the church are sculptures, an iconostasis of the 5th-6th centuries and frescoes dating to the 14th century.

After leaving the *Rest-house,* continue along the road across the desert. 60 km. (37 miles) from Cairo the road skirts round a group of buildings and makes a wide turn to the right. Here there is another patrol post on the road. Soon afterwards the Pyramids of Giza can be seen on the horizon after the road turns to the right. From here it is 25 km. (15½ miles) to the Mena House Hotel, where the desert road joins the road to the Pyramids of Giza.

On the right of the road about 8 km. (5 miles) from Giza, lie the ruins of the pyramids and cemeteries of *Abu Roash*, on the edge of the desert and near to the village of Abu Roash. The most interesting monument here is the limestone Pyramid of Redjedef, the son and successor of Cheops. He did not choose to build his tomb on the Giza plateau, but chose this site for his funerary complex. The mortuary temple lies on the east side of the pyramid, but the causeway,

which is about 1.5 km. (nearly a mile) long, goes to the north side of the enclosure wall. This is probably because the builders came across difficulties when constructing the causeway and had to alter its course. Not far from the mortuary temple is a boat-pit for a solar barque. At the base the sides of the pyramid were each 100 m. (328 ft.) long. The entrance of the pyramid was on the north side where a passage descends 48 m. (157 ft.) to a huge rectangular pit cut out in the rock. There is a splendid view over the surrounding area from the top of the fallen remains of the pyramid. Nearby is a necropolis of tombs and mastabas of the early dynasties.

After passing Giza and having travelled 225 km. (139 miles) from Alexandria, the visitor reaches **Cairo** (see p. 103).

Route n° 3 : Cairo-Asyût (385 km. (239 mi.)

(see plan page 360). Information on the various means of transport i.e. train, bus and boat, for the journey between Cairo and Asyût is given on p. 381.

The railway line and the road are on the left bank of the Nile and follow a course which is parallel to the river to

El-Wasta, which is 92 km. (57 miles) from Cairo. See *Cairo,* excursions n° 4 (p. 163), n° 5 (p. 177) and n° 6 (p. 181), and Route n° 1 (p. 159). On the opposite bank, to the east of El-Wasta, lie the scanty remains of the ancient city of *Aphroditopolis*. Hathor was identified with Aphrodite.

It was at this place that St. Anthony took refuge in a hermitage and fought against the temptations of the devil.

El-Maimum, 97 km. (60 miles) from Cairo. From here a surfaced road on the right bank crosses the Eastern Desert to *Ras Zafarana* on the Red Sea coast. From there the traveller can visit the Coptic monasteries of *St. Anthony* and *St. Paul* (see p. 335) A special permit must be obtained in order to visit these monasteries. From the road on the left bank the traveller can see the fellahîn working in the fields and engaging in their daily activities in the villages.

Beni Suef, 120 km. (75 miles) from Cairo, is a provincial capital and a centre of the cotton and textile industry. Sugar-cane is the main crop of the surrounding area. On the right bank a track road leads off and goes to the Red Sea coast. On the left bank a road leads off towards the Fayûm. About 15 km. (9 miles) to the west of Beni Suef near to the edge of the desert are the ruins of *Heracleopolis Magna*. This was the cult centre of the ram-headed god, Herishef, whom the Greeks identified with Heracles. The ruins extend over a vast area nearly 2 km. (just over a mile) in length, but the remains are in a poor state of preservation.

Biba el-Kobra, 145 km. (90 miles) from Cairo, is situated on the *Ibrahimiya Canal* which irrigates a large area of agricultural land of which the main crop is sugar-cane. On the edge of the western desert is the necropolis in which the princes of the district were buried at the end of the Old Kingdom. The site is called Deshasheh. The visitor may prefer to make a visit to this site from *Beni Hasan* (see p. 276).

El-Fashn, 159 km. (99 miles) from Cairo, is a district capital. To the south-east of the town on the right bank on an eminence which becomes an island during the inundation, are the ruins of the ancient town of *El-Hiba*. The fortified town walls were rebuilt in the Twenty-first Dynasty and are in a good state of preservation. Inside the walls are the remains of a temple of Amun built by Sheshonq I and Osorkon I in the Twenty-second Dynasty.

Maghagha, 180 km. (112 miles) from Cairo. A road starts from here and goes to the small oasis of *Bahariya* (190 km. (118 miles) ; see p. 350), which is the northernmost of the line of oases in the western desert. Some ancient ruins can be seen at the oasis, although they have not been properly excavated. There is a chapel of Amasis and a temple of Alexander, which is more or less covered by sand, and a necropolis. To visit Bahariya and any or all of the other oases a special permit of authorisation must be obtained. To the south of Maghagha on the east bank near the village of *Sharuna*, there are rock-tombs and the ruins of a Ptolemaic temple.

Beni Mazar, 198 km. (122 miles) from Cairo. About 15 km. (9 miles) to the west of the Bahr Yusuf, which is to the west of Beni Mazar, is the town of *Behnesa*, which is situated on the site of the ancient *Oxyrhynchus*. The name of the ancient town was derived from the Oxyrhynchus fish, which was worshipped here. A large number of Greek, Coptic and Arabic papyri were found at the site. In the Christian period the town was the seat of a bishop and had 12 churches and numerous monasteries. Nearly 20,000 monks and nuns lived here in the 5th century. From here a desert route goes to the oasis of *Bahariya* (see p. 350).

Kolosna, 215 km. (133 miles) from Cairo, lies between the Nile and the Ibrahimiya Canal, and there is a good view from here over a large island in the river. On the east bank near to the village of *El-Sirîrîya* are ancient limestone quarries with a chapel cut in the rock dedicated to Hathor. On a rock is a representation of Ramesses III with Hathor and another divinity. To the south of the chapel, at the foot of the « hill of birds », the *Gebel et-Teir*, stands a Coptic monastery.

Deir et-Teir, is reputed to have been founded by the Empress Helen. The sanctuary of the church of the monastery is cut in the rock and curiously decorated in the Byzantine style.

Minya, 245 km. (152 miles) from Cairo, is a provincial capital. The town has an important market for wool and sugar-cane. It is situated between the Nile and the Ibrahimiya Canal. There is nothing of particular interest to be seen here, although there is a small museum, which contains a collection of finds made in the area.

Abu Qurqas, 268 km. (166 miles) from Cairo. On the opposite bank to the town, i.e. on the east bank, are the famous rock-cut tombs of Beni Hasan. After crossing the river by boat, it takes about 15 minutes to walk to the tombs, which are near the Arab village of *Beni Hasan.*

BENI HASAN

The 39 tombs quarried out in the hillside were built by the nomarchs or provincial princes of this district in the Eleventh and Twelfth Dynasties. Twelve of the tombs are decorated with paintings in bright colours on stucco. The tombs are arranged in long rows up the hillside and the scenes in them depict the daily life of Egyptians in the Middle Kingdom. They include scenes of artists and craftsmen at work and scenes of leisure activities - sports, games and dancing. The tombs are numbered continuously.

It would take a long time to visit all the tombs and in fact some are better than others. Tombs n° 2,3,15,17 and 27 are the best preserved and the most typical in an architectural sen-

se. The visitor, who can only spend a short time here, should at least visit tombs n° 2,3 and 17.

Tomb n° 2 : This tomb belonged to *Amenemhat,* who was prince of the *Gazelle Nome* in the reign of Sesostris I. He distinguished himself in various military expeditions to the land of Kush. In front of the tomb is a portico with two octagonal pillars. From the portico the visitor enters the rock-cut tomb which in ancient times had a wooden door. The roof of the main chamber is in three sections with false vaults and is supported by four sixteen-sided columns with shallow fluting, which are a type of proto-doric column. The architraves are at the sides and parallel to the axis of the tomb. There is a niche in the rear wall for a statue of the deceased flanked by two other statues, which are in a poor state of preservation. On the lintel and door-posts are inscribed the names and titles of the deceased and prayers for the dead. The inner doorway is decorated with a chequered ornament.

Painted scenes : on the entrance wall : artists and craftsmen at work ; on the north wall : hunting in the desert, the work of the deceased and

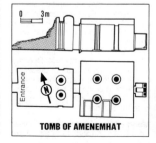

TOMB OF AMENEMHAT

The Caravan of Asiatics

the reception of tribute ; on the east wall : military scenes and the besieging of a fortress, possibly in the land of Kush ; below is shown the pilgrimage to Abydos and Busiris ; on the south wall : offering bearers, the preparation and slaughter of sacrificial animals, Amenemhat and his wife before a table of offerings.

Tomb n° 3 : This tomb was built for the prince *Khnumhotep*. The portico is supported by two sixteen-sided columns without fluting. Four similar columns support the slightly vaulted roof of the main chamber. In the main chamber at the foot of the walls is a long biographical inscription written in vertical columns of hieroglyphs, which are painted in green. In the east wall is a niche which contained a statue of the deceased.

On the north wall is the famous scene of a caravan of Asiatics, who are led by their chief before the prince and who offer to him a variety of presents.

Painted scenes : entrance wall : scenes of the work of various artists and craftsmen ; scenes of offerings ; the mummy of the deceased being taken by boat along the Nile to Abydos ; on the north wall : hunting in the desert ; the caravan of Asiatics ; groups of animals ; on the east wall : scenes of fowling, fishing and games ; on the south wall : scenes of offerings and of the preparation and slaughter of sacrificial animals, which are similar to those in tomb n° 2.

Tomb n° 17 : This tomb belonged to the prince *Kheti*, who was nomarch of the area during the Eleventh Dynasty. The façade of the tomb is very simple in plan. The roof of the main chamber is supported by six lotiform columns with bud-capitals. The architraves are placed transversely. There are two wells dug out in the floor in front of the south wall.

Painted scenes : entrance wall : scenes of fishing and fowling ; on

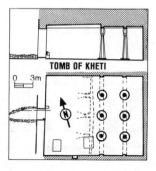

TOMB OF KHETI

0   3m

the north wall : scenes of hunting in the desert with realistic depictions of animals ; craftsmen at work, scenes of games and dancing ; the prince with his wife, sports, wrestling, military scenes and the taking of a fortress ; on the west wall : agricultural scenes, aquatic creatures, offering bearers and scenes of sacrifice ; on the south wall : the prince, his wife and his dogs, musicians, dwarfs, dancers ; Kheti receiving offerings.

Speos Artemidos. This is a rock-cut temple, which lies 500 m. (547 yards) to the south of the tombs at Beni Hasan. A path leads from the tombs to the temple. The temple was built by Hatshepsut and Tuthmosis III and dedicated to the goddess, *Pekhet*, a lion-headed goddess. In plan the temple has a vestibule, a small corridor and a sanctuary and is typical of the small rock-cut temple or sanctuary of the New Kingdom. The vestibule was in the form of a portico and was supported by two rows of four pillars of two different sizes. The pillars and the walls were decorated with religious scenes.

Tuthmosis III erased the representations and name of Hatshepsut from

the temple. In the Nineteenth Dynasty, Sethos I had his name and representations carved in the erased spaces. Nevertheless over the entrance to the temple is preserved a long inscription praising the reign of Hatshepsut. The *reliefs* in the temple show : the king between Amun and Pekhet ; the king receiving the sign of life ; Sethos offering jars of wine and a cynocephalus to Pekhet. Not far from the temple is a cemetery for the burial of sacred cats.

Further along the valley are rock-tombs and caves with a cross at the entrance. Monks and hermits lived in the caves and were buried in the tombs. It is from these monuments that the name of the wadi is derived as it is known as the « Valley of the Anchorites ».

★

The route now follows the west bank of the Nile to
Er-Roda, 286 km. (177 miles) from Cairo. About 6 km. (3¾ miles) to the west is the village of *El-Ashmunein*, near which lie the ruins of *Hermopolis Magna*. A little further to the west, about 10 km. (6 miles) away, is the necropolis of *Tuna el-Gebel*.

HERMOPOLIS MAGNA

This is the name which the Greeks gave to the capital of the Fifteenth nome of Upper Egypt. The patron and god of the city was Thoth, the god of writing, who recorded the words of the gods and wrote down the result of each judgement of the dead. He is usually shown as an ibis-headed man but could also be depicted as an ibis or a baboon, his

SPEOS ARTEMIDOS

sacred animals. The Greeks identified him with their god, Hermes, and therefore called his city Hermopolis. In this area one of his epithets was « Trismegistos », which means « thrice grand ». In the Coptic period the city was called *Shmun* which was derived from its ancient Egyptian name of *Khmunu*, meaning « the Eight ». According to ancient Egyptian mythology this was the birth-place of the eight primordial gods, who appeared on the island which rose out of the primeval waters of chaos. The city, the capital of the Hare nome, is now very ruined and the vast site has as yet been only partially excavated. Unfortunately certain parts of the site are now below the level of the water-table and therefore lost from the archaeological point of view. Other parts of the site have been destroyed by *sabakh* diggers, who have taken away quantities of the ancient mud-brick ruins of the city, which are very good for use as fertilizer on the fields. One of the most interesting monuments at the site is the

Temple of Thoth. The temple was founded by Amenophis III and was situated in the centre of the city. It had a portico with 12 columns. The most remarkable finds made here were several colossal granite statues of Thoth in the form of a crouching baboon. Each statue was about 5 m. (16 ft.) high and weighed nearly 35 tons. Other buildings surrounded the temple on the east and west. To the west lie the ruins of a temple of Amun dating to the New Kingdom. The superb inscriptions and reliefs on the walls and the pylon date to the reign of Sethos II. Behind the temple are the remains of an enclosure wall, which was built by the High Priest, Petosiris.

Further to the south can be seen two *seated statues of Ramesses II*. Between these and the temple of Amun are the ruins of a Middle Kingdom temple dating to the reign of Ammenemes II and a pylon of Ramesses II with a sphinx dating to the Thirtieth Dynasty. A great number of relief fragments from a temple built by Akhenaten, whose blocks had been re-used, were found during the course of the excavations.

The Greek Agora with its columns and porticoes was the most important monument of the Greek city of Hermopolis. Some of the fallen red granite columns have now been re-erected by the Egyptian Antiquities Service. This building stood at the centre of the Greek city and was built on the site of a small temple of Thoth, which had been erected in earlier times by Petosiris. Fragments of this earlier temple have been found in the ruins here. Numerous Greek and Byzantine papyri have been discovered at the site.

Hermopolis Magna : the Greek Agora

Tuna el-Gebel is about 10 km. (6 miles) to the west of Hermopolis and was the site of the necropolis of the city and of the cemetery for the ibises and baboons, the sacred animals of Thoth. Petosiris, the High Priest of Thoth c. 300 B.C. in the reign of Ptolemy Soter, was buried here. His sarcophagus is now in the Egyptian Museum in Cairo. The reliefs in his tomb are extremely interesting. They were executed at a period in Egyptian history when the Egyptians had come under the influence of Greek culture and ideas. The themes of the reliefs are purely Egyptian but they are very Hellenistic in style and character.

A paved road 20 m (65 ft.) long and 4 m (13 ft.) wide, on which stands an altar 8 ft. high with horn-shaped decorations at the four corners, leads to the *tomb of Petosiris*. The façade of this tomb, resembling a temple façade, is decorated with representations of *Petosiris* making offerings to the gods of the province. The walls of the vestibule are decorated with agricultural scenes and offe-

rings made to the deceased in a style strongly influenced by Greece. The representations which are found in the chapel, which is supported by four pillars, are here chiefly centred on religious scenes : the funeral, processions of porters with offerings. The texts accompanying the reliefs are an invaluable witness to personal piety and mysticism, elements which are rarely come across in ancient Egypt. The shaft which is now closed leads to a chamber below the chapel.

Behind the tomb of Petosiris, a necropolis was discovered with complete streets of tombs, funerary edifices fairly similar to that of Petosiris. The mingled Egyptian and Graeco-Roman style, is shown chiefly in the façade with its Greek elements and influence from the Egyptian pylon. The interior decoration is often fairly well conserved ; with much painted stucco and camouflage.

Not far from here, notice a large shaft 35 m (115 ft.) deep with a staircase for descent ; perhaps once provided with water to enclose the sacred ibises which are believed to have existed at this place. These ibises, as well as baboons, were interred in immense galleries which have been discovered fairly recently. After descending about a hundred steps, corridors are reached, about 6 m (20 ft.) high, 4 m (13 ft.) wide and they may reach more than 100 m (328 ft.) in length. The mummified ibises and the apes were placed in niches on each side according to the principle of catacombs. In one of these galleries, the well preserved workshop of an embalmer has furnished the dessicated remains of substances used in the process of mummification. In the third gallery, the deepest, an ape's mummy was discovered in a chapel ; it was still intact and sea-

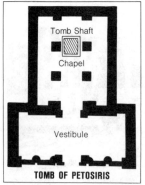

Tomb Shaft

Chapel

Vestibule

TOMB OF PETOSIRIS

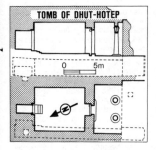

TOMB OF DHUT-HOTEP

0   5m

led in the wall. It can be supposed that this is the « Ibatophion » of Herodotus where, according to the writings of the Greek historians, pilgrims came from afar to give the sacred ibises and apes to the priests for mummification which were then interred in these catacombs.

A little to the south of the tomb of Petosiris stands one of the seventeen frontier stelae of the territory of *Amarna* erected by Amenophis IV (= Akhenaten). They defined the territory of the new capital and at the same time related the foundation of the city. This one has a representation of the king and queen Nefertiti accompanied by three of their daughters in adoration before the solar disc which has extended rays terminating in hands.

★

In following the west bank of the Nile,

Mallawi, 295 km. (183 mi.) is now reached. The rock tombs of *Deir el-Bersha* can be visited on the opposite bank ; after crossing the Nile, the flanks of the valley are reached where the tombs are cut which date

from the end of the Old Kingdom to the Ptolemaic period. The site owes its fame chiefly to the tombs of the nomarchs of the Hare nome of the Middle Kingdom.
Visit

Tomb n° 2 : which belonged to the nomarch *Dhut-hotep*. Its plan is similar to that of the tombs of Beni Hasan. The ceiling of the vestibule was formerly supported by two palmiform columns. A corridor which used to be closed with a door leads to the chapel. The walls were covered with paintings in lively colours, which have now partially disappeared ; notice however the famous representation of the transport of a colossal statue from the quarries of Hatnub to a temple, important because of all its realistic details.

Deir Mawas, 306 km. (190 mi.) Departure point for the excursion to *Tell el-Amarna* on the east bank (a least a half-day is required).

TELL EL-AMARNA

The « heretic » king *Amenophis IV* (XVIIIth dynasty), after having left *Thebes,* the city of Amun, began to erect a new capital including a sun temple, a royal palace and other buildings. The king abandoned the cult of the dynastic god which Amun had become and also the other gods and devoted all his worship to the solar disc of Aten represented with rays which terminate in hands holding signs of life *(ankhs)*. Aten, a form of the ancient solar god Re, became a universal god. The king himself changed his name from Amenophis to *Akhenaten* (« he who is useful to Aten ») and undertook the construction of his new city.
Its site was judiciously chosen, 450

km (280 mi.) from Thebes and about 250 km (155 mi.) from the Delta ; it was a fertile area of about a dozen kilometres (6 miles) long and 18 to 25 km (11 to 15 km.) wide from one desert to the other. Seventeen stelae delineate the frontiers of the territory on the two banks of the Nile. The king called the city *Akhet-Aten*, the « horizon of Aten ». Today the site is called *Tell el-Amarna*. In the new city, the construction began with a temple for the royal mother Tiy, another for the princess Baket-Aten and the great royal temple ; the king's palace was then built and the offices, magazines, houses and villas for the court dignitaries.

Tutankhamun, the successor of Akhenaten, very rapidly abandoned the reforms of his predecessor as well as the cult of the Aten and returned to Thebes. The forsaken royal city of Akhet-Aten was soon abandoned by its inhabitants and rapidly fell into decay. Its temples were de-

molished and the building materials were used elsewhere. Therefore the modern visitor will find almost nothing at the site except for traces of the buildings.

The *temple of Aten [1]*, occupied the centre of the city ; it was a vast edifice almost 800 m (2625 ft.) long by 300 m (985 ft.) wide of which only ruins survive ; other monuments were also discovered : another temple nearby, the king's palace [2] (certain pieces are preserved in Cairo Museum), the *north palace* [3] where Nefertiti lived as well as two other palaces in the south [4]. It was in a building near the royal palace where the famous *Amarna clay tablets* were discovered. They constitute the diplomatic correspondence of Amenophis III and Akhenaten with Babylon, Phoenicia, Syria and Palestine ; they are written in Akkadian and inscribed in cuneiform script. They are invaluable documents for the comprehension of the interna-

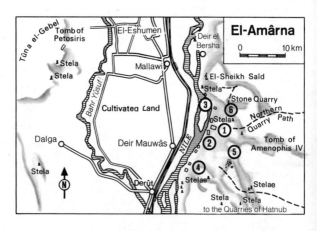

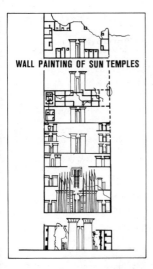

WALL PAINTING OF SUN TEMPLES

tional politics of this period and the difficulties which Egypt had in Palestine with the local rulers. The tablets are now dispersed in different museums, such as Cairo, London and Berlin. The workshop of the sculptor, Tuthmosis, produced several remarkable works of art, sculpter's models and unfinished statues like the limestone bust of queen Nefertiti which is now in the Egyptology Museum of Charlottenburg in Berlin.

The *necropolises* are situated at the north and south of the city. The king himself cut his tomb in the desert in a valley called *Darb el-Melek*. The artists who decorated these tombs tended to use a realistic and intimate style, so that these reliefs tell us more about the city of Aten and its in-

habitants, the royal family and the court, than the ruins of the temples and palaces. A great number of the twenty-five tombs of the necropolis were never finished because Amarna was rapidly abandoned by its inhabitants to the advantage of Thebes. Notice the representation of the Aten on the reliefs ; its rays ending in hands offering the signs of life to the king and members of the royal family. The

South tombs [5]

on the route to the alabaster quarry of *Hatnub*, which was used chiefly in the Old Kingdom and at the beginning of the Middle Kingdom (allow about five hours with a saddled animal for this excursion, which is chiefly of interest to the specialist).

Tomb n° 8 of the chief inspector *Tutu*. Its plan is similar to that of the Theban tombs. Two rows of six columns (the columns in the rear row are united by low stone screens with cornices) supported the ceiling of the large hall. They are papyrus columns with closed capitals decora-

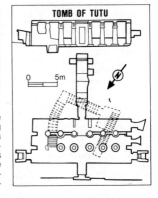

TOMB OF TUTU

0   5m

ted with bands and floral motifs as well as representations of the cult of the Aten. On the lateral walls are small open niches containing statues, opposite the entrance, there is a deep corridor with unfinished niches for statues ; at the left, a flight of steps leads to the funerary chamber. The bas-reliefs of the chamber show the royal couple with Tutu and other courtiers ; Tutu receives a gold collar from the hands of the king in recompense for his good service.

Tomb n° 9 ; belonged to the commander of the military police, *Mahu*. It is a small tomb of cruciform plan with some very interesting reliefs. There are numerous representations of the royal couple (in adoration ; the king on the balcony of his palace, etc...) and the activities of Mahu (a fort in the desert ; troops in displacement). A winding staircase leads to the funerary chamber. Note that this tomb is the only one which was finished and perhaps used in the necropolis of Amarna.

Tomb n° 25 ; is that of Ay, fan-bearer and divine father. He became the successor of Tutankhamun and was buried in his second tomb at Thebes, in the Valley of the Kings (see p. 221). For this reason his tomb at Amarna remained unfinished. Although the twenty-four columns of the great hall were commenced only four of them were finished ; they are papyrus columns with closed capitals with representations of the Aten and the royal couple who reward Ay with gold collars. Notice the representations of Ay and his wife on the door jambs with the famous hymns to the sun above them ; those of Akhenaten and Nefertiti on the north wall ; Ay and his wife receive presents from the king. The officials, soldiers, and servants of Ay's hou-

sehold participate joyfully in the occasion.

North tombs [6]

The quarries were also exploited in this area, where a path leads to the alabaster quarries.

Tomb n° 1. It belonged to *Huya*, superintendent of the royal harem and chamberlain of the palace of queen Tiy. The representations of Akhenaten, Nefertiti and the princesses can be admired here. Other representations show realistic and freely expressed scenes : a meal at the royal court ; Amenophis III and the queen mother Tiy. In the niche for the funerary statue, there is a seated statue of Huya the face of which is destroyed.

Tomb n° 2. Although begun under Akhenaten and continued under Smenkhkare it remains unfinished. The reliefs show the royal couple under a canopy ; groups of foreigners bringing rich tributes to the king ; the deceased is rewarded with gold collars.

Tomb n° 4 of *Merire* I, high-priest of the Aten. It is one of the most important tombs with three rooms, two of

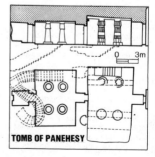

TOMB OF PANEHESY

which are completely decorated. There are numerous representations of Merire at his duties, offering sacrifices in the temple of the Aten beside the king. There is an interesting representation of the temples and palaces of Akhetaten seen according to Egyptian perspective.

Tomb n° 6 ; belonged to *Panehesy*, priest of the Aten, superintendent of the granaries and the herds of the Aten ; although unfinished, it has some beautiful reliefs : the deceased is rewarded ; the king in adoration in the temple ; Panehesy carries offerings to the royal family ; the king and the queen in their chariots in the middle of the troops. On the ceiling, there is geometric decoration with circles, lozenges and zig-zags. Of the four papyrus columns, only two exist now. A staircase leads to the sarcophagus chamber. In the Coptic period, the tomb was transformed into a chapel where a baptistry was placed in a good position.

Tomb n° 26 ; is the royal tomb of *Amenophis IV*, about a dozen km (six miles) to the south in a wadi where access is still difficult (hire a mount) and it is in principle closed to tourists. The plan of the tomb resembles that of the Theban royal hypogea in the Valley of the Kings (see p. 215), but it is pratically destroyed. A long corridor leads straight to the sarcophagus chamber ; in the middle of it a gallery leads off to the right which has a sharp angle and never received any decoration. A little further on, on the right again, three lateral chambers open, the walls of which have reliefs : realistic scenes of the life of the royal couple ; scenes of offerings and adoration ; a badly preserved scene which shows the royal couple crying at the death of one of their daughters, the princess

Meket-Aten ; behind them there are groups of lamenting mourners.

Continue on the west bank of the Nile up to

Nazali Ganub, 330 km (205 mi.). About 9 km (5 ½ mi.) to the north-west, near the village of *Meir*, is a necropolis of the Middle Kingdom (XIIth dynasty). The two most interesting tombs are those of *Senbi*, nomarch of the province, and his son *Ukhhotep*. Both have their entrances at the west ; the statue niche is placed in line with the door at the end of the great hall. This measures most than 5 m (16 ft.) long by 4 m (13 ft) wide and 4 m (13 ft.) high in Senbi's tomb ; 10 m (33 ft.) long by 7 m (23 ft) wide and 7 m (23 ft.) in that of Ukhhotep. There are interesting reliefs which have provincial character but are picturesque : scenes in the fields with very realistic details and sometimes characterisation.

At the limit of the cultivated land, about twelve km (six miles) off the principal route stands the Coptic monastery of *Deir el-Maharraqa*.

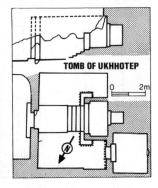

TOMB OF UKHHOTEP

0   2m

According to legend, the chapel with its altar was built on the actual spot where Jesus' mother made a fire with wood. This is the southernmost point of the « Flight into Egypt » of Joseph's family, where they stayed for six years in a house which Joseph built himself until an angel announced the death of Herod to them and told them to return to their own country.

Asyût, 378 km (235 mi.), capital of the province of the same name ; it is one of the important urban districts of Upper Egypt. The old quarters on the edge of the Nile with their upper-class houses and shady roads have retained a certain allure. The rest of the town has nothing of particular interest. Crafts : textiles, potteries (making clay pipes). Above the town is a *barrage* which serves as a bridge as well as retaining the Nile waters (more than 800 m (2625 ft.) long, about 12 m (39 ½ ft.) high. The

Ibrahimiya Canal joins the river here from *Beni Suef.*

The town was the capital of the 13th nome of Upper Egypt in ancient times and the centre of a cult of the jackal god *Wepwawet,* which gave rise to its name Lycopolis in the Greek period. Its prosperity increased during the First Intermediate Period and the beginning of the Middle Kingdom. At the south-west of the town, the tombs of the nomarchs are cut in the sides of the mountain. From the summit a magnificent view encompasses the ancient necropolis, the Muslim cemetery, the town, the cultivated plain and also the desert (access to the mountain is strictly regulated ; enquire on the spot).

Tomb of Hapi-djefa I, nomarch of Lycopolis, 13th nome of Upper Egypt, under Sesostris I (XIIth dynasty).. It is one of the largest tombs of the Middle kingdom, more than 40

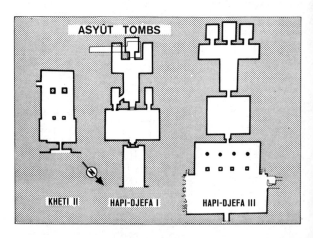

m (130 ft.) long with three large rooms : in the last, three niches are cut, the last of which leads to the subterranean sarcophagus chamber. At the left is the deceased's long panegyric and appeal to the living ; at the right, the texts of contracts which Hapy-djefa made with priests in order to ensure the permanence of his funerary cult. Part of the decoration of the ceilings is preserved. The tomb was never finished and the proprietor was never buried there since he died in the Sudan at Kerma where he had been appointed governor.

Tomb of Hapy-djefa III, is similar to the preceding one. The vestibule is supported by four pillars and four columns at the back. The central chamber and the one at the back with three niches are also similar.

Tomb of Kheti II, dates to the Xth dynasty. It is in a very bad state of preservation with a narrow façade, the entrance of which was flanked by two statues of the deceased. A rectangular chamber is entered, supported by four pillars. On the south wall are the remains of a relief which depicts rows of soldiers.

Route n° 4 : Asyût-Luxor (296 km (184 mi.)

(see plan page 361).

At *Asyût* there is the choice between following the route south of the town which passes through rich cultivated areas, keeping on the west bank, or crossing the Nile on the *barrage* and continuing up to *Nag Hammadi* where the Nile is re-crossed to reach the west bank again. It is recommended that the west bank should not be left because it is much more interesting ; the road follows the railway line.

In the villages notice the high towers made of clay which are used as pigeon houses ; it is a characteristic and picturesque feature of this region ; pigeons are appreciated in Egyptian cooking ; their excrement provides excellent manure for market-gardens. Pigeon-houses are found all over the country, but their appearance differs from one region to another.

Sohag, 92 km (57 mi.), capital of the province of Girga ; wool making and varied textile industry. This is the departure point for visiting the Coptic convents of *Deir el-Abyad* and *Deir el-Ahmar*. A taxi can be hired at the station to visit the two convents, or take a bus from the station to the White Convent (7 km (4 ½ mi.)), then walk to the Red Convent (7 km (4 ½ mi.) ; the latter method is much cheaper but much longer and more laborious.

Deir el-Abyad. The « White Convent », like the « Red Convent », is in a region of Middle Egypt in which the population is still largely Christian and which saw the development of a great number of monasteries and convents. The two which have survived to this day were founded in about the middle of the fifth century. The second is situated in the middle of a village with clay houses which

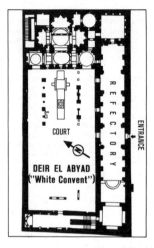

DEIR EL ABYAD ("White Convent")

senting Christ triumphant ; in the lateral domes, the four evangelists, Mary with a star and Christ with the sun. The baptistry which is also vaulted is found on the left of the chancel ; on the other side, a staircase leads to the crypt.

Deir el-Ahmar, the « Red Convent », was built of red bricks and is less well preserved. The frescoes of the chancel were painted in the XIVth century. They represent *Christ* in glory surrounded by the four evangelists, with the twelve apostles below in the central apse ; on the south vault is *Amba Bishoi,* the founder of the convent, transfigured. The plan of the convent is very similar to that of the « White Convent ».

El-Balyana, 143 km (89 mi.) ; point of departure for the visit to the temples of *Abydos,* about fifteen kilometers (nine miles) away on the edge of the Libyan desert (taxis at the station).

mask it completely ; the White Convent itself is built on the edge of the desert and is well preserved in spite of several intrusive habitations.

The « White Convent » is a vast and massive rectangular building of large blocks of white limestone, from whence it gets its name, the name which originally came from the nearby ancient site of Athribis, now completely ruined. The entrance, with a beautiful granite frame, opens on the south side. A very long court is entered which was once occupied by the refectory and the monks' cells. A basilica is then entered with three naves, very badly preserved ; eight of its former forty-two pillars are still in pace ; these are re-used ancient columns. The chancel is surmounted with half domes. Notice in the central dome a fresco representing

ABYDOS

From the beginning of Egyptian history, the city of *Abydos* played a role of political and religious importance. In the archaic period, the kings built their tombs on the neighbouring site of Thinis where the god of the dead *Khentimenty* was venerated. From the Vth dynasty the custom of being brought from all the Egyptian provinces to be buried at Abydos spread, because by then Osiris, the god of life in the underworld and of resurrection, had taken on such importance at the site that he became confused with the ancient local divinity and little by little supplanted him. To be interred in the city of Osiris or, at least to have a cenotaph there was the wish of every Egyptian in order to participate in this way in the resurrection of the god. The pilgrimage and the festivals (mysteries during which the priests carried a statue of Osiris in a barque up to his tomb) were the most solemn times of the religious year at Abydos. Not far from the necropolises, which date from the Archaic period to the New Kingdom, Sethos I and Ramesses II constructed two magnificent temples where different gods appear ; little by little Isis and Horus, then Amun, Ptah and Horakhty had become associated with the cult of Osiris in Abydos.

Temple of Sethos I. The temple was once surrounded by a wall with the principal pylon as the entrance on the north, although there was another door opening at the south to the desert ; both of them are now destroyed. Two courts, the first of which is destroyed, stood before the two hypostyle halls. These are divided into seven processional aisles which correspond to the seven sanctuaries ; this is without doubt unique in Egyptian temple architecture. Note also the existence of an annexe aisle on the south of the sanctuaries which interrupts the symmetry of the plan ; at the front of this aisle, on the exterior of the temple, there are buildings which were no doubt store-chambers. The other remarkable element in this construction is the *Osireion* which is situated behind the temple exactly on a line with it. The numerous reliefs on the walls in an excellent state of preservation appear as master-pieces of Egyptian art, as much for the finesse of the modelling as the perfection of its treatment. Sethos never finished the construction ; Ramesses finished it and added to the front part of the temple.

First court : in the middle of the court, there are two pits surrounded

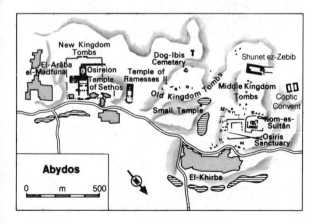

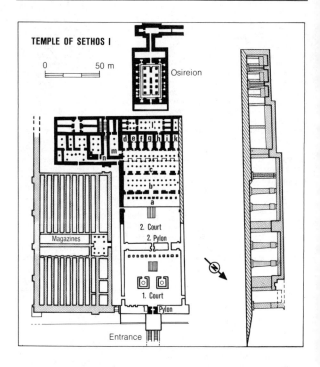

TEMPLE OF SETHOS I

0   50 m

Osireion

Magazines

2. Court

2. Pylon

1. Court

1. Pylon

Entrance

by walls ; at the left reliefs of Ramesses II (the battle against the Hittites ; the hands cut from the dead enemies are counted ; tribute is offered to Amun). A ramp between the two wells leads to a portico with twelve pillars which precedes the second court.

Second court : inscriptions and representations relating to the activities of Ramesses II ; Ramesses offers a sacrifice to the gods ; Rames-

ses smites his enemies in the presence of Amun.

A second ramp leads to a colonnade [a] also with twelve pillars, which served as the vestibule of the temple proper. Ramesses walled up four of the seven doors which led into the temple. Scenes of Ramesses in front of different divinities. A large inscription commemorates the completion of the temple by Ramesses II.

First hypostyle hall [b] : it measures

about 50 m (171 ft.) by 10 m (36 ft.) and is supported by twenty-four papyrus columns with closed capitals. The representations on the shafts of the columns correspond to those in the sanctuaries situated at the back of the temple. Ramesses II is represented each time before the god to whom the sanctuary is dedicated. The gods Horus and Thoth baptize the king ; the king is led into the temple ; a box containing rolls of papyrus is carried to Osiris, Hathor, Isis and Horus.

Second hypostyle hall [c] : This is entered by seven doors, none of which were walled up. Three rows of twelve columns each divide the hall into seven aisles which lead to the seven sanctuaries (two rows of papyrus columns and one row of palm columns). On the right and the left, are djed-pillars which date to Sethos I and are symbols of Osiris. Representations of the king : offering to the goddess of justice, Maat ; the king makes a libation and censes for Osiris and Horus ; Sethos before the sanctuary of Osiris, holding a censer in his hand, accompanied by Maat, Isis, Nephthys, Imentet, the goddess of the west, and nine other divinities.

The seven sanctuaries. These sanctuaries were formerly closed by wooden doors and are symbolically divided into two parts ; the front part contained the barque of the god, the rear part the cult statue. From the left to the right the following sanctuaries are found : *Sethos* deified [d], *Ptah* [e], *Horakhty* [f], *Amun* [g], *Osiris* [h], *Isis* [i], *Horus* [k]. On the walls, there are cult scenes and scenes of offering ; on the back wall, a stela dedicated to the god ; on the ceiling, stars and cartouches of Sethos. The sanctuary of Osiris [h] opens onto an *Osiris hall* [1] (ten columns without capitals) on the right of which are

three sanctuaries dedicated to Sethos with Osiris, Isis and Horus ; behind these is an inaccessible chamber. On the left, there is a small hall with four columns and three sanctuaries (destroyed) which joins onto the larger hall.

Return now into the second hypostyle hall [c], there, between the sanctuary of Sethos and the djed pillar, a door gives access to the chamber of the funerary god *Ptah-Seker-Osiris* [m] (three columns) ; on the reliefs, Sethos adores the god of the dead and other divinities. At the back, there are two sanctuaries dedicated to Ptah-Seker and Nefertum. Beside the djed-pillar, the *King's gallery* [n] opens which leads to the other parts of the temple wing. On the right wall the most famous and well-known relief in the temple can be admired : Sethos holds a censer in his hand, his young son Ramesses in front of him, and pays hommage to 76 kings, his predecessors. All the names are inscribed in two rows above the representation. This is the *king list of Abydos*, often mentioned as a source of the first importance for chronology from Menes up to Sethos I. On the left wall, Sethos and Ramesses offer a sacrifice to their ancestors and to different gods. Notice also in the corridor which leads by a staircase to the Osireion, scenes of the Osiris cult and the Aramaic and Phoenician graffiti left by visitors in antiquity.

A hall of barques (where the barques of the gods were stored), a slaughter court for the sacrificial animals with a door giving direct access to the exterior and various store chambers complete this wing.

Osireion. This was constructed by Sethos I to serve as his cenotaph and play a strictly cult role. It is built

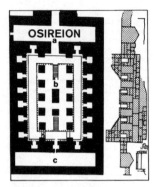

on the same axis as the temple, the line which divides the temple into two equal parts between the sanctuary of Amun [g] and through the Osiris hall. The Osireion is lower than the temple and behind it at a depth of about 8 m (17 ft.) ; it is built in limestone and granite. It used to be hidden from view by an artificial mound covered with vegetation. From the entrance situated on the north-west, a long corridor about 100 m (330 ft.) makes a right turn leading to an antechamber. There are relgious texts on all the walls taken from the *Book of the Dead*, the *Book of the Gates* and the *Book of the Underworld*. This leads to a transverse chamber [a] and then to the

Great Hall [b] ; 30 m (100 ft.) long by 20 m (65 ft.) wide ; supported by two rows of five massive pillars of pink granite which are only 3 m (10 ft.) high and have an almost square section. Around the hall, there is a trench and seventeen small niches cut in the rock. The interior of the hall therefore forms an island which symbolises the primeval mound surrounded by the original ocean from

which the cosmos emerged ; this creation myth was not without connection to the Osiris cult. Two staircases led to the water. It was Nile water which filled the trench, it seems, but only at certain times during the year during antiquity. Two cavities (rectangular and square) were cut in the centre of the island, probably for a sarcophagus and a canopic box, which would therefore simulate the tomb of Osiris.

The last transverse chamber [c] with a saddle-roof possibly symbolised the cenotaph of Sethos with its sarcophagus shape. The reliefs on the walls and the ceiling relate to the Egyptian cosmogony. Shu, the god of air, supports the goddess of the sky, Nut ; astronomical list of the decans and constellations ; nocturnal circuit of the sun in its barque ; resurrection of Sethos.

Temple of Ramesses II. It is situated at 300 m (985 ft.) to the north of that of Sethos I and is destroyed from 2 m (7 ft.) above ground level : it still has remarkable reliefs however which almost have the quality of those of Sethos I. In the first destroyed court, there are the remains of the first pylon and a small chapel. The second court is entered through the second pylon and is surrounded by Osiris pillars on three sides and by a raised colonnade on the fourth. The rest of the temple is laid out according to a symmetrical plan, the two hypostyle halls (each with eight pillars) flanked on the right and left with lateral chambers. The sanctuary is composed of three chapels.

Opening directly from the colonnade are four chapels, two on the right and two on the left, dedicated to the royal cult ; at the left, for the cult statue of Sethos, his barque and the

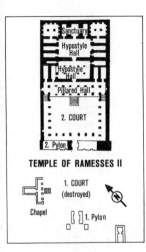

TEMPLE OF RAMESSES II

1. COURT
(destroyed)

Chapel

1. Pylon

king's ancestors ; at the right, for the barque of Ramesses II, his cult statue and that of Hathor. There is an alabaster stela in front of the central sanctuary and at the back of it a group of grey granite consisting of Amun, Sethos, Ramesses and two other figures which are difficult to identify (the group is badly preserved). The other chapels are dedicated to other divinities, in particular Osiris. The temple also had storechambers for cult objects.

Among the *reliefs*, notice particularly those of the first hypostyle hall ; the king makes an offering to Osiris ; the statues of the gods are brought to the temple and are honoured there during the procession of Osiris. On the exterior walls, north and west, there are scenes of war against the Hittites ; on the south there is a long

text concerning the construction of the temple and the donations made in its favour. Here as elsewhere, Ramesses chose the material with care ; the walls are in limestone ; the door enclosures in black granite ; the pillars were all cut in sandstone.

Further to the south stretch the vast necropolises which date to all epochs. Notice the ruins of a small Osiris shrine which was enlarged several times.

From *El-Balyana* continue towards the station of

Oasis Junction (*Muwasla el-Wahat*), 165 km (102 mi.). The railway line divides here, the secondary line goes to *Kharga* oasis (see p. 351). Oasis Junction is a request stop ; warn the conductor if you wish to leave the train at this station ; ask about the times of the trains for Kharga (the train does not run every day). A bus regularly covers the same route. By car choose the road (fairly good) which leaves Asyût and reaches Kharga after crossing the desert. The pleasant oasis scenery, the large village of Kharga with its covered roads, the oasis life itself but also the ruins of the temple of Amun built by Darius at Hibis and the necropolis of the Roman period at El-Bagawat provide the interest in this excursion.

Nag Hammadi, 178 km (105 mi.) The railway and the road cross the Nile here. The route is rejoined on the east bank. The road and the train follow the right bank up to Luxor, then Aswan and Shellal. On the left bank, in a sharp bend of the river, is the large village of *Hû (Diospolis*

Parva). Opposite, at the foot of the escarped slope of Gebel el-Tarif, is *El-Debba.* It was in this region, near the village of *Qasr el-Saiyad,* that an important group of gnostic manuscripts were discovered in 1945 including Coptic texts previously unknown, now preserved in the Coptic Museum in Cairo.

Qena, 234 km (145 mi.) ; capital of the province, famous throughout Egypt for its production of water spouts and porous jars made of clay mixed with ashes. Water keeps fresh in these jars because of evaporation.

In passing through the town, notice the walls of numerous houses faced with pottery sherds, which gives them a strange appearance. From here a good asphalted road, 164 km (101 mi.), goes to *Port Safâga* on the Red Sea. The pilgrims on their way to Mecca choose this route which leads rapidly to the coast. It is the place where the Nile approaches nearest the Red Sea. From Qena, visit the temple of *Dendera* on the other bank of the river. Take a taxi ; over the Nile, on the left bank, a fertile area is crossed (about 7 km (4 mi.) to the temple). Allow a minimum of three hours for the journey both ways and the visit.

DENDERA

The building of the temple was commenced under the last Ptolemies and continued by different Roman emperors. It was dedicated to Hathor, goddess of love and joy ; her consort was also worshipped here, the hawk-headed god Horus and her son, Ihy, a musician god. This cult place existed in the Old Kingdom, but the monuments were constantly enlarged and rebuilt. It is a beautiful example of late architecture in Egypt and is still in a good state of preservation. The nearby town was called *Tentyra* by the Greeks.

A brick wall (nearly 300 m each side (985 ft.)) built under Domitian encloses the temple area. It is entered by the north gate which is preceded by two Roman fountains. Immediately on the right, is the Roman *mammisi* in which the birth of Ihy was celebrated annually. The sanctuary evidently corresponds to the birth chamber where scenes of nursing with the divine nurses are represented ; there are representations of the grotesque god Bes on the ceiling who protected the birth and nursing. The Copts erected a *church* nearby in the Vth century, the sanctuary of which is turned to the east. A little further to the south, is the first *mammisi of Nectanebo I* of the XXXth dynasty. The themes of the scenes depicted on the walls are the same as those in the other birth house. The temple wall was built later over the small sanctuary.

Temple of Hathor. The imposing facade of the great *hypostyle hall* [a] is reached which served as a vestibule. Twenty-four Hathor columns support the ceiling ; the six in the facade are joined together by screen walls. The trapezoidal facade is surmounted by a decorated cornice with a winged solar disc in its centre. The interior walls of the vestibule are decorated with reliefs ; immediately at the right, the king and a priest burn incense in front of the king's *ka* ; Horus and Thoth baptise the king ; the stream of water is symbolised by a line of the signs of life ; the goddesses of Upper and Lower Egypt bless the king. On the four registers above, the Roman emperors dressed as pharaohs adore Hathor and the other gods and make offerings to them : Augustus,, Tiberius, Caligula, Claudius and Nero. The

The Sky Goddess Nut

ceiling of the hypostyle hall is divided into seven bands by architraves and has astronomical representations of the body of the sky goddess Nut.

The *small hypostyle hall* [b] : it receives light through eight square openings in the ceiling. Situated just behind the first hypostyle, it is supported by six columns with composite capitals surmounted by Hathor heads. The various scenes show the ceremonies performed at the foundation of the temple : at the right, the king wearing the crown of Lower Egypt, holds a hoe in the presence of Hathor ; a priest with a censer ; at the left, the king with the crown of Upper Egypt brings Hathor an ingot of precious material which will be deposited in the foundations. All the chambers which open off this small hall were used as store-rooms or treasuries.

Two narrow antechambers now follow ; the first, the *hall of offerings* [c] with staircases on the right and the left which turn and lead to the roof of the temple ; the second [d] was the

vestibule of the sanctuary with a small room on the left for the robes of the goddess. At the right, a small court which is open to the sky is entered, it precedes the kiosk of the New Year. On the ceiling of the kiosk there is a representation of Nut and the birth of the sun the rays of which shine on the temple represented by a Hathor head standing on a hill between two trees.

In the *sanctuary* [e] the barques and statues of the goddess were kept. The scenes on the walls show the succession of daily rites which the king had to accomplish ; he breaks the door seals ; he adores Hathor ; he offers incense ; he presents a statue of the goddess Maat to Hathor and Horus. A narrow corridor runs around the sanctuary from which eleven small chambers open. In the central room behind the sanctuary

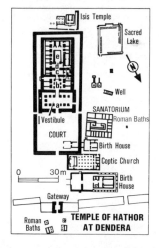

TEMPLE OF HATHOR AT DENDERA

there was a naos with a cult statue of Hathor. In the south-west corner, the crypts can be reached which have beautiful reliefs which show chiefly the objects of the cult which were kept there.

The walls of the staircases which lead to the roof show the procession of the New Year festival in the course of which the statue of Hathor was carried each year to the roof of the temple in order to be regenerated by the solar rays of her father Re which shone on the roof on that day. There is also a small *shrine of Osiris* on the roof from which came the famous « zodiac of Dendera » now in the Louvre Museum, Paris, replaced here by a cast. There is beautiful view from the roof of the temple.

On the *exterior walls* of the temple, there are reliefs of the Roman period. Notice especially Cleopatra and her son Caesarion before Hathor, Horus of Edfu and Ihy (south wall).

The other buildings, the *temple of Isis*, sacred lake, Roman baths also called the *Sanatorium* are interesting, but sometimes less well preserved.

Continue on the right bank of the river Nile up to

Quft (255 km (158 mi.), the town of the god Min, protector of travellers in the desert. It was the central meeting place of the caravans which came from the Red Sea or the land of Punt which furnished incense. Elephant ivory, panther skins, incense and other products destined for the king and the temples accumulated here. It was also from here that the workers and the artists left to exploit the granite and porphyry of the *Wadi Hammâmât*. Quft comes from the ancient name of Coptos ; the ruins are of little interest.

Qûs 265 km. (164 mi.), is on the site of the ancient *Apollonopolis*. A little to the south, on the west bank, next to *Naqada*, stands a brick mastaba in a very bad condition which is attributed to Neithhotep, a queen of Dynasty I.

Then the last bend in the river before *Luxor* follows. The Coptic monastery of *Deir el-Malak* can be seen on the west bank near *Qamula* with its twenty-eight domes. The fertile area on the east bank enlarges, on the west the Libyan mountains approach the river. The *temple of Karnak* will soon be seen, the obelisks and pylons of which emerge from a group of palm trees.

Luxor, 296 km (182 mi.) is then reached. (see p. 196)

Route n° 5 : Luxor - Aswan (232 km (144 mi.)

(see plan page 361)
During the winter season, there is the possibility of a cruise on the Nile between Luxor (see p. 196) and Aswan. The ports of call are generally the following : *Esna, Edfu* and *Kom Ombo.*

The railway and the road, which run parallel, follow the east bank of the Nile to the south. About 20 km (12 mi.) to the south, at a place where the river bends, are the ruins of the town of *Armant* on the west bank, opposite a large island. A temple dedicated to the war god Montu was built there in the Ptolemaic period. A great number of the blocks from this building were used to construct the neighbouring sugar refinery.

Gebelein, 30 km (18½ mi.). (station *El-Shagab*). At the foot of two mountains, one of which is surmounted by the tomb of sheikh Mûsa, *Crocodopolis* once stood. The remains of a temple of Hathor of the XVIIIth dynasty can still be seen here and tombs of crocodiles as well as their sarcophagi.

Ed-Deir, 52 km (32 mi.) ; crossroads ; to the left the road continues through a desert area to *Edfu* and *Aswan* ; to the right the barrage of *Esna* ia reached (nearly 900 m (984 yd.) long) and the town on the other bank.

Esna, 55 km (34 mi.), centre of agriculture and a small textile industry. The kings of the XVIIIth dynasty constructed a temple here dedicated to the ram god Khnum, the chief creator god, to his wife Nebut and

the lion goddess Menhyt. Nothing remains of the temple reconstructed by the Saites and then the Ptolemies except the beautiful vestibule, which dates predominantly to the Roman period.

Temple of Khnum. The vestibule, the only part of the temple which remains today, dates to the Roman emperors Claudius and Vespasian. Their names are incised on the cavetto cornice of the door which is decorated in the centre with a winged solar disc (the temple is actually situated in the centre of the town

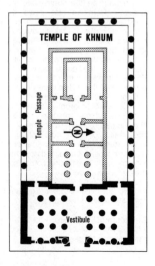

TEMPLE OF KHNUM

Temple Passage

Vestibule

about 9 m (10 yd.) below ground level). The six columns of the façade are connected with screen walls with the great door opening in the centre. The scenes on the screen walls show Horus and Thoth purifying the pharaoh ; the gods lead the king into the temple.

Twenty-four columns more than eleven metres (37 ft.) high with elaborate composite capitals support the ceiling of the hall ; on the ceiling, over the centre aisle there are two rows of vultures in flight ; over the side-aisles there are astronomical representations. Wall reliefs : in the interior, the Roman emperors in pharaonic costume make offerings to the gods ; on the exterior, Trajan, who massacres the enemies of Egypt according to tradition, receives the curved sword from the hands of Khnum ; on the south wall, the Emperor Domitian also slays his enemies in the presence of Khnum. Notice also the list of vanquished peoples given at the base of the wall. In the interior again, there are numerous representations of the king in front of the gods, particularly Khnum ; the Emperor Commodus is represented there. The walls and the column shafts are also filled with very numerous hieroglyphic texts ; they are chiefly religious texts : theological (cosmogony of Esna with the creation of the world by Khnum) or cult (festivals of the liturgical year at Esna). Most of the texts date to the time of Trajan and Hadrian but some were incised under the reign of Decius (IIIrd century A.D.) and are among the last ancient Egyptian texts inscribed in hieroglyphs.

El-Mahamid, 85 km (53 mi.). Alongside the railway line an important wall can be seen (more than 11 m (37 ft.) thick) which is the enclosure wall of the ancient city of *El-Kab*, capital of the third nome of Upper Egypt in antiquity and site of the cult of the vulture goddess Nekhbet. This once protected town, where temples were constructed in the course of the New Kingdom, is now in a bad state ; the temple of Nekhbet was however discovered there. Outside the town, in the desert, it is possible to see the charming building of Amenophis III, the small chapel of Ramesses II and the Ptolemaic rock temple.

Numerous rock tombs were cut in the mountain side in the Arabic desert ; they date to the Middle Kingdom and New Kingdom. To be noted here is the

Rock Tomb of Ahmose, son of Ibana (n° 5). He took part, as an admiral, in the war against the Hyksos and their expulsion from Egypt. His tomb consists simpy of a vestibule orientated north-south and a lateral room with the mummy-shaft. It is decorated with scenes relating to the life of the deceased and includes a long boastful biographical inscription. Nearby is the

Tomb of Pahery, nephew of the admiral (n° 3). It occupies a larger area, but has a similar plan. In the back wall of the principal room, niches

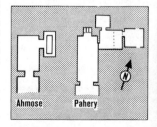

Ahmose   Pahery

destined for statues of the owner, his wife and his mother can be seen. The representations on the walls, in well preserved colours, show here once again scenes from the daily life of the deceased.

EDFU

The town of Edfu, 104 km (64 mi.) stands on the left bank of the Nile now connected to the right bank by a new bridge. A taxi can be taken up to the temple on the left bank.

Edfu was the capital of the second nome of Upper Egypt. The vizier of the Old Kingdom, Isi, was deified here much later. Practically nothing has been discovered of the most ancient buildings of this once famous town ; perhaps some of them remain under the houses of the modern town. Only the monumental temple of the Ptolemaic period still survives.

Temple of Horus. It took many decades to complete as was usual in the Graeco-Roman period. Ptolemy III undertook the construction in 237 B.C. and it was completed in 57 B.C. It is one of the most beautiful examples of late temple architecture. It consists of a pylon, a colonnaded court surrounded by an exterior wall, a vestibule which is wider and higher than the rest of the temple, central chambers with lateral rooms and the sanctuary surrounded by a corridor. The temple, which was exposed by Mariette, is one of the best preserved in Egypt. Its reliefs did not suffer destruction in the Christian period.

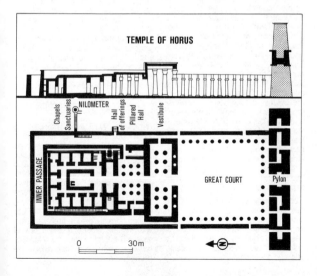

TEMPLE OF HORUS

Chapels / Sanctuaries / NILOMETER / Hall of offerings / Pillared Hall / Vestibule

INNER PASSAGE

GREAT COURT

Pylon

0   30m

The numerous inscriptions incised on the walls have considerably enriched our knowledge of Egyptian civilisation concerning theology as well as cult practices. The temple was dedicated to the sun god Horus, represented in the form of a falcon, accompanied by his wife Hathor of Dendera and his son, the youthful Harsomtus.

Pylon. It is 36 m (118 ft.) high, almost 80 m (262 ft.) wide and after the first pylon of *Karnak* (see p. 204), it is the second largest in Egypt.

In front of the pylon two monumental statues of falcons in black granite still stand. Notice the four wide incisions on the two towers which were used to support large flagstaffs and the small rectangular apertures which served to admit light to the interior chambers. Gigantic reliefs decorate the different faces ; on the exterior face, a horizontal inscription, then two registers below where the king makes offerings to the gods ; below that Ptolemy XII Neos Dionysos, who finished the construction of the temple, slays his enemies in the presence of Horus and Hathor. On the lateral faces of the pylons, in four horizontal registers, the king Ptolemy VIII makes offerings to the gods of the temple. A staircase of more than 200 steps leads to the summit of the pylon (access to which is however fairly strictly regulated). Notice the Egyptian architectural technique which made great use of the dovetail joint to connect the blocks.

Court. There is a good view of the plan from the top of the pylon. The court is paved with an altar in its centre and surrounded on three sides by a covered colonnade. The columns have beautiful floral capitals and their shafts are completely covered with representations of the king in front of the gods. On the internal face of the pylon (court side) there is the usual representation of the king's baptism by Horus and Thoth ; the king is then led into the temple. In front of the entrance to the vestibule, there is a granite statue of Horus, the avenger of Osiris, in the form of a menacing falcon.

Vestibule. The façade is formed by stone screen walls half the height of the columns which they join together with the door in the centre. The screen walls, the shafts of the columns and the architrave are decorated with texts and reliefs : representations of Horus and Hathor ; Ptolemy VIII Euergetes makes offerings to them. The ceiling of the vestibule is supported by twelve enormous columns with elaborate floral capitals. The walls, the column shafts and the ceiling are covered with reliefs : foundation and consecration of the temple ; astronomical representations ; cults of the gods and offerings. Two miniature chapels on the left and the right of the entrance once served as a purification room and a library. At the right a door leads to the corridor which goes around the exterior of the temple.

Hypostyle hall. This is entered by a large door above which is a representation of the sun barque adored by Ptolemy IV and four divinities symbolizing sight, hearing, taste and reason. Twelve columns with floral capitals support the ceiling of this room, pierced with apertures which allow a little light into the hall. The walls, the column shafts and the ceiling here are also entirely covered with reliefs. Notice a small lateral room on the left called the « laboratory » the walls of which evoke the preparation of perfumes and oils destined for use in the cult. Opposite this chamber a staircase leads to the roof of the temple.

Antechambers. Two antechambers each with a raised floor lead to the sanctuary. All the walls are decorated with processions of offerings. A staircase and a corridor connect the second room with a small kiosk the ceiling of which has a representation of the sky goddess Nut and the sun barque ; it is preceded by a court which is open to the sky.

Sanctuary. A naos of black granite which dates to the pre-Ptolemaic period still stands here ; it used to contain the statue of the god. In front of the naos is a pedestal of black granite which used to support the sacred barque. The reliefs on the walls show the different rites of the daily ritual ; among them, the entrance of the king into the sanctuary and the offerings made to Horus. Small chapels dedicated to different divinities surround the central sanctuary and are connected by a corridor ; in the rooms at the corners, behind the sanctuary, openings lead to the crypts.

Corridor. Notice here the representation of a long procession of local divinities, but above all the illustration by a series of scenes of the cult drama of the legend of Horus : representations of the combats of Horus against his enemies, with Seth at their head, transformed into a hippopotamus or a crocodile. This liturgical drama was presented as a type of mystery play during the victory festival, one of the principal occasions of the religious year at Edfu. On the exterior of the temple on the east side, a ritual shaft (nilometer) was filled with Nile water ; it could formerly be reached by an exterior spiral staircase.

At the west, in front of the pylon, stands the *mammisi,* it is very ruined and was built by Ptolemy IX Soter II ; it is decorated with scenes of the birth, nursing and education of the young Horus, but also, as at Dendera (see p. 294), scenes of the creation of the infant on the potter's wheel of Khnum in the presence of Bes, the grotesque god who protected birth.

On the east bank, the visitor reaches

KOM OMBO

Outside the large village (165 km (102 mi.)) on a fairly prominent escarpment which dominates the Nile is the

Temple of Kom Ombo (journey by taxi of about a dozen kilometres (seven miles)). The *double temple* of the crocodile-headed god Sobek and the falcon headed god Haroeris is preceded by a pylon ; its plan is similar to that of the temples of Dendera and Edfu. But here, as it is a double temple, an imaginary line which follows the central axis divides the temple along its length into two equal parts, the right for Sobek, the left for Haroeris, each possessing its series of doors and its sanctuary. Three antechambers instead of the customary two precede the sanctuary. The temple was constructed in the second century B.C. under the auspices of the Ptolemies, but some of the texts date to the Roman period.

Court. The entrance pylon which opens onto the court is virtually destroyed ; of the sixteen columns which formerly surrounded the court on three sides only the bases remain. On the bases of the columns, on what remains of the walls of the court and the internal face of the

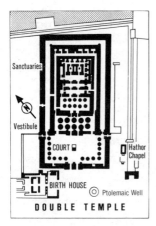

Sanctuaries

Vestibule

COURT

Hathor
Chapel

BIRTH HOUSE
Ptolemaic Well

DOUBLE TEMPLE

in some places the artist did not have time to finish the reliefs which are merely sketched. Admire also the remarkable composite capitals on which a band placed just under the capital separates the shaft in the form of stems of different plants from the flowers which expand on the capital.

Hypostyle. Ten papyrus columns with umbellate (open) capitals support the ceiling. Between the two entrance doors, notice the representation of the sacred crocodile of Kom Ombo, and on the left wall, that of the king receiving the curved sword and a sign of life.

Antechambers. Notice the deeply cut reliefs on the columns here, with representations of different gods and bands of inscription, as well as the walls which have many scenes of the king in front of the gods.

Sanctuaries. The chapels are almost entirely destroyed and nothing but their plan can be recognised today. The pedestals of black granite on which the sacred barques rest are preserved. In the annexe rooms, almost entirely destroyed, it can be seen very clearly how the Egyptian artists worked because of the unfinished reliefs ; there are finished figures (in high relief) between which areas prepared to receive texts have not been incised. The

Mammisi, situated in front of the pylon, is now in a very ruinous condition. A shaft leading directly to the waters of the Nile once served as a nilometer. The crocodiles were interred in special tombs not far from here ; then their mummies were transported to a small sandstone building at the right of the pylon, which was used as a chapel of Hathor.

pylon, fragments of reliefs which still retain their colours can be seen. On the pylon there is a procession of genies carrying agricultural products preceded by the king. In the middle of the court, which is paved, stands an altar which is flanked by two small granite basins sunk into the ground which had a cult purpose.

Vestibule. Columns engaged in screen walls, two large doors and two small doors form an imposing façade surmounted by a cornice with two winged solar discs ; a frieze of uraei with solar discs surmount the screen walls. On the walls, there are beautiful reliefs representing the « baptism » of the king Ptolemy XII Neos Dionysos. On the internal face (at the left), four divinities bless the king. Flying vultures decorate the ceilings of the two principal aisles and astronomical representations decorate the architraves. Notice that

The visit to the temple will not end until the incomparable view over the Nile from the temple terrace has been admired.

In the *district of Kom Ombo* a large number of villages have been created ; they are inhabited by about a hundred thousand Nubians who exploit almost 20,000 ha (44,000 acres) of arable land on the east bank. They had to abandon their old villages, with the construction of the new great Aswan dam, and move further north in this area. The villages have been reconstructed as they were in Nubia retaining their names and their geographical arrangement with their old social and family organisation. They have their own schools and hospitals ; sugar refineries and preserving plants (market-garden produce) have been installed here.

Daraw, 171 km (106 mi.). Motorists have the chance to visit the colourful Nubian market (Tuesdays). Camels are one of the principal local wares. Twelve kilometres (7 1/2 mi.) from Aswan, the first granite blocks will be noticed which, in this region, have not been covered with a bed of sandstone as elsewhere and which rise up from the bed of the Nile where they form the first cataract.

Aswan, 232 km (144 mi.) (see p. 241)

Route n° 6 : Aswan - Abu Simbel (280 km (174 mi.)

(see map p. 304)
From *Shellâl,* the terminus of the railway line 11 km (9 mi.) south of Aswan, it is only possible to reach *Abu Simbel* by the Nile. The hover-craft takes five hours to reach there (stopping very briefly at the site) and returns the same day, in the afternoon, to Aswan (reservations can be made in Cairo and Aswan ; the voyage is rather uncomfortable). An Egyptian-Sudanese connection by boat is gradually being re-established, as it once existed (rather summarily at present) between Shellâl and Wadi Halfa. Interruptions can be expected. It is wise to inquire for the present in the travel agencies in Cairo. The journey by hover-craft or boat no longer provides the opportunity to admire the Nubian villages, which are unfortunately engulfed, but it provides the chance of navigation on the immense stretches of water between the austere, deserted banks totally denuded of life for the present. The second method of travel and much longer excursions departing from Aswan also allows the principal Nubian temples to be seen which have been moved and reconstructed in three main areas.

Bab el-Kalabsha, 49 km (30 mi.). The escarped cliffs of the two banks form a type of mountainous door (Arabic : *bab*).

Abu Hôr, 57 km (35 mi.). The Tropic of Cancer is crossed ; constellations which do not appear in the northern hemisphere can soon be seen.

Wadi es-Sebûa, 163 km (101 mi.). This third rock temple of Ramesses II which used to stand near the Nile

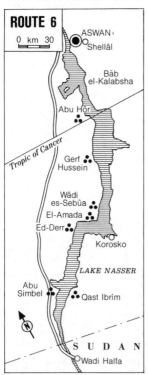

ROUTE 6
0 km 30

ASWAN
Shellâl
Bâb el-Kalabsha
Abu Hôr
Tropic of Cancer
Gerf Hussein
Wâdi es-Sebûa
El-Amada
Ed-Derr
Korosko
LAKE NASSER
Abu Simbel
Qast Ibrîm
N
S U D A N
Wadi Halfa

has been reconstructed at a higher level. The King dedicated it to Amun and Re-Horakhty ; it is a type similar to the temple of Garf Husein a little further north (now partly submerged). The temple of Sebûa is divided into several parts : two courts, standing temple and rock temple. The lions of the sphinx alley in the forecourt gave it its name (Wadi es-Sebûa = Valley of Lions). There were two statues of Ramesses II in front of the brick wall which once enclosed the temple. The central passage of the first court was flanked by sphinxes wearing the double crown (in two rows of three). The sphinxes have different features and hold a representation of the king between their paws. Immediately after the great pylon (virtually destroyed), in the second court, there are four more sphinxes. On the left a small building opens off the court (chapels dedicated to Amun and Re-Horakhty and a storage room).

In the centre of the court there is a staircase which ascends to the temple terrace. The great stone entrance pylon stands in front of the exterior temple, it is 24.5 m (80 ft.) wide, 20 m (65 ft.) high (but partly destroyed). Four monumental statues of the king stood in front of the pylon ; the reliefs (weathered) show the king slaying his enemies in front of the gods. The court of the temple proper measures about 20 m by 20 m (65 ft. square) ; its sides are adorned by two rows of pillars with colossal statues of the king in front of them. On the left of this court there is an entrance to a court reserved for slaughtering animals and for offerings, with perforated walls to which the animals were tethered.

The rock temple consists chiefly of the hypostyle hall with twelve pillars (about $16 \times 13 \times 6$ m ($52 \times 41 \times 19$ ft)), its roof is supported on each side by three pillars with a royal figure with three plain pillars behind them. In the Christian period, a church was installed here, orientated from east to west (remains of frescoes).

A long transverse chamber, terminating on each end with a room and opening onto three chapels completes the temple. The central chamber was the sanctuary where the barque of the sun god was placed. The wall murals here show the king making offerings, on the right to Re-Horakhty (falcon-headed), on the left to Amun (ram-headed) ; the back wall

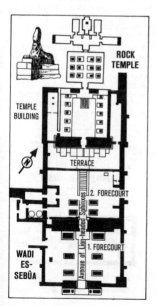

shows Re-Horakhty in the solar barque, in front of him, the king kneeling with three baboons and the king once again in front of Thoth holding a papyrus. Ramesses is shown burning incense and offering wine. Sometimes he practises the rites in front of himself depicted as a divinity. In the narrow niche at the back (with a representation of St. Peter dating to the Christian period) there were once statues of Amun, Ramesses II and Re-Horakhty.

The Temple of Dakka, once further north, has been re-assembled in the neighbourhood. The chapel which proceeds the sanctuary is the most ancient and the most significant part of the temple which was begun by the Ethiopian Ergamenes. The Ptolemies, Philopater and Euergetes II constructed the transverse chamber and the vestibule while the Romans (Augustus) added the pylon and the sanctuary. On the jambs of the door which leads to the sanctuary there is a beautiful relief which shows the goddess of the cataracts, Anukis ; on the right side, she holds a papyrus stalk and on the left the sign of life. A diadem of feathers adorns her head.

Wall representations in the chapel of Ergamenes and in the Roman part include : the king making an offering ; two ibises of the god Thoth and the goddess Tefnut in the form of a lioness ; below, Thoth in the form of a baboon and two lions ; foundation text dedicating an offering of land situated south of Aswan to the goddess Isis of Philae.

In the *sanctuary* is the prayer naos of Augustus and the walls show the emperor as a pharaoh ; he offers perfumed oil and a sphinx to Tefnut ; a diadem and the double uraeus to Thoth ; a field and a necklace to Isis ;

the « Nile » gods follow the pharaoh ; Thoth behind a sacred tree ; a winged sun disc.

The reliefs in the other chambers are less important, badly preserved and also partly destroyed or covered with plaster during the Christian period. Attention should be paid however to the beautiful representations of vultures on the ceiling of the vestibule. From the transverse chamber, a staircase leads to the roof of the temple which gives a good view over the region.

The Temple of Maharraqa has also been re-assembled in this area. This small temple dates to the Roman period and it is dedicated principally to the god Serapis, but also to Thoth, Tefnut and Mandulis. It used to be situated in the town *Hierasykaminos* which was a fortified emplacement on the borders of the empire. Three of its sides are enclosed, in the square court, by types of arcades which, on the temple façade, have their columns connected by stone screen walls. Only some of the wall scenes have survived. Scenes of offerings before Thoth and Mandulis can be recognised. From the interior of the temple, a spiral staircase, a form otherwise unknown in Egyptian architecture, leads to the roof of the colonnade.

Korosko, 195 km (121 mi.), is situated on the southern extremity of a large bend in the Nile (which has now disappeared). During the Mahdi's revolt, it was the departure point for General Gordon when he tried to re-capture Khartum where he fell after several months campaigning (1885). On the rock faces of the region, which once marked the limit of the great Nubian agricultural plain, numerous rock drawings have been discovered, many of them have now

been transported to the museums of Cairo and Aswan.

A little further to the south, two temples which used to be near each other have been re-sited :

The Temple of Amada, 206 km (128 mi.). The temple dates to the XVIIIth dynasty ; it was commenced by Tuthmosis III and finished under Amenophis II. His successor, Tuthmosis IV, erected the pillared court. Three-thousand, three hundred years passed up to the XXth century, then the temple was moved several kilometres (a few miles) to the north and raised 65 m (71 yd.). It was taken to its new emplacement in one piece by means of a hydraulic system. Without its concrete frame built to hold it during transportation, the temple weighed more than 800 tons.

This small building consists of a court or hall of pillars, a transverse chamber and a sanctuary ; the pylon which once preceded the temple is destroyed. On the portal, at the left, Re-Horakhty embraces Amenophis II ; at the right, Tuthmosis III and also the viceroy of Kush kneel before the

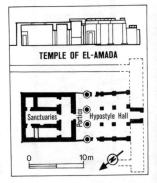

TEMPLE OF EL-AMADA

Sanctuaries   Portico   Hypostyle Hall

0   10m

cartouche of Merneptah. In the door passage, on the right another viceroy and on the left the report of Merneptah's campaign during the war against the Ethiopians. In the original court with four columns (protodoric), Tuthmosis IV finally added twelve pillars which supported the ceiling and had the side walls resting on them. A hypostyle hall was thereby created more than 8 m (26 ft.) wide, 10 m (33 ft.) long and 5 m (16 ft.) high, which was decorated with representations of the king and the gods as well as inscriptions relating to the building of the temple. The walls of the transverse chamber have the most successful representations : Horus and Thoth pour water, the source of life, on Amenophis II ; Amenophis in front of the gods ; worship and offering.

The *sanctuary* is situated in the central chamber which follows. The reliefs depict the cult ceremonies taking place before the gods of the temple, Amun and Re-Horakhty in his barque. An inscription on the back wall of the sanctuary records the completion of the temple and the Syrian campaign of Amenophis II : he captured seven Syrian princes and hung six of them from the walls of Thebes and another on the wall of another town. In the chamber on the right of the sanctuary, the reliefs record the foundation and the dedication of the temple. The representations of the other chamber (stone-room) show the usual scenes of prayers in front of the gods and cult offerings. Amenophis IV/Akhenaten had the figures of Amun effaced, but they were re-cut by Sethos I.

The Temple of Ed-Derr. It was built by Ramesses II and dedicated to Amun-Re. This is the reason it was called the temple of Ramesses in the house of Re. It is a temple cut entirely

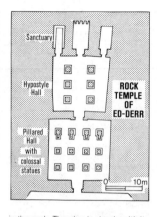

ROCK TEMPLE OF ED-DERR

Sanctuary

Hypostyle Hall

Pillared Hall with colossal statues

0   10m

in the rock. The plan is simple with its two pillared halls and its three chambers in the sanctuary. The pylon and the forecourt have disappeared. In the first hall, twelve pillars, the last four of which were decorated with a royal statue (partly preserved), support the roof. The reliefs on the walls mainly concern the king's Nubian campaign. The most animated scene is found on the back wall : the king smites a group of Nubians he holds by the hair while his lion attacks the legs of another group. In the hypostyle hall which follows, hewn entirely out of the rock, there are the usual scenes of the divine cult and those relating to the jubilees celebrated by the king. Only fragments remain of the four cult statues in the sanctuary. These statues represent Re-Horakhty, Ramesses II, Amun-Re and Ptah. The divine barques are represented on the walls of the sanctuary.

Rock Tomb of Pennut. About forty kilometres (25 miles) to the south, near *Aniba*, this high official's tomb can be visited where particularly well-preserved inscriptions and reliefs are found. This tomb belongs to a certain Pennut, who lived under Ramesses VI and built his tomb according to a very simple scheme (chamber and niche) but paid special attention to its decoration. In the chamber, all the walls deal with themes relating to the life and activities of the deceased on the right side, while the left side is dedicated to the after-life.

On the right, there are two registers next to the donation text (20 lines) for the cult of the statues of Ramesses. The king gives the viceroy of Kush, Pennut (under a canopy) a silver object ; the official and another person in front of a statue of the king ; servants assist Pennut ; he and his wife give prayers and offerings to their parents ; (back wall), other ancestors of Pennut ; he, his wife and their six sons at prayer in front of Re-Horakhty.

At the left : the owner of the tomb in front of the door which leads to the after-life ; Pennut and his wife in the after-life ; they raise their arms in prayer ; Anubis weighs the heart of Pennut and compares it to Maat while Thoth notes the result and the Devourer regards the scene ; « Opening of the mouth » ; funeral procession ; Horus leads the wife in front of Osiris ; Anubis on his shrine ; text taken from the *Book of the Dead* ; Pennut and his wife in prayer ; Anubis and Thoth pour water on the deceased ; the couple pray in front of Ptah, Soker and Osiris ; the solar barque ; prayer text. In the niche, in the centre of the three statues, there is a representation of the goddess Hathor with the head of a cow, the protective deity of the funerary regions.

Qasr Ibrim, 232 km (144 mi.). Remains of a fortress several thousand years old situated on the river route which leads to the African interior, on the summit of a rock promontory on the east bank of the Nile. The Egyptians, the Nubians and the kingdom of Meroe, the Romans, the Byzantines, the soldiers of Bosnia and the Mamelukes held garrisons here ; the last disappeared with the war led against the Mamelukes in 1812. In the interior of this fortified town, Egyptian temples, Coptic churches, mosques and the corresponding necropolises have been found (all of them very ruined). Under the ruins of a large Coptic church, in a cave, the habits of a bishop were found in 1961, also texts relating to the installation of the bishop in the fourteenth century and manuscripts (rolls of papyrus five metres (16½ ft.) long, Coptic and Arabic writing, as well as parchments). Up to the XVth century, the site remained Christian, then it was conquered by Islam.

On the slope of the cliff, above the water, interesting reliefs could be seen in five caves which served as memorial recesses (they are now lost) : the governor of the south, Nehi, brings tribute to the king ; the governor of Nubia, Setaw, before Ramesses II. On the opposite bank, one of the principal towns of Lower Nubia, *Maam*, existed during the pharaonic period.

ABU SIMBEL

At 280 km (174 mi.) south of Aswan, the rock temples of *Abu Simbel* are reached. Ramesses II constructed them, more than 3,000 years ago, in the years 26 to 34 of his reign, very near the river, as his sanctuaries « for eternity ». In the second half of

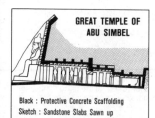

GREAT TEMPLE OF ABU SIMBEL

Black : Protective Concrete Scaffolding
Sketch : Sandstone Slabs Sawn up

the twentieth century, an important international rescue scheme was organised to protect the temples from the rising waters of the reservoir lake. This is why the monuments are found today set back 180 m (600 ft.) from their original emplacement and also raised by 64 m (210 ft.). Protective dams, metal frameworks and resin injections were used, before the mountain above the temples was cut away (without any damage to it) and the monument was cut into pieces of 20 to 30 tons and transported piece by piece, the mass totalling 20,000 tons, to its new site where the whole monument was reassembled according to its original plan. The natural mountain has been replaced by a dome of concrete, forming a framework which is invisible from the outside, on which cut rock rubble has been replaced in order to give the site its original appearance and allure. The astonishing dome can be visited and the supporting devices can be seen.

The visitor who undertakes this long voyage to see the group of temples will possibly wonder why they were erected so far from the royal resi-

The Reconstruction of the Great Temple of Abu Simbel

dence in the Delta and the still prestigious town of Thebes. In fact, there are several reasons : as well as a demonstration of piety and the royal desire for eternal self aggrandizement, it should be stressed that the constructions at Abu Simbel also had a political and economic motive. They were a witness to the strength of Egypt in Nubia, this open door into the African interior from which diverse products were obtained which were of the first importance in the economy and at the same time essential to the luxurious life of the upper classes.

In a sense, the Nubians profited from the higher culture and civilisation of Egypt ; as they assumed its mode of life they contributed to the pacification of the region. Also, it was in Nubia that the principal and most productive Egyptian gold mines were situated (gold-bearing quartz in the Wadi el-Alaqi) ; finally, the region was a connection between the south of Egypt and the land of Punt (outside the maritime route).

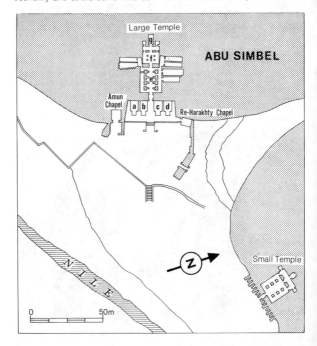

The Façade of the Great Temple

The great temple, orientated precisely towards the west, is dedicated to the great god of the empire, Amun-Re and the sun god Re-Harakhty, as well as the principal gods of the country. The multiple dedication in the temple will often be noticed during the visit.

A small staircase leads to the narrow *temple terrace* which has representations of captives and the dedication text on its balustrade. Behind this are the famous statues of the king and the statue of the falcon-headed man representing Re-Horakhty. The group is well-known because it has often been photographed and reproduced.

The appearance of this famous *temple facade* is really impressive with its height of 31 m (102 ft.). Four colossal seated statues 20 m (65½ ft.) high [a, b, c and d] represent the pharaoh Ramesses II (measurements : forehead,, 0.59 m (2 ft.) ; nose, 0.98 m (3 ft.) ; ear, 1.06 m (3½ ft.) ; width of the face from one ear to the other, 4.17 m (13½ ft.). The façade faces to the east and the statues look in the direction of the rising sun. All the colossi wear the double crown (*peschent*), the royal head-

dress (*nemes*) and the uraeus (a cobra ready to strike, symbol of the burning strength of the sun and the royal power).

A false beard and a loin-cloth complete the king's costume. The name of Ramesses II appears several times : on the chest, the arms and between the legs. The typical form of the nose on the statue recalls that on the royal mummy in the Egyptian museum at Cairo. The artist worked in a realistic manner here, but also gave preference to indicating sensitiveness and calm which is clear from the lines of the mouth, the cheeks and the eyes. Beside the legs of the statues and also between them, are small representations in the round (notice that the latter always have a youthful appearance) of the royal wife Nefertari, the king's mother and several of his sons and daughters (Ramesses II had nearly 200 children by his different wives and concubines).

The colossus on the left of the entrance [b] is broken. Its upper part fell to the ground ; this was due to a fall following an earth tremor in antiquity. The numerous graffiti on the legs of the colossi were left by

Greek soldiers who came to Egypt at the end of the Saite period, as well as mercenaries who came from other eastern countries. These were followed by the addition of graffiti of travellers coming from Europe.

At the north and the south of the façade, two *chapels* were constructed ; the one at the north has an open court where four small obelisks were placed with an altar with statues of baboons in adoration (now in Cairo Museum). The chapel was dedicated to Re-Horakhty to whom in general the whole temple was dedicated. The south chapel was constructed as a speos in the rock and was chiefly consecrated to Amun, whose presence is also well attested at Abu Simbel.

At the left of the feet of the colossus of Ramesses which is best preserved on the south side [a], notice the « marriage » stela, commemorating the union of Ramesses II with the eldest daughter of the Hittite king Khattushilish (XIIIth century B.C.). On this stela Ramesses, between Ptah and Amun-Re, greets his new wife who accompanies her father. An accompanying text records the circumstances (peace treaty) which preceded this occasion.

Above the *entrance door*, which is high and narrow, is a niche holding the statue of the sun god at his zenith, Re-Horakhty, depicted with a falcon head and a solar disc. The god holds a *was* sceptre in his left hand and a representation of the goddess Maat in his right hand. All this forms a sort of play on words to form the name User-Maat-Re which is the « prenomen » of Ramesses II, who therefore appears as the central figure of the temple, its principal divinity. This divine nature of the royal person also appears on the nearby reliefs where the king offers a figure

of Maat to the sun god, symbol of truth and justice, which is also part of his prenomen. Within and below the cornice is an interrupted frieze of royal cartouches and divine figures : Re-Horakhty (at the right) and Amun-Re (at the left) and dedication texts mentioning the two gods, placed symmetrically on either side of the central axis. Above the cornice, twenty-two baboons raise their paws in adoration towards the rising sun. This special temple façade replaces here the pylon constructed in ordinary temples, from which it has borrowed the trapezoidal form.

The reliefs on the *thrones* on which the colossi which flank the entrance are seated show the Nile gods joining the two heraldic plants of Upper and Lower Egypt, as well as Africans and Asiatics attached to the group and symbolising the strength of Egypt and its king. The faces of these peoples are depicted in a realistic manner. Photographers should take note of the fact that the oriented façade, is only well lit in the morning before midday, after that it is plunged into shade.

The entrance is now reached and the interior of the temple is penetrated which was entirely cut in the interior of the mountain. The depth of the temple is about 55 m (180 ft.). The plan has an almost total symmetry and includes the following elements ; two pillared halls with long annexe chambers, a transverse chamber furnished with niches and finally the sanctuary.

The first *hypostyle hall* [e] (it corresponds slightly to the vestibule of ordinary temples) measures a little less than 16 m (54 ft.) wide and 18 m (58 ft.) long. Its floor rises slightly. There are two rows of four Osiris pillars 9 m (29½ ft.) high flanking the central aisle. The statues represent the king Ramesses II with crossed arms, holding the sceptre and the flail in his hands and wearing the white crown of Upper Egypt on the left (south) and the double crown on the right (north). The hall contains reliefs of good quality which are chiefly concerned with war themes here the story of the battle of Kadesh predominates.

Reliefs : (starting from the left and continuing in a clockwise direction) : Ramesses smites his enemies in front of Amun ; the king (five times) in front of the gods ; scenes of a Syrian campaign ; Ramesses charges in his chariot in the direction of an enemy fortress ; he runs through an enemy with his lance ; his triumphal return with captured prisoners ; (back wall) Ramesses leads the captives in front of the gods ; he leads two lines of bound Hittites in front of the gods ; (right wall) the departure of the Egyptian army ; the camp protected by shields ; the camp life ; the king enthroned at a council of war with his officers ; enemy spies are captured ; they are beaten to extort their information ; the battle with the Egyptian chariots opposing the Hittite chariots ; Ramesses leads the charge in his chariot ; the fortress of Kadesh, surrounded by a bend of the Orontes ; Ramesses inspects the mass of hands cut from the Hittites who have fallen in the battle ; the fettered captives are led away ; the king gives his thanks to the gods.

The eight *lateral chambers* served as store-rooms for treasures and cult instruments. Stone benches run around the walls.

In the second *pillared hall* [f] (about 11 × 8 m (36 ft × 25 ft) ; four pillars)

the reliefs show religious scenes : the gods and goddesses embrace the king ; Ramesses burns incense in front of the sacred barque and pays homage to his own divinity ; the queen shakes two sistra.

In the *sanctuary* [g], in front of the back wall of the temple there are four large statues ; they are those of Ptah, Amun-Re, Ramesses II himself and Re-Horakhty. The statues are placed in a position where all of them, with the exception of Ptah (who does not have a solar character), are struck by the rays of the sun during the solstices. This supreme architectural refinement, desired for religious reasons, is possible because of the siting of the temple. Notice finally in the centre of the sanctuary a rock-hewn support for the solar barque.

The Temple of Hathor. A little north of the great temple, Ramesses II cut a second smaller sanctuary in the mountain, which he dedicated to the goddess Hathor and her supreme representative, the great royal wife Nefertari. The supporting pillars 12 m (39 ft.) high, inclined towards the temple, decorate the façade which again imitates the form of a pylon ; six standing colossal figures (10 m (33 ft.) high) are placed in niches in such a way that on each side of the entrance a figure of the queen is flanked by two figures of the king ; all of them are turned towards the sun. At the feet of the great statues, there are smaller ones representing the children of the royal couple. A cobra frieze protects the entrance to the temple.

The plan of the temple is symmetrical and is centred on a pillared hall behind which there is a transverse chamber with lateral chambers and finally the sanctuary. In the great hall, the six pillars are decorated, on the side which is turned towards the temple aisle with Hathor heads (cow ears and a curled wig), on the other side with texts and reliefs showing the royal couple and the gods.

Three doors lead into the transverse chamber which precedes the sanctuary, the latter ends in a niche. In the sanctuary there is a representation of the Hathor cow protecting a figure of the king. All the walls here and in the preceding chamber have scenes showing the royal couple making offerings and practising the cult in front of the goddesses of the temple, Isis and Hathor, but also Anukis, goddess of the Nile cataracts. Notice particularly the characteristic treatment of the figures of the queen, which is almost extreme here, she is depicted as especially slender and delicate. It seems that this was a convention, although it is certain that the figures are a portrait ; the flesh tints are also different here (all the colours are well-preserved), a curious clear and slightly yellow colour predominates ; perhaps it is also an allusion to Hathor called « the Golden ».

Rock Temple of Abahuda. This small re-sited sanctuary once stood on the east bank of the Nile, a little south of Abu Simbel. The rock temple was cut and decorated in the XVIIIth dynasty, under the reign of Horemheb and it was dedicated to the gods Amun and Thoth. Its plan is simple ; a small pillared hall (with four closed papyrus columns) is flanked by two lateral chambers and precedes the even smaller sanctuary. As a church was installed here during the Christian period, many of the pharaonic reliefs have been covered with a layer of plaster on which Christian figures are painted. It has been possible to remove these figures (Christ, the saints and the apostles) so that the Egyptian reliefs appear again : (from right to left in a clockwise direction) : Anukis suckles Horemheb under the gaze of ram-headed Khnum ; Horemheb before Thoth, Horus and other local gods ; Seth and Horus lead the king ; he is presented to Amun ; the king in front of Thoth ; (sanctuary) the king prays before the barque of Amun ; a Nile god ; offerings (among others there is a small calf).

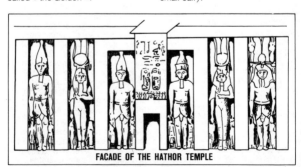

FACADE OF THE HATHOR TEMPLE

ROCK TEMPLE OF ABAHUDA

Memorial Chapel of Pasiur. This small chapel (in fact a niche), which was situated in the rock face of Ge-

bel el-Shams, further to the south, near the Sudan, has also been cut and re-sited on the east bank of the Nile. Pasiur was a governor of Kush who served under Ay and Horem-heb, at the end of the XVIIIth Dynasty ; unfortunately the good quality reliefs are partially destroyed : (door) name and titles of Pasiur ; (from the left in a clockwise direction) Pasiur at prayer, opposite the cartouches of king Ay ; servants carrying offerings ; Pasiur in front of a table loaded with offerings ; he prays ; prayers (texts) ; priests and other people (family) near the deceased before the offering table ; Pasiur, kneeling, addresses an invocation to Anukis and the other divinities of Nubia.

Route n° 7 : Cairo - Bubastis - Tanis (173 km (107 mi.)

The traffic on the roads in the Delta is still subject to strict controls and therefore the visitor should make enquiries in Cairo before embarking on the journey.

Leave Cairo along *Port Said Street* and follow the course of the *Ismailia Canal* towards the north. The railway line is almost parallel to the road but is some distance away. The road crosses the fertile countryside of the Delta and beyond *Bilbeis* (61 km (37 milles) from Cairo) reaches the

Wadi et-Tumîlat. The Ismailia Canal now runs along the Wadi and on the east flows into Lake Timsah. There was probably a canal linking the Nile and the Red Sea during the Middle Kingdom and such a canal certainly

existed in the reign of Ramesses II. It gradually became silted up and was cleared and re-opened in the reign of Necho II in the Twenty-sixth Dynasty. The discovery of blocks of stone from the edges of Necho's canal indicate that it was nearly 45 m (147 ft wide and 5 m (16 ft) deep. The canal was repaired in the reign of Ptolemy II Philadelphus, and then redug and restored in the time of Trajan, when it was renamed Trajan's canal. Some centuries later it had again become silted up and was cleared and restored by Amr ibn el-As for the purpose of sending supplies along it to his army. Thereafter the canal was neglected and quickly became silted up again and in need of repair. It was not until the nineteenth century, when the Suez Canal was being built, that this canal was redug and restored. It was named the Ismailia Canal and provided a supply of drinking water for the workmen at the Suez Canal. It is now used for irrigation purposes. Around Abu Hammad, Zagazig and Bilbeis is the area which has been known since the time of Moses as the « Land of Goshen », where the Israelites were forced to work for the Pharaoh. A short distance to the south-east of Zagazig (103 km (64 miles) from Cairo is the site of

Bubastis. On the mound of *Tell Basta* lie the debris and ruins of Bubastis, one of the most ancient cities of Egypt. The city was mentioned by the prophet Ezekiel and was the cult-centre of the goddess, Bastet. The kings of the Twenty-second Dynasty, which is known as the Bubastite Dynasty, came from this city

MEDITERRANEAN

Damietta
Damietta Branch
PORT SAID
Mansala
MANSURA
Abusir
Tanis
Suez Canal
Horbêt
Qantir
Wâdi Tumilât
Zagazig
Bubastis
SUEZ
Bilbês

Heliopolis

ROUTE 7
0   km   150   N
CAIRO

and it was during their reigns that many of the tombs and temples were built. Earlier monuments have also been found at the site and include buildings dating to the reign of Ammenemes III in the Middle Kingdom and the ruins of a building of the Sixth Dynasty inscribed with the name of king Pepi I. An important cemetery of the Late Period was also discovered here. The mummies were either buried without sarcophagi or in sarcophagi made of wood or pottery. Many of the bodies were those of children. All of them had been buried with *wedjet* eye amulets. The deity of the city was the cat-headed goddess, Bastet, who was a pleasant and benevolent divinity. This was her principal cult-centre and noisy and joyful festivals were held here in her honour. Herodotus records that more than half a million Egyptian men and women took part in the procession to her temple during the festival. Today nearly the whole of the city is below the level of the water-table in the Delta, which has risen considerably since ancient times. The walls of the ancient mud-brick buildings have crumbled and it is difficult to imagine how splendid the city must have been in its heyday. Furthermore all the important fragments, which were discovered here, were taken away and are now in various museums. In 1905 a large number of silver objects were found at Zagazig. This important treasure is now in the Egyptian Museum in Cairo.

The *Great Temple* of Bastet was begun in the Fourth Dynasty by the kings Cheops and Chephren, altered over the centuries and finished magnificently decorated by Osorkon II and Nectanebo II. The temple covered a vast area and the remains of a hypostyle hall and numerous chapels can be seen. As the ruins indicate, the city suffered a number of violent attacks, particularly by the Hyksos, who entered Egypt at the end of the Middle Kingdom. Nevertheless limestone statues and beautiful fragments of walls inscribed with the names of Pharaohs of the Fourth, Twelfth, Eighteenth, Nineteenth and particularly of the Twenty-second and Thirtieth Dynasties have been found here. Mummies of the New Kingdom were also discovered, who had been provided with numerous faience and gold magical and protective amulets. Many of these finds are now preserved in the Egyptian Museum in Cairo.

The *necropolis* of the city lies nearby and extends over a vast area. The tombs are of various different types and the dead were buried with canopic vases containing their viscera, statues of themselves and other funerary equipment. Although all the tombs had been robbed, some inscribed statues, various amulets and a small amount of funerary material was found in the cemeteries.

To the west of the Great Temple, the remains of a temple of Pepi I were discovered. This had eight pillars. On the plain at the foot of the mound of Bubastis lay a huge cat-cemetery. The cat was the sacred animal of Bastet and a large number of statues of cats or of the goddess with the head of a cat were recovered from the graves. (Before continuing northwards along the road, the visitor should go to the office of the Egyptian Antiquities Service in Zagazig and enquire about visiting the city of Tanis and buy an entrance ticket for the site.)

Qantir, 148 km (92 miles) from Cairo. The existence of a palace of Ramesses II here only 25 km (15 miles)

from Tanis, has led a number of Egyptologists to suggest that Qantir was the site of the Ramesside city of Pi-Ramesses. This theory is an attractive one, although there is no concrete evidence yet to support it. Only very limited excavations have been conducted at the site. There is little to see at the site itself but the visitor can admire the polychrome faience tiles which decorated the walls of the palace at the Egyptian Museum in Cairo.

Tanis *(San el-Hagar)*, 173 km (107 miles) from Cairo. The flat table land which extends to the south of *Lake Manzala* was formerly covered by profuse vegetation. Above this in the centre of the plateau rose the mound of San el-Hagar. For a long time it has been maintained, although without any real proof, that this was the site of the Hyksos fortress of Avaris and also the site of the Residence of Pi-Ramesses, which was founded and built by Ramesses II and was called « The Mansion of Ramesses, beloved of Amun ». This name was inscribed on an obelisk found at the site. However, it is possible that the ancient Pi-Ramesses was at Qantir (see above). It was only from the Twenty-first Dynasty onwards that the city was called Tanis. It covered an area of more than 30 hectares (74 acres) and was still flourishing in the Roman period. Today it is the most impressive area of ruins in the Delta and an extremely interesting site. The finds made here were mainly divided between the Egyptian Museum in Cairo and the Louvre in Paris. Of particular interest are the objects, including many gold and silver items, which were excavated from the royal tombs. This treasure ranks second only to that of Tutankhamun and is displayed in special rooms in the Egyptian Museum in Cairo.

At the centre of the site of Tanis is the *temple area*. This is surrounded almost entirely by a strong brick wall 10 m (32 ft) thick. The enclosure measures 300×400 m (328×437 yds) and lies parallel to the axis of the Great Temple which was oriented east-west. A large number of fragments bearing the name of Ramesses II were found here. They had been re-used in the building of a later temple. Near to the north gateway were found two colossal statues of

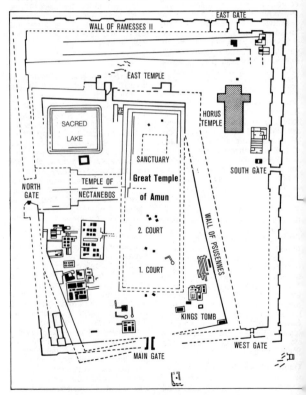

Ramesses II and two statues of lions with their front paws crossed. The main gateway on the west, which was a sort of propylon, was partly decorated by Sheshonq III. The main temple at Tanis was the Great Temple which was dedicated to the Theban god Amun. The name of Seth on the Ramesside columns which were re-used was erased and these erasures can still be seen.

Inside the enclosure is the sacred area containing the *Great Temple*, the *North Temple*, the *East Temple*, the *Temple of Horus*, the *Sacred Lake* and the *Royal Tombs*. Outside the enclosure to the south-west is the *Temple of Anat*. The whole area is now very ruined and it is difficult to determine the exact position and plan of the buildings. Nevertheless the ruined site is very impressive with its scattered decorated blocks, broken statues, columns, stelae, fallen architraves, remains of altars and shrines, fallen and shattered obelisks and bases.

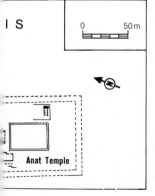

Before the court of the Great Temple stood the second pylon with two pairs of pink granite obelisks in front of it. Further on in the court are fragments of colossal statues of Ramesses II. The sanctuary is now very ruined. The remains of high monolithic columns can be seen. These were palmiform columns with very fine capitals.

The interior enclosure wall was built by Psusennes I. Within this smaller enclosure were a group of *Royal Tombs*. They date to the Twenty-first and Twenty-second Dynasties and belonged to Sheshonq III, Amenemope, Osorkon II, Psusennes and Heqakheperre Sheshonq II. The tomb of Psusennes was still undisturbed and its contents intact when Pierre Montet discovered it in 1940. Psusennes was a king of the Twenty-first Dynasty, who ruled over the north of Egypt, while the dynasty of Priest-kings governed the south of Egypt from Thebes. The tomb contained not only the body of Psusennes but also the bodies of Queen Mutnodjmet, the Twenty-first Dynasty King Amenemope, King Heqakheperre Sheshonq II and the general Ankhefenamun, an official and contemporary of Psusennes. The silver coffins, gold funerary masks, gold silver and precious stone amulets and funerary vessels were all of superb quality and these and the rest of the funerary equipment indicate the high standards of Egyptian art and craftsmanship of this period. This funerary equipment is certainly worthy of comparison with that of Tutankhamun.

Of the buildings which lay outside the large enclosure, the best known is the *Temple of Anat,* which was also dedicated to Mut and Khonsu, and which was surrounded by an enclosure wall. Anat was the consort of Seth and a war-goddess of Asiatic origin who had been assimilated into the Egyptian pantheon of gods. The axis of her temple is perpendicular to that of the Great Temple. The temple was built by the the Pharaoh Siamun in the Twenty-first Dynasty and many earlier blocks, particularly from the reign of Ramesses II, were re-used in its construction. Here can be seen a large granite group-statue of the reign of Ramesses II and beautiful palmiform columns of the same type as those in the Great Temple.

Route nº 8 : Cairo - Suez - Ismailia - Port Said (305 km (189 m.)

(see map on p. 321). Before embarking on this journey, the visitor should enquire in Cairo as to whether it is possible to travel on the road along the Suez Canal. Leave Cairo along *Ramesses Street* and passing the station, continue to *Heliopolis* and turn to the right onto the desert road. The desert road follows a course slightly to the west of the ancient caravan trail along which the pilgrims travelled to get to Mecca ; 66 km (41 miles) from Cairo there is a rest-house with a petrol station, which is situated near to the mausoleum of a sheikh. The road then goes through a high valley which separates the mountain chain of Gebel Ahmed Taher on the left and Gebel Ataqa on the right and reaches the Gulf of Suez.

Suez, 134 km (83 miles) from Cairo. The town was founded in the 15th century and expanded greatly when the Suez Canal was built. In Pharaonic and Ptolemaic times there was a settlement on the hill, Kom el-Qulzum, to the north of the town. From the summit of the hill there is a good view over the town and the sea, to the east as far as the Sinai Peninsula and to the west over the mountains of Gebel Ataqa. The Suez Canal runs into the Gulf of Suez, where the channel has been deepened in the Red Sea so that the ships can pass into and through the Canal at low tide. From the pier there is a magnificent view over the Gulf of Suez, the desert coast of Asia to the east and the mountains of Africa on the right. The ships which can be seen come from all over the world, passing through the Canal to their various destinations. The town of Suez is a lively and colourful place but contains no monuments of particular interest to the tourist. The town suffered considerable damage during the wars of June 1967 and October 1973. The inhabitants were evacuated but are now gradually returning and the town is being redeveloped and rebuilt.

To the north of Kom el-Qulzum, the southern branch of the Sweet Water Canal, which comes from the Nile, flows into the Red Sea through a system of conduits. Here the level of the canal is 2 m (6 ½ ft) above that of the Red Sea. On the other side of the Gulf of Suez is Port Taufiq, which is situated on an artificial peninsula, which was built with the earth which was dug out when the Suez Canal was constructed. The town is linked

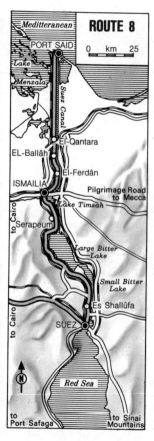

ROUTE 8

0   km   25

southwest and like Suez its harbour and docks are used by the ships passing through the canal.

THE SUEZ CANAL

Even as early as the New Kingdom, the Egyptians realised the advantages of a canal between the Mediterranean and the Red Sea. Ramesses II tried to establish such a link by using the branches of the Nile. His ships left the Nile and travelled along a canal through the Wadi Tumilat to Lake Timsah. Around 600 B.C. Necho began the construction of a canal between Lake Timsah and the Red Sea. Herodotus states that 120,000 Egyptian workmen died during the course of the work and the whole scheme was abandoned when an oracle predicted that the Persians would use such a canal to invade and conquer Egypt. Although the king obeyed the oracle, the Persians did invade Egypt in 525 B.C. and Darius I completed the cutting of the canal. He set up commemorative stelae inscribed in Egyptian and Persian along the canal. The text proclaims grandly that Darius, the great king of the Persians, who had conquered Egypt, gave the order for the canal to be cut, which would link the river called the Nile, which flowed in Egypt, with the sea which extended to Persia. A flotilla of triremes loaded with Egyptian tribute left the Nile, travelled along the canal, sailed across the Red Sea and around Arabia and arrived safely at a Persian port.

At the end of the 1st century A.D. Trajan restored the canal, which by then had fallen into a state of disrepair. It was renamed « Trajan's Canal ». The canal was then neglected until c. 650 A.D. when the general of

to Suez by a pier 2 km (½mile) long across which run the road and the railway. *Port Ibrahim* lies to the

the Caliph, a man called Amr ibn el-As, had it cleared and it remained open to shipping for a short time. After that it became silted up again. In later times the Venetians, Leibnitz, Sultan Mustapha III, Ali Bey and Napoleon Bonaparte all considered the possibility of a direct link between the Mediterranean and the Red Sea without starting from the Nile and going along the Wadi Tumilat. For a long time it had been believed that the level of the Red Sea was 9 m (29 ½ ft) above that of the Mediterranean. This assumption was proved incorrect by the precise measurements and calculations of Waghorn and the Frenchman, Ferdinand de Lesseps. Lesseps devised a scheme for the construction of a direct canal and this had a favourable reception. The Suez Canal Company was founded and obtained a concession to construct the canal and to take the dues from it on a 99 year lease. The work began on April 25th 1859. There were many difficulties during the course of the work. The Suez Canal was officially opened on November 17th 1869 amid general rejoicing.

The canal is 171 km (106 miles) long. The channel has been widened eight times since it was opened and is now 90 m (98 yds) wide. The width of the canal from bank to bank is 140 m (156 yds). A scheme to widen the channel further, which would allow ships to pass along it in both directions at once is being considered. Ships drawing 11 m (36 ft) of water can cross the isthmus in 15 - 20 hours and this means that two such ships can pass through the canal every day in each direction. The new scheme which is envisaged would include waiting areas or passing-places every 10 km (6 miles) along the channel. At present ships can only pass by each other at the branch canal between El-Firdan and El-Qantara. The Suez Canal is one of the most used waterways in the world. It was re-opened on June 5th 1975 after being closed for 8 years. Normally more than 20,000 ships representing a total of 200 million tons of shipping pass through the canal every year. The dues and charges levied for using the canal amount to a considerable annual sum. In 1960 the total raised was about 170 million American dollars. The Suez Canal was taken over and nationalised by the Egyptian Government in 1956.

Crossing the Isthmus of Suez (a journey of 171 km (106 miles)) by ship is an interesting experience and can be highly recommended. The crossing can also be made by car or train along the western bank and shore. The crossing by ship is described below. The journey by car or train is slightly different but the visitor travelling by these methods will still be able to follow the description without any difficulty.

The Suez Canal

The Isthmus of Suez :

1 km (c. 1/2 mile) - Suez/Port Taufiq. Here stands the *Indian War Memorial*, a granite obelisk, which was erected in 1926 to the memory of the Indian soldiers who were killed in Egypt and Palestine during the First World War. Right at the entrance to the Canal from the Red Sea is a large relief sculpture. It depicts President Nasser in the symbolic act of handing back the Suez Canal to the Egyptian people and commemorates the nationalisation of the Canal by the Egyptian Government.

26 km (16 miles) - Esh Shallufa. Here the canal can be crossed by ferry-boat.

36 km (22 miles) - Gineifa, Where there is a signal station. On the left the hills of the Gebel Gineifa rise to a height of 250 m (820 ft). Beyond the signal station at Gineifa the canal enters the *Bitter Lakes*, the Small Bitter Lake and the Great Bitter Lake, which are 37 km (23 miles) long. At the shores of the lakes are sandy, flat beaches. These lakes were dried-up salt beds when in 1869 the waters of the Mediterranean flowed into them along the newly constructed canal and filled the basins. It is here that the tidal waters of the Red Sea are absorbed into the Lakes in such a way that the differences in the volumes of water in the various tides do not affect the ships. The area which is between 56 and 71 km (34 and 44 miles) from the Red Sea is a zone where ships can pass by each other. The deepened channel across the Lakes is clearly marked out.

73 km (45 miles) - Le Deversoir, which is a signal station at the end of the *Great Bitter Lake.*

81 km. (50 miles) - Serapeum, where the canal has been cut through the rock. At 87 km (54 miles) the canal passes the foot of the *Gebel Maryam* on the left. According to an Arab legend Miriam spent seven days on this mountain when she was afflicted with leprosy after disapproving of the marriage of her brother, Moses, to an Ethiopian woman. Beyond Gebel Maryam the canal enters Lake *Timsah.*

91 km (56 miles) - Ismailia, which is a very pleasant town with a number of green parks and public gardens. At one time the offices of the Suez Canal Company were situated in the town and today part of the administration is still controlled from here. The inhabitants were evacuated from the town during the Arab-Israeli Wars and have only recently gradually returned to their homes. On the shores of Lake Timsah (« crocodile lake ») there are pleasant beaches and bathing areas. At Ismailia every ship is required to change its pilot in order to conform with the regulations governing the work of the Canal employees. During the cutting of the canal and the transport of the materials for its construction, a great number of interesting finds were made in the area. Many of these dated to the Ptolemaic and Roman periods. They are displayed in a small Museum in the town.

The Museum (the building is being renovated and some items may have been temporarily removed from display).

Room 1 : Ptolemaic wooden sarcophagus from Asyût ; Roman mosaics ; diorite statue with the wig surmounted by a scarabeus ; prehistoric tools ; seals ; bronzes ;

Coptic textiles ; outline drawings on plaster and stone and sculptors' model carvings ; statues.

Room 2 : Greek pottery ; coins ; lamps ; Byzantine glass ; Roman pottery ; various statuettes ; statuettes of the god, Bes ; Arabic papyri from Akhmim ; grind-stone and mortars ; black granite naos from *El-Arish*, Sinai, inscribed with interesing mythological texts ; in the centre of the room is a mosaic with a mythological scene.

Museum garden : Here stands one of the stelae erected by Darius I along the canal which he had constructed between the Nile and the Red Sea (see on p. 321). On the stelae he boasts proudly of this great work. The text is inscribed in four languages - Egyptian hieroglyphic, Babylonian, Elamite and Ancient Persian.

Garden of the Stelae. This is situated not far from the museum and contains finds of the Pharaonic period, most of which date to the reign of Ramesses II. The most important items are : a pyramidion ; a granite pedestal for a statue of the falcon-god, Horus, which dates to the reign of Sethos I but which bears inscriptions of Ramesses II ; the remains of a naos of Ramesses II ; a black granite lid of a sarcophagus ; sphinxes of Ramesses II, one of which is dedicated to Atum and Harakhty ; a group statue of Ramesses II seated between the gods Atum and Khepri ; a representation of Ramesses II offering Maat to the god Re-Harakhty with an accompanying inscription ; Ramesses before the god Atum ; various stelae, etc.

Nearly all of these finds come from the « hill of images », *Tell el-Maskhuta,* and from *Pithom.* The two sites

were situated along the canal which flowed in the Wadi Tumilat during the pharaonic period and are about 20 km (12 miles) to the west of Ismailia near Nahsama. The name Pithom is derived from the Egyptian Per-Atum, « House of Atum ». It was a frontier town on the eastern boundary of the Delta in the Ramesside period. The ruins of a temple were found here during early excavations. The most interesting finds from the site are now in the Museum at Ismailia (see above).

98 km (60 miles) - El-Gisr (« the embankment »). The constantly shifting sand dunes can reach a height of 30 m (98 ft) but cannot be seen from the road. The shifting sand caused many problems during the building of the canal. To stop the sand moving Lesseps covered the dunes with wooden planks, using a whole ship's cargo of them, the canal was then dug out and its sides were built up with masonry so that the sand could not encroach into the canal. From the top of the sand dunes there is a good view of the Sinai Peninsula, Lake Timsah, the Bitter Lakes and over to Gebel Ataqa to the south of Suez.

106 km (65 miles) - El-Firdan, the « needle's eye ». This used to be one of the most difficult parts of the canal for the passage of large ships because of the pillars of the great swing-bridge. The bridge is more than 300 m (984 ft) long and across it run the road and the railway. Since 1951 there has been a branch canal between El-Firdan and El-Qantara and convoys of ships one behind the other can travel along it easily but in one direction only at a time. The branch canal, which is 11 km (6 miles) long (between 110 and 121 km (68 and 74 miles) from Suez) was constructed between 1949 and 1951 across the salt beds of *Lake Ballah*, the « lake of dates ».

127 km (78 miles) - El-Qantara, « the bridge ». The branch canal rejoins the main canal. This is still the only place where two ships can pass by each other in the canal itself. On the Asiatic bank is the starting point of the railway which goes to El-Arish, Gaza and Jerusalem. The canal now continues in a straight line towards the north. On the left is the northern branch of the Sweet Water Canal and further on is *Lake Manzala*, part of which has been drained near the canal. Across Lake Manzala in the Roman period still flowed the three eastern branches of the Nile, the Mendesian, Tanitic and Pelusiac Branches. At the centre of this then very fertile region was situated the city of Tanis while Pelusium, the famous ancient sea-port, lay to the east of modern Port Said.

171 km (106 miles) - Port Said, 305 km (189 miles) from Cairo. The town was founded in 1859 when work on the construction of the Suez Canal commenced, and lies on a sandy, marshy tongue of land between Lake Manzala and the Mediterranean. It is practically surrounded by water on all sides and is bordered on the east by the canal and on the south by lake Manzala. The harbour and the entrance to the Suez Canal are protected by two large piers, more than 2 km (1 ¼ miles) and 1,5 km (nearly a mile) in length. On the seaward side of the Lighthouse, which is 56 m (184 ft) high, at the end of the western pier there stood a large statue of Lesseps. The statue itself was taken down during the Suez Crisis of 1956 but the pedestal remains and is inscribed with the words : *Aperire terram gentibus,* « to open the world to the nations ». Port Said is the second largest port in Egypt after Alexandria and has always been a very cosmopolitan town. The various quarters of the town and the port itself are therefore interesting places to visit. The town has suffered some damage and destruction during the course of three wars but reconstruction work has begun and the town is being redeveloped and enlarged.

On the east bank of the Suez Canal are the residential quarters and buildings of the town of Port Fuad. The town was founded in 1926 as Port Said could not profitably be expanded any further to the west. In crossing from Port Said to Port Fuad, the visitor leaves the continent of Africa and steps onto the soil of the continent of Asia. In this area on the Mediterranean coast there are numerous pleasant sandy beaches and the water is clear and calm.

Route n° 9 : Cairo - Suez - Sinai (392 km (243 mi.)

(see map, on p. 363). Since the wars of 1967 and 1973 it has not been possible to visit the Sinai Peninsula from Egypt. Only the east bank of the Suez Canal and its neighbouring area have been accessible from the Egyptian side. A peace treaty has now been signed between Egypt and Israel (1979). Therefore in the hope of continuing peace and future agreements which may once again lead to free access to the Sinai Peninsula, a description of the area is given below as it was before 1967. At that time it was necessary to obtain a permit to visit the area from the offices of the Frontiers Administration.

The journey from Cairo to Suez, a distance of 134 km (83 miles), has already been described (p. 320). From Suez continue northwards and cross the Canal by ferry-boat at Esh-Shallufa. Owing to the traffic passing along the Canal, it is wise to allow at least three hours for the crossing. After crossing the Canal, travel southwards along the Red Sea coast.

THE SINAI PENINSULA

The Sinai Peninsula is one of the most interesting and attractive areas of Egypt. The landscape is varied and the area has many connections with events in Biblical history. There is plenty to see and admire from the sandy plains of the north, the mountainous region in the centre to the high hills in the south. The wild life includes gazelle, leopards, hares, falcons and pigeons and these can still be hunted here.

In ancient times the Pharaohs came to Sinai in search of gold, copper, malachite and turquoise and the goddess, Hathor, was considered as the Lady of the Land of Turquoise. It was here that the Egyptian soldiers escorted the workmen to the mines and protected them from the Bedouin. It was in Sinai that Moses received the Ten Commandments after the Exodus. The Holy Family passed through here on their Flight into Egypt and under the Roman Empire the persecuted Christians came to seek refuge in the wild mountains. In modern times plants and equipment for finding and exploiting the oil fields have sprung up on the Red Sea coast and in the sea itself.

The Sinai Peninsula is in effect shaped like an equilateral triangle. The southern part with the cape of Râs Mohammed at the tip lies between the two gulfs of the Red Sea, the Gulf of Suez and the Gulf of Aqaba. In the northern part of the peninsula is the Wadi el-Arish, which has many branches radiating outwards like the fingers of a hand. In the southern part of the peninsula there are high coastal mountains with high valleys often with steep sides, formed of ancient rocks of the earliest Geological periods : gneiss, granite, syenite and porphyry - all crystalline rocks. In the south these are partly overlaid by the sedimentary rock, sandstone. The granite mountains of Gebel Serbal, Katerin and Mûsa are the high places with many religious connections and the charming oasis of Firan also has many religious associations. The Sinai Peninsula has very few inhabitants. It is populated by at the most 20,000 people and these are mainly Bedouin.

The distances given below are those from Suez.

31 km (19 miles) - a road leads off on the right to the Springs of Moses, *Ayun Mûsa*, which are situated about 1 km (just over half a mile) from the coast. The luxuriant vegetation grows here on account of the twelve springs of water which irrigate the small oasis. The southermost spring is said to be that from which Moses drew a spring of water when he struck the rock with his stick.

72 km (44 miles) - on the left a road branches off to the *Wadi Baba*, which is a valley with caves in the rocks. About 20 km (12 miles) along the valley are the turquoise mines of *Om-Bogma*. This was one of the valleys of Sinai which during antiquity

The Spring of Moses

was constantly explored by bands of Egyptian workmen whose task was to find and exploit the rich veins of copper, malachite and above all turquoise. The inscriptions of pharaoh after pharaoh were left here and elsewhere in Sinai and some of them date to the oldest periods of Egyptian history. In this particular valley with its rock-caves there are inscriptions recounting the expeditions of the King Sekhemkhet of the Third Dynasty and his skirmishes with the Bedouin tribesmen when he was protecting his workmen at the mines.

About 15 km (9 miles) further along the valley is Serabit el-Khadim, the most important Pharaonic site in Sinai with the ruins of a temple dedicated to Hathor, mistress of Sinai and « Lady of the Turquoise ». An important relief of King Sneferu of the Fourth Dynasty was found here and is now preserved in the Egyptian Museum in Cairo. This find indicated that even in the Fourth Dynasty there was a sanctuary here. The temple itself was founded in the Twelfth Dynasty and was a small speos or rock-cut sanctuary with an open court in front of it. After the troubles of the Second Intermediate Period, the kings of the New Kingdom in the Eighteenth and Nineteenth Dynasties decided to enlarge the building and added to it a court and a pylon preceded by a certain number of rooms. The commemorative stelae set up at this period give valuable information on the paramilitary working parties, the gangs of workmen and the various adventures of the expeditions who came here. In later times next to the speos of Hathor, a sanctuary was constructed and dedicated to the god of the deserts, Sopdu. Sopdu was identified with the Pharaoh Sneferu who had by them been deified. The Hathor columns

SERABIT EL-KHADIM

are carved in differing styles. On one of them the goddess is shown wearing a smooth, straight wig but on another she is shown with a curly wig. Some of the columns are carved in sunk relief, while others are carved in raised relief. Not very far from the temple are commemorative stelae standing in the open air. They date to the Twelfth, Eighteenth, Nineteenth and Twentieth Dynasties and stood along the path which led to the temple. The texts inscribed on them tell the stories of the various expeditions to Sinai. The stela of King Sethos I stands on the summit of a hill. The ground-plan of this sacred place had to be adapted to the configurations of the valley, and therefore the approaches to the temple were nearly 1/2 km (1/3rd mile) in distance and an alteration was made in the axis of the temple. Many of the workmen who were employed here seem to have been Asiatics as an Asiatic influence is evident in some of the architectural details.

At the **sign-post** which stands at the junction for the road to *Wadi Sedri*, turn left off the coast-road and go along the valley to the south-east.

204 km (126 miles) - the Oasis of Fîrân, which lies 600 m (1,968 feet) above sea-level. The oasis is extremely fertile and date-trees, tamarisks, maize and other cereals grow here. By the spring of water at the centre of the oasis there is a small monastery. It stands on the site where the Hebrews under the command of Joshua defeated the Amalekites. The oasis lies at the foot of Mount Horeb, known today as the Gebel Serbal (2078 m (6,818 ft) high), where Moses spoke with God and where Aaron and Hur supported the arms of Moses during the battle with the Amalekites. Immediately to the right of the road is a hermitage belonging to the monastery of St Catherine. It is one of the two hermitages which the monastery maintained permanently for the benefit of the needy. From the 4th to the 7th centuries Firan was the seat of a bishop and here can be seen the remains of a basilica, a church, houses, a fortified wall and several rock-tombs.

Leave the oasis and continue north-westwards into a valley carved out between two high porphyry rock walls. This is the *Wadi Maghara*, which contains the remains of turquoise mines of the Pharaonic period and the *Wadi Moqqatib*, the « valley of inscriptions », which is of great interest to archaeologists and philologists. The smooth walls of the rocks are covered with inscriptions written in various ancient languages - Egyptian hieroglyphic, Nabatean, Greek and a Semitic language similar to Canaanite. The inscriptions written in this last language are the famous *Inscriptions of Sinai* and are proto-Semitic. The signs which are used are apparently borrowed from Egyptian hieroglyphic and employed as consonantal signs. From these signs was developed the later Phoenician alphabet, then the Greek and finally our modern alphabet.

From the valley the road rises in a series of hair-pin bends above the area covered by tamarisks and « Manna trees ». The latter trees supply a sweet scented honey, which is probably the Manna mentioned in the Bible. After passing through the rocky pass of El-Buweid the road enters the Wadi Sheikh. In the Wadi is the domed tomb of Nebi Salih, the national saint of the Bedouin of Sinai. The valley then widens out and ahead at an altitude of 1 600 m (5,249 ft) can be seen the Monastery of St Catherine.

THE MONASTERY OF ST CATHERINE

258 km (160 miles) - The Monastery or convent of St Catherine is situated 1530 m (5,020 ft) above sea-level in a valley surrounded by mountains - Gebel Safsaga, Gebel Mûsa (the mountain of Moses), Gebel Katerin and Gebel Moneiga. Saint Mark introduced Christianity into Egypt and was the founder of monasticism in the Egyptian deserts. By the beginning of the 4th century there was a small community of monks living at the foot of Mount Sinai. During the 4th century the Empress Helen, the mother of Constantine, visited the Holy Mountain and gave orders for a small church to be built there. This small church was situated at the foot of the mountain on the site where in ancient times the Hebrew people had heard the voice of God and on the site where God had manifested himself to Moses by the sign of the burning bush.

In 527 A.D. the Emperor Justinian I, who built the Cathedral of St Sophia in Constantinople, officially founded the monastery here. The church was surrounded by a fortress with rampart walls to protect the monks from the attacks of marauding Bedouin and a small garrison of Roman and Egyptian soldiers was stationed at the site. Originally the church and the monastery were dedicated to the Mother of God and to the Transfiguration of Christ. The name Monastery of St-Catherine comes from the legend concerning a young Christian woman called Catherine who was martyred for the faith at Alexandria. The relics of the saint were brought to Sinai around the 8th century and the monastery was named after her. However, it seems certain that her relics were not placed in the monastery itself until the Middle Ages.

Between the 7th and the 18th centuries the monks were driven from the monastery on several occasions. The beginning of the Islamic period saw the beginning of the decline of the monastery. However, until 1575, the monastery was an independant archbishopric, and the smallest see in the world. The monks elected the Archbishop from among themselves and he with the help of four archimandrites administered the wealth and incomes of the monastery. The wealth was derived from various sources, among which was the ownership of property in the Greek Islands. Today in the monastery and in its other buildings there are less than fifty monks. They follow the teaching of St Basil the Great (331-379 A.D.), who came from Caesarea and was the founder of eastern monasticism. The principles of his teaching were « solitude, silence and mortification ». They are not Coptic monks but belong to the Greek Orthodox Church. Today the monastery is like an oasis enclosed by ramparts and lies in a setting of almost tragic grandeur in a place of

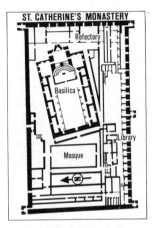

Originally the buildings within the enclosure were designed for the Latin Church services, but they are now all used for the celebration of the services of the Greek Orthodox Church. These buildings and the others which have been added over the centuries are crowded together and the plan of the interior of the enclosure appears very confused.

The mosque, which was built in about the 11th century, contains some interesting antiquities. There is a wooden throne with kufic inscriptions and a minbar of the Fatimid period. These two items date from the reign of the seventh Fatimid caliph, El-Mustali who ruled from 1094-1101.

The Basilica Church. A beautiful gateway in the Fatimid style dating to the 11th century leads to the narthex or long arcaded porch and then to

utter peace far from the troubles of modern civilisation, preserving within it its tradition of piety, its frescoes, icons, manuscripts and treasures.

The enclosure wall of the monastery is of granite and the enclosure is more than 90 m (295 ft) in length and 75 m (246 ft) in width. The wall was built as a rampart and is similar to the walls of the fortresses built by Justinian. It is 12-15 m (39-40 ft) high and more than 1.50 m (5 ft) thick. The path along the top of the wall is protected by battlements and loop-holes and there are projecting towers at each corner. On the north wall at the top can be seen the openings through which men and provisions were hauled by a pulley and rope during the long period when there was no gateway into the monastery. Today the north gateway is at ground-level below these openings.

The Monastery of St Catherine

an ancient Byzantine gateway of the 6th century beyond which lies the catholicon. The polychrome floor is of porphyry and marble and is relatively modern as it dates to the 18th century. Twelve granite columns divide the interior of the church into three aisles. There are chapels leading off from the side-aisles. On the left are the chapels of Cosmas, Damian and Simeon and on the right those of Marina, Constantine and Helen, and Antipas. The gifts of the pious are placed along both sides of the 13th century iconostasis. There are large candlesticks and precious silver chandeliers, which are not particularly interesting in an artistic sense, ostrich eggs, a great number of lamps, etc.

In the apse is a magnificent Byzantine *mosaic* of the 6th century. The scenes on the front wall show : Moses in front of the Burning Bush ; he receives the Tablets of Law from God ; the angels look down from on high ; portraits of the Emperor Justinian and his wife Theodora. The scenes on the vault show : the Transfiguration of Christ ; on his right is Moses, on his left, Elias, and at his feet are the apostles, Peter, James and John.

The magnificent altar is of wood inlaid with mother-of-pearl and was a gift to the monastery. It came from Damascus. To the right of the altar, beneath a canopy is a marble reliquary in which are preserved the relics of St Catherine. Inside the reliquary are two gold ossuaries containing the head and a hand of the saint. The relics are taken out of the reliquary on special Holy days and shown to the faithful. Two silver reliquaries inlaid with costly precious stones stand behind the icon ostasis. These were gifts to the monastery

and were presented by the Empress Catherine of Russia in the 17th century and by Tsar Alexander II of Russia in the 19th century. One of them was given with the express wish that it should contain the relics of the saint but the monks preferred to place these two reliquaries with their collection of precious gifts.

The walls of the chapels on either side of the apse are decorated with frescoes. The paintings are well preserved, particularly in the chapel of St James on the left. The scenes in this chapel show : Moses and St Basil the Great ; Mary in the burning bush ; Chrysostomas, St James. It is possible though by no means certain that the relics of St James were at one time preserved in the monastery.

The Chapel of the Burning Bush is immediately behind the chancel. It is the holiest and most famous part of the monastery. Beneath the permanently lit lamp is the reputed site where the Burning Bush of the Bible stood. The actual site is covered by silver plaques, which are engraved with scenes from the Old and New Testaments, from the life of Jesus and from the legend of St Catherine. In the apse there is a simple cross on a golden pedestal. Before entering the holy place of the chapel of the Burning Bush the visitor must take off his shoes as God instructed Moses to do this. Behind the chapel there grows a bush of broom, which is believed to be an offshoot of the Burning Bush and which lies to the side of the source of the sacred bush.

The mills and bakeries of the monastery stand next to each other. In the bakeries can still be seen the old wooden carved moulds in which the bread for the holy festivals was shaped. To the south-east is the refectory, which is a vaulted room 17 m (55 ft) long with wall-frescoes of scenes depicting the Last Judgement. The paintings date to the 16th century. The Knights who came here as pilgrims from Europe during the Middle Ages carved their names and coats-of-arms on the available clear surfaces of the walls

The Library is one of the richest monastic libraries in the world and is now installed in the new wing of the monastery. It contains more than 3,500 manuscripts in Greek, Arabic, Hebrew, Armenian, Georgian, Syriac, etc. Most of the texts are religious, but some of them are historical or medical writings. During his work in the library between 1844 and 1859, the German scholar, Tischendorf, discovered a Biblical manuscript of the 4th century, which is known as the *Codex Sinaiticus*. This document is now preserved in the British Museum in London. Visitors can see a facsimile of the manuscript at the monastery. They can also see the Syriac version of the Gospel of St Luke and the edicts affording protection to the monastery. One of these came from the prophet, Mohammed and another bears the signature of Napoleon Bonaparte.

The Museum contains more than 2,000 icons of incalculable value. They range in date from the period of iconoclasm in the 8th century to the end of the Byzantine period in the 15th century. The interesting and rare paintings on wax of the 5th and 6th centuries are quite remarkable. Among the treasures are beautiful sacerdotal ornaments. In the garden of the monastery the crypt of the chapel of St Tryphon is the ossuary or charnel-house which contains the last remains of the monks. The piles

of bones are a striking reminder of the past life and history of the monastery.

Every day between the hours of 4.30 and 7.30, the monks gather together to celebrate the main daily service. The wooden gong rings out in the belfry to announce the hour of prayer. It sounds again before the afternoon service. Its rhythmic sounds echo the unchanging life of the monks, a life devoted to simplicity, renunciation and piety in a place of historical and religious importance for Jews, Christians and Moslems.

THE THREE HOLY MOUNTAINS

(The visitor who can only spend one day here should go up *Mount Moses*.)

1. Mount Moses (*Gebel Mûsa*), 2285 m (7,497 ft) also called *Mount Sinai*. This is reputed to be the mountain where God Gave Moses the Ten Commandments. It is very likely that the mountain of the Law, known as Mount Horeb in the Old Testament, was in fact Gebel Serbal. However, pre-Christian Nabatean inscriptions describe Gebel Mûsa as a sacred mountain.

The climb up the mountain takes at least three hours. To the east of the monastery follow the winding camel track which passes beyond and above the *hermitage of St Stephen*. Here there is a small plateau with a cypress tree growing beside a spring of water. This was where Moses, Aaron and the seventy elders of Israel supposedly stopped to worship God from afar. Two small chapels on the plateau are dedicated to Moses and Elias. Camels should be left here and the visitor continues on foot to the *staircase of Moses*, a flight of more than 3,000 granite steps. It is said that these were carved in the mountain by a monk who had made a vow to accomplish this task. From the steps the visitor reaches the « Gate of Confessions ». Pilgrims had to make their confession to the hermit who lived here and when they had received absolution for their sins from him, they could continue on their way to the summit. Higher up the mountain just below the summit is the « Gate of the Law » Here the pilgrims took off their shoes and finished the climb bare-footed. Since the 4th century there has been a small chapel on the summit of the mountain. Justinian enlarged it and made it into a church and it was on the site of the ruins of the church that a new chapel was reconstructed in 1934. Not far from the chapel on the summit is a ruined mosque.

The Bedouin believe that Nebi Salih was taken up to heaven from the summit of the mountain. Just below the mosque is the cave, where according to tradition Moses took refuge. The view from the summit extends across Sinai and southwards to the Gulf of Aqaba.

2. Mount Moneiga, 1854 m (6,083 ft). Follow the winding path at the beginning of the ascent of *Mount Moses*. On one of the bends a path leads off on the left. The path is marked and leads to the summit of Mount Moneiga. The small chapel on the summit is dedicated to Mary, Mother of God. From the summit there is a very good view over the monastery of St Catherine. The ascent of the mountain takes about an hour.

3. Mount Catherine (Gebel Katerin), 2639 m (8,658 ft) The long climb to the summit takes at least five hours. The route passes the chapel of Aaron, the monastery of the garden convent of the Holy Apostles and the pavilion built by King Fuad, which is now a rest-house, the monastery of the Forty Martyrs and thence to a staircase which leads to the summit. On the summit stands the Chapel of St Catherine which was built by the monk Callistes. According to legend the angels brought the headless body of the martyred virgin Catherine from Alexandria and laid her on the summit of this mountain. A hollow in the rock is said to be the imprint of her body. It is possible to spend the night on the summit in two small rooms built for that purpose. Permission to do so must be obtained in advance from the monastery of St Catherine. The view from the summit extends over the mountainous landscape of the peninsula and across to the Red Sea and the Gulf of Aqaba.

On the neighbouring summit of Gebel Sebir, a climb of about 25 minutes from Mount Catherine, stands an observatory, which belongs to the Smith Institute of Meteorology of California. Solar radiation was measured here for the first time between 1933 and 1938. A path descends from the summit to the monastery of the Forty Martyrs.

Route n° 10 : Suez - Hurghada - Mersa Alam (679 km (421 mi.)

(see map, on p. 335). Before embarking on a journey to the Red Sea coast, it is necessary to obtain any relevant information from the Tourist Office in *Cairo, at N° 5 Adly Pasha Street,* or at the office of the Egyptian Automobile Club in *Cairo, at n° 10, Qasr el-Nil Street.* The movement of traffic along the Red Sea coast and across the Eastern Desert is subject to strict controls. Bathing in the Red Sea is allowed only in certain areas and even then the bather has to be careful as there are sharks in these waters. The coastal road to *Mersa Alam* is a surfaced road for most of the way and is in good condition. Leave Suez on the road to the west of the town. On the right of the road lie the cemeteries of the town and on the left is the Gulf of Suez. The road follows along the Gulf towards the south.

The *Red Sea,* in Arabic *Bahr el-Ahmar,* is part of the Indian Ocean and lies between Africa and Arabia. It is linked to the Mediterranean Sea by the Suez Canal. In geological terms the sea bed is a fault dating from the Tertiary Era and is a depression with sheer sides. The depth of the depression reaches 2000 m (6,562 ft) in parts, although the average depth is about 500 m (1,640 ft) and the coastal areas of the sea are built up with shelfs and coral reefs. The water is very saline, containing about 4 % salt and is astonishingly warm. The average temperature of the water is 22 °C (72 °F), but the surface temperature in summer can reach 34 °C (93 °F). This is why the Egyptian coast of the Red Sea has become over a period of time more and more popular with tourists and holiday-makers. It is particularly popular with fishermen and under-water divers today and in the past people also came here in search of antiquities. *Fishing :* This can be done all along the coast. Shark-fishing is particularly popular in summer when the sharks surface close to the coast as in winter they stay in the depths of the sea. Many varieties of fish can be caught. The corals are particularly interesting for under-water divers.
Sites of interest : The monasteries of St Anthony and St Paul ; Mons Porphyrites ; Mons Claudianus ; the route to Luxor and Karnak ; the Wadi Hammâmât.

Ain Sukhna, 55 km (34 miles). At the foot of the range of mountains not far from the coast there is a hot sulphurous spring from which the place takes its name as *sukhna* means « hot » in Arabic. This is a tourist centre with hotels, bungalows and tents and there is a petrol station here. There is a road across the desert between Ain Sukhna and Maâdi, a southern suburb of Cairo (a distance of 90 km (55 miles)) and thus from Cairo bathing areas on the Red Sea coast can be reached by car in about one hour. However, the movement of traffic on this road is subject to strict controls. As well as

ROUTE 10

the possibilities of bathing in the Red Sea or in the sulphurous spring, excursions can be made into the nearby mountains. It never rains here and the climate is very pleasant in winter.

The road continues along the Red Sea coast, where there are various rare species of palms growing and the sea is a beautiful turquoise-blue in colour.

Abu Darag, 87 km (54 miles). From the lighthouse there is a magnificent view over the small port, the sea and the coastline of the Eastern Desert.

Râs Zafarana, 125 km (77 miles). Here there is a lighthouse and a small port. A good surfaced road goes from Râs Zafarana across the desert to the Nile Valley, 33 km (20 miles) further along the road a track leads off on the left to

THE MONASTERY OF ST. ANTHONY

All the buildings of the monastery are surrounded by a wall 12 m (39 ft) high and the enclosure covers an area of about 10 hectares (24 acres). Behind the monastery is a high wall of rock from the foot of which runs a stream. The water is only slightly salty and the existence of this natural supply of water explains why the monastery was founded in this particular spot. The monastery is dedicated to the « father of monasticism », the hermit, St-Anthony the Great. He was born about 250 A.D. in a town in Upper Egypt and died during the 4th century, c. 356 A.D. After St-Mark had brought the message of Christianity to Egypt, it was St Anthony who founded the first Egyptian hermitages. In the Christian world he was revered as a great worker of miracles and as a helper and consoler of the persecuted and those who were held captive. In later times he was the saint who protected people against fire, plagues and the diseases caused by domestic animals, particularly the pig. This aspect of the saint is shown in a painting by Jerome Bosch. The temptations suffered by St Anthony have often been the subject of artistic work, e.g. by Flaubert. His cross in the shape of a T, the cross of Saint Anthony became the sign of his order. The events of his life were recorded by his friend Athanasius.

The Monastery of St Anthony survived the period of the Arab Conquest without suffering any damage as it was situated in a remote spot and was not near the important military routes. Thus it continued to flourish for several centuries after the Arab Conquest. Pilgrims and invalids came to the monastery and made special visits to the cell of St Anthony. His small hermit's cave is situated half-way up the mountain above the monastery. Near to the stream can be seen the millstones used to grind corn, an old oil-press and the refectory with its stone tables and benches and the seat of the abbot. These are the remains of the earliest buildings at the site.

The Monastery of St Anthony

There is a path along the top of the enclosure wall, which is defended by towers. From the path there is a good view of the various buildings of the monastery, the garden and the mountain. In the wall can be seen the openings of the granaries and the winch by means of which goods and visitors entered the monastery. As at the other monasteries in the desert and in Sinai, provisions and men were hauled up the outside of the wall. The entrance with its impressive gateway is below the winching

apparatus on the north side and is relatively recent in date. Inside the monastery after passing the granaries there is a fairly narrow path which goes across the enclosure from north to south. On the right are the houses for visitors and nearby are the little houses of the monks. They live alone and are not obliged to follow strict rules. Some of their houses are two-storied. There are various other monastic buildings and seven churches. Among these is the church of St Anthony, the domed church of St Mark and the church of St Peter. The smallest church is situated in the lower part of a tower and is dedicated to St Michael. This church should be visited as from the tower above it there is a superb view over the whole monastery, the surrounding area and the beautiful gardens.

The main path inside the monastery leads to the church of St Anthony which dates to the 6th century but which was restored and rebuilt in later centuries. The inside of the church is decorated with frescoes. Some of them are badly preserved and very dirty and would be seen more easily if they were well lit. The frescoes on the dome show : the Transfigured Christ with four angels who hold four shields bearing representations of a lion, an eagle, a bull and a man, the symbols of the Evangelists ; Mary and the Evangelist John. The frescoes on the walls depict : hermits, saints of the desert, Knightly saints ; Alexandrian patriarchs. On the arches is a fresco of the archangel. In the apse is a fresco of Christ and an angel.

An abbot is in charge of the small society of monks. Until 1951 a monk from this monastery was chosen by the Patriarch and appointed to a high position in the Abyssinian Church.

From Râs Zafarana, provided that all the necessary authorisation permits have been obtained in advance and the visitor has considerable knowledge of the country and its language, he may hire a camel and set out to explore the Wadi Arabi or the valleys on either side of it. There the impressive silence and grandeur of the desert can be fully experienced. 153 km (95 miles). A sign-post indicates the way to the *Monastery of St Paul*, which is 14 km (8 ½ miles) away along a track road. On the way on some of the rocks can be seen the inscriptions left there by Bedouin caravans. The track is very enclosed as it follows the bed of a wadi and there is a danger of landslides. Eventually after a turn in the track the monastery can be seen perched on its rock. This first view of the monastery in the middle of the desert rocks is a unique sight.

THE MONASTERY OF ST PAUL

St Paul of Thebes who lived from the 2nd to the 3rd century was buried at this site. During the persecution of Christians by the Emperor Decius, St Paul took refuge in a natural cave and remained there for the following sixty years of his life. During this time he was occasionally visited by St Anthony. St Jerome described his life, isolated from the world, and the things associated with him — the palm-tree, the crow who brought him his bread every day and the two lions who befriended him. The first church which housed his tomb was a small one dating to the 5th century, when the monastery was surrounded by a wall. The present wall was rebuilt in the Middle Ages, but like all the monastic buildings, it has been repaired and restored many times over the years.

As at the Monastery of St Anthony, there is a small stream here which provides water, but the Monastery of St Paul seems smaller, older and poorer than that of St Anthony. The gardens and utilitarian buildings are near to the stream, the source of which has a roof shelter over it. Behind a transverse wall is the main church, which is a two-storied building. The church on the ground-floor is dedicated to St Paul and that on the upper floor to St Anthony. It is possible to visit the church of St Paul on the lower floor. The church was in fact built on the site of the cave of St Paul and the cavity can be seen inside. It contains a white marble sarcophagus which according to tradition contains the body of St Paul. Behind it are three tiny chapels and in front of it is the iconostasis. There are frescoes in both churches but these are very badly preserved and have been greatly retouched and repainted. The scenes depict episodes from the life of the saint, angels, the apostles, Mary, the Evangelists, the Apocalypse and Christ. In the tower on the wall of the monastery there is another little church. From the tower there is a really superb view across to the Red Sea and beyond in the distance can be seen the Sinai Peninsula and its mountains.

Râs Gharib, 235 km (146 miles). At the oil-fields of Râs Gharib there are 150 oil-wells. Owing to the complex underlying geological structure of the area it was necessary to sink a number of exploratory wells to find the oil which is now being exploited successfully. There is a petrol station near to the rest-house and a very good beach nearby. The modern settlement with its villas is grouped around the small new mosque.

The road continues across deserted wild country and runs inland for a time and then at the foot of the mountains reaches

Râs Gemsa, 326 km (202 miles). Here there is a small oilfield and as well as oil, phosphates are also exploited. This is where the Gulf of Suez ends and the Red Sea proper begins. Anybody bathing in the sea here should be extremely careful. There are many sharks in the area and they come right up into shallow water.

10 km (6 miles) to the north of *Hurghada* between two golden sand dunes by the turquoise-blue sea lies

El-Ghadarsqa, 385 km (239 miles). The Institute of Hydro-biology is very interesting and should certainly be visited. The Aquarium and the Museum house a complete collection of the flora and fauna of the Red Sea. The warm temperature of the water provides favourable living conditions for rare species of multicoloured fish and superb coral reefs. Either here or at Hurghada it is possible to hire a boat for a trip to the coral reefs. These boats have a flat transparent bottom through which the living things on the reefs can be seen in much the same way as they are seen by under-water divers. The colours of the fish passing along the reefs are iridescent and beautifully reflected by the clear water. Schools of blue-striped « surgeon » fish with lanceolate orange caudal fins dart in and out of the reefs and rocks. Baracudas and small sharks watch the boat gliding past above them. The *rais* or captain handles the small boat or *houri* with great expertise and guides it over the shallows and coral reefs.

Hurghada, 395 km (245 miles). The town is near to the southernmost Egyptian oilfield on the Red Sea coast and is rapidly becoming the main tourist centre on the Red Sea. Bungalows and hotels have been built and there is an airport. The port will shortly be developed and enlarged. From Hurghada a visit can be arranged to

On the Red Sea

Mons Porphyrites, the « mountain of porphyry », also called *Mons Hadrianus.* The journey is 130 km (80 miles) there and back and involves travelling over difficult terrain. *Gebel ed-Dukhkhan,* 1 661 m (5,449 ft) was quarried in the Roman period for porphyry. The stone which is normally purplish-red in colour was used for statues, columns, architraves and sarcophagi. Hadrian built a temple at the quarries and also modest houses for his quarrymen, stone-cutters and engineers. The settlement was grouped irregularly round two reservoirs of water. The remains of some houses and workshops can still be seen, but most of the site is very ruined. The surrounding landscape is wild and impressive.

Between Hurghada and *Port Safaga*, the mountains of the Eastern Desert rise to a height of more than 2000 m (6,560 ft). From certain points on the road it is possible to make excursions lasting a day into the wild rocky heights of the desert region. However, travellers undertaking such excursions should remember that there are no sources of water at all in this region and that in the case of an accident occuring they cannot rely on any help arriving quickly, if at all.

Port Safaga, 460 km (285 miles), is a small port and there are phosphate mines nearby. Fishing boats can be hired for a trip out to the reefs and rocky islands. From here an interesting excursion can be made to

Mons Claudianus, the mountain of Claudius, a distance of 95 km (59 miles) there and back. The road is surfaced up to the turning for the *Roman camp* in the *Wadi Umm Husein*. There is a sign at the turning for the camp. The camp was situated near to a quarry where quartzy diorite, a good quality granite was extracted. At Rome a number of Imperial buildings from the reign of Nero, but principally in the time of Trajan and Hadrian, were decorated with architectural elements carved from this « granite of Claudius ». The stone was much sought after and very popular. It can thus be seen in the columns of the portico of the Pantheon, the columns and floor of the temple of Venus, in the villa of Hadrian, in public baths built by Caracalla and Diocletian, and elsewhere.

At the site there is the Roman camp itself, stables, a dromos, dwellings

and workshops. The temple which occupied an elevated site on high ground has collapsed in ruins. It was built by Trajan. A staircase led to it and the remains of this can still be seen. Wells were dug all around the site and there was a bath-house. The camp was within a square enclosure, whose sides were 70 m (229 ft) long. The camp was surrounded by a granite wall with towers at the corners so that it could be defended against Bedouin attacks. The stables were similarly protected as the animals were essential for transporting men and loads. Troughs large enough for 300 beasts to eat from had been constructed with some care and a little further away large silos had been built. To the north-east of the camp there was a bath enclosed by a wall and a temple of Serapis, which is now destroyed. This site and its buildings right out in the desert were obviously completed at considerable expense. The provision of water for the men and animals must have been difficult and there was also the problem of transporting the quarried stone to its various destinations. The quarries themselves were large with ramps and apparatus for pulling along the blocks of stone and in them today can be seen lying around the remains of inscribed columns, half-finished architraves, and flooring slabs, etc.

The road to Qena. The new road to Qena (Port Safaga - Qena, 175 km (108 miles)) is a well-surfaced road which passes through a number of valleys in the Eastern Desert, where in Pharaonic times gold was mined and granite was quarried. From the road the changing colours of the landscape of this region can be admired. For holiday-makers on the Red Sea coast, the road to Qena is the best route for visiting the sites in the Nile Valley between *Dendera* and *Thebes.* (For Luxor and Karnak, see, on p. 196).

*

Qoseir, 545 km (338 miles) is a fairly sleepy small port and there are some phosphate workings in the neighbourhood. In the Ptolemaic period this was called the « White Harbour » and it was the end of the desert route for caravans who had crossed the *Wadi Hammamat* carrying goods from Middle Egypt and Nubia. In later times the town was fortified by Selim. Today there are colourful bazaars in the narrow streets with a distinct Bedouin influence, which are of great interest. A trip can also be made out to sea on a sailing-boat, an excursion which can be highly recommended.

*

The road to Quft. (Qoseir - Quft, 190 km (118 miles)). The road is surfaced for most of the way and crosses the desert through the famous *Wadi Hammâmât*. In ancient times there was intensive quarrying in the wadi for stone for the Pharaohs, particularly during the Old and Middle Kingdoms. At that time Qoseir was a busy port for ships coming from the Sinai Peninsula with cargos of turquoise and malachite and for trade with the Land of Punt.

The ancient caravan route across the desert went between *Leukos Limen* (Qoseir) on the Red Sea coast and *Coptos* (Quft) in the Nile Valley.

The rock consists of strata of Nubian sandstone between which are embedded primary crystalline rocks pushed up into peaks up to 2000 m (6,560 ft) high. These are the hard stones, black and green basalt, breccia, and fine stone like carnelian and rock crystal, which were much sought after during the Pharaonic period.

After passing through the *Wadi Ambagi*, where there is a spring of brackish water, the road goes along the *Wadi Beida* and climbs up into the mountains to *El-Itema-Hokheben*. It goes through the *Wadi Rôsafa*, where there is a large well, and then through the *Wadi Abu Siran*. There are now a number of bends in the road as it climbs to the top of a wild pass. On the way down is *Bir es-Sidd*, where there is a spring around which the Ababda Bedouin have settled. They belong to the tribe of the Baga Bedouin and were formerly nomads but have now settled here permanently and become peasants. They raise camel, sheep and goats and lead a very simple life. They are very hospitable and always invite strangers who stop to take a meal with them.

Beyond Bir es-Sidd lie the *Hammâmât Mountains*, a picturesque region of high plateaux in an area of sandy terraces with abrupt rocky peaks and deep valleys. Near *Bir el-Hammâmât*, where there was an important desert settlement in Roman times, lie the remains of five unfinished sarcophagi, which are now broken into fragments. From the Fifth Dynasty Egyptians came to this valley to quarry the hard, dark granite for the sarcophagi and statues of the Pharaohs. King Isesi and later Mentuhotep III sent expeditions to these quarries. Ramesses IV sent a great expedition of nearly 9,000 soldiers and workmen here to quarry out and transport blocks of sandstone and granite from Hammâmât for the construction of the temple of Amun at Thebes. On the rocks in the valley and in the neighbouring valleys the inscriptions left by ancient expeditions can be seen. The texts describe the expeditions and offer prayers and thanks to the gods. There are stelae showing the king worshipping the gods and there is also a representation of the sacred boat of Sokaris.

In the pass of *Mutraq es-Selâm* there is a commemorative inscription of Amenophis IV and near it are a large number of graffiti left here by soldiers, quarrymen, travellers and Bedouin. Further along at *Qasr el-Banât* the sandstone rocks are covered with inscriptions in Greek, Coptic and Arabic. The Qasr el-Banât or « castle of the maidens » is a rock which has been eroded into the shape of a tower. The road now passes the remains of a Roman watering-station and down on the plain reaches *Laqeita*. This is a village of the Ababda Bedouin, and through here passed the Roman road, *Via publica*, which linked Coptos and Berenike. Near the main well is a fragmentary inscription bearing the name of Tiberius. The road continues to Quft.

To reach Qena from here follow the line of semaphore-towers, many of which are now in ruins, which were built by Muhammed Ali. They were the signalling towers of an optical telegraph along which messages were sent.

The road between *Qoseir* and *Mersa Alam* is not a very good one and therefore it is necessary to ensure that the vehicle used is running perfectly. Travellers should also take with them a reserve supply of petrol in addition to a full tank and plenty of drinking water.

Mersa Imbarak, 628 km (390 miles) is a small fishing port. Nearby at the end of the *Wadi Umbarek* are the ancient gold-mines of *Umm Rus*.

Mersa Alam, 679 km (421 miles). The small port is an ideal fishing centre from which to set out on trips to catch sharks, muraena, turtles, lobsters, crayfish, tunny fish, etc. The « Fishing and Hunting Club of Egypt » maintains a rest-house at the port.

The road to Edfu (Mersa Alam - Edfu, 230 km (142 miles)). This desert road is surfaced and goes through the *Wadi Abu Karalia* to *Bir Besah*, which is encircled by mountains. The road then passes the ruins of ancient abandoned mines and goes through the *Wadi Baramia* and into the *Wadi Miah* to

The temple of El-Kanâyis. The partly rock-cut temple was built by Sethos I near to a well and dedicated to the god, Amun-Re. The temple has a portico supported by four columns with lotiform capitals and behind lies a rock-cut hall with three niches.

The central span of the ceiling is decorated with vultures with their wings curved downwards. The reliefs in the portico of the temple are scenes of

EL KANÂYIS TEMPLE

carved out in the rock of the king and the two gods. This type of sanctuary is similar to those in the great Ramesside rock-temples in Nubia. Three important inscriptions are carved on the walls of the temple. One of them records a visit made by the king to the gold-mines and his anxiety and sympathy for the difficult life of the miners in this desert region. The king founded this temple and an establishment to which he awarded certain privileges around 1300 B.C.

the King's victories over foreign peoples — Asiatics and Nubians. The hall is completely carved out of the sandstone rock and is about 8 × 6 m (26 × 19 ft) in size. The ceiling is supported by four pillars. The reliefs on the walls describe the construction of the temple, its foundation, its siting near the well, the laying of the first stone etc., and show Sethos I making offerings to the gods. A few steps lead up to the three cult-niches at the rear of the hall. The central niche was dedicated to Amun, that on the left to Sethos, and that on the right to Re-Harakhty. Each of these niches contained a small niche for a group statue

The coastal road south of *Mersa Alam* is not in good condition but continues 145 km (90 miles) further southwards to *Berenike* on the bay of Ras Benas. The town is built on coral and today is partly covered by sand and appears rather desolated. It was founded as a port c. 275 B.C. by the Ptolemies for trade with the ports on the eastern shore of the Red Sea and with those in the Indian Ocean. The ruins of a temple of Serapis built by Tiberius and Trajan can still be seen. Just to the north of Berenike in the *Wadi Sakeit* and in the desert nearby are the remains of the Emerald Mines, which were worked until the Middle Ages.

Route n° 11 : Alexandria - El Alamein - Mersa Matrûh - Siwa (592 km (367 mi.)

(see map below)

For a distance of about 300 km (186 miles) the whole way between *Alexandria* and *Mersa Matrûh*, the road follows the coast and the shore and its beaches can be seen from the road for most of the way. The beaches are sandy and large and the pure, almost white sand contrasts beautifully with the intense blue and green colours of the sea. A cool, fresh North breeze blows across the shore throughout the year, even in the summer. It blows the sand up

into the numerous dunes which can be seen along the coast and also makes this part of the coast more pleasant and less hot in summer than the beaches on the northern shore of the Mediterranean. However, despite the cool breeze the sun is still very hot and those who are not accustomed to a hot climate should take care to protect themselves against its burning rays. Along the road among the palm-trees, pines and fig-trees there are small towns with little harbours and ancient hal-

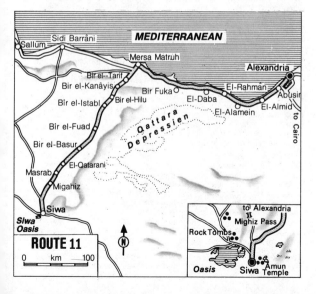

ting-places for caravans. These caravans used to travel all over the Maghreb. Caravans still cross the desert areas but today they cannot travel so freely between one country and another. Natural sponges are harvested from the sea along this coast. There is sufficient rainfall in winter for vegetables, melons, olives and figs to be grown successfully. In the Graeco-Roman period this part of the coast was famous for its vines and in certain areas corn was grown for export to Rome. Since ancient times this coastal area has been strategically important for the defence of Egypt and such defence involved controlling the road to the *oasis of Siwa*, where the Temple of Jupiter-Ammon, famous throughout the Classical world, was situated.

The railway and a road go from Alexandria to Mersa Matrûh. The journey by train is slow and therefore rather impractical. The road passes through *Bir Fuqa*. It starts from Alexandria in the industrial quarter of *Mex*. (It is also possible to avoid Alexandria and get on to this road by coming from the direction of Cairo on the Desert road.) The main road to Mersa Matrûh is surfaced and from it the coast and its scenery can be easily seen. The trees grow right up to the sand dunes and then stop abruptly.

After negotiating through the heavy traffic in *Mex*, outside the city the road is fairly clear and good progress can be made along it. It is not long before *Agami* and *Hannoville* are reached. These are very popular places with beautiful beaches and holiday chalets, but very few hotels. Further along among the trees is

Burg el-Arab, 17 km (10 ½ miles). The landscape here is beautiful and the village itself is a very colourful

place as Bedouin peoples live here. Some of them have settled here permanently and others stay here for a short time before moving on elsewhere.

Abusir, 48 km (29 miles). In the Graeco-Roman period there was a town here which was dedicated to the cult of Osiris and which was named *Taposiris Magna*. The town also had a harbour of some importance. Today the coastline has altered and the ruins of the town lie some distance inland. The great temple was dedicated to Osiris and its remains are well-preserved and worth visiting. Although it was a temple of some importance, it was apparently not decorated with scenes and no inscriptions can be seen either. The walls and the pylons with their interior staircases are particularly well-preserved. To the north of the temple are the ruins of a Roman tower, which was undoubtedly a lighthouse. It gives some impression of how the lighthouse at Alexandria must have looked although of course that was much larger and higher than this one. There is a good view from the top of the tower. In the area of the ancient harbour there are several Roman tombs. Along the road in several places the sites of ancient abandoned quarries can be seen. The countryside is dotted with trees and the road passes vegetable fields before reaching

El-Hammâm, 63 km (39 miles), which is a picturesque little village. There are numerous wells from which the water is raised by pumps. A large animal market is regularly held here.

El-Almid, 85 km (52 miles), lies at the west end of the dried-up part of *Lake Mareotis*. On the coast are the remains of an ancient lighthouse from which there is a good view. After leaving here the road passes near to the *Qattâra Depression* which lies to the south-west in the desert. This is the most important depression in the Egyptian part of the Libyan Desert and reaches a depth of 133 m (436 ft) below sea-level. In the not too distant future it is intended to construct a canal between the Mediterranean and the Depression and to flood the Depression and at the same time harness the electric power from the water as it races down to the Depression.

Not far along the road from El-Almid is the area where considerable fighting took place in the Second World War around

El-Alamein, 110 km (68 miles). The site of the great battle can be easily recognised by the huge cemeteries and commemorative monuments. There is also a small village nearby. Between October 23rd and November 4th 1942 a bitter and bloody struggle took place here between the German and Italian forces under the command of Rommel and the British 8th Army, representing the Allied forces, commanded by Montgomery. The outcome of the battle had an important effect on the future course of the War. The crushing advance of the Africa Corps towards Egypt was finally checked. After this battle the Allies assumed the offensive and advanced westwards and were able to recapture Libya and Tunisia from the Germans.

During the fighting at El-Alamein several thousand men were killed. Not all of their bodies were buried in the cemeteries which were built afterwards as many men had lost their lives further out in the desert and their bodies were never recovered.

Imposing monuments were built to their memory and as a reminder to future generations of the bitter fighting which took place here. The cemetery of the British Empire forces, which also contains the graves of other nationalities, is sombre and memorable. The 7,500 graves within it show how many nationalities fought here together and gave their lives to stop the advance of Nazism. As well as the graves of British soldiers there are those of Australians, New Zealanders, South Africans, Poles, Frenchmen and so on, of all religious denominations. The vast extent of the cemetery is awesome and saddening. In the centre of the grouped graves is an altar inscribed with the words : « Their Name Liveth for Evermore. »

At *Tell el-Eisa,* 115-119 km (71-73 miles) are the German and Italian cemeteries and monuments. In the German cemetery there is a monument over the tomb of an unknown soldier which bears the inscription : « Death knows no country. » With the inscription there is a carving representing German, French, British and Italian helmets.

In the village of *El-Alamein,* which has a small hotel and a restaurant, there is a museum in which the circumstances and events of the fighting in 1942 are described and are illustrated by various military objects of the period. In the other rooms the displays illustrate Egyptian military events.

Continuing along the road, the traveller comes to a really beautiful part of the coast, where there is a superb beach and a really good hotel. *Sidi Abd er-Rahman,* 154 km (95 miles). In the village is the *Mosque of Abd er-Rahman* in which a local Moslem saint is buried. He is much venerated by the Bedouin. From here the road rises and crosses the sand dunes which extend along the coast. The green fields and pastures which can be seen contrast with the vast yellow extent of the desert and the bright blue sea.

The road passes through *El-Daba*, 160 km (99 miles) and reaches

Bîr Fuqa, 214 km (132 miles), where a less important road joins the main one. The branch road goes past *Râs el-Heqma*, an old royal rest-house, to the end of a cape jutting out into the sea (a journey of 20 km (12 miles) there and back). From the cape there is a good view across the bay between *Ed-Daba* and *Bîr Fuqa*.

Mersa Matruh, 290 km (180 miles) is one of the main towns on this magnificent coast, which remains relatively unexploited. The town is situated at the end of a bay which has huge and superb beaches along it. The white sand extends a long way out to the turquoise-blue sea. The tide comes in very slowly and bathers have to go some way to reach the water.

The town has many historical associations. Alexander left from here when he set out to visit the Temple of Jupiter-Ammon at Siwa. Cleopatra and Anthony lived here for a time. The famous queen built herself a superb residence here and from it commanded the army which she sent out to do battle with Octavian Augustus. After his victory over the queen at Actium in 31 B.C., the victorious Octavian stopped at the town and admired its beautiful location and pleasant climate. A little way outside Mersa Matruh is « Cleopatra's beach ». A natural basin in the rocks on the beach contains sea-water and is known as « Cleopatra's baths ». According to tradition Cleopatra is supposed to have loved to bathe here.

Mersa Matruh is the capital of the Western Desert province of Egypt and the seat of the governor. From here excursions can be made to Siwa. The best time to go by car to the oasis is from October to November and from February to the middle of May. In December and January there are often violent rainstorms in the area and the track road can be flooded. In the summer months the excessive heat makes the journey unbearable. It is best to set out from Mersa Matruh very early in the morning at dawn as only the first 120 km (74 miles) of the road is surfaced and the total distance to be travelled is 302 km (187 miles). The journey takes about eight hours. Enough petrol and drinking water should be taken to last for the journey out and the journey back. Vehicles should not travel alone. At least two vehicles should leave together, so that in case of an accident or breakdown occuring help can be fetched. The necessary permits for the trip should be obtained in advance in Cairo.

For the first 120 km (74 miles) the road goes directly southwards and is rather narrow but fairly well-surfaced. It then becomes a dirt track and follows the line of telegraph posts. About 25 km (15 miles) from Siwa, the road is surfaced again. Below is a list of the main points of interest and places on the journey with the distances as a guide. The distances in brackets at the end are those from Mersa Matruh.

Airport, 294 km (182 miles)) from Alexandria ; (4 km (2½ miles) from Mersa Matruh).

Wadi er-Raml, 299 km (185 miles) ; (9 km (5½ miles)

Road junction, 305 km (189 miles) ; (15 km (9 miles)). The right fork is the road to Libya. The left fork is the road for *Siwa.*

Wadi el-Haraiq, 330 km (205 miles) ; (40 km (24 miles)). Here is the well of *Bir el-Tarif.* The road climbs up onto the mountain plateau of the Libyan Desert and passes a number of cisterns, which in Arabic are called *bir.* They are filled with rain water but it is brackish and not really suitable for use.

Bir el-Kanâyis, 347 km (215 miles) ; (57 km (35 miles))

Bir el-Gallaz, 363 km (225 miles) ; (73 km (45 miles))

Bir-el-Hilu, 376 km (233 miles) ; (86 km (53 miles))

Bir-el-Istabl, 389 km (241 miles) ; (99 km (61 miles)). End of the surfaced part of the road.

Bir el-Fuâd, 415 km (257 miles) ; (125 km (77 miles))

Bir el-Nuss, 439 km (272 miles) ; (149 km (92 miles)) - about half-way between Mersa Matruh and Siwa.

Bir el-Basur, 485 km (301 miles) ; (195 km (121 miles))

Khalda, 502 km (311 miles) ; (212 km (131 miles))

El-Qatarani, 522 km (324 miles) ; (232 km (144 miles))

Aerodrome, 571 km (354 miles) ; (281 km (174 miles). Not long after passing here the road again becomes surfaced.

Pass of Nabg, 583 km (362 miles) ; (293 km (182 miles))

Siwa, 592 km (367 miles) from Alexandria ; (302 km (187 miles)) from Mersa Matruh.

THE OASIS OF SIWA

The Oasis of Siwa has a population of about 5,000, many of whom live in the village of *Aghurmi.* It is the furthest west of the desert oasis and the most distant from the Nile Valley. It is 20 m (65 ft) below sea-level and is like an island in the desert, lying in a protected valley and totally isolated. It is a pleasant place with shady palm-trees and olive-groves and it is possible to bathe in its blue waters. There are nearly 200 sources of water here, pools and lakes of which 80 are used for irrigation purposes. In the oasis there are nearly 100,000 date palm-trees and some 40,000 olive-trees. Most of these fruits are exported. In addition cereals, vines and oranges are grown.

Young girl at the Oasis of Siwa

The inhabitants are Berber in origin and have intermarried with Bedouin and Sudanese peoples. They speak a Berber dialect as well as Arabic. As they have lived for centuries isolated from foreign influences, they have succeeded in preserving their native culture and dignity and retain many of their ancient traditions.

The women lead a quiet and isolated life. Outside their houses they hide their faces behind a veil. Their bodies are also completely covered from head to foot by a traditional garment called a *melayah*, which is a large rectangular piece of grey woollen cloth with a multi-coloured border. The young girls do not wear the veil and wear gay garments of yellow, red or orange. Under their coloured melayah they wear a simple coloured cotton garment and beneath that a pair of pantaloons with an embroidered border. Their hair is parted and braided into numerous plaits with coloured ribbons at the ends. Sometimes their hair is very elaborately done and arranged on the head and forehead rather like a kerchief. While young girls remain unmarried they wear a silver pendant which hangs down on their breasts.

The Berber customs which are ancient in origin are very interesting. In general they tend to marry within their own families and the parents meet to arrange marriages a long time in advance for their children. The betrothed couple do not see each other before the wedding day, but if they do then they meet secretly. On the day of the wedding the girl puts on her prettiest dress and goes with her friends to *Ain Tamusi*, a pool in the oasis where the waters are famous for their purity and clear colour. The older women with her help her to bathe herself and they take

from her the silver pendant which was the sign of her virginity. On the way back to the village she sees her fiancé who is on his way to the pool for his bath. During the ceremonies the girl will be welcomed by the parents of her future husband and given various wedding presents. Among these she receives 40 garments and must wear seven of them on the wedding day. Her hair is then braided into forty plaits. While she is getting ready her fiancé receives his wedding presents from his friends and aquaintances.

The ancient history of Siwa is also interesting. In 525 B.C. Cambyses ordered an expedition of 50,000 Persian soldiers to march to Siwa, take the inhabitants captive to make them slaves and to destroy their temples. But the expedition was lost in a sandstorm and never reached the oasis. All the men perished in the desert. The oasis was eventually taken by the Persians in 500 B.C. A little later the Athenian general Cimon send a delegation to consult the famous oracle at Siwa, while he was besieging the town of Kition in Cyprus. The oracle told the delegation that Cimon had gone before them and when they were on their way back from Siwa, they learnt that Cimon had died during the siege. In 331 B.C. Alexander the Great came to consult the oracle of Amun. It told him that he would be master of the world and that he was the son of the god, Amun. This is why Alexander is represented on Hellenistic coins with the ram's horns of the god Amun.

The houses of the *village of Siwa* are grouped picturesquely around a square and the village lies at the foot of a rock more than 50 m (164 ft) high. Some of the houses are perched on the rock. They are simple huts made of baked bricks and are situated along a network of tangled alleyways most of which are roofed. Nearly all the houses are not completely covered by roofs, there is usually an opening in them as it never rains here. The ancient capital of the oasis of Siwa is on the site of the modern village of *Aghurmi*. Some remains of an ancient temple can be seen there, probably the Temple of Jupiter-Ammon which was very famous in the ancient world. Only a few hieroglyphic inscriptions have been found on some walls. It was here that the priests of Amun, who were intelligent, perceptive and very politically aware, proclaimed Alexander as the son of Amun. A little further away among the palm-trees there are some more ruins which are perhaps connected with the temple or were part of it and its famous oracle.

In the north of the oasis is the great *lake of Siwa*, the *Birket Siwa*. In this area some rock tombs of the Pharaonic necropolis of Gebel Mota, « the mountain of the dead » have been found. They date to the time of the last native Egyptian dynasties and are decorated in an individual and unusual local style of art.

One of the gastronomic specialities of Siwa is a dish called *meshui*, which is a whole lamb roasted on a spit with aromatic herbs and young vine leaves, which give the meat a special and exotic flavour. The custom is to eat this meat with home-baked bread, ewe's milk cheese, black olives and sweet Siwa dates as a dessert. With the meal the slightly salty well water is drunk either on its own or with the juice of the small Siwa lemons which taste rather like an apple and which can be eaten whole, the skin as well. The inhabitants also drink very strong, sweet tea and *Lupki,* which is fresh palm juice. This juice can also be fermented to make palm wine.

There is a marked difference between the temperature during the day and that at night. At night the temperature can drop by 20-25 °C. Visitors are therefore strongly advised to take some warm clothing with them to Siwa.

The Libyan Desert Oases

In the desert where there is a subterranean or surface source of water, there is an oasis. These islands in the desert are fertile, covered with rich vegetation and are often densely populated. The word « oasis » is derived from an Ancient Egyptian word like some other words which have survived into modern usage. An oasis is a depression in the desert and the most fertile part of it is in the deepest part of the depression. The water table is about 100 - 170 m (328 - 557 ft) below the surface in a stratum of sandstone and the water is brought to the surface either by natural springs or by deep artesian wells.

In this immense Egyptian part of the Libyan desert, which covers about two million square kilometres (about 772,000 sq. miles), and which is one of the most arid parts of the world with no rain except for a very occasional storm, there are seven main oases ; *Siwa, Baharîya, Farâfra, Dakhla, Kharga*, and also the *Fayûm* and the *Wadi Natrûn*. The New Valley *Sahara Development* project has been trying with evident success for a long time to create an area of cultivated land which would link the oases. The search for wells and the digging of irrigation canals will help to create fertile land in the desert. This new fertile valley parallel to the Nile Valley will cover an area of 42 million hectares (103 million acres) when the project is finally completed. Visits to Siwa, the Fayûm and the Wadi Natrûn have already been described. A detailed description of Kharga oasis is given below and only brief descriptions of the other oases.

BAHARIYA, the northernmost of the oases is extremely fertile. Dates, vegetables and onions are grown and poultry, particularly turkeys, are bred. All the produce is sent to the Nile Valley to be sold. At the oasis are the remains of a temple of the Twenty-sixth Dynasty built by the Kings Apries and Amasis and not far from the main village of *El-Qasr* there are some tombs. In another village are the ruins of a *temple of Alexander*, several chapels of the Twenty-sixth Dynasty, and underground tombs with some interesting wallpaintings. The oasis is reached by car, either from Cairo, the Fayûm or from Beni Mazar in the Nile Valley. The road is surfaced for only part of the way. Otherwise it is a dusty, sandy track road and this is not an easy journey in an ordinary small car. When undertaking a journey to this and any of the other oases, it is recommended that two cars at least should travel together.

FARAFRA. There are scarcely 1,000 inhabitants at this small oasis and they make their living by growing dates and olives. There are no antiquities to see here except for some very insignificant remains. The oasis can be reached either from Dakhla or Baharîya. The road to it is a very bad track which is often covered by sand and it is really necessary to use a suitable vehicle like a land-rover for the journey.

DAKHLA. The cultivation of dates and market gardening, and the breeding of poultry are the main occupations of the inhabitants. Amidst the spectacular scenery of the oasis can be seen monuments of the Old Kingdom, Roman and Islamic periods. At the eastern end of the oasis are the large, mud-brick mastabas of the VI th dynasty, one of which contained the intact burial of a ruler of the oasis. These are situated near the modern village of Balat. At the opposite end is the temple of Deir el-Haggar. The temple was dedicated to Amun, Mut and Khonsu and was built in the classical Egyptian style, with a colonnaded court, a hypostyle hall, a pronaos and a sanctuary. Built by the Roman emperors Titus, Vespasian, Nero and Domitian, the quality of the reliefs varies considerably ; although intact, the roof has been removed for safety. Nearby, at Mussawaka, are two decorated tombs of the Roman Period. The decoration is well preserved and the scenes depict representations of the oasis and a remarkable astronomical ceiling. The medieval city of el-Qasr, still inhabited, preserves the architecture and atmosphere of its period almost unaltered.

The oasis of Dakhla is easily reached from the oasis of Kharga along a surfaced road.

KHARGA. The main settlement at this oasis, which is about 200 km (124 miles) long and 20-50 km (12-31 miles) in width, is the town of *Kharga*. The principal wealth of the oasis lies in its date-palm trees but cereals and vegetables are also grown. The town is very picturesque and individual with its maze of narrow streets and alleys which are roofed with palm trunks and branches. This roofing acts as a protection against the burning heat of the sun and against the frequent sandstorms. In the north and the south of the oasis there are remarkable an-

cient monuments, 4 km (2½ miles) to the north of the town of Kharga lie the remains of a temple of the Persian period, practically the only surviving monument of this period in Egypt. This is the great

Temple of Hibis, which was dedicated to Amun. It was built by Darius I and lies near to later Roman remains. The temple is approached through four gateways, covering an area of 42 × 20 m (127 × 65 ft). On the second gateway is a long Greek inscription, which is a decree of the Roman Emperor, Galba, dating to 69 A.D. The temple has a colonnade, a colonnaded court, a hypostyle hall supported by four columns, a sanctuary, a pronaos and a small side chapel on the right. All the walls of the temple and the doorways are covered with varied reliefs. On the doorways : dedicatory texts ; Darius I presenting offerings to various divinities. Colonnade : texts relating to the construction of the temple ; dedications ; Nectanebo I making offerings to the gods. Hypostyle hall, built by Nectanebo I : offering scenes with the king before the gods ; Seth and the serpent Apophis. Pronaos : the eight primordial gods of Hermopolis ; a royal hymn in honour of Amun-Re ; Darius, Thoth and Harsiesis pull along the sacred barque of Sokaris ; Geb and Nut embrace the king ; Darius travels through the thickets of papyrus ; Sekhmet embraces and anoints the king ; numerous texts are inscribed in long vertical columns. Sanctuary : all the known Egyptian gods with their symbols and sacred animals are depicted on nine registers. Side chapel : Khnum and Ptah shape the king on the potter's wheel ; Neith suckles the royal child. Chapel of Osiris : the classic themes of the death, burial and resurrection of Osiris are shown ; the grief and lamentations of Isis and Nephthys ; hymns to Osiris. From the roof of the temple there is a good view over the oasis.

About a kilometre (just over half a mile) to the north of the temple is the Christian cemetery of

El-Bagawat. The tombs date from the Roman period to the end of the 7th century. The domes and apses of the circular tombs and chapels contain some superb examples of Coptic paintings illustrating themes from the Old and New Testaments which are painted with a wealth of detail. Most of the paintings are done in shades of mainly red and violet and are executed in a very naive style. Among the most remarkable paintings are those in the *Chapel of Peace* and the *Chapel of the Exodus*.

About 1 km (half a mile) to the north of the cemetery are the vast remains of a Coptic monastery of the 5th century, which is extremely well preserved. It is known today by the name *Qasr Ain Mustafa Kâshif*.

To the south-east 2 km (1¼ mile) beyond Kharga are the remains of the *Temple of Nadura*, which was built by Hadrian and Antoninus Pius in the 2nd century. The pronaos, which was preceded by a court, is still well preserved. Further to the south are the remains of various temples dedicated to Serapis and Isis at *Qasr Dush*. In the area there are other remains of temples of the Graeco-Roman period.

The oasis can be reached by train from Oasis Junction (Moasla el-Wahat, see on p. 293) or by road.

Plans, Maps
and Coloured
Photographs

The site of Giza and the famous Sphinx is very near Cairo.

CAIRO

to Heliopolis
Airport

N

1000 m

354

NILE

GEZIRA

ZAMALEK

RÓD-EL-FARAG

EL DOQQI

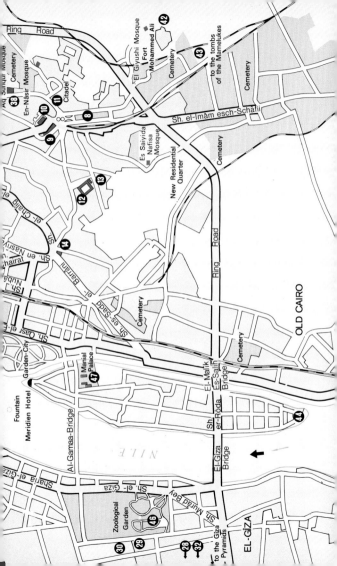

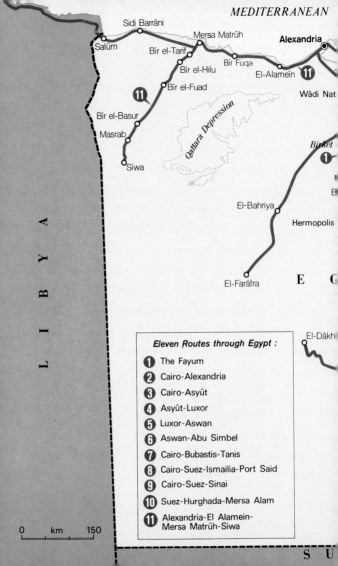

MEDITERRANEAN

Sidi Barrâni

Mersa Matrûh

Alexandria

Salûm

Bir el-Tarif

Bir Fuqa

El-Alamein

Bir el-Hilu

Bir el-Fuad

Wâdi Nat

Bir el-Basur

Qattara Depression

Masrab

Birket

Siwa

El-Bahriya

Hermopolis

El-Faráfra

E   G

El-Dâkh

Eleven Routes through Egypt :

1. The Fayum
2. Cairo-Alexandria
3. Cairo-Asyût
4. Asyût-Luxor
5. Luxor-Aswan
6. Aswan-Abu Simbel
7. Cairo-Bubastis-Tanis
8. Cairo-Suez-Ismailia-Port Said
9. Cairo-Suez-Sinai
10. Suez-Hurghada-Mersa Alam
11. Alexandria-El Alamein-Mersa Matrûh-Siwa

L   I   B   Y   A

0   km   150

S   U

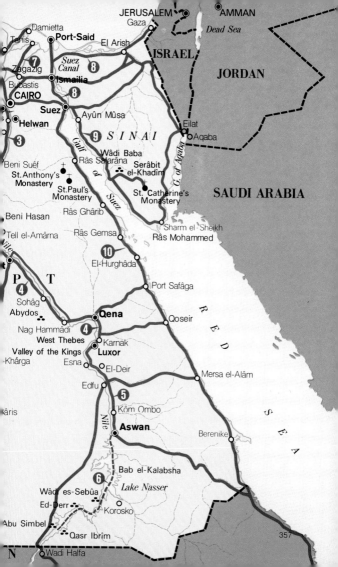

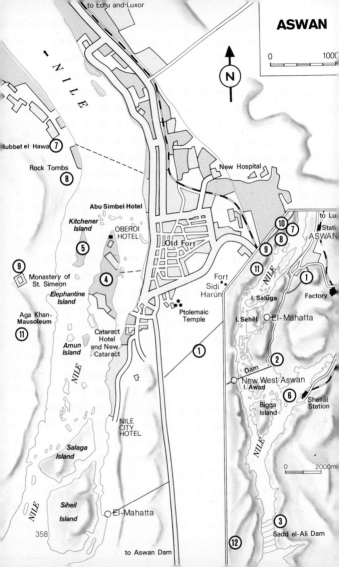

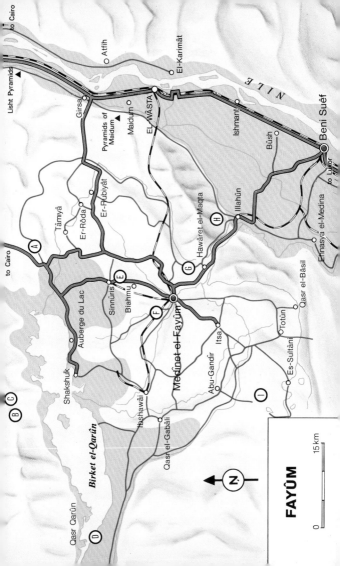

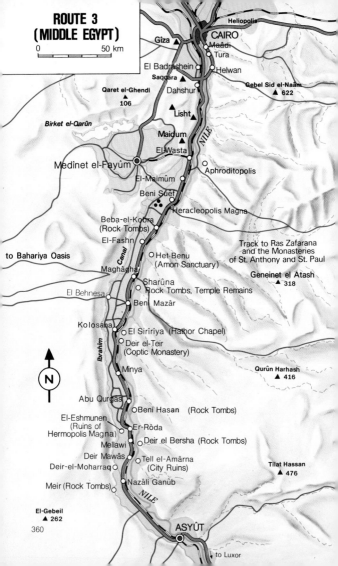

ROUTE 3
(MIDDLE EGYPT)

0   50 km

Heliopolis

CAIRO

Gîza

Maâdi

Tura

El Badrashein

Helwan

Saqqâra

Gebel Sid el-Naâm
▲ 622

Dahshur

Qaret el-Ghendi
▲ 106

Lisht

Birket el-Qarûn

Maidum

El-Wasta

NILE

Medînet el-Fayûm

El-Maimûm

Aphroditopolis

Beni Suêf

Heracleopolis Magna

Beba-el-Kobra
(Rock Tombs)

El-Fashn

Het-Benu
(Amon Sanctuary)

to Baharîya Oasis

Canal

Track to Ras Zafarana
and the Monasteries
of St. Anthony and St. Paul

Maghâgha

Geneinet el Atash
▲ 318

Sharûna
Rock Tombs, Temple Remains

El Behnesa

Beni Mazâr

Kolosana

El Sirirîya (Hathor Chapel)

Ibrahim

Deir el-Teir
(Coptic Monastery)

Qurûn Harhash
▲ 416

Minya

Abu Qurqâs

Beni Hasan   (Rock Tombs)

El-Eshmunen
(Ruins of
Hermopolis Magna)

Er-Rôda

Mellawi

Deir el Bersha (Rock Tombs)

Deir Mawâs

Tell el-Amârna
(City Ruins)

Tilat Hassan
▲ 476

Deir-el-Moharraq

Meir (Rock Tombs)

Nazâli Ganûb

NILE

El-Gebeil
▲ 262

ASYÛT

to Luxor

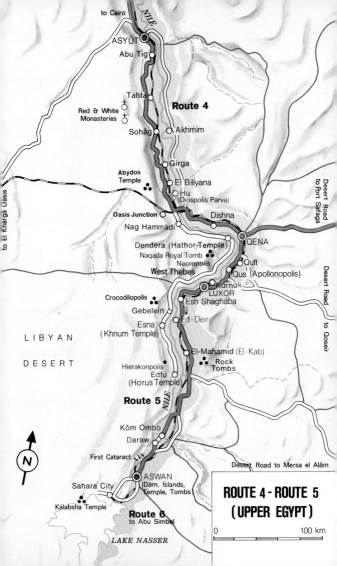

NILE DELTA

0   50 km

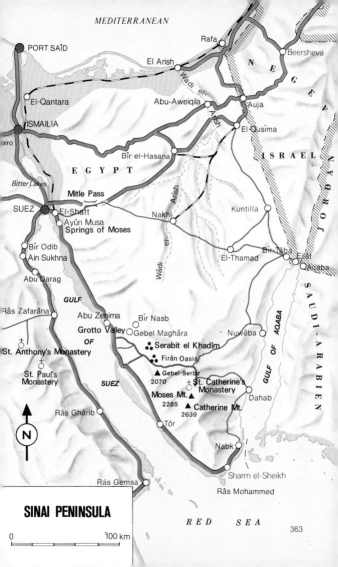

SINAI PENINSULA

0   100 km

Water is present everywhere in the Nile valley and the Delta which is furrowed by nume-rous canals. Irrigation is accomplished by manual labour as is the case with the double shaduf which is still used in Egypt for raising water.

Water once again, but as a means of communication in Egypt from antiquity. The Nile, but also the sea and the Suez canal, forms a vast domain for felukas with characteristic silhouettes.

A traditional Cairo street with its mosques and ancient buildings among which a busy crowd often mills forming a constantly changing spectacle.

Cairo has gradually extended towards the Nile and even beyond today. The minarets are always present but, near the great river, there are also gardens, the cornice road, residential buildings and great modern hotels.

367

Nothing remains of ancient Memphis, which was once of the greatest cities of its time, except great cemeteries in the desert and some ruins which are often immersed in the rising subterranean waters.

The Step Pyramid of king Djoser at Saqqara is a unique monument built by the great Imhotep. The huge architectural complex which surrounds it is the object of suggestive restoration.

369

In the ruins of Karnak, the columns and pylons, the walls and obelisks, the visitor sometimes comes across statues of gods or kings. Here is Amun with the features of Tutankhamun.

The tomb of Sethos I, in the Valley of the Kings, is covered with superbly coloured paintings with chiefly represent the funerary books with their processions of gods and genies of the after-life.

371

The temple of Horus at Edfu is in an extremely good state of preservation. In front of the entrance to the hypostyle, in the court, the god is depicted in the form of a falcon wearing the double crown.

Aswan has one of the most beautiful landscapes. This view, taken from the Island of Elephantine, shows a branch of the Nile and, further on, the west bank where the desert begins almost immediately.

373

The queen is often represented as a small figure at the base of a colossus, protected by her royal spouse. Here is Nefertari and Ramesses II at the entrance of the great temple of Abu Simbel.

Sheltered behind his surrounding wall, the Monastery of St Catherine remains indissociable from the Mount Sinai, the typical silhouette of which overlooks the country.

The people are often represented on the base of columns in the form of a hieroglyph which serves to transcribe their name : the lapwing. The bird is depicted with human arms in the attitude of adoration.

Practical Information

Time to Travel

The winter is an excellent season to visit Egypt, and particularly Upper Egypt. Alexandria and the Mediterranean coast are fairly pleasant in summer. The very brief autumn (October-November) is still hot, but it is one of the best times to travel.

In any case, it should be noted that the nights are fresh, even in summer, and distinctly cold during the winter in Cairo (with rare but consequently spectacular rainstorms). The contrast is even more noticeable in the desert areas.

How to reach Egypt
Travel Prices

By Air

From its international airport situated 26 km (16 mi.) north-east of the city (Heliopolis), Cairo is connected to the principal cities of the world by the great world airlines. From London, according to the type of jet used, it takes from 5 to 7 hours for the journey with EGYPTAIR (31, Piccadilly London, W.1. Tel. 734-2864) or BRITISH AIRWAYS.

Prices (September 1980) in pounds sterling.

Return	1st Class	Tourits	Student/Youth
From London	£ 768	£ 524 £ 416,50	£ 236

By Boat

Few boat companies connect Alexandria (and gradually Port-Said) with the great ports of the western Mediterranean. But on the other hand there are numerous organised cruises with Egypt as a port of call (for a short time).

The companies specialising in the Italy-Egypt route (none of them from France) with agencies in London are :

DFDS SEAWAYS (Danish company) : Mariner House, Pepys Street, London, E.C.3. Tel 481 3211. Regular weekly service leaving from Ancona (Italy) for Alexandria by the air conditioned ferry-boat « Dana-Sirena » (3 - 4 days).

ADRIATICA (Italian Company), represented in London by Milbanke Travel, 104, New Bond Street W.1. Tel. 493 8494. Twice monthly departing from Venice by the ferry-boat « Espresso Cagliari » (3 - 4 days).

These companies offer several classes of travel with a range of prices, meals are not always included. The boats are equipped to transport passengers' cars. It is necessary to make reservations a long time in advance.

By train

It is possible to reach Beirut from Istanbul by train and then to take a boat (24 hours) for Alexandria, but it is a long and difficult journey due to the present political conditions.

Here are the rail fares to the two italian ports which have connections to Egypt (single prices only) :

From		to Venice	to Ancona
London	1st	£ 64,5	£ 72
	2nd	£ 47,9	£ 50
Glasgow	1st	£ 93	£ 100,6
	2nd	£ 67,7	£ 97,9
Paris	1st	394 FF	409 FF
	2nd	252 FF	261 FF
Brussels	1st	3285 FB	
	2nd	2139 FB	
Genova	1st	86 FS	99 FS
	2nd	53 FS	60 FS

By Car

It takes a long time to reach Egypt, from Spain, Morocco, Algeria, Tunisia and Libya (frontier is sometimes closed to foreigners at Solum (inquire)), or from Yugoslovia, Bulgaria, Turkey, Syria, and the Lebanon (then a ferry-boat from Beirut to Alexandria). The solution most often adopted is to take the car by boat from Venice, or even Piraeus (port of Athens).

Note also that the frontier between Israel and Egypt is now open and it is possible to take a ferry-boat to Israel and then reach Egypt by road (inquire about formalities).

Organised Travel at Reduced Prices

Many travel agents, who sometimes specialise, as well as cultural and other associations organise « package » travel to Egypt. These often have the advantage of being cheaper than independent travel and also make reservations in hotels and on cruises easier to obtain (several months in advance at Christmas and Easter). But these tours are most often organised in groups (with however the possibility of individual organised holidays) which leave little time for personal discovery.

Holiday Clubs

Egypt is still largely closed to holiday clubs, but the situation is expected to change within the next few years.

Le Club Méditerranée - Connaissance du Monde is the only one to have developed its « holiday club » activities together with traditional tourism. There are many possibilities between the hotel club in Cairo (Manial Palace), the village club at Hurghada on the Red Sea, the hotel village and the boat club at Luxor (with cruises). Inquire at the Club Méditerranée, Greater London House, Hampstead Road, London, N.W.1. Tel. 387 9321.

Passport and Visa

A valid passport is necessary for entering Egypt and also a visa. The individual tourist can obtain one from the Consulates of the *Arab Republic of Egypt.*

In London, the visa is provided in 48 hours from the Consulate of the Arab Republic of Egypt, 19 Kensington Palace Gardens, W.8. Tél. 229 8818. It is valid for three months and costs. £ 2. In New York, the visa is provided by the Consulate of the Arab Republic of Egypt, 900 Park Avenue, N.Y. 21 (Photograph necessary).

On arrival in Egypt, it is necessary

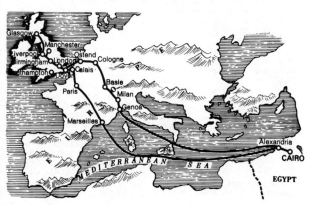

to register with the police within three days. Hotels look after this formality.

Otherwise, it can be done in person at *Mogamma* el-Tahrir Square in Cairo (or in the town of arrival). This is also the place to ask for a visa extension when your stay has to exceed the authorised time.

Health

The usual precautions which are taken in hot or tropical countries are particularly recommended in Egypt. Be careful to eat well-cooked meat, and well-washed salads. Do not drink iced drinks and reserve alcohol for the evening, particularly in the hot season.

In the evening and the night, chills which may spoil the visit can be avoided by wearing extra woollens. Air conditioning is often a source of trouble to those who are not used to it.

Only bathe in the swimming-pools or the sea, and never in the Nile or in the ·canals, which are infected with bilharzia fluke and other germs.

From the point of view of vaccinations an international certificate of vaccination against smallpox is no longer necessary. The anti-cholera injection (valid for six months) is only needed during special, very rare alerts. The Egyptian health authorities require those who have travelled from Africa or the Near East to be innoculated against yellow fever and cholera.

Take your usual medicines with you and pills to prevent stomach upsets.

It is a good idea to be vaccinated against polio and tetanus.

Customs

Articles purchased in Egypt can be exported up to the value of £ E 100. Antiquities, carpets and old objects can only be exported under strict authorisation.

Currency and Exchange

The *Egyptian pound* (£ E) is divided into 100 *Piastres* (PT) or 1,000 millimes. There are 10, 5 and 1 £ E notes, as well as 50, 25, 10 and 5 PT. The coins in circulation are 10, 5, 2, 1 and 0,5 PT. The regulations have been much simplified. The circulation of currency is particularly easy (but remember to check current British restrictions before you leave). One can still declare jewellery and valuables on entry if desired. The import and export of Egyptian pounds remains forbidden. Money is exchanged at banks. The official exchange rate of the *Egyptian pound* varies according to the economic situation. 1 £ Sterling = about 165 PT. $ 1 = about 69 PT.

International credit cards often make things easier (payments, purchases, withdrawing money by cheque).

Internal Transport

Air

Internal air traffic is controlled by the *Egyptair* (Or *Misrair*) company. Luxor is little more than an hour from Cairo and Aswan two and a half hours. Information and reservations can be obtained from the agencies in Cairo or the company's offices in the Hilton or Sheraton hotels. Prices of some single journeys :

Cairo-Luxor . . . . . about 19,600 £ E

Cairo-Aswan . . . . about 27,500 £ E
Cairo-Abu Simbel . about 39,000 £ E
Cairo-Hurghâda . . about 21,300 £ E

Trains

The Egyptian railways cover a network of about 4,500 km (2,800 mi.), serving nearly all the important centres. This method of travel is very practical, although not very quick. If you are used to a certain amount of comfort, travel first or second class. But a journey by the very cheap third class provides an excellent opportunity to get to know the Egyptians, and to appreciate their politeness and humour.

There are important reductions for students. Inquire at the stations in Cairo and Alexandria.

Cairo - Alexandria (3 hours)
1st cl. air conditioned :
about 325 PT
2nd cl. air conditioned :
about 200 PT

Cairo - Aswan (16 hours), via Luxor 1st cl. air conditioned and sleeping berth : about 1700 PT

1st cl. air conditioned :
about 1100 PT

2nd cl air conditioned :
about 600 PT

Boats

There are no regular internal connections by boat. On the other hand, the organisation of cruises is developing and several days travel on the Nile remains an unforgettable experience. Unfortunately this method of travel is not very cheap and has to be booked a long time in advance. The most common cruise is that which goes from Luxor to Aswan or vice-versa.

There are numerous boats of every description cruising up and down the Nile, some of which are very modern. They belong to the large travel agencies or the Hilton and Sheraton hotels. The passenger list however is almost always made up of people on tours organised in Europe or Great Britain.

For sometime the fashion of taking short cruises on felukas (sailing boats) has developed with various ports of call and summary comforts (it is possible to arrange these trips on the spot).

Finally, the *Sudan* can be reached from Aswan (Shallal-Wadi Halfa), in about two days. Inquire at Cairo, 8, Qasr el-Nil Street (Sudanese railways).

MERSA MATRUH   106¾   63½   ALEXANDRIA   PORT SAID
115   73¾   EL ALAMEIN   138   137½   148
186½   130   87½   ISMAILIA
CAIRO   99¼
SIWA OASIS   238   83¼   88   SUEZ   161¼
DISTANCES   DAKHLA OASIS   231¼   237½
(miles)   ASYUT   MOUNT SINAI
= by rail   213   LUXOR
= by road   185   163¾   93¾
= by steamer   ABU SIMBEL   184¼   130   PORT SAFAGA
ASWAN

Coaches

Except for the coaches which run between Cairo and Alexandria and to the large towns on the Suez Canal, there are no regular comfortable coach services for long-distance travel; but excursions from Cairo by pullman air-conditioned buses are organised by some agencies (and their routes will eventually cover the whole country).

Car Hire

A hired car with a driver is relatively easy to obtain (enquire in travel agencies or at hotels). Self-drive hire cars are becoming more common, but you will need to be familiar with Egyptian traffic conditions, signs, etc. Hire firms like Herz, Avis, Bita, etc., have agencies in the towns or in large hotels.

Taxis

Ordinary taxis are numerous (except in peak or rush-hour periods, when you will have to share one with other passengers). Prices are very reasonable; in Cairo, the minimum charge is 12 PT. There is no special night tariff. There are also taxis which can be hired by the hour, or for a journey to a specific place, and there is one company which runs luxury taxis with radio-telephone (« Misr Cars »).

City Buses

With very few exceptions, these buses are usually crowded and it can be almost impossible to even get on one. For this reason tourists should not rely on them as a mode of transport.

Private Cars - Petrol - Roads

A tourist travelling in his own car must have a custom's pass in the name of the driver, an international driver's licence and a nationality badge on the vehicle. The green international insurance card is not valid in Egypt, and you must obtain a third party insurance on entry to the country and then all risks cover. Motorists can obtain full information and all the permits they will require from the « Automobile Club of Egypt » (10, Qasr el-Nil Street, Cairo, tel : 77.243). It is foolish to travel on the desert roads unless there are two cars undertaking the journey. The main routes are asphalted roads in a reasonable state of repair, but the secondary roads can be more difficult. in any case, you will need a car in good mechanical order for driving in Egypt, a fair degree of concentration for the different traffic conditions, and a smattering of Arabic will certainly be useful if you intend driving other than on main routes and outside large towns. Driving at night, except in towns, is not advisable. The Egyptians drive on the right. Petrol is cheap, but the octane rating is insufficient (regulate and slow down the ignition). Price : ordinary 11 PT ; super (recommended grade) 13 PT.

What to wear

The type of clothes required will obviously depend on the time of year at which you visit Egypt. In the hot season, light cotton garments will be adequate with one or two woollens for the cool evenings. In winter, a coat will be useful for the evening, and woollens and a raincoat will probably be necessary items to take. Whatever the time of year, comfortable walking shoes and a hat are essential. Evening dress may sometimes be required, especially for women ; men should take with them a jacket and tie. Very brief clothing, e.g. shorts, should be avoided and women should ensure that they are fairly conservatively dressed when visiting public areas and mosques.

Equipment

As well as appropriate clothes (see above), a good pocket torch, sunglasses, sun-lotion, a pair of binoculars) for viewing the upper parts of temple walls), and a small first-aid kit will be useful items to include in your luggage.

Time

Egyptian time is two hours in advance of GMT, noon in London is 2 pm in Cairo. From May 1st to october 1st, summer time, the time is 3 hours ahead of GMT.

Hotels and Restaurants - Prices

Hotels and other accomodation are listed at the end of the guide under the heading 'Tourist Information by Region', and their classification is given in each case. It is wise to plan your itinerary with your accomodation in mind as the standard and availability of places to stay does differ quite considerably in some parts of the country.

The official classification for hotels in Egypt divides them into 5 categories : De luxe, 1st class, 2nd class, Tourist, 3rd class. Our classification (see p. 387) distinguishes between hotels of 1st, 2nd and 3rd class only. 1st and 2nd class hotels are very good. Some average prices are given below, but costs vary from one area to another and according to the time of year (local and government taxes not added).

In the hot season and in upper Egypt, it is more pleasant to have an air-conditioned room (for this a small supplement is charged : about 50 PT).

An important point to note is the tremendous growth in tourism in Egypt in recent years and although a number of new hotels have been built, there is still not enough accomodation available, especially in high season. It is therefore essential to book your room well in advance and to bear in mind that reservations made by tourists travelling alone and not in a group may not be honoured, particularly at Christmas and Easter.

Hotel restaurants have international cuisine menus, but there are numerous places to eat in Cairo and Alexandria which offer a wide variety of different cuisines at all kinds of prices (see the lists at the end of the guide).

Category	Single room with bath	Double room with bath
🏨 L	from 20 - 30 £ E	30 - 35 £ E
🏨	10 - 15 £ E	19 - 21 £ E
🏨	6 - 10 £ E	9 - 15 £ E
🏠	2 - 5£ E (without bath)	4 - 7 £ E (without bath)

Food and Drink (see on p. 29)

Youth Hostels

See under tourist information by region (p. 387), under the principal towns (Alexandria, Cairo, Luxor, Aswan).

Camping and Caravanning

Camping is only just becoming known in Egypt and therefore there are as yet few facilities provided in most of the country. Outside Cairo (camp-site at Giza) and Alexandria, campers should check with the tourist police for permission and suitable sites to camp. Caravanning is not very practical because of the traffic problems and the condition of the roads. At present using a dormobile would be preferable to towing a caravan in Egypt, but in the next few years it is likely that the situation will change and caravanning will become much easier.

Service and Tipping

Generally 10 to 15 % is given. Taxi drivers, hotel staff and porters expect a tip which may rise to 20 % if the bill is small. When a mount (camel, donkey) is hired, give a 15 % bakshish immediately.

Electric Current

Although it is still very often 110-120 volts, the electric current is tending to become 220 volts, chiefly in Cairo. The wall-plugs are the same as those used in Europe.

Weights and Measures

Except for a few local survivals, the metric system of weights and measures is currently in use.

Post

The postal service is completely separate from the telecommunication service (telegraph and telephone). Besides the offices in the towns, some services can be obtained in the large hotels.

Price of stamp :
Britain :
for a postcard by air : 12 PT ;
for an air letter : 16 PT.

The cost of a local telephone call is between 5 to 10 PT according to whether the call is made from a public telephone or from a hotel. The French and English telephone directories are no longer available. A telephone call lasting 3 minutes to Great Britain costs about 11 £ E.

Relations with the People

Relations with the Egyptians are excellent. Travellers from the United Kingdom and America should be patient and not expect the same standards of efficiency in a country of such established traditions as at home. Finally, bakshish should always be given to reward a service.

Holidays

Friday is the day of rest in Muslim countries, but Sunday may also be celebrated (chiefly shops). The great religious festivals (Bairam, Aïd el-Kebir, Muled el-Nabi) fluctuate (lunar calendar), as well as the « spring festival » (Sham el-Nessim), which is typically Egyptian. There are also great, fixed national festivals (Solar calendar) : 23rd July, 26th July (Revolution), anniversaries of recent wars.

During the month of Ramadan (a lunar month which fluctuates from year to year) (e.g. mid July to mid August in 1980) the pace of life seems slower during the day but becomes more animated in the evenings.

Shops, banks, offices - hours of opening

Shops generally open from 9.0 am to 1 pm ; in the afternoon they re-open about 4-5 pm (according to the season) and do not close until late evening. Banks and offices are only open in the morning (except in some hotels). Friday is the holiday for banks, government offices and some commercial establishments.

Tourist information ⑦

The Tourist Office of the A.R.E. in London (62a Piccadilly W.1., Tel. 493 5282, 10 am to 4 pm) and New York (630, Fifth Avenue, N.Y. 20) are in a position to give the tourist all the information he should need. In Egypt itself, the Ministry of Tourism is represented in the principal towns. The tourist police are also at the service of travellers. The Ministry of Tourism in Cairo is at 5 Adly Street.

Embassies and Consulates

United Kingdom : Embassy, Ahmed Ragheb Street, Garden City, Cairo Consulate, 8 Sharia El-Zahra, Garden City, Cairo (Tel, 28 850). Consulate, 3, Mina Street, Ramleh Alexandria (Tel. 47 166).

United States of America ; Embassy and Consulate, 5. Latin American Street, Garden City, Cairo (Tel. 28 219).

Guides

At the entrance to monuments and museums, the official guides wear a badge which allows them to be identified. They are often called *dragomen*. There are some very good guides in Egypt (who chiefly accompany the organised tours). With the others, it would be preferable to refer to a good serious guide-book, unless it is a case of walking through a site or unknown quarter where historical and archaelogocial explanations are not required.

Souvenirs-Antiquities

In the *Khan el-Khalili* for example, ancient and artistic objects are found (jewellery, leather, cloth, copper, silver, etc.) which are more interesting than the shoddy goods which abound at the tourist sites. Avoid the « pharaonic » objects, which are generally ugly. It is not necessary to have a souvenir which has a vague resemblance to Nefertiti to prove that you have been to Egypt. The cost of objects is interesting. Compare the price in several shops before purchasing and then you will not be under the illusion of securing a bargain, or have the impresson of being cheated, if you are well informed on the prices.

Antiquities constitute the most excellent souvenir of Egypt, but their purchase poses certain problems. Nine out of ten which are offered at the sites, overtly, or « under the counter » are fakes and sometimes very crude fakes. On the other hand, it is difficult to buy a pharaonic object without a very specialised knowledge of the art. Also, this country, like so many others, is aware of the number of thefts and acts of vandalism and imposes a strict control on the export of antiquities (a permit is necessary, ask at the Museum). All these reasons mean that it would be wise to look only in some shops, which have a Government licence (as well as *Khan Khalili* in Cairo). These shops provide certificates of authenticity and display pretty objects at varied prices. Even there, a good bargain is exceptional and there is a market price founded on fairly strict criteria.

Plaster reproductions are on sale in the Egyptian Museum, Cairo.

Photography

The light is often excellent. It is possible to take photographs in the mosques, when there are no religious services. On the other hand, photography is not allowed in the Cairo Museum or near public buildings, military installations, bridges, ports, etc. It is also better to avoid taking photographs in the native quarters. Proceed with tact and reward the subject with *bakshish*. It is better to take films with you (particularly colour).

Entrance Tickets to the Monuments

On sale at the sites or at the entrances of museums. Special free entrance tickets can be obtained from the Public Relations Service of the *Antiquites Service* (for some professors and students), Abbasiah Square, Cairo (1st floor).

Authorised Areas and Forbidden Areas.

For reasons of security, inquire before leaving the main routes, particularly if you wish to travel in the Delta, outside Alexandria, or in Middle Egypt and especially if you are an independent tourist using your own car. The Red Sea coastal area is still subject to certain restrictions as is the route into Libya and you should enquire about these before starting out on a journey to either area.

Tourist Information by Region

In this chapter, practical details are given on the numerous places described in the various itineraries or on the large towns which may be interesting for the tourist because of their architectural and artistic treasures or because of their importance as excursion centres.

Instead of an alphabetic order, the usual division into large centres of interest has been followed here, which is more practical for travel in Egypt. For this reason the main information given concerns the two most important cities in the country, Alexandria and Cairo (with its surroundings). Then, leaving Cairo and travelling to the south, the large towns situated in the Nile Valley up to Aswan follow, corresponding to the classic itinerary of a tour through Egypt. We have grouped the remaining places as follows :

« Mediteranean Coast », « Red Sea Coast » and « Suez Canal ». The symbols used for hotel classification conform to those used by Editions Marcus and follow in a general way the official classification of the Egyptian Ministry of Tourism, although personal experience has made a few small changes possible. Here are the symbols together with the other signs which are used in the following pages :

- 🏰 De-luxe Hotel
- 🏚 First Class Hotel
- 🏚 Second Class Hotel
- 🏠 Third Class Hotel
- ⑦ Tourist Office
- 🏠 Youth Hostel
- 🚒 Railway
- 🚌 Cars and Buses
- 🚢 Sea or River Connections
- ✈ Air Connections

ALEXANDRIA

Information

⑦ State Tourist Office, Midan Saad Zaghlul, tel. 25 985 ; at the port, tel. 25 977 ; at the passport office ; at the Automobile Club, 15 Sharia Sherif, tel. 26 730/61 996 ; at the Touring Club, 21 Sharia Sesostris, tel. 24 676. There and in all the travel agencies and hotels, a free periodical can be obtained « Two Weeks in Alexandria » (with a calendar of events and the principal addresses of interest to the tourist).

Tourist Police

Information and urgent help everyday from 8 am to 8 pm (Friday from 8 am to 2 pm) at the port and the Palace of Montaza, tel. 60 000.

Post

Principal post-office in the Midan Ismail, open from 8 am to 8 pm every day ; night service ; *poste restante*. Stamps can also be purchased in the large hotels (reception). There are other post-offices in the rest of the city and they are open each day (except Friday) from 8 am to 12 am and from 3.30 pm to 5.30 pm. In general there are seperate telecommunication offices.

Transport

🚍 From the central station (« Cairo station »), on Midan el-Gumhuriya, there are regular connections with Cairo (2½ hours : the prices vary according to the speed of the train ; take the « diesel »), Rosetta and the Delta and with Mersa Matrûh. From Ramleh station on Saad Zaghlul Square, connections with the principal places on the coast and the eastern beaches (tram-lines).

🚌 Long distance connections, chiefly towards Cairo, several times each day ; from the bus station in Saad Zaghlul Square (tel. 29 683), by the desert route (3½ hours) or by the Delta route (5 hours). The price varies between 2 and 3 £. Details in the brochure « Two weeks in Alexandria ».

✈ The airport of Nuzha south of the city has only dealt with civil traffic for several years ; another airport is planned. For connections between Cairo and Upper Egypt, the office of Egyptair on Saad Zaghlul Square (tel. 20 773).

🚢 In principle there are sea connections with the whole world. The boats leaving for Europe or arriving from there are found in the west port. Passport control and police on the boat (on arrival) and customs upon landing. For the main formalities of entry and departure, see on p. 319. From the port, there are taxis to the town which is fairly distant (ascertain the price in advance).

Municipal Transport

Other than the tramway leaving from Ramleh station (see above), many bus lines cover the town (principal bus-stops in el-Tahrir and Saad Zaghlul squares). But the mass of passengers usually makes this method of transport impractical.

Accommodation

🏨 « Palestine », Montaza Palace.

🏨 « Cecil », 16 Saad Zaghlul Square ; « Hannoville », Agami (west of the city) ; « El-Alamein » (with private bungalows) at Sidi Abd el-Rahman (west side).

🏨 « Mediterrane », Tarek el-Gish / Saba Pasha ; « San Stefano », Tarek el-Gish ; « El-Salamlek », Montaza Palace ; « Beau Rivage », Tarek el-Gish / el-Laurens ; « Windsor » el-Shoada Street ; « El-Mamura Palace », Mamura ; « Agami Place », El-Bitar-Agami ; « Borg el-Saghr », el-Horreya Street ; « Ziro », Tarek el-Gish ; « Swiss Cottage », Tarek el-Gish.

🏨 « Champs Elysées », Tarek el-Gish ; « Capri », Mina el-Sharkiah Street ; « Cleopatra », Tarek el-Gish ; « Darvich », Tarek el-Gish ; « El-Amawi » el-Nasr Street, « Eleima », Amin Fikry Street ; « Faida Place », Tarek el-Gish ; « Hyde-Park » ; Amin Fikry Street ; « Philippe », Tarek 26th July ; « Piccadilly », Tarek el-Horreya ; « San Giovanni », Tarek el-Gish ; « Villa Nana », Tarek el-Gish.

🏠 13, Port Said Street (Shatby). Camp-site at Abuqir.

Restaurants and Tea Rooms

Besides the large hotel restaurants,

the following establishments are recommended : « Au Privé », El-Horreya Street ; « L'Union », 1 Borsa el-Kadima Street ; « Santa Lucia », 40, Saad Zaghlul Street ; « Pastroudis », 39 el-Horreya Street ; « L'Élite », Saad Zaghlul Street ; « Andrea », (on the cornice, near Montaza, fish) ; the small fish and sea-food restaurants at Abuqir, on the east of the town. Also : « Aiglon », 236, 26th July Street ; « Athineos », 21, Midan Saad Zaghlul ; « Baudrot », 2, el-Horreya Street ; « Calithea », 180, 26th July Street ; « Délices », 29, Saad Zaghlul Street ; « Grand Trianon », 52, Saad Zaghlul Boulevard ; « Mayfair », 43, Zafia Zaghlul Street ; « Nassar » (Chamber of Commerce) ; « Omar Khayyam », Midan Saad Zaghlul ; « Pam-Pam », 33 Saad Zaghlul Street ; « Taverna », 1 Saad Zaghlul Street ; « Trianon », 53, Saad Zaghlul Street ; « San Giovanni », Stanley Beach.

Night Life

Gaming casinos in the Montaza Palace and at « Cecil » (closed for reconstruction). Night-club of the Hotel Palestine. Also « Aiglon », 236, 26th July Street ; « Chatby », Tarek el-Gish ; « Élite », 43, Saad Zaghlul Street ; « Grenouille », 225, el-Gish Street ; « Monseigner », 15, Midan Saad Zaghlul ; « Pam-Pam », 33, Saad Zaghlul Street ; « Pastroudis », 39, el-Horreya Street ; « Santa Lucia », 40, Saad Zaghlul Street ; « Windsor Palace », 17, el-Shohada.

Museums

Graeco-Roman Museum, 5, el-Mathaf el-Rumani Street, daily from 9 am to 4 pm and Friday from 11.30 am to 1.30 pm. Museum of Fine Arts, 18 Mensheya Street, daily from 9 am to 1 pm and from 5 pm to 8 pm (excluding Monday). Entrance free.
Râs el-Tin Palace Museum ; at present closed to visitors.
Montaza Palace Museum ; daily from 10 am to 5 pm.
Aquarium, at Anfushi, daily from 9 am to 2 pm ; entrance free. Catacombs of Kom el-Shughafa, daily from 9 am to 5 pm.
Necropolis of Anfushi, daily from 9 am to 5 pm. Possibility of entrance tickets valid for the museum, Kom el-Shughafa, Anfushi, and Kom el-Diq.

Important Addresses

British Airways, 15, Midan Faad Zaghlul ; Adriatica, 33 Salah Salem Street ; Turkish Maritime Lines, 28, Salah Salem Street ; British Consulate, 3, Mina Street, Ramleh ; United States Consulate, 110, el-Horreya Street ; The Egyptian Automobile Club, 15 Salah Salem Street.

Cairo

Information

℗ State Tourist Office, 5, Adly Street, tel. 923 000 ; at the central station, tel. 41 827 ; at the airport, tel. 66 475 ; at the Pyramids, tel. 850 259 ; at the Egyptian Automobile and Touring Club, 10, Qasr el-Nil Street. The weekly paper « Cairo this Week » with a calendar of events and important addresses is given free at the above addresses and in the hotels.

Tourist Police

In the numerous places frequented by tourists (station, airport, Pyramid area, bazaars), the tourist police can be recognized by their armbands and badges ; they can give all the help necessary to the tourist (they generally speak more than one foreign language). Main Headquarters, 5, Adly Street, tel. 912644.

Post

Central post-office on the Midan el-Ataba, open daily from 8 am to 8 pm ; night service ; *poste restante*. Stamps can be obtained in the large hotels and mail can be sent from them. The other post-offices are open from 8 am to 12 noon and from 3.30 pm to 5.30 pm (except Friday). The telephone directories in European languages are no longer available. The telegraph and telephone offices are separate from the post-offices ; apart from the large hotels, you can send telegrams or telephone abroad at the office in the Midan el-Tahrir. Telex facilities available in large hotels.

Transport

➤ From the central station (double), there are connections with the Delta and Alexandria as well as with the south (Fayûm, Middle and Upper Egypt) up to Aswan. From Limun Bridge station (just nearby), direct line to Suez. From Bab-el-Luq station (Muhammed Pasha Mahmud Street), local train for Maâdi and Helwan.

➤ Principal lines to the important places in the country depart from el-Tahrir Square. The fares are fairly cheap. Choose pullman coaches. Cairo airport (about 30 km (17 mi.)) is used by the principal airlines serving the entire world. Reached by bus, but chiefly by taxi.

➤ To Helwan and the Nile barrages from Rod el-Farag ; an hour or a day's sail in a feluka from the embarking point situated in front of Shepheard's Hotel. Nile cruises take about twelve days to reach Luxor, but the usual itinerary is from Luxor to Aswan or vice-versa. Information and bookings in your own country or at the « Eastmar » agency, 13, Qasr el-Nil Street, or in the other travel agencies.

Municipal Transport

The trams, trolleybuses and buses in Cairo are usually extremely overloaded. It is therefore practically impossible to use them. Only the tourist lines which leave from el-Tahrir Square may be usable. On the other hand, taxis (insufficient numbers to cope with the demand) are cheap 12 PT is the basic charge ; there is no night tariff ; service (tip) is not obligatory). Even long distances are reckoned on the meter. Ascertain the price for excursions in advance. There is also the possibility of hiring a car with a driver (and self-drive) ; inquire in the hotels.

Accommodation

➤ « Meridien », Roda island ; « Nile Hilton », Nile Esplanade and Midan el-Tahrir (« Ramesses Hilton » being built just to the north) ; « Sheraton », Midan Elgala (a second « Sheraton » is being built at the southern end of Gezira Island) ; « Mena House Oberoi », Pyramids ; « El-Salam», Héliopolis ; « Heliopolis-Sheraton », (on the airport road) ; « Holiday Inn », Pyramids.

➤ « Shepheard's », Nile Esplanade ; « Jolie Ville », Pyramids ; « President », Taha Hussein Street, Zamalek ; « Cleopatra Palace »,

Midan el-Tahrir ; « Rehab Hotel », Mohandesin, Dokki.

🏨 « El-Borg », Gezira ; « Atlas », Opera Square ; « El-Nil », Nile Esplanade ;« Cosmopolitan », Ibn Talaab Street ; « Continental », Opera Square ; « Sheherazade », Agouza Esplanade ; « Longchamp », Ismail Muhammed Street, Zamalek ; « Lotus », Talaat harb Street ; « Garden City House », Kamal el-Din Salah Street (near to « Shepheard's ») ; « Windsor », el-Alfi Street.

⚓ « Carlton », 26th July Street ; « Tulip », Talaat Harb Square ; « Golden », Talaat Harb Street ; « Everest », Ramesses Square ; « Ambassador », 26th July Street ; « Grand Hotel », 26th July Street ; « Khan el-Khalili », el-Bosta Street ; « Horus House », Ismail Muhammed Street, Zamalek ; « El Hussein », Midan el-Hussein (Khan el-Khalili) ; « De Rose », Talaat Harb Street ; « Gresham House », Tallat Harb Street ; « Luna Park », el-Goumhouria Street ; « Minerva », Talaat Harb Street ; « Green Valley », Abdel Khaleq Saruat Street ; « Ismailia House », el-Tahrir Square ; « Omayad », 26th July Street ; « Scarabee », 26th July Street.

⚓ Abdel Aziz El-Seoud Street, Manial, Roda Island (near University bridge).

Camp-site at Sahara City, near the Pyramids, Giza.

Restaurants

In the large hotels the restaurants are usually of three types : snackbars or pizzarias, grills (for entry to which a jacket and tie is often required for men), and dinner with floorshow. There are a large number of restaurants where you can sample local cooking, but these are not as well patronised by foreign tourists ; recommended places are : « Felfela », Oda Shaaraui Street ; « Felfela Village » (just before the Pyramids) ; « El-Hatti », Halim Square ; « Abou Shakra », Qasr el-Aini Street ; « Hag Mahmoud el-Sammak », Abdel Aziz Street ; and small kebab restaurants near the Khan el-Khalili.

There are also a number of very pleasant restaurants which serve European food, often of very good quality, and Egyptian specialities, for example : « Arabesque », Qasr el-Nil Street ; « Swissair », Nile Esplanade at Giza (with « Le Chateau », a luxury restaurant, and on the ground floor, « Le Chalet », a snack bar) ; « Caroll », Qasr el-Nil Street ; « Estoril », Tallat Harb Street ; « Le Grillon », in an alleyway off Qasr el-Nil Street ; « Rex », Abdel Khaleq Saruat Street ; « Groppi », Talaat Harb Square ; « Andrea », near the Pyramids ; « Andrea Seahorse », by the Nile on the road to Maadi ; « The Farm », near the Pyramids ; « Sofar », Adly Street ; « Paprika », Nile Esplanade, near the Radio-Television Centre ; « Okamoto » (Japanese restaurant), Ahmed Orabi Street, Agouza ; « Chateau de Versailles », Muhammed Sakeb Street, Zamalek ; « Casino des Pigeons », by the Nile at Giza ; « The Cairo Cellar », President Hotel, Taha Hussein Street, Zamalek.

Snack-Bars and Tea Rooms

Other than the large hotels, the following should be mentioned : « Groppi », Suliman Pasha Square and Saruat Street ; « A l'Américaine », 26th July Street and Talaat Harb Street ; « Indian Tea House », Talaat Harb Street ; « Lappas », Qasr el-Nil Street ; numerous open-air cafés (called « casinos ») along the Nile, pleasant in the high season at night and during the day in winter.

Cabarets and Discotheques

Dancing and floor-shows in the large hotels (♨), generally on the terraces. You can dine there whilst watching a « belly-dance » and a show and also dance to an orchestra playing western music. The best stars of Oriental dancing appear there. There are other comparable places : the « Omar Khayyam » boat at Geziar and « l'Auberge des Pyramides » on the Pyramid road. At Sahara City, a few kilometres from the Pyramids, you can sit under a vast tent and watch an essentially Oriental and picturesque floor-show. There are also numerous night-clubs situated along the Pyramid road, as well as in certain parts of the city, such as those of the Opera and Elfi Bey Street (« Granada ») or the establishments which are not quite so popular. The discotheques in Cairo should also be mentionned such as the « Saddle », Mena House Oberoi ; « After-Eight », Qasr el-Nil Street ; « Salt and Pepper », headland north of Zamalek and « Goha », Gezira. Finally, Cairo has American gaming casinos (in transferable foreign currency) at the Hilton, and Sheraton Hotels.

Museums

Egyptian Museum (Pharaonic Antiquities), Mariette Pasha Street (next to the Hilton) open daily from 8.30 am to 1.30 pm (Friday up to midday). Entrance fee (separate ticket for the mummy room).

Coptic Museum, Old Cairo (Mari Girgis Station), open daily from 8 am to 1 pm (Sunday from 10 am to 1 pm) ; entrance fee.

Museum of Islamic Art, Midan Ahmed Maher ; open daily from 9 am to 1 pm (Friday from 9 am to 12 noon) ; entrance fee.

Agricultural Museum, Doqqi ; open daily from 9 am to 4 pm (except Monday and Friday) ; entrance fee.

Abdine Palace Museum, el-Gumhuriya Square ; daily from 9 am to 5 pm ; entrance fee.

Gohar palace Museum, Citadel, open daily from 9 am to 4 pm ; entrance fee.

Manial Palace Museum, Rôdâ Island ; open daily from 9 am to 5 pm ; entrance fee.

Museum of Egyptian Civilization (and Automobile Museum), Gezira Island ; open daily from 9 am to 4 pm (except Monday and Friday) ; entrance fee.

Geology Museum, 13/15 Sharia Rian ; open daily from 9 am to 1 pm (except Friday) ; entrance free.

Military Museum, Citadel ; open daily from 9 am to 1 pm (except Friday and festival days) ; entrance free.

Museum of Hygiene, 2 Madbuld Square ; open daily from 9 am to 3 pm (except Monday and festival days) ; entrance free.

Railway Museum, principal station ; open daily from 9 am to 1 pm (except Friday and festival days) ; entrance free.

Mokhtar Museum, Gezira ; open daily from 9 am to 3 pm ; entrance free.

Mahmud Khalil Museum (modern painter), Gezira ; open daily from 9 am to 1 pm (except Friday) ; entrance free.

Cotton Museum, Gezira ; open daily from 9 am to 4 pm (except Monday and Friday) ; entrance free.

Gayer-Anderson Museum near the Mosque of Ibn Tûlûn ; open daily from 9 am to 1 pm (Friday up to midday) ; entrance free.

Amusements

National Theatre near Ezbekiya ; chiefly Arab repertoire.

The Opera was burnt down in 1971 and is being reconstructed. There are concerts in the Sayed Darwiche auditorium and the Ewart Memorial Hall of the American University in Cairo. Various Arab theatres in the city. Puppet theatre at Ezbekiya Square.

Cinemas in the town (European or American programmes predominate). Shows (films, music) in the foreign Cultural Centres.

« Son et Lumière » (Sound and Light) at the Pyramids. Every night after sunset, in different languages according to the evening. Inquire in the hotels. Cars leave from el-Tahrir Square.. Wrap-up carefully because the nights are cold in the desert.

Sport

The large clubs of Gezira (Gezira sporting Club), Maâdi, and Heliopolis are well-equipped for every type of sport. Membership is necessary for entry, or ask for a temporary card (there is also the possibility of buying day-tickets).

The « Nile Hilton » has a swimming-pool and tennis courts generally reserved for its clients ; there are also facilities at the Mena House Oberoi Hotel.

Important Addresses

British Embassy, Ahmed Ragheb Street, Garden City ; British Consulate, 8, Sharia el-Zahra, Garden City ; United States Embassy, 5, Latin American Street, Garden City ; British Airways, 1, Bustan Street ; TWA, 1, Qasr el-Nil Street ; Thomas Cook Ltd.,4, Champollion Street ; American Express, 15,Qasr el-Nil Street ; Anglo-Egyptian Bookshop, Muhammed Farid Street ; Automobile Club, 10,Qasr el-Nil Street.

Surroundings of Cairo

HELWAN

Old treatment centre which is becoming progressively transformed into an industrial town. It is 25 km (15 1/2 mi.) from Cairo. Do not go there however expecting to find a thermal station like those in Europe.

🚂   Terminus of the Helwan railway line leaving from Bab el-Luq Station in Cairo.

🚌   Bus line Tahrir-Maadi-Helwan. But it is advisable to take a taxi.

🏨   « Evergreen », 26, Zaki Street.

🍴   « Antonio », 25, Burhan Street ; « Des Princes », 16, Mustapha Safuat Street ; « Excelsior », 5, Mansur Street ; « Glanz », 25, el-Maraghi Street.

Information at the Treatment Centre (« Cabritage »).

Museums

Rest-house museum on the Nile ; open daily from 9 am to 5 pm ; entrance free. Wax Museum in the thermal zone ; daily from 9 am to 3 pm ; entrance free. « Japanese Gardens ».

Observatory : opening hours are often changed.

Nile Valley

FAYÛM

🚂 From El-Wasta or Beni Suef, there are branches to Medinet el-Fayûm (also called simply El-Fayûm). Then secondary lines for Sennuris and the other villages.

🚌 Several buses each day from Cairo (el-Tahrir Square) to Medinet el-Fayûm and « Auberge du Lac ». A taxi is also possible.

🏨 « Panorama », Shakshuk, « Auberge du Lac » and « Pavillon de chasse » (on the banks of Quarun Lake). Small local hotels at El-Fayûm and the other localities ; very basic comforts.

🏛 at Medinet el-Fayûm.

MINYA

🚂 on the principal line along the Nile Valley, 245 km (152 mi.) south of Cairo. Departure point for excursions to Beni Hasan, Tell el-Amarna, Hermopolis, Tuna el-Gebel and the rock tombs of the region.

🏨 « Lotus », « Palace », « Savoy » (near the station). Other small hotels in the town (« Sathi », « Ibn Khasib »).
Local Museum on the banks of the Nile ; entrance free ; open in the morning.

MELLAWI

🚂 on the principal railway line, 300 km (186 mi.) south of Cairo. This town will be an excellent departure point for excursions at present leaving from Minya when the « Nefertari » hotel is open.

Local Museum, open every morning (except Wednesday) ; entrance free.

SOHAG

🚂 on the principal Nile Valley railway line, 470 km (292 mi.) south of Cairo. Important Coptic town (with Akhmin on the other bank of the Nile). Departure point for visiting the monasteries in the region.

🏨 « Atlas », « Hilton », « El-Khayyam », « Semiramis » (very basic comforts).

NAG HAMMADI

Hotel of the « Aluminium Company ».

LUXOR

Information

ℹ at the Tourist Office, el-Bahr Street (cornice), at the station, airport, Antiquities Inspectorate, el-Karnak Street (Tel. 2215) ; tourist police, Tel. 2120.

Post

Principal office in station street (Sharia el-Mahatta). Stamps and post-boxes in the hotels.

Transport

🚂 important station in the Nile Valley, 674 km (419 mi.) from Cairo ; the journey takes about 12 hours ; 232 km (144 mi.) north of Aswan. Local transport : taxis on the tourist sites chiefly on the left bank (necropolises), less common in Luxor itself. On the left bank it is also possible to hire a donkey.

On the right bank (Luxor itself), horse carriages can be used to reach Karnak (about 150 PT). At west Thebes, it costs about 4 £E for a morning's visit by taxi and 150 PT for a donkey.

✈ the airport is 11 km (6 mi.) north-east of the town. There is a bus to the terminus at the Winter Palace. There are several flights each day to Aswan and Cairo and less often for Abu Simbel (timetable and length of flights variable.

🚢 Cairo-Luxor cruises and vice-versa take place chiefly in the autumn and towards April-May. On the other hand, there are numerous cruises from Luxor to Aswan (or vice-versa). The boats stop at the quay in front of the Winter Palace. It is possible to hire a feluka for a sail (« banana island »). Embark in front of the hotels to cross the Nile to west Thebes. It is also possible to take the local ferry-boat.

Accommodation

🏨ᴸ « Etap »,
🏨 « Winter Palace » and « New Winter Palace » (swimming-pool, gardens, etc.). The de-luxe boats « Osiris » and « Isis » (Hilton chain) are regularly moored at Luxor. The « Sudan » boat is controlled by the Club Connaissance du Monde (Manial Palace in Cairo).

🏨 « Luxor Hotel », « Savoy Hotel » (with bungalows and a swimming-pool).

⚓ « Horus » « Mina Palace » « Hotel des Familles ». Very simple hotels near the station.
On the left bank : « Sheikh Ali » (Qurna) « Kings Valley » and « Habu » (Medinet Habu).

⌂ Sharia el-Manchia.

Restaurants

Other than the hotels, « Chez Farouk » and « Marhaba ».

Museum

Nile Street open from 4 pm — 9 pm in winter (5 pm — 11 pm in Summer) ; entrance fee.
« Son et Lumière » : every evening at Karnak in several languages.

Guides

Even though it is possible to go alone and tour the chosen monuments by taxi or by donkey, with the help of this guide, it is possible to hire the services of a dragoman for about 5 £E a day.

Entrance Tickets

To visit the ruins of Luxor and Karnak you pay on the right of the entrance (ticket-box). For the necropolises and temples of west Thebes you must buy a group ticket at the landing-stage of the tourist ferry-boat. Take some change for « bakshish » during your visit to the tombs. A general entrance ticket for the Theban monuments can be requested at the Antiquities Service, el-Karnak Street.

EDFU

For the moment Edfu can not be visited from the « Edfu » hotel. You have to take a taxi or a carriage from the station or the landing stage. The temple is on the opposite bank of the river, but it can be crossed by a bridge. There is a buffet-restaurant at the station where tourists can obtain any information they require.

ASWAN

Information

☎ Tourist Office at the station and Sharia el-Manchia (tel. 3297). Tourist police : tel. 3163.

Post

On the Nile cornice near the National Bank. Stamps and post-boxes in the large hotels.

Transport

🚌 The town of Aswan is situated 232 km (144 mi.) south of Luxor and nearly 900 km (560 mi.) south of Cairo. The terminal station of the Nile Valley line is about twelve kilometres (7 mi.) further south at Shellal.

Local transport : taxis and buses serve the town and its surroundings. There are donkeys and camels on the west bank. Hotels and tourist offices can give information and prices (and guides).

✈ Several connections each day to Cairo and Luxor ; less often to Abu Simbel. The airport is 15 km south-west of the town (9 mi.). There is a bus to the town terminus. This airport is sometimes closed to tourists and replaced by the one at Kom Ombo (a very pleasant drive).

🚢 Principal landing-stage in front of the « Grand Hotel », but there are numerous felukas plying for trade along the Nile. It is possible to cross to the islands or the west bank. Prices are given in the tourist offices or in the hotels. Daily hovercraft excursions to Abu Simbel (fairly uncomfortable journey) ; about 25 £E. River connections between Shellal and the Sudan (Wadi Halfa).

Accommodation

🏨 « Oberoi », island of Elephantine.

🏨 « New Cataract » « Old Cataract ».

🏨 « Amun » (on Amun island) ; « Kalabsha » ; « Nile City » (with bungalows). « Nefertari » (at Abu Simbel).

🏠 « Abu Simbel » (at the north) ; « Grand Hotel » « Philae ». Less comfortable small hotels near the station and in the town.

🏕 in the town, near el-Manchia Street.

Mediterranean Coast

RAS EL-BAR

Very popular family beach, on a strip of land between one branch of the Nile and the sea.

🚢 From Cairo or Alexandria up to Damietta, then bus.

🚌 Bus directly from Alexandria or Cairo.

Accommodation
Small, simple hotels (🏠).

EL-ALAMEIN

Historic site and a peaceful place to rest. It can be reached by train, bus, or taxi from Alexandria.

🏠 « Rest-House » with restaurant.
Military museum open daily in the morning ; entrance free.

SIDI ABD EL-RAHMAN

Marvellous holiday resort with a superb beach, just outside the town. It can be reached by train, bus or taxi from Alexandria (or possibly Cairo).

🏠 « El-Alamein » Hotel with ten bungalow annexes.

MERSA MATRÛH

Holiday resort with superb white sand beach. Departure point for excursions to Siwa.

🏨 « Beau Site » ; « Des Roses » ; « Lido » ; « Riviera » (most of them are only open in the summer).

🏠 « Bel Air » ; « Cleopatra » ; « Mathrûh Palace » ; « Miami » ; « Rio » ; « Zephyr ».

SIWA

The oasis can be reached by air (inquire in Cairo ; the lines are irregular) or by car from Mersa Matrûh. The road from this town, which crosses the desert, is only asphalted at the beginning and the end of its length ; the rest is a rough, pitted track. Accomodation at Siwah, « Governmental Rest-house », moderate price. There is no restaurant. Take some food (supplement from local provisions). Allow nearly six days for the journey and the stay. An excursion to Siwa is still subject to prior permission being obtained in Cairo.

Red Sea Coast

At present the Red Sea is an area still strictly forbidden to foreigners. It is difficult to obtain permission to travel there. Therefore only some brief indication is given here. For more information, ask at the information offices in Cairo or « Red Sea Tours », 11 Mahmud Bassiuni Street.

AIN SUKHNA

🏛 « Ain Sokhna Hotel ».

RAS GHARIB

🛏 Rest-House

HURGHADA

🏛 « Sheraton » Club Mediterranée
🏛 « Dolphin Club Centre »
« Hurghâda Rest House »

PORT SAFAGA

🛏 Rest-House

QOSEIR

🛏 Rest-House.

MERSA ALAM

🛏 Rest-House.

Suez Canal

PORT SAID
Information

☎ Tourist Office, Sultan Hussein Street, tel. 3100
🏛 « Holiday » Gumhuriya Street ; « Abu Simbel » Gumhuriya Street ; « Vendôme » Gumhuriya Street.
🛏 « Akry », Gumburiya Street ; « Al Ghazl », 23rd July Street ; « Grand Hotel », Salah Salem Street.
🚋 23rd July Street.

ISMAILIA

🏛 « Sinaï » « Nefertari » « Grand Hotel » ; « New Palace » ; « Des Voyageurs ».

Museum

Antiquities Museum open daily from 9 am to 4 pm (except Monday and Friday from 8 am to 11 am and 2 pm to 4 pm) ; entrance fee. Undergoing rebuilding.

SUEZ
☎ Information Office, Canal Street, Port Taufiq.
🏛 « Al Suez », Port Taufiq ; « Bel Air », Salah el-Din Street.
🛏 « Beau Rivage », Saad Zaghlul Street ; « Misr Palace », Saad Zaghlul Street.

Index

Printed in 1981 by

Brodard Graphique - Coulommiers

Photocomposition : Imprimerie Marchand - Paris

Colour Photogravure : La Photochromie - Gentilly

Binding : Reliure Brun - Malesherbes.